D1620379

Palgrave's Critical Policing Studies

In a period where police and academics benefit from coproduction in research and education, the need for a critical perspective on key challenges is pressing. Palgrave's Critical Policing Studies is a series of high quality, research-based books which examine a range of cutting-edge challenges and developments to policing and their social and political contexts. They seek to provide evidence-based case studies and high quality research, combined with critique and theory, to address fundamental challenging questions about future directions in policing.

Through a range of formats including monographs, edited collections and short form Pivots, this series provides research at a variety of lengths to suit both academics and practitioners. The series brings together new topics at the forefront of policing scholarship but is also organised around who the contemporary police are, what they do, how they go about it, and the ever-changing external environments which bear upon their work.

The series will cover topics such as: the purpose of policing and public expectations, public health approaches to policing, policing of cybercrime, environmental policing, digital policing, social media, Artificial Intelligence and big data, accountability of complex networks of actors involved in policing, austerity, public scrutiny, technological and social changes, over-policing and marginalised groups, under-policing and corporate crime, institutional abuses, policing of climate change, ethics, workforce, education, evidence-based policing, and the pluralisation of policing.

Tereza Østbø Kuldova ·
Helene Oppen Ingebrigtsen Gundhus ·
Christin Thea Wathne
Editors

Policing and Intelligence in the Global Big Data Era, Volume I

New Global Perspectives on Algorithmic Governance

Editors
Tereza Østbø Kuldova ⓘ
OsloMet – Oslo Metropolitan University
Oslo, Norway

Helene Oppen Ingebrigtsen Gundhus ⓘ
University of Oslo
Oslo, Norway

Christin Thea Wathne ⓘ
OsloMet – Oslo Metropolitan University
Oslo, Norway

ISSN 2730-535X   ISSN 2730-5368   (electronic)
Palgrave's Critical Policing Studies
ISBN 978-3-031-68325-1   ISBN 978-3-031-68326-8   (eBook)
https://doi.org/10.1007/978-3-031-68326-8

Acknowledgements

This edited volume springs from the research project *Algorithmic Governance and Cultures of Policing: Comparative Perspectives from Norway, India, Brazil, Russia, and South Africa* (AGOPOL) funded by The Research Council of Norway under project no. 313626. This project sought to investigate the implications and ways in which police departments and private sector security and intelligence actors collaborating with the police, across the globe, have been embracing artificial intelligence (AI), machine learning, and various forms of automation to support decision-making in preventing crime, security threats, and disorder. The use of digital technologies and the growing role of private security, tech, and consultancy companies, are continually reshaping policing and the ways in which we ensure social order and security, enforce law, and prevent and investigate crime. To investigate these dynamics, we brought together a team of established scholars and researchers from cultural and area studies, anthropology, criminology, sociology, history, literature, and law, and over the course of the project, we engaged with many other scholars, some of whom are also represented in this volume. The project was based on qualitative and ethnographic research on policing in Norway, Russia, India, Brazil, and South Africa, but these two volumes go beyond, as we have invited scholars focusing on other locations as well. We have tried to shed new light on the diverse consequences of algorithmic governance for society, police forces, and those policed: from the transformation of knowledge cultures and organizations, to algorithmic injustices and their impact on legitimacy and societal trust. This volume also springs from several conferences we have organized over the course of 2021–2023. We would like to thank all our colleagues engaged in and having engaged with this project—you know who you are, and The Research Council of Norway for funding this project and enabling these inspiring encounters which, we hope, open new fields of research and new perspectives on algorithmic governance and policing.

Contents

Notes on Contributors

Marcos César Alvarez is a Professor of Sociology at the University of São Paulo (USP), where he also coordinates the Center for the Study of Violence (NEV). Previously, he held research and teaching positions at the École des Hautes Études in Sciences Sociales, France; at the Universidad de Salamanca, Spain; at the Universidad Nacional de Cuyo and at the Universidad Nacional del Litoral, both in Argentina. His current research focuses on the sociology of violence and punishment. Marcos received his Ph.D. from the Department of Sociology, USP.

Bruno Cardoso is an Associate Professor in the Department of Sociology at the Federal University of Rio de Janeiro (UFRJ) and in the Post-graduate Programme in Sociology and Anthropology (PPGSA/UFRJ). Cardoso holds a Ph.D. in Human Sciences from UFRJ and has experience in the areas of Sociology and Anthropology, with research and publications on technology, surveillance, public security, violence, cities, governmentality, mega-events, power, media, and the internet. Cardoso is also a Researcher at the Centre for the Study of Citizenship, Conflict and Urban Violence (NECVU - IFCS/UFRJ), member of the Latin

American Network for Studies on Surveillance, Technology and Society (Lavits), and coordinator of the Digital Studies Laboratory (LED/UFRJ).

Simon Egbert is a Postdoctoral Researcher at the Faculty of Sociology, Bielefeld University, Germany. He is part of the ERC-funded research project 'The Future of Prediction', working on the sub-project on predictive policing. He is also PI of a project on police bodycams in the project network 'Visions of Policing. How visual technologies influence police surveillance and training'. Prior to joining Bielefeld University, he was a postdoctoral fellow in the graduate programme 'Innovation Society Today' at the Technische Universität Berlin and a postdoctoral fellow in the research project 'Predictive Policing. An ethnographic study on new technologies for predicting criminal offences and their consequences for police practice'. He completed his Ph.D. in 2018 with a dissertation on discourse and materiality using the example of drug testing applications. He published widely on predictive policing and the sociology of prediction as well as police data integration and analysis platforms.

Vasilis Galis is an Associate Professor in the Technologies in Practice (TIP) group at the IT University of Copenhagen. His research on the digitalization of the welfare state, and on law enforcement, is informed by STS and qualitative methods. Galis is the principal investigator of Welfare after digitalization (funded by the Velux foundation in Denmark) and Critical Understanding of Predictive Policing (funded by Nordforsk). Galis has published in leading international journals including *Political Geography, Science, Technology and Human Values, Science as Culture, Journal of Cultural Economy, Social Media + Society, Social Movement Studies*. Galis' research is interdisciplinary and is impregnated by a strong epistemological solidarity with social movements.

Helene Oppen Ingebrigtsen Gundhus is a Professor of Criminology at the University of Oslo, and professor II at the Norwegian Police University College. She has published on issues to do with police methods and technology, police professionalism, crime prevention, risk assessments, migration control, and transnational policing. Her research interests lie in the intersection of criminology, critical security studies, and science and technology studies. Gundhus is, among others, author of *Moral* *issues in intelligence-led policing* (co-edited with N. Fyfe and K.V. Rønn; Routledge, 2018). Gundhus is a core researcher of the AGOPOL project.

Kjetil Klette-Bøhler is a Professor of Music at the University of South-East Norway. He has published 43 articles and book chapters, including two research anthologies as co-editor. Most of his scholarly publications deal with music and politics and his publications have appeared in internationally leading peer-reviewed journals such as *Popular Music, Music Perception, Latin American Music Review, Musical Quarterly* and *Twentieth Century Music,* among others. Most of his research examines music's cultural and political meanings in Cuba, Brazil, and Norway, and he is currently exploring related studies in the USA, the EU, and in Mozambique. Bøhler is a core researcher of the AGOPOL project.

Tereza Østbø Kuldova is a Research Professor based at the Work Research Institute, Oslo Metropolitan University and a social anthropologist. She is the author of, among others, *Compliance-Industrial Complex: The Operating System of a Pre-Crime Society* (Palgrave, 2022), *How Outlaws Win Friends and Influence People* (Palgrave, 2019), *Luxury Indian Fashion: A Social Critique* (Bloomsbury, 2016), and co-author of *Luxury and Corruption: Challenging the Anti-Corruption Consensus* (Bristol University Press, 2024), in addition to many edited volumes and journal articles. She has written extensively on topics ranging from fashion, design, branding, intellectual property rights, philanthropy, India, to outlaw motorcycle clubs, subcultures, organized crime, corruption and anti-corruption. She is the founder and editor-in-chief of *the Journal of Extreme Anthropology* as well as of the Algorithmic Governance Research Network. Kuldova is a co-leader of the AGOPOL project.

Shivangi Narayan is a Fellow at IT for Change and former Researcher with the Algorithmic Governance and Cultures of Policing Project (AGOPOL) 2021–2024. She has a Ph.D. in Sociology from Jawaharlal Nehru University, New Delhi (2021). She is interested in the use of AI in policing and security along with the use of identification systems such as the UID in India. She is the author of *Predictive Policing and the Construction of the Criminal: An Ethnographic Study of Delhi Police*

(Palgrave MacMillan 2023) and *Surveillance as Governance* (People's Publication, 2021).

Matthew Nesvet is an anthropologist, author, and Professor at the Indiana University School of Medicine and Miami Dade College. You can read more of his work at MattNesvet.com.

Jardar Østbø is a Professor and the head of Programme for Russian Security and Defence Policy at the Institute for Defence Studies, Norwegian Defence University College. His articles on Russian politics and society have appeared in journals such as Post-Soviet Affairs, Journal of Extreme Anthropology, Cultural Politics, Demokratizatsiya: Journal of Post-Soviet Democratization, and Social Movement Studies. Østbø is the author of *The New Third Rome. Readings of a Russian Nationalist Myth* (Ibidem, 2016) and co-author of *Luxury and Corruption: Challenging the Anti-Corruption Consensus* (Bristol University Press, 2024). He is the leader of the international project RUSINTELSTATE (2024–2027), which studies the intelligence-politics nexus in Russia. Østbø is a core researcher of the AGOPOL project.

Alcides Eduardo dos Reis Peron holds a Ph.D. in Scientific and Technological Policy at Unicamp. He is the coordinator of the International Relations department at FECAP; member of the advisory board of the Latin American Network on Technology, Surveillance and Society (LAVITS); and Researcher at the Center for the Study of Violence at USP (NEV). Previously he held research positions at the Lancaster University and the King's College London, both in the UK. His current research focuses on AI-based Surveillance Systems, Policing and Security.

Paulo Cruz Terra is a Professor at the History Department of Federal Fluminense University in Brazil. He was an Alexander von Humboldt Foundation fellow at the Bonn Center for Dependency and Slavery Studies in Germany between 2019 and 2020. Currently, he is a research fellow of National Council for Scientific and Technological Development (CNPq), of Research Foundation for the state of Rio de Janeiro (FAPERJ), and part of the project Algorithmic Governance and Cultures of Policing, financed by the Research Council of Norway. In 2022, he was elected an affiliated member of the Brazilian Academy of Science. Terra is a core researcher of the AGOPOL project.

Ashwin Varghese is a sociologist studying algorithmic governance, power relations, policing, and state development. He is currently a CGHR Postdoctoral Scholar at the University of Cambridge, former Assistant Professor of Sociology at O.P. Jindal Global University India, and former Researcher in the Algorithmic Governance Research Network. His broader research interests include political sociology, sociology of law, governance, political economy, theories of everyday, and ethnographic methods. Varghese is a core researcher of the AGOPOL project.

Christin Thea Wathne is a Research Director and Research Professor at Work Research Institute, Oslo Metropolitan University in Norway. Her research interests include leadership and management, New Public Management, organizational development, organizational learning, professions, social identity and working environment and mastering. She has published extensively on policing and regularly contributes to public debate on policing in Norway. Wathne is a project leader of the AGOPOL project.

List of Figures

1

Introduction to Volume I: Algorithmic Governance, Policing and Intelligence in the Global Big Data Era

Tereza Østbø Kuldova⬤,
Helene Oppen Ingebrigtsen Gundhus⬤,
and Christin Thea Wathne⬤

The rise of big data, machine learning, and artificial intelligence (AI) has not only ushered in a new era of 'surveillance capitalism' (Zuboff, 2019), where the ever-growing digital exhausts of our daily online activities translate into new sources of profit, but also into new modes, forms, and possibilities of social control, surveillance, monitoring, intelligence-gathering, regulation, and governance. While many of these forms of policing and governance of the social have deep historical roots and precedents, the scale and speed at which ever more granular data can be collected, processed, analysed, and integrated have been rapidly

T. Ø. Kuldova (✉) · C. T. Wathne
OsloMet—Oslo Metropolitan University, Oslo, Norway
e-mail: tereza.kuldova@oslomet.no

C. T. Wathne
e-mail: wach@oslomet.no

H. O. I. Gundhus
University of Oslo, Oslo, Norway
e-mail: h.o.i.gundhus@jus.uio.no

© The Author(s), under exclusive license to Springer Nature
Switzerland AG 2024
T. Ø. Kuldova et al. (eds.), *Policing and Intelligence in the Global Big Data Era,
Volume I*, Palgrave's Critical Policing Studies,
https://doi.org/10.1007/978-3-031-68326-8_1

increasing, with profound consequences, both intended and unintended. As the social, economic, and technological complexity increases, so does the speed, complexity, variety, and volume of data, making analysts overwhelmed and in search of various forms of augmentation of analytics, from various smart dashboards to artificial intelligence (AI). This goes, too, for technologies designed for various purposes of social control and management of the social, be it crime or consumer behaviour. While we are being promised data-driven decision-making with razor-blade precision, we are, in reality, often overwhelmed, confused, and disoriented when facing the massive amounts of data. Hence, we are facing new forms of 'uncontrollability' (Rosa, 2021), which are inadvertently generating new vulnerabilities and threat scenarios as we are increasing our dependence, in all aspects of life, on these ever more complex technological products and managerial and governance *systems*—not to mention ever more complex supply chains within an increasingly tense geopolitical landscape marked by wars and violent as much as ideological conflicts. The risks stemming from these new vulnerabilities, dependencies, and complexities are then typically sought managed or eliminated through new layers of control systems and products designed to tackle these new vulnerabilities with their inherent potential for exploitation by criminals and other threat actors. The solutions thus often take the form of technological, managerial, intelligence, and compliance 'fixes' (Kuldova, 2022; Kuldova et al., 2024), supplied by the tech, security, and consulting industries which typically address various symptoms of systemic issues rather than tackling causes. These trillion- and multi-billion-dollar global industries, respectively, have over the past decades amassed immense power—not only capital power, but epistemic and ideological power. In crucial ways, these industries have been shaping the very ways in which we are being governed, surveilled, monitored, managed, controlled, nudged, and so on—designing both algorithmic and managerial systems of control used both by private and public sectors (the distinction remaining only as an ideal type and becoming ever blurrier in reality).

The growth of what some have called the 'regulatory state' (Veggeland, 2009) and others 'regulatory capitalism' (Braithwaite, 2008; Levi-Faur, 2017)—pointing to the frenetic (re)regulatory activity of states, the

European Union (EU), and a whole range of other actors involved in governance—has created new markets both for big tech companies and for consulting and audit firms and their products. The concept of regulatory capitalism tries to capture the increased legal and regulatory complexity, which is today of such technobureaucratic detail that not only cannot citizens be any longer expected to understand applicable laws and regulations, but even large teams of legal experts often fail, feeling notoriously overwhelmed by this complexity—and thus, again, looking to technological solutions, such as LegalTech, legal automation, or the promise of large legal models (LLMs) (Bent, 2023; Susskind, 1996), while at the same time fearing that much of the profession and lower-ranking jobs will be automated. Meanwhile, we have seen the growth of the so-called regulatory technologies (RegTech) (Barberis et al., 2019; Waye, 2019) that seek to automate compliance with various laws and regulations—from anti-money laundering (Verhage, 2011), anti-corruption (Kuldova et al., 2024), or security compliance (*see* Kuldova, this volume) to compliance within police departments (*see* Nesvet, this volume).

What is crucial for us to recognize here is the degree to which the technologies used by various policing and intelligence agents, public and private—or even technologies to which these policing agents have to submit—have become first and foremost 'techno-managerial', i.e., they are technologies that in various ways seek to automate management, governance, and compliance. And that the way in which they seek to achieve this typically takes the form of surveillance, monitoring, prediction, risk profiling and risk-flagging, or else, data-driven predictive and pre-emptive modes of de facto policing. This is also why we prefer to speak of the cultures of policing—beyond the police (Crawford, 2003)—since we not only have to consider the new hybrid and rhizomatic assemblage that is policing today, but also the (transforming) cultural logic of policing spilling into new domains as it becomes embedded in self-learning algorithms (Nagy & Kerezsi, 2020). *Cultures of policing and intelligence*, as we use the concept, are not to be confused with the traditional inward-looking studies of 'police culture' ('canteen culture', 'cop culture', etc.), 'occupational' and 'organizational' culture typical for policing studies (Westmarland, 2011). Instead, across these two volumes, we aim to transgress these and pave new way towards a comparative cultural analysis of policing, intelligence, and algorithmic governance that affords a much larger place to the cultural and global context—and to the epistemological and institutional transformations as a consequence of the movement towards *pre-emption* in crime, risk, threat, and security management (Arrigo & Sellers, 2021; Kuldova, 2022; McCulloch & Wilson, 2016; Zedner, 2007; Zedner & Ashworth, 2019).

Policing tech, surveillance and intelligence tech, and management tech on the market tends to be predicated on the same logic and epistemology—this is also why Palantir, Peter Thiel's notorious software company best known for supplying its analytics platforms to military, law enforcement, and intelligence agencies, has been able to rapidly diversify from the security fields into supply chain management, healthcare sector management, financial industry risk management, and compliance, or, for that matter, into any other industry looking to leverage one's 'ontology's semantic and kinetic graphs to simulate operations, automate processes, and federate decision-making across operators, devices, and environments'.[1] This is yet another reason why it is worthwhile conceiving policing beyond law enforcement agencies, and as increasingly embedded into techno-managerial architectures. This policing—be it conducted by the police itself or by corporate actors, in turn, resembles more and more data-driven risk management; the foundations and evolution of this phenomenon have been eloquently described by Ericson and Haggerty several decades ago, as they managed to put a finger on likely the most important shift in policing—the shift to expert systems of risk, the progressive legalization of risk, and increased importance of compliance-based law enforcement (Ericson & Haggerty, 1997). Today, these managerial and statistical epistemologies are being built into ever more advanced algorithmic systems and platforms designed to collect, process, integrate, and analyse data and churn out automated risk assessments, be it of individual workers within a corporation or hot-spot areas designated for increased policing efforts. This is precisely why concepts such as 'algorithmic governance' (Kalpokas, 2019;

---

[1] The Foundry Ontology, *Palantir*, https://www.palantir.com/platforms/foundry/foundry-ontology/.

Katzenbach & Ulbricht, 2019) can help us understand and perceive contemporary data-driven and intelligence-led modes of policing (or ambitions).

Considering all these developments together, it comes as no surprise that policing has become more hybrid: new players proliferate while technological companies embed behavioural nudges, laws, regulations, and managerial principles into the code (Susskind, 2018). We could go as far as arguing that we live in times marked by the pluralization and privatization of policing and intelligence (Boels & Verhage, 2015; O'Reilly, 2015) wherein an ever greater number of actors and organizations, public and private, are taking on various policing and intelligence-gathering tasks (Ben Jaffel & Larsson, 2022)—both on behalf of the state and for their own purposes (be it protection of physical and intellectual property or increased productivity sought achieved through monitoring and policing of workers). By privatization we thus do not only refer to the growth of private security companies, private prisons, or private military contractors which may immediately come to mind (Bureš, 2015; Button, 2019), but also to deeper processes which can be linked to the aforementioned regulatory state and capitalism where the state tries to leverage private managerial infrastructures for its own crime-fighting and intelligence-gathering purposes. To take a few examples, financial institutions are required to generate 'suspicious activity reports' for Financial Intelligence Units (FIUs) under anti-money laundering regulations (Amicelle & Iafolla, 2018), schoolteachers in the UK are obliged to report suspicious activity or signs of radicalization under the counter-terrorism Prevent Duty (Kaleem, 2022), or HR-departments in designated organizations are to screen, background check, and monitor both existing and prospective employees as part of security compliance and feed information about suspicious actors to various state agencies (*see* Kuldova, this volume). These processes of privatization and pluralization of policing have been, again, greatly accelerated not only neoliberal reforms, the rise of New Public Management (Hansen et al., 2002; Wathne, 2015, 2020), or privatization and outsourcing, but precisely by the co-evolution and global diffusion of 'surveillance capitalism' (Zuboff, 2019) and 'regulatory capitalism' (Levi-Faur, 2005). In trying to unpack contemporary modes of 'algorithmic governance' and the ways in which they both intersect and underpin pluralized policing, we thus need to consider these larger trends. But we also need to question the normative and epistemic power of algorithmic architectures, in particular in areas such as policing.

The *normativity* of computational algorithms (even self-generated normativity in the case of AI), their 'epistemic power' (Kuldova & Nordrik, 2023), and their capacity to define the limits of our actions and imagination needs to be understood as a form of *governance*, which encompasses the increasingly 'liquid' security and policing (Bauman & Lyon, 2013; Zedner, 2006). But not only are algorithmic decisions value-laden, they have fundamentally shifted our thinking away from causality to thinking in terms of probabilities and correlations (Amoore, 2013)—a normative shift embedded into these technologies and challenging established rule of law principles (De Gregorio, 2023). Algorithmic governance can then be seen as a mode of 'ordering, regulation and behaviour modification, as a form of management, of optimisation', a form of social control based on rules involving particularly complex computational epistemic procedures 'characterised by inscrutability, the inscription of values and interests, by efficiency and effectiveness, by power asymmetry' (Katzenbach & Ulbricht, 2019, p. 11). Algorithmic governance thus refers to the new and more granular ways in which we are sought governed, managed, policed, risk assessed, punished, nudged, or made more efficient and productive, speaking to the inherent normativity of these systems (beyond questions of reproduction of social biases for instance). Given all the above, we could thus argue that algorithmic governance as it manifests in the multiplying products of the tech industry, has accelerated the global spread and social embedding of pre-existing visions of techno-managerial and seemingly apolitical 'governance by numbers' (Supiot, 2017), or else, visions of 'engineering' the social and humanity (Frischmann & Selinger, 2018) that see the world as ultimately programmable and humans as imperfect and fallible in comparison to machine perfection. Again, while not radically new, the scale and speed is something that does transform these ideologies into a new force to reckon with. In this sense, it is the combination of institutional, infrastructural, market, and epistemic power aligned around the key assumptions upon which these technologies rest that must be challenged and better understood.

Given precisely this infrastructural power, we are not only subjected by but also *subjectivated* by (Kuldova, 2021) these more or less opaque algorithmic architectures and 'roboprocesses' (Besteman & Gusterson, 2019). But this does of course not mean we are all subjectivated or governed in the same way merely because we are subject to more or less the same technologies circulated across the globe by big tech and big audit and consulting firms. The adoption of these technologies of course does not happen in a cultural, political, or economic vacuum. In many countries, to take an example, police forces are experiencing financial cuts and/or organizational reform at the same time as demands on response time, results, performance, and efficiency are increasing (Gundhus, 2017; Gundhus et al., 2018; Wathne, 2018). In the context of these multiple pressures, predictive policing tools promise to 'optimize effective use of the scarce human resources available' (Camacho-Collados & Liberatore, 2014, p. 25), while parts of police work are outsourced to private companies. Economic management by numbers, bureaucratic oversight, benchmarks, statistics, audit, and performance evaluation—or else the 'audit culture' (Shore & Wright, 2015, 2024) where new modes of 'gaming the stats' become ingrained, be it in Russia or Norway (Fyfe et al., 2018; Paneyakh, 2014)—albeit in different ways and with very different consequences for the policed.

Across this volume, algorithmic governance thus manifests in different iterations and modes across different cultures, from the Russian 'intelligence-driven technopoly' (Østbø, this volume), via militarized managerialism during Bolsonaro's rule in Brazil (Cardoso, this volume), to e-governance and smart policing in Kerala, India (Varghese, this volume), to name a few. Reading across these chapters, we can consider both the similarities and the differences as policing, surveillance, and monitoring-cum-managerial technologies predicated on largely the same principles and informed by largely the same theories embed themselves differently across these different social, political, cultural, economic, and organizational contexts. Even in more proximate countries, such as Germany, Denmark, and Norway, the introduction of policing platforms can play out very differently, as the comparative chapter by Egbert,

Galis, Gundhus, and Wathne shows (this volume). These culturally and sociologically informed analyses *in themselves* break with the widespread naïve positivism and fetishization of data 'neutrality' or universality of standardized management and governance procedures. But they also show us that it is not only the technologies as such that are appropriated differently, but that also the very narratives, fantasies, and mythologies surrounding these technologies are reshaping policing, intelligence as much as governance.

The commercial and marketing promises of BigTech companies and start-ups, and of consulting companies, such as the Big Four audit firms (Deloitte, EY, PwC, KPMG) and hundreds of thousands of other management consulting firms—whether they are 'hype', 'puffery', or real—have been in themselves reshaping contemporary policing and policing cultures and the ways in which we ensure security, enforce law, and prevent, pre-empt, and investigate crime and relate to security threats and other risks (*see* Narayan, this volume). The widespread cultural faith in big data and data-driven decision-making, in particular among decision-makers across both public and private sectors, and the view itself that artificial intelligence is *the* technology of both now and future which will radically transform everything—every aspect of the world we inhabit (Mayer-Schönberger & Cukier, 2013), has in itself been reshaping policing, intelligence, and governance well before the actual implementation of these technologies (which, as several chapters across these volumes show, are often far from impressive). The *ideological* force of what some have deemed 'technosolutionism' (Morozov, 2013)—the notion that the solutions to most of our problems are merely technological—thus cannot be underestimated. After all, it is also the *faith* invested in commercial promises and marketing narratives that drives valuations of tech firms on the stock market and attracts venture capital. The phantasmatic and the real are also increasingly difficult to tell apart—no less as policing agents themselves like to flaunt their latest AI-powered superweapons and jump on the rhetorical bandwagon of the AI hype—whatever motivations may drive them, be it the fear of missing out, reputation building, quest to attract more investment capital, or any other more or less noble goal.

This technosolutionism has taken hold of law enforcement agencies across the globe, well-supported by the growth of public–private partnerships (PPPs), the influence of consulting companies over public reform efforts, and the influence of private security firms and the growing range of intelligence providers. Police departments across the globe (as much as corporate security departments) have turned to new technologies to support decision-making through algorithmic risk assessments and predictions based on big data and real-time analytics, facial recognition, or intelligent surveillance (Ferguson, 2017; Joh, 2016, 2017; Peron & Alvarez, this volume; Narayan, this volume; Terra, this volume). The growth of the global private security industry and of private risk and threat intelligence firms, both in numbers and ideological force, is inevitably impacting both public and private policing worldwide (Abrahamsen & Leander, 2016; Diphoorn & Grassiani, 2018; Joh, 2004; King, 2020; Krahmann, 2009; Liss & Sharman, 2015; Meerts, 2020; Morrow, 2022; O'Connor et al., 2008; O'Reilly & Ellison, 2006; Rønn & Søe, 2019; Schneider, 2006; Schreier & Caparini, 2005; Williams, 2014). Public–private partnerships have also been shown to drive police reforms, the global consulting firms in turn shaping the visions of future policing (Kuldova, 2022), while public policing models have been commodified and globally marketed (Ellison & O'Reilly, 2008), pointing to a dynamic of cross-fertilization of policing ideas across the private and public sectors. Recent scholarship has begun seriously engaging with the ways in which these technologies and new public–private partnerships are reshaping the ways we police societies, organize police work, produce criminal intelligence, and prevent crime (Brayne, 2017, 2021; Dencik et al., 2018; Egbert & Krasmann, 2019; Egbert & Leese, 2020; Ferguson, 2017, 2018; Joh, 2016; Kaufmann et al., 2018; Marda & Narayan, 2020; Wilson, 2019). This volume builds on these works, while expanding both into new theoretical and geographical territories.

Law enforcement agencies across the globe have thus—to a greater or lesser degree, and with varying motivations and outcomes—come to embrace the commercial promises of the likes of Palantir that if trained on data sets large and 'clean' enough, predictive algorithms will be able to deliver expert intelligence within milliseconds, outperforming the best experts, the best field-experience of policemen, or security personnel. While the technologies in themselves and the epistemologies and governance approaches embedded in these are without doubt transforming cultures of policing within and beyond the police—as we show across these two volumes, so are the ideological and cultural narratives. Technological fixes, as we amply document, not only go often hand in hand with 'managerial fixes' but are propelled by cultural fantasies of ever-accelerating efficiency, rationalization, and optimization. These fantasies can hold such power that we even no longer ask—efficient at what exactly? Rationality can flip into irrationality as quickly, while the never-ending quest for ever more granular optimization makes us lose sight of the bigger picture, becoming disorienting, increasing our confusion in proportion with the increase and multiplication of possible variables.

The implementation of new technologies often not only results in organizational change and internal restructuring but *is* first and foremost organizational (and cultural) change. This is precisely how technologies transform organizations and societies and, as in the case of the police, can end up challenging established hierarchies, transforming notions of professional discretion (Ericson & Haggerty, 1997; Gundhus, 2017; Joh, 2019; Terpstra et al., 2019, 2022), or the very notions of what constitutes good and efficient policing or intelligence work. As a consequence of the implementation of these various techno-managerial systems, we have thus for instance seen increased organizational and cultural privileging of formalization, a favouring of rigid systems and of information and data over embedded and local knowledge (and knowledge as such, understood as more than data analytics)—in the context of the police, this has been analysed as the shift to 'abstract policing', to a police 'more at a distance, more impersonal and formal, less direct, and more decontextualised (…) less dependent on personal knowledge of officer(s), as this is increasingly being replaced by "system knowledge", framed within the "logic" and categorisations of computer data systems', ultimately impacting on 'the dominating views about what is "good" policing and about police professionalism and leadership' (Terpstra et al., 2019, p. 340).

The turn to big data analytics, machine learning—from their real capabilities to the phantasmatic projections of the future possibilities of AI—must therefore also be seen in terms of the (re)valorization of different forms of knowledge and knowing, and thus in terms of epistemology (the second volume is dedicated to some of the questions pertaining to knowledge in the global big data era). The increasing cultural valorization of 'data', of statistics, of modelling, of quantification, and so on, as a superior mode of understanding the world—manifesting in the fetishization of 'data-driven decision-making'—has by now become undeniable. But while data-driven decision-making is often presented as 'objective', 'neutral', 'apolitical', 'bias-free', 'smart', efficient, 'targeted', and so on, numerous critical scholars across disciplines have, time and again, shown the opposite to be the case (as do also multiple chapters across these two volumes).

Data-driven predictions, risk assessments, and algorithmic decisions have been sold for several decades now by tech companies as 'evidence' and 'intelligence'—as something 'solid' in 'liquid times' (Bauman & Lyon, 2013) as the 'transparent truth', as 'pure', unspoiled by human emotion, prejudice, discretion, and judgement (Kuldova, 2020). However, as critical scholars we are well aware that what counts as data and how it is collected, what is included and what excluded, reflects historical, representational, cultural, gender, and other biases. Prejudices about criminality of certain groups can be built into crime data, resulting in strengthening of prejudices (Marda & Narayan, 2020; Narayan, 2023). Bias has been shown to be endemic to the criminal justice system and to data-driven 'actuarial justice' (Paneyakh, 2014). Bias thus does not disappear through the use of technology, to the contrary, we risk that it will be magnified, with profound consequences for human rights and privacy (Murphy, 2017; Risse, 2019). Critical scholars have discussed many of these unintended harms related to the use of algorithmic technologies (Benjamin, 2019), discussing the perils of systems trained on biased and 'dirty' data (Valentine, 2019), 'rogue algorithms' (O'Neil, 2016), 'algorithmic injustice' (Mbadiwe, 2018), and 'algorithms of oppression' (Noble, 2018). This research has shown how algorithms can reinforce existing racist biases and inequalities and create 'a pernicious feedback loop', where 'policing itself spawns new data, which justifies more policing' (O'Neil, 2016, p. 87). This results in an algorithmic self-fulfilling statistical prophecy—not 'prediction' (Brayne, 2021), further criminalizing those marginalized. Algorithmic injustices can in turn trigger a deeper crisis of legitimacy and declining societal trust. In the United States, citizens have mobilized to challenge the opaque predictive policing systems, questioning their accuracy, accountability, and transparency: for example, LASER (*Los Angeles Strategic Extraction and Restoration*), a predictive policing tool used by LAPD, was discontinued under the pressure of civil rights groups. In Brazil, activists mobilize against facial recognition systems in the service of law enforcement (see Terra, this volume). Critical scholars, across social sciences and humanities, and beyond, have thus not only shown that technology *neither* neutral *nor* apolitical, and that technological change is best understood as simultaneously social, organizational, cultural, and political change (Postman, 1993).

While grassroots resistance has emerged, the need to regulate the use of these technologies, especially in areas such as policing, has come to the forefront of the regulatory agenda in recent years, with the EU AI Act being often seen as pathbreaking. In the meantime, there has been— in line with the logic of regulatory capitalism—a 'whirlwind of new AI regulation' where 'it feels like every day, there's another AI task force, regulatory body, or other group being created or proposed to tackle AI regulation' making it 'increasingly hard to follow what's happening, who's in charge of what, and what progress is actually being made' (Lazzaro, 2024). As soft and hard instruments proliferate, the paradox already emerges—to keep track of regulatory complexity and to comply with these new regulations, we already look to the same tools and technologies that are its subject. It is not likely that the tensions between the rule of tech and the rule of law will be resolved any time soon. But we can start with analysing these tensions and investigating the effects of the expansion of tech-driven punitive solutionism that aims to anticipate, predict, and control (future) human behaviour, and punish deviance based on quantified risk, predictive models, and algorithmic decisions/suggestions (Brayne, 2021; Kuldova, 2022). Moreover, while much literature exploring these subjects has been focused on developments in the West, it is time to draw in perspectives from other locations, while transgressing the methodological nationalism that has in particular shaped studies of policing. These two volumes aim to do just that, while not pretending to be exhaustive in any sense, they seek to open up new paths of investigation while contributing the evolving critical literature on policing in contemporary societies across the globe. These volumes spring from the research project *Algorithmic Governance and Cultures of Policing: Comparative Perspectives from Norway, India, Brazil, Russia, and South Africa* (AGOPOL) which ran from 2021 to 2024 and was funded by The Research Council of Norway (no. 313626). During these years, we have organized several workshops and conferences, in Norway, Brazil, and India, others online due to the COVID-19 pandemic; this volume springs from these encounters and the authors across these two volumes comprise project members as well as those we met at these events. These volumes would not have been possible without these encounters, generous discussions, and commitment of all scholars to understanding the complex realities of the cultures of policing in the global big data era.

Towards a Transversal Reading of Volume I

While each chapter can of course be read in a stand-alone manner, we very much encourage the readers to read across the volume, finding their own connections and frames, beyond the above. Each chapter is provided with a brief abstract summarizing the key gist of the argument, hence there is no need for repeating the same here as readers can simply scroll through these and get an overview. In the following, therefore, we will just very briefly introduce the chapters with an eye to the points of connection and lessons that can be drawn from reading the chapters in context of each other.

In Chapter 2, *National Security, Insider Threat Programs, and the Compliance-Industrial Complex: Reflections on Platformization in Corporate Policing, Intelligence, and Security*, Kuldova extends upon some of the initial reflections in this introduction, drawing us into the hybrid world of corporate policing, intelligence, and security compliance. This chapter shows on the example of insider threat programs what hybridization of crime and security governance and its platformization and datafication can mean in the Western context, building on examples from US and Norway, while drawing predominantly theoretical conclusions. Most interestingly, the chapter shows how certain ways of conceiving, analysing, and understanding the world, embedded and programmed into the algorithmic architectures designed to predict and pre-empt insider threats, represent and are reproductive of 'epistemic closure' which can result in intelligence failure. This logic of 'epistemic closure', however, can be found well beyond this particular case, and speaks precisely to the ways in which algorithmic governance at large operates. In Chapter 3, *Russian Intelligence-Driven Technopoly: Efficiency, Positivism and Governance by Data in an Authoritarian State,* Østbø draws us into the world of Russian 'new intelligence' analysing the ways in which the old *chekist* culture and practices interweave with 'hybrid surveillance capitalism' (Østbø, 2021) and the postmodern, technology-driven pluralization of intelligence, expanding existing and offering new possibilities for surveillance and repression. This chapter shows precisely how the intelligence-driven technopoly in the Russian context is not merely a product of global trends and of technological development but 'also of the power dynamics of the authoritarian system, with which it lives in a peaceful, even synergetic coexistence' (Østbø, this volume). If read together, these two chapters in particular can be read as sounding a warning to liberal democracies increasingly seduced by the promises of 'smart' and 'anticipatory' governance. In Chapter 4, *Smart Security? Transnational Policing Models and Surveillance Technologies in the City of São Paulo,* Peron and Alvarez draw us into the Brazilian context, showing how the discourses of the 'smart city' have been reshaping surveillance and governance in São Paulo (resonating with the discussion of Moscow as a 'smart city' in Østbø's chapter). Again, the authors speak to the various practices of pluralization of policing and security, and distribution of security governance, speaking even of 'securitized sociality' which has emerged in the wake of introduction of various smart and intelligence surveillance and security systems. The chapter shows how transnational security and consulting companies, with their 'universal' solutions and 'best international practices' actually embed themselves into the local contexts and with what consequences, reinforcing local disputes and hierarchies while introducing new dilemmas into security governance, while these new 'arrangements between policing practices and technologies redefine the role of the city's infrastructure as devices for information production and risk control' (Peron & Alvarez, this volume).

In Chapter 5, *Militarized Managerialism and the Bolsonarist Dystopia in Brazil*, Cardoso draws us even deeper into Brazilian context, analysing the rise of the far right under the former president Jair Bolsonaro and the implications of 'militarized managerialism', which treats public security as war and a targeted portion of citizens as enemies, for the larger logic of policing and governance in the country. Drawing on ethnographic research with the Rio de Janeiro Military Police and Integrated Command and Control Centres, Cardoso paints a vivid picture of how techno-managerial systems have come to operate within this context, as the ideals of efficiency and technological precision become invoked 'when violently managing the death of a part of the population'. In Chapter 6, *'For Your Own Safety': The Soft Push of Surveillance by the Private Sector in India*, Narayan draws us into the contemporary Indian context, considering the increasing power of the private security and surveillance industry in shaping both state and everyday governance and policing in India and the role of public–private partnerships. The chapter also unpacks the cultural tropes, ideologies, and phantasms invoked by the industry to sell its products, create new markets, and legitimize these, showing that rather than responding to pre-existing needs and demands of the public sector, the industry is effectively creating and shaping these needs. This again speaks to the hybridization, privatization, and pluralization of policing discussed earlier in this introduction, and can also be read in the parallel to the developments and role of private security providers in policing discussed in Brazil by Peron and Alvarez. In Chapter 7, *E-Governance and Smart Policing in Kerala, India: Towards a Kerala Model of Algorithmic Governance?*, Varghese continues this discussion by drawing us into the dynamics of the ambitious e-governance program launched by the Kerala Government, which, among others, seeks to transform policing under the promise of 'efficiency' and modernization of state infrastructure, digitizing police practices, integrating everyday policing with ICT and AI as part of its vision. Again, these algorithmic technologies play a double role, seeking to surveil and govern both the population and the police itself, being a managerial tool. In particular, within the Indian context of policing and management of the police as workers, algorithmic techno-managerial infrastructures, as Varghese shows, seek to sanitize decision-making (precisely through the presumed technological neutrality), while inducing 'automatic docility' in the lower-ranking police officers, revealing their considerable disciplining power and speaking to the shift to some of the aspects of 'abstract police' (Terpstra et al., 2019). In Chapter 8, *Musical Policing in Today's Brazil: A Study of Jingles in the Bolsonaro Movement*, Bøhler draws us back to the Brazilian context, opening up a unique perspective on policing informed by scholarship on the power of music and of jingles in particular. Brazil is likely impossible to think without music, and this goes also for the context of policing and political programming, the intersection of the latter two discussed earlier by Cardoso. Bøhler develops a new and exciting perspective on algorithmic governance and musical policing by exploring the phenomenon of earworms that 'expose us to political imaginations beyond our own will as melodies play on repeat in our own bodies', a phenomenon actualized by the rise of both social media and AI, and their particular role in the context of electoral politics in Brazil. In Chapter 9, *A Historical Perspective on Civil Society Activism and the Campaign to Ban Digital Facial Recognition Technologies in Public Security in Brazil*, Terra probes into both the history and present of resistance to facial recognition technologies in Brazil. In this unique and historically contextualized perspective on civil society resistance and mobilization against surveillance technologies, and vis-à-vis the power of private security and tech firms, the unique interplay between the transnational and local dynamic of these movements comes to fore, as questions of policy transfer across different sites of activism (e.g., US) and regulatory efforts (e.g., EU) come to fore. But the chapter also proves the need to consider the role of civil society and resistance in shaping cultures of policing and modes of algorithmic governance in any given location. In Chapter 10, *Algorithmic Police Reform: The Political Economy and Social Lives of a Police Early Intervention Algorithm*, Nesvet follows up on the theme of reform as a result of civil society and political pressure following events of police violence, zooming on the so-called early intervention systems (EIS), algorithmic systems used in the US as a compliance tool to flag and predict bad behaviour by police employees. While these systems, albeit directed at the police, share some features and resonate with the 'insider threat programs' described by Kuldova in Chapter 2, in Nesvet's chapter we get a closer understanding of how such compliance measures may work (or rather not) in practice—in his case paradoxically normalizing violence, foreclosing organizational change, public knowledge, and democratic deliberation. This chapter sheds unique light on how the lower-ranking police are sought to be policed (and individually responsibilized) through computational compliance software supplied by private tech firms, while high-ranking police are typically let off the hook (a design feature of the software). But it also speaks to the ways in which both cultures of accountability and of policing become transformed in the process of automation. And finally, in Chapter 11, *The Platformization of Policing: A Cross-National Analysis*, Egbert, Galis, Gundhus, and Wathne, draw us into both the internal and cultural dynamic of 'desiloisation' of police databases and the way it played out in the three close but different contexts of Germany, Denmark, and Norway as the local police departments worked to implement the Palantir Technologies platform. In the process, the authors analyse these processes of implementation— some more or less successful, others failed—within the local cultural, economic, and political contexts. But irrespective of success or failure, in all cases it is beyond doubt that these platforms 'restructure, and reprogram the police organizations and work by (re-)introducing a new type of scientific rationality based on the desire for a powerful data integration' (Egbert et al., this volume), while reconfiguring work practices, professional cultures, and work conditions. Thereby, we return to our introductory remark on the techno-managerial nature and effects of these software products, wherein their capacity for social, organizational, and cultural change also resides, reflecting their infrastructural and epistemic power.

We hope that this volume opens up new perspectives on the multiple dynamics of algorithmic governance and policing and intelligence in the big data era and we shall also continue this discussion in the volume II, which revolves around the questions of politics and ethics of knowledge.

Funding Statement This work was supported by The Research Council of Norway project no. 313626—*Algorithmic Governance and Cultures of Policing: Comparative Perspectives from Norway, India, Brazil, Russia, and South Africa* (AGOPOL).

References

Abrahamsen, R., & Leander, A. (Eds.). (2016). *Routledge Handbook of Private Security Studies*. Routledge. https://doi.org/10.4324/9781315850986

Amicelle, A., & Iafolla, V. (2018). Suspicion-in-the-Making: Surveillance and Denunciation in Financial Policing. *The British Journal of Criminology, 58*(4), 845–863. https://doi.org/10.1093/bjc/azx051

Amoore, L. (2013). *The Politics of Possibility: Risk and Security Beyond Probability*. Duke University Press. https://doi.org/10.1515/9780822377269

Arrigo, B., & Sellers, B. (Eds.). (2021). *The Pre-Crime Society: Crime, Culture and Control in the Ultramodern Age*. Bristol University Press. https://doi.org/10.1332/policypress/9781529205251.001.0001

Barberis, J., Arner, D. W., & Buckley, R. P. (2019). *The RegTech Book: The Financial Technology Handbook for Investors, Entrepreneurs and Visionaries in Regulation*. Willey & Sons Ltd.

Bauman, Z., & Lyon, D. (2013). *Liquid Surveillance: A Conversation*. Polity.

Ben Jaffel, H., & Larsson, S. (Eds.). (2022). *Problematising Intelligence Studies: Towards A New Research Agenda*. Routledge. https://doi.org/10.4324/9781003205463

Ben Jaffel, H., & Larsson, S. (2023). Why Do We Need a New Research Agenda for the Study of Intelligence? *International Journal of Intelligence and Counterintelligence*, 1–25. https://doi.org/10.1080/08850607.2023.2222342

Benjamin, R. (2019). *Race After Technology: Abolitionist Tools for the New Jim Code*. Polity Press. https://doi.org/10.1093/sf/soz162

Bent, A. A. (2023). Large Language Models: AI's Legal Revolution. *Pace Law Review, 44*(1), 91–138. https://doi.org/10.58948/2331-3528.2083

Besteman, C., & Gusterson, H. (Eds.). (2019). *Life By Algorithms: How Roboprocesses Are Remaking Our World*. University of Chicago Press. https://doi.org/10.7208/chicago/9780226627731.001.0001

Boels, D., & Verhage, A. (2015). Plural Policing: A State-of-the-Art Review. *Policing: An International Journal of Police Strategies & Management, 39*(1), 2–18. https://doi.org/10.1108/PIJPSM-05-2015-0069

Braithwaite, J. (2008). *Regulatory Capitalism: How it Works, Ideas for Making it Better*. Edward Elgar. https://doi.org/10.4337/9781848441262

Brayne, S. (2017). Big Data Surveillance: The Case of Policing. *American Sociological Review, 82*(5), 977–1008. https://doi.org/10.1177/0003122417725865

Brayne, S. (2021). *Predict and Surveil: Data, Discretion and the Future of Policing.* Oxford University Press. https://doi.org/10.1093/oso/978019068 4099.001.0001

Bureš, O. (2015). *Private Security Companies: Transforming Politics and Security in the Czech Republic.* Palgrave Macmillan. https://doi.org/10.1057/978113 7477521

Button, M. (2019). *Private Policing.* Routledge. https://doi.org/10.4324/978 1351240772

Camacho-Collados, M., & Liberatore, F. (2014). A Decision Support System for Predictive Police Patrolling. *Decision Support Systems, 75*, 25–37. https:// doi.org/10.1016/j.dss.2015.04.012

Crawford, A. (2003). Plural Policing in the UK: Policing Beyond the Police. In T. Newburn (Ed.), *Handbook of Policing* (pp. 147–181). Routledge.

De Gregorio, G. (2023). The Normative Power of Artificial Intelligence. *CGSL Working Papers, 4*, 1–27. https://repositorio.ucp.pt/bitstream/10400. 14/43016/1/88166160.pdf

Dencik, L., Hintz, A., & Carey, Z. (2018). Prediction, Pre-emption and Limits to Dissent: Social Media and Big Data Uses for Policing Protests in the United Kingdom. *New Media & Society, 20*(4), 1433–1450. https://doi.org/ 10.1177/1461444817697722

Diphoorn, T., & Grassiani, E. (Eds.). (2018). *Security Blurs: The Politics of Plural Security Provision.* Routledge. https://doi.org/10.4324/978135112 7387

Egbert, S., & Krasmann, S. (2019). Predictive Policing: Not Yet, But Soon Preemptive? *Policing and Society,* 1–15. https://doi.org/10.1080/10439463. 2009.1611821

Egbert, S., & Leese, M. (2020). *Criminal Futures: Predictive Policing and Everyday Police Work.* Routledge. https://doi.org/10.4324/9780429328732

Ellison, G., & O'Reilly, C. (2008). 'Ulster's Policing Goes Global': The Police Reform Process in Northern Ireland and the Creation of a Global Brand. *Crime, Law and Social Change, 50*, 331–351. https://doi.org/10.1007/s10 611-008-9126-4

Ericson, R. V., & Haggerty, K. D. (1997). *Policing the Risk Society.* Clarendon Press. https://doi.org/10.3138/9781442678590

Ferguson, A. G. (2017). *The Rise of Big Data Policing: Surveillance, Race, and the Future of Law Enforcement.* New York University Press. https://doi.org/ 10.2307/j.ctt1pwtb27

Ferguson, A. G. (2018). Illuminating Black Data Policing. *Ohio State Journal of Criminal Law, 15*, 503–525.

Frischmann, B., & Selinger, E. (2018). *Re-engineering Humanity.* Cambridge University Press. https://doi.org/10.1017/9781316544846

Fyfe, N., Gundhus, H., & Rønn, K. V. (Eds.). (2018). *Moral Issues in Intelligence-led Policing.* Routledge. https://doi.org/10.4324/9781315231259

Gundhus, H. (2017). Discretion as an Obstacle: Police Culture, Change, and Governance in a Norwegian Context. *Policing, 11*(3), 258–272. https://doi.org/10.1093/police/pax012

Gundhus, H., Talberg, N., & Wathne, C. T. (2018). Konturene av en ny politirolle: politiansattes erfaringer med Nærpolitireformen. In V. L. Sørli & P. Larsson (Eds.), *Politireformer: Idealer, realiteter, retorikk og praksis* (pp. 199–222). Cappelen Damm Akademisk.

Hansen, H. K., Salskov-Iversen, D., & Biselev, S. (2002). Discursive Globalization: Transnational Discourse Communities and New Public Management. In M. Ougaard & R. Higgott (Eds.), *Towards a Global Polity* (pp. 107–124). Routledge.

Joh, E. E. (2004). The Paradox of Private Policing. *Journal of Criminal Law and Criminology, 95*(1), 49–132. https://doi.org/10.2307/3491382

Joh, E. E. (2016). The New Surveillance Discretion: Automated Suspicion, Big Data, and Policing. *Harvard Law & Policy Review, 10*, 15–43.

Joh, E. E. (2017). Artificial Intelligence and Policing: First Questions. *Seattle University Law Review, 41*, 1139–1144.

Joh, E. E. (2019). The Consequences of Automating and Deskilling the Police. *UCLA Law Review Discourse*, 1–34.

Kaleem, A. (2022). Citizen-Led Intelligence Gathering under UK's Prevent Duty. In H. Ben Jaffel & S. Larsson (Eds.), *Problematising Intelligence Studies: Towards a New Research Agenda* (pp. 73–95). Routledge. https://doi.org/10.4324/9781003205463-6

Kalpokas, I. (2019). *Algorithmic Governance: Politics and Law in the Post-Human Era.* Palgrave Macmillan. https://doi.org/10.1007/978-3-030-31922-9

Katzenbach, C., & Ulbricht, L. (2019). Algorithmic Governance. *Internet Policy Review, 8*(4), 1–18. https://doi.org/10.14763/2019.4.1424

Kaufmann, M., Egbert, S., & Leese, M. (2018). Predictive Policing and the Politics of Patters. *The British Journal of Criminology*, 1–19. https://doi.org/10.1093/bjc/azy060

King, M. (2020). Out of Obscurity: The Contemporary Private Investigator in Australia. *International Journal of Police Science & Management, 22*(3), 285–296. https://doi.org/10.1177/1461355720931887

Krahmann, E. (2009). *Private Security Companies and the State Monopoly on Violence: A Case of Norm Change?* (PRIFF Reports, 88, Issue). http://nbn-resolving.de/urn:nbn:de:0168-ssoar-292745

Kuldova, T. (2020). Imposter Paranoia in the Age of Intelligent Surveillance: Policing Outlaws, Borders and Undercover Agents. *Journal of Extreme Anthropology, 4*(1), 45–73. https://doi.org/10.5617/jea.7813

Kuldova, T. (2021). The Cynical University: Gamified Subjectivity in Norwegian Academia. *Ephemera: Theory & Politics in Organization, 21*(3), 1–29.

Kuldova, T. (2022). *Compliance-Industrial Complex: The Operating System of a Pre-Crime Society.* Palgrave Macmillan. https://doi.org/10.1007/978-3-031-19224-1

Kuldova, T., & Nordrik, B. (2023). Workplace Investigations, the Epistemic Power of Managerialism, and the Hollowing Out of the Norwegian Model of Co-determination. *Class and Capital.* https://doi.org/10.1177/030981 68231179971

Kuldova, T., Østbø, J., & Raymen, T. (2024). *Luxury and Corruption: Challenging the Anti-Corruption Consensus.* Bristol University Press. https://doi.org/10.56687/9781529212426

Lazzaro, S. (2024). Good Luck Keeping Up With the Whirlwind of New AI Regulation. *Fortune.* 28 March 2024. https://fortune.com/2024/03/28/ai-regulation-un-eu-us-biden/

Levi-Faur, D. (2005). The Global Diffusion of Regulatory Capitalism. *Annals AAPSS, 598*, 12–32. https://doi.org/10.1177/0002716204272371

Levi-Faur, D. (2017). Regulatory Capitalism. In P. Drahos (Ed.), *Regulatory Theory: Foundation and Applications* (pp. 289–302). ANU Press. https://doi.org/10.22459/RT.02.2017.17

Liss, C., & Sharman, J. C. (2015). Global Corporate Crime-Fighters: Private Transnational Responses to Piracy and Money Laundering. *Review of International Political Economy, 22*(4), 693–718. https://doi.org/10.1080/096 92290.2014.936482

Marda, V., & Narayan, S. (2020). Data in New Delhi's Predictive Policing System. *FAT* '20: Proceedings of the 2020 Conference on Fairness, Accountability, and Transparency,* 317–324. https://doi.org/10.1145/3351095.337 2865

Mayer-Schönberger, V., & Cukier, K. (2013). *Big Data: A Revolution that Will Transform How We Live, Work, and Think.* Houghton Mifflin Harcourt.

Mbadiwe, T. (2018). Algorithmic Injustice. *The New Atlantis: A Journal of Technology & Society, Winter,* 3–28.

McCulloch, J., & Wilson, D. (2016). *Pre-crime: Pre-emption, Precaution and the Future*. Routledge. https://doi.org/10.4324/9781315769714

Meerts, C. (2020). Corporate Investigations: Beyond Notions of Public-Private Relations. *Journal of Contemporary Criminal Justice, 36* (1), 86–100. https://doi.org/10.1177/1043986219890202

Morozov, E. (2013). *To Save Everything, Click Here*. Public Affairs.

Morrow, M. A. R. (2022). Private Sector Intelligence: On the Long Path of Professionalization. *Intelligence and National Security, 37* (3), 402–420. https://doi.org/10.1080/02684527.2022.2029099

Murphy, M. H. (2017, 2017/05/04). Algorithmic Surveillance: The Collection Conundrum. *International Review of Law, Computers & Technology, 31* (2), 225–242. https://doi.org/10.1080/13600869.2017.1298497

Nagy, V., & Kerezsi, K. (2020). Introduction—Critical Reflection in Policing Studies. In V. Nagy & K. Kerezsi (Eds.), *A Critical Approach to Police Science: New Perspectives in Post-Transitional Policing Studies*. Eleven International Publishing.

Narayan, S. (2023). *Predictive Policing and The Construction of The 'Criminal': An Ethnographic Study of Delhi Police*. Palgrave Macmillan. https://doi.org/10.1007/978-3-031-40102-2

Noble, S. U. (2018). *Algorithms of Oppression: How Search Engines Reinforce Racism*. New York University Press. https://doi.org/10.2307/j.ctt1pwt9w5

O'Connor, D., Lippert, R. K., Spencer, D., & Smylie, L. (2008). Seeing Private Security Like a State. *Criminology & Criminal Justice, 8* (2), 203–226. https://doi.org/10.1177/1748895808088995

O'Neil, C. (2016). *Weapons of Math Destruction: How Big Data Increases Inequality and Threatens Democracy*. Crown.

O'Reilly, C. (2015). The Pluralization of High Policing: Convergence and Divergence at the Public-Private Interface. *British Journal of Criminology, 55* (4), 688–710. https://doi.org/10.1093/bjc/azu114

O'Reilly, C., & Ellison, G. (2006). 'Eye Spy Private High': Re-Conceptualizing High Policing Theory. *British Journal of Criminology, 46*, 641–660. https://doi.org/10.1093/bjc/azi090

Østbø, J. (2021). Hybrid Surveillance Capitalism: Sber's Model for Russia's Modernization. *Post-Soviet Affairs, 37* (5), 435–452. https://doi.org/10.1080/1060586X.2021.1966216

Paneyakh, E. (2014). Faking Performance Together: Systems of Performance Evaluation in Russian Enforcement Agencies and Production of Bias and Privilege. *Post-Soviet Affairs, 30* (2–3), 115–136. https://doi.org/10.1080/1060586X.2013.858525

Postman, N. (1993). *Technopoly: The Surrender of Culture to Technology*. Vintage Books.

Ratcliffe, J. H. (2016). *Intelligence-Led Policing*. Routledge. https://doi.org/10.4324/9781315717579

Risse, M. (2019). Human Rights and Artificial Intelligence: An Urgently Needed Agenda. *Human Rights Quarterly, 41*(1), 1–16. https://doi.org/10.1353/hrq.2019.0000

Rønn, K. V., & Søe, S. O. (2019). Is SOCMINT Private? Privacy in Public and the Nature of Social Media Intelligence. *Intelligence and National Security, 34*(3), 362–378. https://doi.org/10.1080/02684527.2019.1553701

Rosa, H. (2021). *The Uncontrollability of the World*. Polity.

Schneider, S. (2006). Privatizing Economic Crime Enforcement: Exploring the Role of Private Sector Investigative Agencies in Combating Money Laundering. *Policing & Society, 16*(3), 285–312. https://doi.org/10.1080/10439460600812065

Schreier, F., & Caparini, M. (2005). *Privatising Security: Law, Practice and Governance of Private Military and Security Companies*. Geneva Centre for the Democratic Control of Armed Forces (DCAF) Occasional Paper No. 6.

Shore, C., & Wright, S. (2015). Audit Culture Revisited: Rankings, Ratings, and the Reassembling of Society. *Current Anthropology, 56*(3), 421–444. https://doi.org/10.1086/681534

Shore, C., & Wright, S. (2024). *Audit Culture: How Indicators and Rankings are Reshaping the World*. Pluto Press. https://doi.org/10.2307/jj.10819589

Supiot, A. (2017). *Governance by Numbers: The Making of a Legal Model of Allegiance*. Bloomsbury.

Susskind, J. (2018). *Future Politics: Living Together in a World Transformed by Tech*. Oxford University Press.

Susskind, R. (1996). *The Future of Law: Facing the Challenges of Information Technology*. Oxford University Press.

Terpstra, J., Fyfe, N. R., & Salet, R. (2019). The Abstract Police: A Conceptual Exploration of Unintended Changes of Police Organisations. *Police Journal: Theory, Practice and Principles, 92*(4), 339–359. https://doi.org/10.1177/0032258X18817999

Terpstra, J., Salet, R., & Fyfe, N. (Eds.). (2022). *The Abstract Police: Critical Reflections on Contemporary Change in Police Organisations*. Eleven International Publishing.

Valentine, S. (2019). Impoverished Algorithms: Misguided Governments, Flawed Technologies, and Social Control. *Fordham Urban Law Review, 46*(2), 364–427.

Veggeland, N. (2009). *Taming the Regulatory State: Politics and Ethics.* Edward Elgar Publishing Ltd. https://doi.org/10.4337/9781848447509

Verhage, A. (2011). *The Anti Money Laundering Complex and the Compliance Industry.* Routledge. https://doi.org/10.4324/9780203828489

Verhage, A., Easton, M., & De Kimpe, S. (Eds.). (2022). *Policing in Smart Societies: Reflections on the Abstract Police.* Palgrave Macmillan. https://doi.org/10.1007/978-3-030-83685-6

Wathne, C. T. (2015). *Like Being a Stranger in Your Own House: How the Police Perceives Meaning and Motivation in Light of New Public Management.* University of Oslo.

Wathne, C. T. (2018). Welfare Professionals in Transformation: The Case of Police Officers in Norway. In H. Hvid & E. Falkum (Eds.), *Work and Wellbeing in Nordic Countries: Critical Perspectives on the World's Best Working Lives* (pp. 260–282). Routledge. https://doi.org/10.4324/9781351169967-18

Wathne, C. T. (2020). New Public Management and the Police Profession at Play. *Criminal Justice Ethics,* 1–22. https://doi.org/10.1080/0731129X.2020.1746106

Waye, V. (2019). Regtech: New Frontier in Legal Scholarship. *Adelaide Law Review, 40,* 363–386.

Westmarland, L. (2011). Police Cultures. In T. Newburn (Ed.), *Handbook of Policing* (pp. 253–280). Routledge.

Williams, J. W. (2014). The Private Eyes of Corporate Culture: The Forensic Accounting and Corporate Investigation Industry and the Production of Corporate Financial Security. In K. Walby & R. K. Lippert (Eds.), *Corporate Security in the 21st Century: Theory and Practice in International Perspective* (pp. 56–77). Palgrave Macmillan. https://doi.org/10.1057/9781137346070_4

Wilson, D. (2019). Platform Policing and the Real-Time Cop. *Surveillance & Society, 17*(1), 69–75. https://doi.org/10.24908/ss.v17i1/2.12958

Zedner, L. (2006). Liquid Security: Managing the Market for Crime Control. *Criminology & Criminal Justice, 6*(3), 267–288. https://doi.org/10.1177/1748895806065530

Zedner, L. (2007). Pre-crime and Post-criminology? *Theoretical Criminology, 11*(2), 261–281. https://doi.org/10.1177/1362480607075851

Zedner, L., & Ashworth, A. (2019). The Rise and Restraint of the Preventive State. *Annual Review of Criminology,* (2), 429–450. https://doi.org/10.1146/annurev-criminol-011518-024526

Zuboff, S. (2019). *The Age of Surveillance Capitalism: The Fight for a Human Future at the New Frontier of Power.* Profile Books.

2

National Security, Insider Threat Programs, and the Compliance-Industrial Complex: Reflections on Platformization in Corporate Policing, Intelligence, and Security

Tereza Østbø Kuldova ⓘ

The post-Cold War age of unrestricted globalization and international cooperation, or rather the naïve belief in their unquestionable benefits, as manifested in the thesis of 'the end of history' (Fukuyama, 1992), appears to have received a final blow with the ongoing war in Ukraine. After several decades of hyperglobalization, intense integration of markets, and minimization of trade barriers, we are witnessing a rapid geopolitical transformation. Russia, China and other authoritarian regimes emerge as a serious threat to US hegemony, the international liberal order, and to globalization as we knew it (or fantasized about—as a force of democratization and peace). As national security interests return to the fore, we are witnessing the *remoralization* of (geo)politics, of capitalism and of markets, and a bifurcation of the world along the lines of good and evil (Kuldova et al., 2024), arguably in a more profound way than during the George W. Bush administration's 'war on terror'.

T. Ø. Kuldova (✉)
OsloMet—Oslo Metropolitan University, Oslo, Norway
e-mail: tereza.kuldova@oslomet.no

© The Author(s), under exclusive license to Springer Nature
Switzerland AG 2024
T. Ø. Kuldova et al. (eds.), *Policing and Intelligence in the Global Big Data Era,
Volume I*, Palgrave's Critical Policing Studies,
https://doi.org/10.1007/978-3-031-68326-8_2

This remoralization in turn depends on the active and increasing *securitization* of liberal values by many Western liberal and democratic states (Buzan et al., 1998; Østbø, 2017), which manifests in, among other things, the Western rhetoric surrounding financial and military support for Ukraine and economic sanctions. But the trouble is that after decades of neoliberal reforms, globalization, privatization, outsourcing, and 'assetization' of (critical and public) infrastructure (Birch & Muniesa, 2020; Christophers, 2023), the world is more interconnected and interdependent than ever. Threats are thus no longer external and contained within hostile nation states, but can lurk anywhere and at any time in both the digital and physical realms. Hence the heightened concerns about 'insider threats', hybrid warfare and 'weaponized interdependence' (Drezner et al., 2021). In this context, national security interests can only be pursued in collaboration with the private sector and civil society. Or else, by enlisting multiple 'stakeholders', in particular large market actors, as *partners* in the pursuit of the state's security interests. Henry Kissinger even argued that 'we are now living in a whole new era', as *Spiegel International* commented, 'this new era, many expect, could be that of strong state' (Schulz et al., 2022). *Wall Street Journal* opinion makers fear the rise of this strong state and 'state capitalism' in U.S. under the Biden Administration (Henninger, 2023). Scholars speak of a far longer genealogy of 'authoritarian liberalism' which is not thinkable without contemporary corporate governance and management structures (Chamayou, 2021). Strong or not, there is no doubt that we are witnessing a transformation of the state under the renewed concerns about national security. But the question is rather the following: how is this state actually pursuing national security interests after decades of neoliberal reforms? While this question could be answered in different ways, in this chapter we will reflect on insider threat programs, which are particular preventive security compliance measure that U.S. and other Western states increasingly impose on private sector and other entities, or 'expect' them to comply with, and which is being established as 'best practice' well beyond those subject to any hard laws. Unlike any of the literature available on this subject, we shall link these programs to the larger socio-cultural, economic and geopolitical context, while also reflecting on the epistemic premises of these programs and their inherent flaws. This analytical and reflexive exercise may reveal the contours of the Western state (understood here as an ideal type) reorienting itself around national security in this 'new era'.

Insider threat and risk management programs and the accompanied digital platforms have become popular 'technosolutions' and managerial fixes for companies, critical infrastructure operators as well as governmental organizations well beyond the defence sector. Insider threat and risk programs and platforms promise to detect organizational betrayal, crimes, malicious behaviours, and subversive activities by insiders, 'disgruntled employees' and other 'enemies within'—and thus to tackle corporate and foreign espionage, intellectual property (IP) theft, financial crimes, corruption, fraud, insider trading, (cyber)security breaches, 'leaking', sexual harassment, and more. This is, indeed, a grand promise—especially if all this is to be achieved through a (single) platform and standardized management procedures. In this chapter, we shall consider insider threat programs and platforms as an 'exemplary example' (Højer & Bandak, 2015) of how this new security state seeks to operate *through* organizations and at the organizational level. In this regard, it may be helpful to think of states, corporations and of artificial intelligence (AI) as three types of 'artificial agents' in the sense developed by David Runciman, as artificial agents to which we, in different ways, delegate decision-making and to think of the transforming relations between these agents (Runciman, 2023). The neoliberal state has already outsourced much of its core tasks, and even decision-making and agency to corporations, while it is increasingly seeking to automate its central functions through data-driven and AI-powered technologies. Now, this neoliberal state, operating in the new geopolitical landscape, seeks to preserve its core ideology while pursuing its national security interests with new vigour. And it does so by trying to leverage the artificial agency of the corporates and the private sector, which has for the most part been limited to narrow profit-oriented activity, for much more comprehensive security purposes. The corporates, in turn, increasingly rely on different forms of automation and AI-powered systems to comply with these demands of the state. Under these conditions, the artificial agency of the state, corporations, and AIs become ever more deeply integrated and decisions delegated to both human and inhuman agents, layered and overlaid in ways that make it increasingly difficult (if not impossible) to determine where power and accountability lies (and where justice is to be had).

I would argue that the defining feature of this neoliberal security state in the new geopolitical situation is its quest to eliminate threats by (among others) weaponizing corporate governance and management (infra)structures. This is attempted through compliance-oriented regulations—sanctions regimes, security compliance obligations for critical infrastructure, or anti-money laundering are just some examples of this type of regulation where the state takes up the role of a supervisor (Petersen, 2012). In contemporary corporate security governance and management, these become translated into anticipatory and 'targeted governance' (Valverde & Mopas, 2004). This form of governance is oriented towards almost 'surgical' detection and pre-emption of 'enemies within'.

This chapter is grounded in extensive hybrid ethnographic fieldwork (2020–2024) across the Western compliance industry (with focus on US, UK, EU, and Norway), which has included interviews with compliance professionals, attending numerous conferences online and offline, taking a number of certifications in compliance, including several different insider threat management trainings (Kuldova, 2022). This chapter also relies on extensive review of primary sources such as public documents, security strategies as well as course material analysis, and secondary literature review. As across my other work (e.g., Kuldova & Nordrik, 2023), I utilize a reflexive methodology which approaches critical theory as a 'triple hermeneutics' (Alvesson & Sköldberg, 2018). Reflecting on this rich material, this chapter raises critical questions pertaining to the nature of the (Western) state, in particular as exemplified by U.S. and Norway, in relation to the privatization, pluralization, and professionalization of private sector intelligence and policing, the securitization of compliance and management, and the consequent platformization of this form of management—which could be argued to mirror the logic of platformization of policing (Egbert et al., this volume; Egbert, 2019). Extending on my earlier work on the 'compliance-industrial complex' (Kuldova, 2022) and our work that has challenged the 'anti-corruption consensus'

(Kuldova et al., 2024), I encourage us to take a critical posture vis-á-vis systems, such as insider threat programs, introduced in the name of protecting us against crime and security threats that, we are told, undermine our democracy and rule of law. I argue that these systems may themselves end up posing these very same risks—not merely perpetuating insecurity (Jacobsen, 2020), but also resulting in (increasingly automated) injustice and intelligence failure. Before we turn to the insider threat programs, let us consider the governance logic which has enabled them in the first place. Since, as we shall see later, there is to date no critical literature on insider threat programs, this is an even more important and necessary exercise.

Governance *Through* Crime and Security: The Logic of Compliance

As national security interests make their presence intensely felt, we can see more clearly the contours of the state that accelerates its efforts to leverage private management infrastructures—the corporate artificial agency—to pursue its security interests. Economic sanctions regimes can serve as an example, by now familiar to all: sanctions compliance requires all citizens, companies and organizations of the sanctions issuing state to *comply* with sanctions regulation (under the threat of prison time, fines, and reputational damage). The recent sanctions regimes aimed at Russian individuals, businesses and exports to Russia have so far largely failed to achieve their initially stated maximalist goals, that is changing Russia's aggressive behaviour or at least crippling its economy—the war is still raging, the Russian war economy experienced growth and new structures of sanctions evasion, reconfiguring supply chains, quickly emerged (Busvine, 2023). But sanctions regimes have still managed to expand the state's hold of the internal governance and management structures of Western companies. For transnational corporations, businesses, and organizations, sanctions regimes translate into implementing sanction screening software and new practices of due diligence, KYC (know-your-customer), intelligence gathering, background checks of clients, customers, suppliers, financial transactions, and more. Anti-money laundering (AML) and countering the financing of terrorism (CFT) regulations are another example: herein the state requires banks, financial institutions and other regulated entities to perform due diligence on clients and transactions, detect 'risky clients' and generate 'suspicious activity reports' (SARs)—or else, intelligence—for the national Financial Intelligence Units (FIUs) (Amicelle & Iafolla, 2018; Marlin-Bennett, 2016; Verhage, 2011). Similarly, anti-corruption regulations require the implementation of internal compliance programs, whistleblowing channels, and more that seek to detect and mitigate corrupt individuals and practices (Hansen & Tang-Jensen, 2015; Jeppesen, 2019; Kuldova, 2022; Kuldova et al., 2024); they are legitimized by the hegemonic view of corruption as a threat to 'the stability and security of democracy, rule of law and human rights' (Zamfir, 2023, p. 7).

As US, UK, and other countries are elevating the fight against corruption to a matter of national security (Kuldova, 2022), we not only see the integration of anti-corruption *into* sanctions regimes—such as in the US, the UK and Canada, but also the emergence of new hybrid task forces—think the US Task Force KleptoCapture. These task forces consist of experts across fields and departments which were, up until rather recently, 'siloed'. These multiagency teams mirror, in a sense, the logic of the platform and of integration of disparate data and expertise and the efforts at 'de-siloing' crime and security governance (*see also* Egbert et al., in this volume). This has also resulted in increasing legal hybridization.

In 2022, in the EU, Ursula von der Leyen for instance proposed to include corruption into EU's human rights sanctions regime, an idea repeatedly pushed by Open Society Foundations (OSF). But what does this mean? Effectively, this would be a novel legal tool that would integrate crime and security governance (corruption now being elevated from a 'mere' criminal offense to a security threat) into the 'governance through human rights' (Hamilton & Lippert, 2020) and into sanction regimes. In a report funded by OSF, 'Why European Union Needs Anticorruption Sanctions', preceding von der Leyen's statement, this is legitimized by the now standard refrain that 'corrupt proceedings have a corrosive impact on Western societies and pose a national security risk to democratic governance and the rule of law' while also invoking the notion of targeted governance when arguing that 'by detaching measures from a country's name, the EU *can surgically target wrongdoers and shift the blame to individuals rather than countries*' (OSEPI, 2022, p. 3; emphasis mine).

This example already reveals three key dynamics in contemporary crime and security governance which have set the stage for the proliferation of insider threat programs and for the platformization of security governance: (1) the *hybridization* of crime and security governance, (2) the quest to govern *through* crime and security by imposing compliance obligations onto market actors and citizens alike (which has stimulated the privatization and pluralization of intelligence), and (3) the ideological fantasy of 'targeted governance' (Valverde & Mopas, 2004). Let us unpack these in turn, as they are a precondition for understanding the compliance logic behind insider threat programs.

Hybridization of Crime and Security Governance

To the first point: It is no overstatement to say that we are witness to a rapid proliferation of regulatory regimes that seek to combat various transnational crimes and security threats. This larger phenomenon of proliferating regulation has been described as 'regulatory capitalism' (Braithwaite, 2008; Levi-Faur, 2017). These regimes are of such techno-bureaucratic complexity and detail that they require armies of experts to interpret, to translate these, and to turn them into compliance, management, and software products. These products are typically designed to both satisfy these detailed regulations and arm's-length governance of the state through supervisory and audit bodies, *and* to contribute to the profit-oriented activities of the corporates. In other words, regulations are commodified; and their rapid proliferation generates new markets for consulting firms and big tech (Kuldova, 2022; Shore & Wright, 2015, 2018). Over the time, these regulatory regimes have become so hybridized that even lawyers routinely struggle to draw boundaries between legal concepts and hierarchies (Sunde, 2023; Tuori, 2014; Valasik & Torres, 2022). Legal debates also increasingly revolve around how to legitimize these legal hybrids or make them (retroactively) compatible with the notion of 'rule of law' and due process; this requires 'legal creativity' (Shagina, 2023). Legal and regulatory hybridization also means that the compliance products on the market—such as insider threat programs—are, too, increasingly hybridized, seeking to tackle crimes, security threats as much as ethical breaches through the same technologies and managerial methods. Compliance thus becomes plat-formized and the managerial siloes between combatting and pre-empting very different forms of risks, threats and crimes—from corruption, via cyber threats and leaking to sexual harassment—are attempted to be dismantled. But compliance products do not only seek to satisfy complex and often conflicting regulatory demands. Increasingly, they also seek to provide added value and serve internal organizational (profit-oriented) interests: e.g., enhanced control and surveillance of workers, performance management, and increases of efficiency and productivity. There is an inherent tension between the *national* security interests which the state seeks to pursue by imposing compliance-oriented regulation on compa-nies and the profit interests of the (often multinational) companies. This inherent tension between profit and state interests is something we need to always keep in mind when thinking about how regulations are trans-lated into compliance products (Notaker, 2023). In this respect it must be noted that while the hybridization of crime and security governance by the state results in 'frictional security governance' (Johansen et al., 2021), it is even further hybridized as it incorporates corporate risk management, which blurs approaches to security and safety (Ericson & Haggerty, 1997), among others. The latter, of course, also feeds back into the security practices of the state. While it is beyond the scope of this chapter to exemplify this through a concrete case study, we will see how this plays out in a broader sense on the case of insider threat programs. But first, we need to address the quest to govern *through* crime and security.

The Quest to Govern *Through* Crime and Security

To the second point: Regulations that impose compliance obligations and stimulate privatized intelligence tradecraft are often driven by anti-policies and counter-strategies (e.g., anti-money laundering, anti-corruption, anti-terrorism, anti-human trafficking etc.). *Anti*-policies seek to combat various crimes, while *counter*-strategies reflect the practices of state *security* apparatuses: such as counterintelligence, counterterrorism, and now also 'counter-insider threat'[1] and seek to combat security threats. In theory, we could argue that counter-strategies respond to 'governance through security' (Valverde, 2001), while anti-policies respond to the 'governance through crime' (Simon, 2007). In practice, however, the two are becoming increasingly hard to tell apart. Regulations driven by anti-policies and counter-strategies, are easy to embrace—after all, who could be for corruption, for terrorism, for human trafficking and so on (Kuldova, 2022; Kuldova et al., 2024; Perkowski & Squire, 2019; Walters, 2008)? Therefore, they frequently fall within the realm of the apolitical or the populist, mobilizing *morality* as the source of their legitimacy. While it is easy to be against crimes, harms and security threats, the real question we need to pose is what we are actually being *for* when we embrace these forms of governance *through* crime and security (Kuldova, 2022; Kuldova et al., 2024). This is where we discover products such as 'insider threat programs'—for it is products such as these that the quest to combat these threats and risks is in practice translated into. We are, thus, effectively being for insider threat programs—among other techno-managerial solutions. Already in 2007, Simon argued that the effects of governance through crime can be felt in the workplace, in organizations that have enormous power over our lives:

> There is a new emphasis on screening potential employees for illegal behavior of almost any sort. Fraud has become a pervasive concern for large information and financial services companies. In all workplaces,

---

[1] The US Department of Defense offers 'Certified Counter-Insider Threat Professional (CCITP) Program', which has been in many respects emulated across the private sector, as we shall see later. https://dodcertpmo.defense.gov/Counter-Insider-Threat/.

there is a heightened concern about violent crime, a concern that leads in turn to yet more efforts at surveillance. There is also a tendency to define workplace conflicts—say, between two employees or a subordinate and more managerial employee—into categories of misbehavior that have crime-like terms and structure, e.g. malice, harm, victim. Sanctions, including dismissal, once thought of as the capital punishment of labor relations, are again becoming an increasingly important part of workplace governance. (Simon, 2007, pp. 9–10)

Through compliance-oriented regulation the state seeks to leverage managerial infrastructures of the 'private government' (Anderson, 2017; Chamayou, 2021) of corporations, businesses, non-profits and other organizations. In other words, rather than merely regulating these actors and their actions, it seeks to govern *through* them by appropriating their governance capacities for its own aims—such as intelligence gathering. At the same time, compliance-oriented regulations are heavily influenced and shaped by corporate lobby, the regulated themselves, and the consulting industry (Schmidt, 2018; Tsingou, 2018; Wedel, 2014) which tends to build its own interests (which may not necessarily be compatible with national security interests) into the regulations from the outset; not to mention the multistakeholder collaborations around regulation and various 'regulatory sandboxes'.

The state—under the changed geopolitical situation and under the conditions of dependence on the private sector and on complex supply chains—thus uses its regulatory power to harness the more immediate managerial power and intelligence-gathering *potential* of corporations and other organizations over workers, clients, suppliers, customers, volunteers, and others for its own purposes. To do so, it has to delegate, at least partially, its policing, crime-fighting, and intelligence gathering powers to an ever-broader range of private, public, non-profit, and corporate actors—and increasingly also automated systems, software and other artificial and automated agents. This further contributes to the deepening of the processes of pluralization and privatization of policing and intelligence described by others (Arrigo & Sellers, 2021; Ben Jaffel & Larsson, 2022; Boels & Verhage, 2015; Henninger, 2023; Joh, 2004; Kuldova, 2022). The challenge posed by this form of governance through crime and security is clear: it boils down to the problem of the privatization of justice and absence of due process guarantees. Accountability, responsibility and decision-making becomes distributed among and delegated to corporations and (semi-)automated systems, difficult to trace. Despite the underlying assumption of alignment of interests between the state and the private sector, the reality is often one of diverging interests and function creep of these technologies. The state's security interests, which it seeks to achieve *through* the governance, managerial and algorithmic infrastructures of private actors, often clash with the private actors' profit interests and their multijurisdictional ambitions.

The Ideological Fantasy of Targeted Governance

To the third point: Governance through crime and security which imposes compliance obligations often invokes various tropes of 'targeted governance' (Valverde & Mopas, 2004), which can be deemed an 'ideological fantasy' of neoliberal governance at large (Žižek, 1989). Targeted governance promises to predict, detect, pre-empt, and eliminate threats and manage risks in a surgical manner by targeting a problem, individuals or groups with laser-like precision. The rhetoric of 'surgically' targeting wrongdoers (and removing them from the healthy body politic), as exemplified in the OSEPI report cited above (OSEPI, 2022), invokes and extends the counterterrorism rhetoric of 'surgical strikes' using precision weapons and drones to 'take out' the terrorists (Chamayou, 2015; Suchman, 2020). We are promised a surgical removal of the corrupt, the criminal, and the insiders threatening and undermining our security, democracy and rule of law; the same promise is inherent to the 'smart sanctions' regimes, echoing the precision of 'smart bombs'. With the rise of big data analytics, machine learning and AI, targeted governance increasingly takes the material form of anticipatory, pre-emptive, and proactive automated systems. This targeted governance thus aligns with what Supiot analyzed as 'governance by numbers' and the culturally hegemonic technosolutionism that views society and humans as *programmable*, and the social order as ultimately engineerable (Frischmann & Selinger, 2018; Morozov, 2013; Supiot, 2017). But, as Valverde and Mopas argue,

> targeting does not necessarily mean governing less. There are always more targets; and there are endless ways of fiddling with existing "smart" weapons, smart drugs, and targeted social programmes. The logic of targeted governance is in its own way as endless, as utopian, as the better-known logic of totalitarian control. (Valverde & Mopas, 2004, p. 248)

This totalitarian drive can be also discerned in the proliferation of 'zero visions' and 'zero trust' architectures in the cyberspace, euphemized through the language of targeted governance. In practice, targeted governance translates into data-, metric-, indicator- and intelligence-driven management, where quantifications of risk and other imperatives of audit culture, due diligence and compliance, reign supreme (Craig et al., 2014; Han, 2015; Merry, 2011, 2016; Power, 1997; Shore & Wright, 2015, 2018; Spira, 2002; Strathern, 2000a, 2000b). It takes the concrete form of algorithmic management and compliance platforms, and other so called regulatory technology (RegTech)[2] solutions (Barberis et al., 2019; Waye, 2019); or else, managerial and technological *products* and *services*.

Regulation is thus commodified by accounting and consulting firms, the tech industry and various private security and intelligence vendors operating across the 'compliance-industrial complex' (Kuldova, 2022). The massive growth, both in size and importance, of these intermediaries, experts, and knowledge brokers, is still widely underappreciated by critical scholars. And yet, it is precisely these actors who not only translate regulation, inform the content, develop managerial knowledge, and embed it in algorithmic control architectures, but also lobby for and shape the same regulations which they consequently turn into products (Edelman & Suchman, 1999; Tsingou, 2018). There is little doubt that

---

[2] RegTech refers to regulatory technologies, which is a booming market which promises to automate regulatory compliance, effectively platformizing both hard law and soft law, along with ethical codes of conduct, internal guidelines and regulations created by the employers, and enables automated flagging of various breaches. These solutions increasingly encompass the field of (cyber)security next to compliance.

technology, especially data-driven intelligence and analytics, in combination with organizational and managerial reforms, legal and ethical compliance, audit, and HR, are seen as *the* solution (Morozov, 2013) to crime and security problems—as well as in other areas of governance. In other words, the preferred 'solutions' are *techno-managerial* and are sold as apolitical, neutral, and objective *because* technological and mathematical (see also Narayan, in this volume)—despite the wealth of evidence to the contrary. Even though the political nature of technology or the complex forms of algorithmic injustice and threats posed by these technologies to our rights and freedoms are no secret (e.g., Besteman & Gusterson, 2019; Mbadiwe, 2018; O'Neil, 2016; Postman, 1993), we still act as if technology were neutral, despite this better knowledge. Having laid out the general dynamics of contemporary governance *through* crime and security and the logic of compliance, let us turn to how insider threat programs came into being.

Insider Threat Programs, National Security, and Targeted Governance

Insider threat programs and insider risk management systems are likely the most illustrative of the new modes of *securitization* of organizations in the age of algorithmic management and 'regulatory' (Braithwaite, 2008; Levi-Faur, 2017), and 'surveillance capitalism' (Zuboff, 2019). They are indicative of the proliferation of *criminalized* (Haugh, 2017) and *securitized* compliance *as* a form of management (Nelson, 2021) which I have discussed at great length elsewhere (Kuldova, 2022). Insider threat programs and insider risk management systems, as their name suggests, seek to combat 'insider threats' and predict, detect, pre-empt, and mitigate 'insider risk'; the conceptual distiction between 'threat' and 'risk' is often ignored in these programs. That is, risk and threats that stem from and are posed by 'insiders': employees, third parties, visitors, suppliers, and others with authorized access to physical premises, facilities, information systems and data, resources, people, networks, critical assets and more who can become potential, witting or unwitting, 'enemies within', and who, by virtue of having legitimate access, are capable of causing great harm, financial losses, and reputational and brand damage, if not directly endangering national security. Insider threat programs, insider risk management and insider detection software and various platforms are today a popular product on the market, both independently and as an integrated part of larger (security) compliance platforms.

The integration of insider threat management systems into compliance platforms and 'algorithmic management' (Besteman & Gusterson, 2019; Rosenblat, 2018; Todolí-Signes, 2019; Wood, 2021) speaks directly both to governance through crime and security and to the ideological fantasy of targeted governance. Therefore, we must further illuminate the drivers *behind* the introduction of these systems—from policy and regulation, historical evolution, professionalization, and commodification to their epistemology. We need to consider insider threat programs as both discursive and non-discursive *dispositif* of social control (Foucault, 1980). Understanding these systems, requires an interrogation of their 'epistemic power' and its sources (Kuldova & Nordrik, 2023). That is, understanding the ways in which insider threat programs categorize, measure, evaluate, and see the world in *particular* ways and often at the expense of alternative modes of understanding. Understanding their epistemic power will also shed light on why it is immensely difficult to meaningfully challenge these systems without sounding endlessly naïve vis-à-vis the 'technostrategic language' of their expert makers (Cohn, 1987).

Rather tellingly, and speaking to the hegemonic nature of this knowledge, there has so far been no *critical* scholarship attempting to understand the evolution of insider threat programs. There has been, to my best knowledge, no research directly interrogating the epistemic power of these systems and the intersections of the 'military-industrial complex' (Roland, 2007) and the 'compliance-industrial complex' (Kuldova, 2022) in the context of the evolving geopolitical instability and market dynamics, or the ways in which these epistemologies shape *managerial* systems and corporate governance, and fuel worker surveillance. In fact, the very existence of these systems is not widely discussed, despite the increasing focus on workplace surveillance and algorithmic management (e.g., Ball, 2010; Noponen et al., 2023; Sempill, 2001). The surveillance and monitoring of *white-collar* professionals has only recently become a subject of public debate. But even here, it has not as yet been placed within its rightful context of state and corporate governance through crime and security. *The New York Times,* for instance, ran (at the time of writing) only one critical article on insider threat management system, published in 2022, under the heading 'Your Bosses Could Have a File on You, and They May Misinterpret It' (Scoles, 2022). The majority of news coverage on the subject has taken place in specialized tech and security media outlets. *Forbes* has featured several articles on insider threat management systems written by industry actors marketing (cyber)security software and consulting services. The hybrid reality on ground transgresses disciplinary silos, which may explain why we see so few critical scholars interrogating both the antecedents and consequences of the rapid expansion of these systems across organizations, private and public. This chapter can be read as an attempt at *reframing* the discussion (which may also excuse the somewhat lengthy introduction into the subject). I argue that we need to question the basic premises of insider threat programs, but to do so, we also need to understand the larger socio-economic, geopolitical, and cultural context within which they emerge and operate.

National Security Strategies, Threat Assessments, and Security Compliance

The heightened focus on national security interests manifests in the increased spending on military, intelligence, security, and protection of critical infrastructure, know-how, and technology. Much of this spending is channelled to public private partnerships (PPPs) as the neoliberal state has outsourced and become dependent on the private sector to provide critical infrastructure and basic needs (Garland, 2001; Valverde, 2022). But while privatization and outsourcing of certain functions and services have been there for several decades, the drive to enlist the private sector in national security and crime-fighting more actively is coming more and more to the fore in national security strategies. We can take the example of Biden Administration's *National Cybersecurity Strategy* from March 2023. The strategy directs our gaze at a broad range of 'malicious actors' that threaten our democratic values, from China, Russia, Iran, North Korea, to organized criminal syndicates, and their malicious cyber activities ranging

> from nuisance defacement, to espionage and intellectual property theft, to damaging attacks against critical infrastructure, to ransomware attacks and cyber-enabled influence campaigns designed to undermine public trust in the foundation of our democracy' (The White House, 2023, p. 3).

Consequently, we are told that 'effective disruption of malicious cyber activity requires more routine collaboration between the private sector entities that have unique insights and capabilities and the Federal agencies that have the means and authorities to act' (The White House, 2023, p. 15). Big tech players—Amazon, Meta, Google and Apple—are now positioned as strategically key actors in the pursuit of national security interests and in securing of the 'American way of life' (McCarthy, 2021).

This way of thinking, while prevalent in the U.S., is of course not limited to it. The same logic can be discerned also across Nordic countries, often juxtaposed to U.S. due to their social welfare reputation. A 2023 report by The Norwegian National Security Authority (NSM), offering professional security guidance for a resilient Norway, makes a similar point, worth citing at length:

> The dividing lines between state security, societal security, security in businesses and individual security are increasingly being erased. There are strong interdependencies between these levels. This is partly due to the digitization of society and the technological development that are linking more and more functions and infrastructure in complex value chains and dependencies. State security is also challenged the blurring of the boundaries between the civil and the military, partly as a result of overlapping value- and supply chains. (…) Norwegian organisations and businesses are at the heart of preventive security work. Assets of importance to national security are mainly owned and managed by organisations, both private and public. With the support of the authorities, organisations

must be able to detect, prevent and manage security-threatening incidents. (…) The authorities' task is thus to ensure that the national security work strengthens organisations' ability to achieve an acceptable level of security. An acceptable state of security is achieved when assets of importance to national security are so well protected against security-threatening activity that the risk is acceptable. (NSM, 2023, 8-10; translation mine)

A whole chapter in this guidance is thereafter dedicated to insider risk management by businesses—following up on an earlier theme report dedicated solely to 'insider risk' (NSM, 2020), and to the threats businesses and other organizations face from foreign espionage, insiders, hackers and political hactivists, criminals, and terrorists (NSM, 2023). NSM recommends increased investments into competence building and research on insider risks, the introduction and improvement of insider risk and threat management programs across public and private sector, in particular in critical national infrastructure (CNI), and evaluation of possibilities to develop legal basis for background checks outside of the security clearance institute, along with a host of other evaluations of legal basis for corporate reporting on security threats (for the purposes of state intelligence). This guidance must also be read in the context of re-establishing 'total defense', which was dismantled after the end of Cold War in Norway; but this revival is taking place under radically transformed social and economic conditions of globalization (Rongved & Norheim-Martinsen, 2022). The report implicitly reflects the obvious challenges of re-creating 'total defense' in a globalized economy where the state depends on private infrastructures and services (Lallerstedt, 2021). The imposition of security compliance obligations by the 'supervisory' state thus presents itself as the only viable solution. Private actors and other organizations are thus either obliged or encouraged to introduce insider risk or threat management programs and other preventive security measures and 'best practices' in the name of national security. These tools, one images, could be in the future be leveraged to generate intelligence for the state—in the same manner that suspicious activity reporting by the financial sector already does for financial crime, only this time in respect to national security and threats such as foreign espionage. This can be read as a manifestation of the quest to re-establish total defense in a globalized world—through an imposition of security compliance which is envisioned to act in national security interests and tighten collaboration between the state and corporate actors.

In the current market environment, such strategic guidance—be it by NSM or other state agencies—necessarily and immediately opens up new markets for security, consulting, audit, and RegTech companies. Their consulting and software products promise to ensure regulatory compliance, deliver necessary training, and implement necessary security upgrades and so forth. Compliance with the underlying ideals of 'total defense' becomes de facto outsourced to expert third parties—if we were to play along with the logic of insider risk, we could argue that this adds another layer of risk, for trusted *third* parties are often flagged high-risk. While transnational consulting and security companies may already have insider threat or insider risk management systems among their offerings, local regulations stimulate the growth of local and often more specialized start-ups[3] (many of which are eventually bought by larger, typically transnational players). The paradox of outsourcing national security compliance to transnational corporate actors, whose loyalty to any one nation can be easily doubted (as corporates are largely registered in tax-favourable jurisdictions), does no longer seem to strike the regulator as odd, or as a source of risk, and vulnerability. The complex supply chains behind security (and other) compliance have not yet been thematized by regulators, despite rising awareness about supply chain risks. This *commodification* of regulation must be truly appreciated if we are to make sense of the disproportionate power of private sector knowledge, norm, and data brokers and professionals (Clarke, 2019; Tsingou, 2018; Wedel, 2014).

---

[3] Following the introduction of the Norwegian Transparency Act in 2022 which imposes various compliance obligations on companies to perform human rights and supply chain due diligence, numerous local RegTech companies sprang up offering software to ensure compliance, while larger market players simply offered tech developed earlier for other legal contexts. The same was the case following the EU Whistleblower Directive, which was translated into whistleblower platforms across the whole EU and EEA. These are just a few concrete examples; we see the same dynamics with the majority of regulation.

The boom of the market for insider risk management systems in the U.S. can be traced back to the Executive Order 13587[4] issued by President Barack Obama in October 2011, which imposed the obligation on all federal departments and agencies working with classified information to establish insider threat programs. This led to rapid development of research, managerial knowledge, best practice for deterrence, detection, and mitigation, and awareness raising on the subject of insider threats. While the concept of 'insider threat' pre-dated this Executive Order, evoking the double agents of the Cold War Era, it was the notion of the *'program'* to combat this threat that rapidly evolved thereafter. Similarly, the scope of the 'insider threat' concept expanded in lockstep with its appropriation by different actors, organizations, and industries, and its integration into consulting and management products and software. While 'insider threat' used to be largely associated with the protection of classified information and while cleared defense contractors are legally *required* to have insider threat programs fulfilling the same minimum criteria as select federal agencies, having an insider threat program quickly spread as part of 'best' managerial-cum-(cyber)security practice and came to encompass very different insider threat scenarios. From unauthorized disclosures and foreign and corporate espionage, the concept has come to encompass corruption and bribery, embezzlement, fraud, insider trading, network sabotage, IP theft, fraud, negligence, workplace violence, self-harm, extremism, terrorism, sabotage, unintentional incidents, data exfiltration and data loss, policy violations, sexual harassment, microaggressions, vandalism, negligence, anti-social and counterproductive workplace behaviour, and more. Insider threat programs can also be found under different names. The Insider Threat Subcommittee of Intelligence and National Security Alliance (INSA)[5] even evaluated the possible benefits of renaming insider threat programs,

---

[4] CERT Insider Threat Program Manager Certificate, Carnegie Mellon University, https://www.sei.cmu.edu/education-outreach/credentials/credential.cfm?customel_datapageid_14047=15170.

[5] INSA is a US '501(c)3 nonprofit organization dedicated to addressing contemporary intelligence and national security challenges, facilitating public discourse on the role and value of intelligence for our nation's security, and advancing the intelligence field as a career choice.' https://www.insaonline.org/foundation.

since the word 'threat' turns out not very popular with the work-force. Using case studies, they identified the following alternative names: Insider Threat Program, Insider Risk Management Program, Counter-Insider Threat Program, Insider Trust/Trusted Workforce, and C.A.R.E. Program (INSA, 2022). But other names are as common: Employee Reliability Program, Employee Risk Mitigation Program, Workforce Reliability Program, Human Capital Protection Program, Asset Protection and Compliance Program, Corporate Responsibility and Compliance Program, and so on. There is a perpetual slippage between the concepts of threat and risk, which are, too, increasingly blurred.

Amidst this maze of very different security, crime, and harm scenarios, and operating under slightly different professional titles, the insider threat and risk professionals, researchers and pracademics search for 'classifications', 'indicators' and 'red flags' of all these very different, intentional and unintentional, malicious behaviours. Most of these experts have background in computer science, psychology, behavioural analysis, psychometrics, intelligence and law enforcement, HR, and management—or various combinations thereof. In line with the logic of targeted governance discussed above, they seek to develop models, increasingly using supervised and unsupervised learning, that could predict with a great degree of precision an 'insider threat' or at least automatically flag high-risk individuals for further follow-up. The reliance on this form of expertise, in particular that combining psychology, behavioural science, psychometrics and computer science is not accidental. To the contrary, it reflects the historical trajectories of research for the military in the U.S. and the milieus that have come to dominate it during and after the Cold War, in particular since the end of the Vietnam war. While social anthropologists, area studies experts and others no longer viewed research funded by the military establishment as ethically acceptable, psychologists, political and computer scientists increasingly came to dominate and shape the military's understanding of the social world (Rohde, 2013, 2017). While this history is indeed complex, the hegemony of computer science and the psy-sciences is striking when it comes to insider threat programs originally developed by researchers funded by the U.S. military and intelligence agencies and later appropriated by the consulting and tech industry, which often relies on similar forms of expertise.

What the psy-sciences, computer science and management had, which social anthropology lacked, was the promise of universal and standardized approaches and practices—applicable to any human in any culture. This is reflected in contemporary 'good governance' or ISO standards of management, as much as in the individualizing focus that dominates both contemporary technology, management, and security governance.

The same forms of expertise are consequently built into the software. Moreover, the logic of the digital *platform* also aligns well with the standardized management *procedures* that dominate the field. This platformization means that very different crimes, threats, risks, and social phenomena are sought pre-empted, detected and even combatted through the same standardized and seemingly universal approaches. Corruption comes to sit in the platform next to terrorism, workplace violence or sexual harassment—as it becomes merely a matter of detecting the 'insider threat' or managing 'insider risk' (or else, suspicious individuals). As an example, we can take the Microsoft Purview insider risk and compliance platform solution, part of Microsoft 365, which offers, among others, communication compliance and sentiment analysis, and flagging of 'risky users'. It is also built with stimulating 'holistic' perspective in sight, catering to multidisciplinary teams: legal, compliance, HR, IT security. While new functionalities are being continually added, for technical specifications and possibilities see *Microsoft 365 Compliance: A Practical Guide to Managing Risk* (Toelle, 2021).

The 'compliance-industrial complex' (Kuldova, 2022) is a crucial driver behind the (global) dissemination of these practices; its armies of professionals are *interpreting* and *translating* state regulation, multilateral and national guidance, private sector standards, codes, and voluntary self-regulation and more into managerial products, training, certifications, and software promising either to comply with these regulation or anticipate forthcoming regulatory actions and 'best practices' (Fig. 2.1).

But these technologies also emerge in response to 'compliance risk', particularly in the U.S., where having satisfying compliance management systems can lead to reduced fines in case of non-compliance; legal instruments such as Deferred Prosecution Agreements (DPAs) also impose compliance systems (*see also* Nesvet, in this volume). A case in point

Insider risks are one of the top concerns of security and compliance professionals in the modern workplace. Industry studies have shown that insider risks are often associated with risky activities. Protecting your organization against these risks can be challenging to identify and difficult to mitigate. Insider risks include vulnerabilities in a variety of areas and can cause major problems for your organization, ranging from the loss of intellectual property to confidential data, and more. The following figure outlines common insider risks:

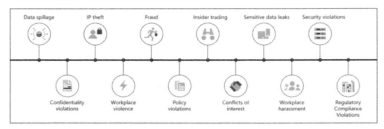

Microsoft 365 risk prevention features are designed and built-in to our insider risk products and solutions. These solutions work together and use advanced service and 3rd-party indicators to help you quickly identify, triage, and act on risk activity. Most solutions offer a comprehensive detection, alert, and remediation workflow for your data analysts and investigators to use to quickly act on and minimize these risks.

Fig. 2.1 As an example, we can take the Microsoft Purview insider risk and compliance platform solutions, part of Microsoft 365, Image: Screenshot from Microsoft website: 'Microsoft Purview insider risk', Microsoft, 21 February 2023, https://learn.microsoft.com/en-us/microsoft-365/compliance/insider-risk-solution-overview?view=o365-worldwide

is Goldman Sachs, which, following the involvement of its employees in the notorious 1Malaysia Development Berhad (1MDB) corruption, embezzlement, and money laundering scandal (Gabriel, 2018), had to increase, as part of remediation and as stipulated in the DPA, its focus on compliance and ethics program, which included, among others, increased focus on its Insider Threat Program. In its Securities and Exchange Commission (SEC) filing we can read in great detail about measures taken,

A key initiative was the firm's creation of an Insider Threat Program in 2015 to help prevent, detect, and mitigate potentially harmful actions by employees (...) While the Steering Group itself was created before the problems with 1MDB came to light, the firm has taken steps to enhance it specifically in response to 1MDB and its assessment that there were opportunities to enhance the firm's efforts to detect employee wrong-doing. (...) Developing and enhancing cyber surveillance and monitoring to better identify malicious or careless behavior by employees, as well as to enhance controls that leave open exploitable weaknesses. Studying changes in employee behavior to identify meaningful trends and data points of potential and likely insider threats, using analytical models that harness historical employee data, such as the location, tenure and role of employees and executing forensic reviews of varied higher risk employee populations to identify signs of potential misconduct, and conducts "lessons learned" analyses to uncover new behavioral risks. (...) Developing and maintaining an insider threat risk taxonomy and conducting gap analyses in respect of insider threats, including collecting data from across the firm in respect of insider threat risks, analyzing this data and presenting it to the Steering Group. (...) GS Group also established in 2019 a dedicated Insider Threat Team, under the sponsorship of the Insider Threat Steering Group, with several full-time employees representing the firm's control functions that have primary responsibility for administering the Insider Threat Program, including Financial Crime Compliance, Conduct Risk Compliance, Operational Risk Management and Analysis, and Technology Risk. The team is also supported by Compliance Engineering. The Insider Threat Team ultimately reports to the global Head of Financial Crime Compliance. (...) GS Group believes that it is an industry leader in having a permanent Insider Threat Team devoted solely to detecting and rooting out threats posed by employees.[6]

Since large corporations are *Too Big to Jail* (Garrett, 2014), prosecutors have introduced legal innovations such as DPAs, reaching extrajudicial agreements in place of criminal prosecutions. Upon this vision, corporate crime, criminogenic structures or managerial incentives that reward risk-taking simply do not exist, what exists are 'bad apples', or else, 'malicious insiders'. The only failures that exist upon this view, are the failures of the corporation and corporate managers and leaders (themselves conveniently too often left off the hook) to detect these 'bad apples'

---

[6] Goldman Sachs (Malaysia) Sdn. Bhd., GOLDMAN SACHS ASSET MANAGEMENT, L.P., GOLDMAN SACHS ASSET MANAGEMENT INTERNATIONAL, GS INVESTMENT STRATEGIES, LLC, GOLDMAN SACHS & CO. LLC; 40-APP of filed (2020–10–22), SEC: https://www.sec.gov/Archives/edgar/data/769993/000119312520274177/d75479d40 app.htm, pp. 17–18.

(by default their subordinates) within their organizations in a timely manner. DPAs such as this end up expanding 'corporate sovereignty' (Barkan, 2013; Diphoorn & Wiegnick, 2021) of the very same corporations fined for misconduct, rather than curtailing it. This imaginary, however, is not unique to DPAs under the Foreign Corrupt Practices Act (FCPA). We could argue that insider threat programs in this sense come with a built-in 'special liberty' features for the elites and leaders who are by default beyond suspicion and can transgress rules with impunity (Hall & Wilson, 2014); similarly, systemic harms remain untouched by preventive security compliance. Let us now turn to a deeper exploration of the epistemologies that underpin insider threat programs.

Pracademics and the Professionalization of Private Sector Intelligence

For our purposes, existing 'grey', policy and academic literature on insider threats is part of the field that we seek to understand. This literature is central to the forms of knowledge that shape practices in security management and the management of workers and other 'insiders' *as* a potential threat and risk. In this sense, we understand here this literature as a part of the *dispositif* of (insider) threat and risk management within the larger context of techno-managerial governance *through* crime and security (Jacobsen, 2020). Or else, as an important part of

> a thoroughly heterogeneous ensemble consisting of discourses, institutions, architectural forms, regulatory decisions, laws, administrative measures, scientific statements, philosophical, moral and philanthropic propositions – in short, the said as much as the unsaid' (…), a 'formation which has as its major function at a given historical moment that of responding to an *urgent need*' and 'has a dominant strategic function (Foucault, 1980, pp. 194–5).

The research and grey literature and 'expert knowledge' on this subject shapes key discursive elements of the power apparatuses at play. These must be understood in conjunction with non-discursive practices and material expressions (e.g., software platforms or security gadgets). The epistemic power of these apparatuses serves the reproduction of *particular* 'regimes of truth', thus foreclosing alternative understandings and solutions to the problems of crime and security.

Existing literature on insider threats is predominantly concerned with the following: categorizing insider threat actors, generating taxonomies, models, and risk scenarios, behavioural, psychological, and psychometric profiling and modelling of 'critical pathways' (Lenzenweger & Shaw, 2022), proactive threat detection and positive deterrence (Moore et al., 2022), developing strategies of monitoring, risk management, data-driven analytics, and anomaly and early detection, development of insider threat mitigation software and deep learning models, and cybersecurity and managerial and organizational best practices and codes of conduct (e.g., Baweja et al., 2022; Bishop et al., 2010; Costa et al., 2014; Elifoglu et al., 2018; Guido & Brooks, 2013; Homoliak et al., 2019; INSA, 2018; Wall, 2013; Yuan & Wu, 2021). Technological solutions are often informed by psychological research and behaviour analysis and utilize concepts such as 'Dark Triad personality traits', 'counterproductive workplace behaviour', 'behavioural antecedents' and more (Maasberg et al., 2015; Kandias et al., 2010). This power nexus of the 'psy-complex' (Klein et al., 2021), management, cybernetics and security/intelligence informs not only insider threat management systems, but is discernible across much of governance through crime and security and governance by numbers (Godard, 2014; Rose, 1999; Supiot, 2017). It is also reflected in the composition of the multi-disciplinary teams that seek to tackle 'malicious insiders'. Much of this literature is generated by pracademics, such as behavioural, security or computer scientists funded by the military-industrial complex and/or who are financially invested in the various risk management and consulting firms and ideologically invested in national security missions; much of the research is also conducted by private security and intelligence experts representing commercial interests, and seeking the legitimation of scientific publishing to enhance their market offerings, by corporate Research & Development teams, particularly in security, or a combination thereof. This knowledge is then turned into software and what are ultimately hostile algorithmic infrastructures of control that aim to manage, track, influence and predict not only behaviours, motivations, emotions, sentiments, and actions, but also the unconscious.

While much of this pracademic output is published in academic journals, conference proceedings (as is more common in computer science) and corporate research papers, we see also new specialized industry-driven academic publications emerge. A case in point is the *Counter-Insider Threat Research and Practice (CITRAP)* open-access, peer-reviewed, and unclassified journal launched in 2022, founded by Frank L. Greitzer, a principal scientist at PsyberAnalytix,[7] a consulting firm at the intersection of social and behavioural sciences and information security and insider threats, and a former research psychologist at the Department of Defense (DoD). Among other contributors are academics affiliated with another provider of similar services and training, the Insider Risk Group, LLC,[8] defense and intelligence pracademics, such as from the Office of People Analytics' (OPA)[9] Personnel and Security Research Center (PERSEREC)[10] at the DoD, software engineers from Carnegie Mellon University, a central player in this field, and academics from the Pacific Northwest National Laboratory specializing on critical (energy) infrastructure security.

This reflects a longer tradition for R&D driven by the intelligence community and the military. Project Slammer (1985–1998) has been particularly influential in this respect: a project where the US intelligence community, psychologists, psychiatrists, and others conducted interviews with 45 convicted US spies to trace the 'psychosocial history of these malicious insiders.'[11] This project was released by FBI in 2010 for approved researchers, predominantly at the MITRE Corporation, established in 1958 as a military think tank and now a non-profit

---

[7] PsyberAnalytix https://psyberanalytix.com/.

[8] Insider Risk Group, LLC https://www.insiderriskgroup.com/.

[9] 'About OPA': The Office of People Analytics (OPA) was established in 2016 to develop cutting-edge analytical methods and solutions for more effective personnel management in the Department of Defense (DoD).' https://www.opa.mil/about-opa.

[10] 'The Defense Personnel and Security Research Center (PERSEREC) is a Department of Defense entity dedicated to improving the effectiveness, efficiency, and fairness of DoD personnel suitability, security, and reliability systems' https://www.dhra.mil/perserec/.

[11] 'Insider Threat Psycho-social Indicator Research: Project Slammer Dataset Analysis', MITRE: Insider Threat Research & Solutions, https://insiderthreat.mitre.org/project-slammer/.

R&D organization, and, according to Fast Company, 'the most important company you have never heard of.'[12] MITRE has now a dedicated Insider Threat Research & Solutions team, 'recognized as national and international experts', 'Building, growing, and maturing Insider Threat/ Risk Programs for government, critical infrastructure organizations, industry, and academia.'[13] MITRE has contributed significantly to the mainstreaming of research on psycho-social indicators of insider threat. In 2022, MITRE also entered a public–private partnership with DTEX Systems, the Workforce Cyber Intelligence & Security Company™ 'to elevate insider risk awareness and human-informed cyber defense strategies through behavioral-based research and the launch of the MITRE Inside-R Protect™ program.'[14] RAND Corporation has, too, contributed to knowledge production within this field, with a number of reports, which reproduce the same focus on insider threat classification, behavioural indicators, detection and mitigation strategies, continuous monitoring and more (Brown et al., 2020; Black et al., 2022; Luckey et al., 2019).

Another influential player in R&D on insider threats is the Insider Threat Center at the Software Engineering Institute' at the Carnegie Mellon University; it produces 'research-based' and 'evidence-based' knowledge and 'best practice' on insider threat management, and is known for its *Common Sense Guide to Mitigating Insider Threats* (CERT, 2022), which is widely adopted and adapted across a wide range of consulting products by the likes of the Big Four accounting firms (Deloitte, EY, PwC, KMPG), and other consulting and compliance services providers, and RegTechs. Carnegie Mellon also offers the *CERT Insider Threat Program Manager Certificate* to satisfy the requirements

---

[12] https://www.fastcompany.com/3017927/30mitre.

[13] 'About Us', MITRE, https://insiderthreat.mitre.org/.

[14] 'MITRE and DTEX Systems Announce Public–Private Partnership to Elevate Insider Risk Programs & Advance Human-Centric Security', MITRE, https://www.mitre.org/news-insights/ news-release/mitre-and-dtex-systems-announce-public-private-partnership-elevate.

under the aforementioned Executive Order 13587,[15] which not only imposed the obligation on federal departments and agencies working with classified information to establish insider threat programs, but also constituted the interagency National Insider Threat Task Force (NITTF).[16] NITTF has, too, over the course of the past decade become an important source of knowledge, training, and best practice, again translated by consultants and management professionals, and cybersecurity and open-source intelligence (OSINT) experts into new products for wider use beyond federal intelligence agencies, military, and defense contractors; it is currently housed at the National Counterintelligence and Security Center (NCSC) and co-led by FBI. While focusing predominantly on deterring, detecting and mitigating insider threats related to unauthorized disclosures, exploitation, and compromise of classified information, the knowledge, training, guidance, and best practices that it promotes are translated into other domains of 'insider risk management' and protection of critical assets across sectors, well beyond the critical national infrastructure (CNI). NITTF and NCSC, key actors in knowledge, certification, training and awareness raising on insider threats (among other subjects), also team up with the Office of the Under Secretary of Defense Intelligence and Security, the Defense Counterintelligence and Security Agency, and the Department of Homeland Security to organize the annual 'National Insider Threat Awareness Month' (NITAM),[17] which is a month-long campaign that seeks to raise awareness in both government and industry about insider threat programs and risks posed by insider threats.

The Defense Counterintelligence and Security Agency also runs the Center for Development of Security Excellence (CDSE), established in 2010, 'the premier provider of security training, education, and certification for the Department of Defense, federal government, and cleared contractors under the National Industrial Security Program (NISP)';

---

[15] CERT Insider Threat Program Manager Certificate, Carnegie Mellon University, https://www.sei.cmu.edu/education-outreach/credentials/credential.cfm?customel_datapageid_14047=15170.

[16] National Insider Threat Task Force (NITTF) Mission, https://www.dni.gov/index.php/ncsc-how-we-work/ncsc-nittf.

[17] Organized for the fourth time in September 2022, https://securityawareness.usalearning.gov/cdse/nitam/.

CDSE offers a range of certifications, courses, e-learning, awareness raising games and an app for the general public with up-to-date information on insider threats, posters, and training on insider threat, the curricula of many of these are freely available, while some basic courses do not require registration and are accessible through the Security Awareness Hub (Fig. 2.2).[18] Another source of 'best practice' in this field, is the US Cybersecurity and Infrastructure Security Agency (CISA), with its influential *Insider Threat Mitigation Guide*.[19] This guide is also reposted on the website of the European Commission.[20]

Fig. 2.2 Screenshots of awareness raising games on insider threats developed by CDSE, as well as author's certificate from one of freely available training courses. For more games, and other materials, visit: https://www.cdse.edu/Tra ining/Security-Awareness-Games/

[18] Insider Threat, CDSE, https://www.cdse.edu/Training/Insider-Threat/; for the Security Awareness Hub, see: https://securityawareness.usalearning.gov/itawareness/index.htm.

[19] CISA, 'Insider Threat Mitigation Guide', https://www.cisa.gov/sites/default/files/2022-11/Insider%20Threat%20Mitigation%20Guide_Final_508.pdf.

[20] 'Insider threat mitigation guide,' https://ec.europa.eu/newsroom/cipr/items/713830/en.

Research, guidance, 'best practice' and insights generated by these researchers, pracademics, federal and state agencies, leading university research centres, non-profit research institutes, and others, have rather quickly trickled into the managerial discourse, appropriated by accounting and consulting firms such as the Big Four, and integrated into their services, as well as into compliance and managerial platforms. This is likely also the reason why institutions such as the Norwegian NSM are now encouraging the implementation of insider risk programs in Norwegian businesses as well as public sector. Once these best practices emerge, they become difficult to challenge or question and are likely to travel across jurisdictions—even if somewhat altered on the way. The annual threat assessments issued by intelligence agencies, be it the *Annual Threat Assessment of the US Intelligence Community*[21] or the Norwegian *National Threat Assessment*,[22] serve also as an important source of information for consultants and RegTechs alike, providing not only guidance on which risks and threats to commodify and on the likely evolution of the risk landscape, but also offering a powerful legitimatory force for their products—as I have observed time and again in the marketing of these products. While regulations, guidance, and best practice are translated into products in the name of compliance (as in the case of AML, sanction screening, anti-corruption, supply chain due diligence, whistleblowing platforms, GDPR, and so on), threat assessments are commodified into security and intelligence products (from country-based risk of operations to insider threat management). In practice, and in line with the aforementioned platform logic and the logic of hybridization, security, compliance, and intelligence products come to merge into each other in practice, in the product design and marketing.

In a report by E&Y, *Managing Insider Threat*, which seeks to sell services in insider threat management, we can thus read that '56% of respondents view employees as the second most likely source of an attack, closely following criminal syndicates (59%).'[23] KPMG offers consulting

---

[21] For 2023 version, see: https://www.odni.gov/files/ODNI/documents/assessments/ATA-2023-Unclassified-Report.pdf.

[22] For 2023 version, see: https://www.pst.no/alle-artikler/trusselvurderinger/ntv-2023/.

[23] https://assets.ey.com/content/dam/ey-sites/ey-com/en_gl/topics/assurance/assurance-pdfs/EY-managing-insider-threat.pdf.

services and development of gold standard insider risk management systems and 'trusted workforce' programs for their clients.[24] PwC offers advice on how to build an 'effective insider risk management program' in collaboration with Microsoft.[25] Deloitte offers a holistic and risk-based insider threat mitigation program[26] along with advice on how to 'unmask insider threats.'[27] We could go on. And while we have already touched upon Microsoft's compliance and security platform, there are numerous other significant RegTechs, specializing in compliance and security, and offering data-driven insider threat mitigation solutions. Among the most well-known is Proofpoint:

> As the leading people-centric Insider Threat Management (ITM) solution, Proofpoint's ITM protects against data loss and brand damage involving insiders acting maliciously, negligently, or unknowingly. Proofpoint correlates activity and data movement, empowering security teams to identify user risk, detect insider-led data breaches, and accelerate security incident response.[28]

Other notable companies in the field are: Teramind,[29] Forcepoint,[30] DTEX Systems,[31] DoControl,[32] or Ekran Systems,[33] to name just a few;

---

[24] E.g. 'Client Story: The Gold Standard of Trust' https://advisory.kpmg.us/client-stories/aut omotive-insider-risk-management.html.

[25] 'Building an effective insider risk management program: A joint report from PwC and Microsoft', PwC, https://www.pwc.com/us/en/services/alliances/microsoft/cybersecurity/insider-risk-management.html.

[26] 'Insider Threat Mitigation: A holistic & risk-based program', Deloitte, https://www2.deloitte.com/in/en/pages/risk/articles/Insider-Threat-Mitigation-A-holistic-and-risk-based-program.html.

[27] 'Unmasking insider threats CFO Insights', Deloitte, https://www2.deloitte.com/us/en/pages/finance/articles/unmasking-insider-threats.html.

[28] 'Insider Threat Management', Proofpoint, https://www.proofpoint.com/uk/products/inform ation-protection/insider-threat-management.

[29] Those interested in detailed tour of the surveillance features on offer, are encouraged to try out the demo version. Teramind Live Demo https://democompany.teramind.co/#/report/Focus+ Dashboard.

[30] 'Insider Threat Solutions', Forcepoint, https://www.forcepoint.com/security/insider-threat.

[31] 'Insider Threat Management', DTEX Systems, https://www.dtexsystems.com/solutions/ins ider-threat-management/.

[32] 'Insider Risk Managemet', DoControl, https://www.docontrol.io/insider-risk-management.

[33] 'Full Cycle Insider Risk Management', Ekran Systems, https://www.ekransystem.com/en.

while some are more oriented towards cybersecurity and data loss, others have more expansive offerings, integrating regulatory compliance, flagging of breaches of internal ethical codes of conduct, monitoring and behavioural analytics of all activities and (or through) meta-data (the latter enables evasion of privacy regulations such as GDPR, as we can learn in a report by Enterprise Management Associates, *The Evolving Dynamics Between Insider Risk, Privacy, and Compliance,* featured by DTEX[34]) (Fig. 2.3).

The proliferation of these market actors speaks to the wider trends of professionalization of private sector risk, security, threat and financial intelligence and compliance through professional associations such as Association of Threat Assessment Professionals (ATAP),[35] Association of International Risk Intelligence Professionals (AIRIP),[36] Association of Certified Financial Crime Specialists (ACFCS),[37] International Compliance Association (ICA),[38] Society of Corporate Compliance and Ethics (SCCE),[39] ASIS International (ASIS)[40] and others, many operating transnationally, with local chapters, while others being nationally

---

[34] https://www.dtexsystems.com/solutions/insider-threat-management/.

[35] 'The Association of Threat Assessment Professionals (ATAP) was founded in 1992 as a non-profit organization comprised of law enforcement, prosecutors, mental health professionals, corporate security experts, probation and parole personnel and others involved in the area of threat and violence risk assessment.' https://www.atapworldwide.org/page/aboutus.

[36] 'Association of International Risk Intelligence Professionals (AIRIP) is a 501(c)(6) nonprofit professional association that empowers members to unlock the value of intelligence in their organizations by connecting, developing and engaging international risk intelligence professionals.' https://www.airip.org/.

[37] 'ACFCS was borne along with its Certified Financial Crime Specialist, CFCS, examination covering a robust AML training program in addition to addressing cyber-crimes, fraud, bribery, corruption, tax evasion, sanctions, terrorist financing, compliance programs, asset recovery, crypto crimes, and investigations.' https://www.acfcs.org/about.

[38] 'The International Compliance Association (Ica) Is The Leading Professional Body For The Global Regulatory And Financial Crime Compliance Community', https://www.int-comp.org/about-ica/.

[39] 'Society of Corporate Compliance and Ethics® (SCCE®) is a member-based association with 7,000+ compliance and ethics members worldwide.' While the association evolved from the health sector, it is increasingly providing training also in financial and threat and risk intelligence, https://www.corporatecompliance.org/about-scce.

[40] 'Founded in 1955, ASIS International is a global community of security practitioners, each of whom has a role in the protection of assets—people, property, and/or information.' https://www.asisonline.org/footer-pages/about-asis/

oriented. 'Corporate crime-fighters' (Liss & Sharman, 2015) thus proliferate in lockstep with the professionalization of corporate security,
private intelligence, and 'privatized spying' (Kaleem, 2022; Keefe, 2010;
Morrow, 2022) and the evolution of criminalized and securitized compliance, reliant on (financial) intelligence, (forensic) investigatory practices
and behavioural analytics (Kuldova, 2022).

Fig. 2.3 Screenshots from Teramind's Live Demo of the software and its capabilities, which also offer productivity optimization and data loss prevention. Those
interested in detailed tour of the surveillance features on offer, are encouraged to try out the demo version. Teramind Live Demo https://democompany.
teramind.co/#/report/Focus+Dashboard

Combatting the 'Enemy Within': Loopholes and Weaknesses

Democracy, freedom, the integrity of financial markets, and the rule of law are in Western policy (circles) viewed as being *undermined* by a broad range of malicious and evil actors: kleptocrats, authoritarian regimes, 'spy-rich nations'[41] and foreign intelligence services, criminals and criminal organizations, corrupt individuals, private sector spies, and more. These malicious actors are thought to exploit and abuse 'loopholes' and 'weaknesses' of our system to their advantage—be these weaknesses legal, regulatory, cyber, infrastructural, organizational, or what is referred to in insider threat literature as 'human factor' (Colwill, 2009; Lang, 2022). Due to this dominant imaginary, the solutions that present themselves take the form of regulatory and technological fixes, of surveillance and monitoring, of securitization of the social and, ultimately, the (global) crime and security governance *through* transnational and market actors (Jakobi, 2013; Liss & Sharman, 2015; Nieto Martín, 2022; Schuilenburg, 2011). These *fixes* seek to improve our defence systems and boost our immunity, to close (the ever proliferating) loopholes, and make us more 'resilient'. Closing these loopholes—it is imagined—will eventually restore the integrity of our system and/or prevent its *corruption* by these actors who seek to penetrate it time and again and undermine it (Kuldova et al., 2024). Our system is therefore seen as *inherently* pure, good, and moral, but dirtied, corrupted, and undermined by countries plagued by systemic corruption (the Other), criminals, or malicious actors. The quest is to make it whole, to endow it with *integrity* (or else, wholeness); the rhetoric of targeted governance and risk management that goes hand in hand with the perpetual closing of various loopholes euphemizes the underlying totalizing and totalitarian fantasies of a perfectly enclosed system of surveillance. In this sense, this totalizing drive mirrors the logic of platformization—new threats, harms and crime scenarios are being

---

[41] For an example of this perspective, see for instance the reports on 'Economic Espionage' by *The National Counterintelligence and Security Center* (NCSC), United States' 'premier source for counterintelligence and security expertise and a trusted mission partner in protecting America against foreign and other adversarial threats', https://www.dni.gov/index.php/ncsc-what-we-do/ncsc-threat-assessments-mission/ncsc-economic-espionage.

added to the same platform, becoming just another risk or insider to detect or cut off from the (pure) system through the same compliance, managerial, intelligence, or technological fix.

While most threats are still largely deemed *external* to our system (with the exception of criminals), the undermining of this system would not be possible (upon this view) without these malicious actors exploiting loopholes and 'trusted insiders.' These trusted insiders then turn, intentionally or not, into malicious insiders: a threat to national security, corporations, businesses, and other organizations. In other words, in the interconnected and digitized world, the 'trusted' insider is seen as likely a source of threat as an outsider. And the better cyberdefences get, the higher the likelihood that a malicious actor will need to penetrate an organization physically. This logic manifests in the security discourse. In an article on the challenges to re-establishing total defense in Sweden we can thus for instance read that:

> Non-ethnic Swedes are playing a dominant role in much of organized crime, and this has raised the prospect of crime becoming an instrument of foreign powers (…) ensuring domestic stability has become a much more important component of total defense than it was historically. (Lallerstedt, 2021, p. 99)

The 'crimmigrant' (Franko, 2020) is simultaneously also cast as potentially *vulnerable* to exploitation by foreign powers and secret services, thus representing an additional risk to national security. This makes the crimmigrant likely to be risk flagged for additional 'targeted' surveillance or subjected to other policies. This, too, falls within the logic of insider threat. Risk *indicators* key to detection of insider threat focus, too, on individual weakness and vulnerability understood as a risk of potential victimization, be it through social engineering, or by corporate espionage or foreign secret services. This became visible also in several highly mediated instances of Russian and Chinese espionage and 'unlawful knowledge transfer' under export control regulations in the Norwegian higher education sector. In the media, we could read of a research institute putting a halt to hiring researchers from any 'red countries' deemed too risky. Another research institute, employing more individualized risk assessments, rejected a top-candidate with Norwegian citizenship, but Russian background, precisely on the grounds of his *vulnerability*: family members in Russia, as the management explained, could be used by the regime to exert pressure on him (Løkeland-Stai, 2023). This is how insider threat prevention can work in practice, here at the point of recruitment. Security interests of any given organization take priority over anti-discrimination laws—as is typical in cases of securitization (Buzan et al., 1998). This case also tells us a great deal about how insider threat is imagined: not only as intentionally malicious threat actors, but as individuals that represent a certain *weakness*—be it psychological (e.g., PTSD) or circumstantial (e.g., divorce), which can be either detected through background checks, or through perpetual monitoring which is increasingly favoured as circumstances change over time. But the same logic is again present in the larger security discourse. Returning to the Swedish 'total defense' paper, we can further read that:

> the focus must be on identifying those particular firms where foreign ownership is considered problematic from a security perspective. The crass reality is that there are firms that could be swayed by foreign or domestic hostile actors. (…) Key personnel or owners need to be screened, and legal mechanisms developed to exclude potentially problematic actors on security grounds. (Lallerstedt, 2021, p. 102)

The Norwegian government has in the meantime amended the *Security Act* to strengthen the investment screening regime, following the same logic.[42]

The paradigmatic examples of 'insider threats'—regularly and almost religiously cited in policy reports, training materials, best practice manuals, practice-oriented research, and reports by private security providers, and consulting and audit firms—are still famous spies such as CIA's Aldrich Ames and FBI's Robert Hanssen (O'Neill, 2019) who have been selling secrets and passing classified information to the Soviet Union. While the figure of the spy still looms large, the category of

---

[42] For a summary of these ammendments, see 'Significant amendments to the Norwegian investment control regime', *Arntzen de Besche*, https://www.adeb.no/en/post/significant-amendments-to-the-norwegian-investment-control-regime.

'insider threat' has expanded also as a result of a series of impactful events. These events made it obvious to the national security apparatuses in the West that one needs to abandon the Cold War mentality oriented around the sole focus on combatting *external* threats. The 9/11 and other terrorist attacks sparked a larger rethinking about the 'enemy within.' This resulted in new forms of intelligence- and data-sharing, background check practices, and organizational reform of intelligence services and the state security and military apparatuses—well beyond the United States. Chamayou argued that anti-terrorism has reshaped the logic of the military into the individual-centered logic of policing, security and 'manhunting' (Chamayou, 2012, 2015)—again, a logic discernible across the insider threat management systems and 'best practices'. In a sense, these systems can be understood as new techno-managerial scientifically informed forms of (privatized) 'manhunting'. This speaks also to the *scientization* of policing, public and private (*see* Egbert et al., this volume). While the terrorist threats have been partly overshadowed in the recent years by other iconic 'insider threat' cases—such as Edward Snowden and his revelations about the NSA program (Lyon, 2014; Snowden, 2019) or Chelsea Manning who leaked classified diplomatic cables and documents about the wars in Iraq and Afghanistan to WikiLeaks—these have only made arguments for insider threat *programs* stronger.

For the U.S. military, the case of the radicalized Army major Nidal Malik Hasan who killed 13 Defense Department employees and wounded 43 others at Fort Hood, Texas, in 2009 while shouting 'Allahu akbar', has revealed the degree to which the Army and even FBI were as organizations poorly adapted to preventing insider threats (Zegart, 2016). This event sparked a rethinking around the detection, preemption, neutralization and elimination of insider threats and malicious actors from one's own ranks. As Zegart puts it,

> During the Cold War, nuclear annihilation focused priorities and clarified tasks. That is no longer the case. "What would Moscow think?" has given way to "We need a special coordinator for that." In an age of increasing threat complexity, government leaders and agencies cannot

just think deeply and go it alone. Today's demands require greater collaboration within agencies, across them, and between the government and nongovernmental sectors. In short, organizations matter more. (Zegart, 2016, p. 72)

The changed socio-economic and technological realities, the increased complexity and interdependencies of the interconnected world and market economy, and the rise of new communication technologies and proliferation of cyber threats, have led to the expansion of private security apparatuses. But they have also been translated into the imperative to develop *multi-agency and multistakeholder programs* to tackle these threats. Better collaboration, across agencies, and private and public sector was required, and so was better threat and insider risk management. The neoliberal state has become dependent not only on the private sector expertise and products, but also on the *willingness* of the private sector to use its internal governance structures to serve national security interests. This is also why we have seen the emergence of the supervisory state, seeking to pursue its will through compliance-oriented regulations and issuing of guidelines for such compliance. This is also why the regulator and the regulated find themselves more and more often negotiating about the costs of this compliance, where the private sector wants there to be something in it for them as well. This dynamic is, also, likely at the core of the 'function creep' (Koops, 2021) of these systems as they become used for instance for performance management as opposed to security—they have to make themselves useful beyond the original purpose (Fig. 2.4).

These are just some of the factors that have contributed to the growth of networked and multistakeholder security governance. Of course, we find this form of governance in other sectors as well. Multistakeholderism has in many ways emerged as a key path to *consensus* which largely favours techno-managerial solutions (Garsten & de Montoya, 2008; Garsten & Jacobsson, 2012; Garsten & Sörbom, 2018). In the fields of security and crime-fighting this resulted in the favouring of *multi-disciplinary* teams and *multistakeholder* teams and in new forms of 'knowledge' and 'intelligence' sharing. This coincided with the rise in popularity of evidence-based and data-driven policies, and of the larger

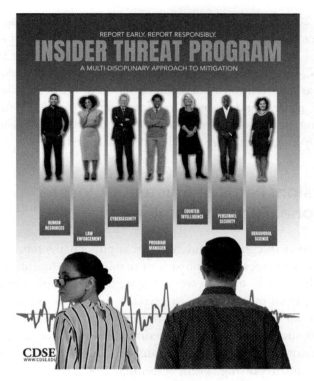

Fig. 2.4 Awareness raising poster by the Center for Development of Security Excellence (CDSE), Defense Counterintelligence and Security Agency. For this and more 'Insider Threat Security Posters', see: https://www.cdse.edu/Training/Security-Posters/Insider-Threat/Article/2753600/insider-threat-vigilance/

governance by numbers, metrics, and indicators (Head, 2008; Merry, 2011, 2016; Supiot, 2017); and with the increasing popularity of RCTs in studies of the social (Donovan, 2018). One could even argue that we have reached a point where the motto 'if it cannot be measured, it cannot be managed' can no longer be challenged. Quantification, measurement, and modelling of risk in the field of security has come to reign supreme (Amoore, 2013). The blurring of boundaries between policing and intelligence as seen in the proliferation of the ideals of predictive, pre-emptive, data-driven, and *intelligence*-led policing has by now become well-documented (Ferguson, 2017; Fyfe et al., 2018; Joh, 2017;

Ratcliffe, 2016). These ideals are also embedded into managerial practices under headings such as 'intelligence-driven decision-making' and propagated by the private intelligence professionals seeking to make it into the C-suite. This managerial intelligence-driven decision-making also increasingly relies on surveillance (be it of workers, clients, trade unions or others) and open-source intelligence (OSINT) supplied by the growing industry of private business and security intelligence companies and in-house corporate intelligence departments.

Conclusion: Perils of Epistemic Closure in National Security Thinking

Global market integration and complex supply chains represent a great number of challenges to the pursuit of national security interests—especially if the aim is to preserve the system while eliminating threats. Since there is an overall desire to preserve the globalized markets (with exceptions for designated goods subject to export control and other restrictions such as investment screening), many of the proposed solutions amount to new rigorous forms of control, monitoring, audit, disclosure, and reporting. From screening, risk assessments, to surveillance, these controls are also meant to *generate* necessary information and threat and risk *intelligence*. This intelligence is then to serve both the respective organizations and the state and identify, detect, and target—and eliminate or manage—(potential) 'enemies within'. But of course, what is deemed an 'insider threat' by a profit-oriented corporation and by nation state tends to differ greatly. Despite this, and irrespective of how the corporations or the state defines insider threats, the solution—by both—is seen to reside in finetuning of techno-managerial and intelligence-driven solutions. These technosolutions are to perpetually and dynamically, in a manner of a smart missile detecting a moving target, identify risks and threats in a rapidly changing regulatory and geopolitical landscape. While these techno-managerial solutions may present themselves as apolitical, and their recalibrations to new regulatory demands or threat assessments a mere technical exercise, they are deeply political and moral devices. In a globalized and interconnected world, where the boundaries between good and evil no longer neatly coincide with the nation states such as during the Cold War, these techno-managerial technologies of control promise to protect us from enemies within and sort the good from the bad apples in our midst.

As the example of insider threat program shows, the shift from government (politics) to (ever more technocratic) governance has brought with it various forms of hybridization and blurring of fields previously thought separate, but now to be unified under the (scientifically informed) umbrellas of 'good (organizational and security) governance', collaboration and information sharing, and management (hence the need for a *program*). Management has of course, over the past century, evolved into a highly professionalized field, to the point where it no longer matters *what* type of organization is to be managed (be it university, nuclear facility, army or a bakery), for the same principles of management and leadership are thought to apply (hence managerial ISO standards). In other words, the *telos* of the respective organization, counts for little if not nothing (Kuldova et al., 2024). This managerial way of thinking easily aligns with the cybernetic logic (and the logic of the platform mentioned earlier), and with the focus on the *individual* (such as the management of 'bad apples'), which is particularly pronounced in HR, as much as in law, psy-sciences, and computer science. As we have seen, it is precisely these disciplines that inform insider threat management systems. The epistemic power of the framework of *individual deviance* is thus propped up by several coinciding factors: (1) the regulatory imaginary, (2) the hegemonic managerial paradigms and the ideological power of Big Audit, (3) the cultural valorisation of technological solutions and the ideological power of Big Tech, (4) the cultural ideals of intelligence-led and data-driven policing, security, and decision-making, and the (5) increased preference for apolitical and evidence-based policies over politics and democratic debate. The combined force of these factors manifests in the widely observed individualization, juridification, psychologization, and securitization of workplaces and society at large (Kuldova & Nordrik, 2023).

The framework of *individual deviance* and its epistemic hold also manifests in the prevalent social imaginary of our inherently good liberal market order being undermined by malicious actors. These malicious actors who become insider threats or their enablers are said, as noted earlier, to exploit loopholes or weaknesses in our legal and control architectures and in 'human capital.' Those vulnerable (and not resilient and robust enough) and thus extra susceptible to what psychologists call 'stressors', need to be detected and at best offered counselling and psychological help, at worst dismissed and made someone else's problem. The fact that these 'stressors' are more often than not pressures generated by the system and organizations only rarely figure in the discourse. This is, of course, a perfect expression of neoliberal individual responsibilization. Alternative solutions to what in many cases are systemic problems are foreclosed by this alliance of techno-managerialism and psychology. Instead, this alliance keeps on generating and churning out more and more managerial and technological products and commodities predicated precisely upon this fundamental foreclosure. We could call it an epistemic closure: certain and very particular ways of understanding the world have gained dominance, and are being reinforced by both policy-makers and industry at the expense of other possible ways of understanding, knowing and governing the social. Most problematically, within this multistakeholder consensus perspective conflict does not seem to exist; alternatively, it is to be eliminated, supressed and undercommunicated, and turned into harmony. This is also why the state can, in all seriousness—but we could also argue in all naivety—believe that imposing security compliance obligations onto the private sector will make profit-oriented (often transnational) corporations align with national security agendas of any particular state. Even the fact that these, often diverging and conflicting, expectations are placed on multinational corporations from multiple states simultaneously does not appear to figure as potential source of conflict. In the world of intelligence, one likes to speak of 'cognitive closure', a concept taken (unsurprisingly) from psychology (Hatlebrekke & Smith, 2010). Epistemic closure, in the sense in which I launch it here, is a broader social concept positioning 'intelligence failure' in a more complex socio-cultural framework that considers market dynamics, relations between the public and private sector, and cultural ideology as much as geopolitics.

The understanding that our 'good' system is being undermined by criminal and malicious 'individuals' (or their networks) as the supreme explanation for our crime and security problems has become so ingrained, so common sense, so hegemonic, that few appear to question it. That is, the fundamental *premise* of insider threat and risk programs, despite their individual variations, is never questioned. Instead, these narrow understandings are built into platforms and software—in the algorithmic architectures of our increasingly automated governance and management. These products lead us to focus on the detection of malicious insiders and promise to tackle very different crimes, harms, and security threats by flagging suspicious and risky *individuals*. There is no contextual and susbtantial understanding possible of the vastly different phenomena. Insider threat programs (as many other such solutions) effectively posit that defences against foreign espionage are the same as the defences against sexual harassment, corruption or cybercrime, or just a matter of tweaking risk indicators. From an anthropological or sociological point of view, this is nothing less than a striking absurdity. Of course, nobody is arguing that foreign and corporate espionage are not real, or that social engineering, hackers, criminals, or corruption do not exist. What I argue is that it is theoretically flawed to try to tackle these issues as *solely* a matter of individual deviance that can be predicted or pre-empted through the same platform—and this is just one example of this technosolutionist logic.

Another striking implication of the 'insider threat' logic is that the leadership and management, be it of a state or of a corporation, is by default cast as pure and good. Of course, with the exception of occasional and almost purifying scandals that only confirm rather than undermine the perception of purity by default. The majority of bad apples is, not accidentally, to be found, among the *lower* ranks. It is those *below*, those to be managed, who are seen as those threatening and undermining those above, and their good 'system': be it 'rule of law', 'good (corporate) governance' or the 'integrity of the financial system'. Even if we would accept the flawed premise of 'insider threat'—would these systems not, by design, lead to ignoring 'insider threats' at the top level of any organization? Elites and top-level management not only define who is to be seen as a threat, risk, or as an illegitimate actor, propped up the epistemic power of pracademics and their expertise. In the process, they position themselves as by default good, legitimate, and beyond doubt (where everyone else is deemed suspect by default), and as almost naturally aligned with national security interests. Time and again we can hear in the rhetoric of state agencies expressions of worry about small businesses and organizations that lack 'robust' compliance and internal security systems. And we are told that it is these small local actors that are particularly vulnerable and prone to being exploited and weaponized by criminal actors or foreign secret services—if not themselves deemed illicit and otherwise problematic. Large, transnational actors such as multinational corporations or financial institutions, on the other hand, are seen as reliable, 'robust', 'resilient', and trustworthy, as natural 'partners' in crime-fighting, as well-run organizations with elaborate security and compliance processes to handle and mitigate threats and risks. This is fascinating, given that so many scandals and systemic harms are routinely connected to these large organizations. But again, this can be explained by the epistemic power of the framework of individual deviance ('bad apples' in Western organizations). For systemic corruption, upon this security imaginary, exists only among the radically Other (Russia, Nigeria, and so on).

Critical literature on corporate crimes and harms (e.g., Glasbeek, 2002; Hall, 2012; Tombs & Whyte, 2007; Whyte, 2003; Woodiwiss, 2005) refuses to see crimes, security threats and harms as a result of a 'few bad apples'. But it is a marginalized view; instead, the logic of 'insider threat' is being entrenched at both micro- and macro-levels of governance—within organizations and at the level of state policy. While framing the fight against crimes and security threats through 'insider threats' might be in the interest of capital (accumulation), it is not necessarily the case for national security interests—for are we not, in this obsessive reliance on profiling and targeting of *individuals*, digging our own graves of a forthcoming massive 'intelligence failure'? For if there is something utterly implausible, no matter how common sense now, is it not precisely the notion that all our problems can be explained by internal and external malicious actors undermining our 'good' system, and hence something that can be solved by targeting, managing or eliminating these 'evil actors', and eventually reaching a state of (neoliberal?)

bliss? This is likely where our national security apparatuses have been listening too much to their private sector suppliers of 'wisdom', expertise, and tech.

Multinational corporations, businesses, or even non-profits have their own goals and their own strategic interests, from increasing shareholder value, increasing efficiency and productivity, cutting costs, sourcing in low-cost countries, maintaining supply chains that cut across the divisions of good and evil in security politics, to the minute control and surveillance of workers. In other words, while the state wishes these organizations to act in national security interests, corporations are driven by their own, primarily financial, interests. This raises the question of the limits of the national 'total defense' imaginary (as we find it in contemporary Norway) within the global market economy. And it also brings into sharp focus the challenges of the state trying to have its cake and eat it, too.

This chapter has tried to show that 'insider threat programs' are not neutral, disinterested, objective, or ideology-free, but to the contrary, materialize both the epistemic, financial, political, cultural, and social power of the actors who enforce them, and reflect their interests. If we were to take the security threats seriously, we would need to collectively break the ideological fantasies of multistakeholder consensus as much as the technosolutionist logic of platformization, for the two are intertwined. This would also require breaking the epistemic hold of certain disciplines over how we know and understand the world. This may prove difficult in the information world increasingly dominated by AI-powered stochastic parrots.

Coda: On the Need for Positive Visions

A more fundamental question we must ask is not merely what kind of a world these security architectures are creating, but what kind of a world we actually envision and want. We need positive visions that push beyond the *anti*-policies and *counter*-strategies that seek to detect, preempt, and eliminate threats. Visions that go beyond the policing logic of 'zero tolerance' and the cybernetic logic of 'zero trust', likely visions that go beyond the security logic itself. For, what kind of visions are these, what do they offer apart from a perpetual state of war on … (insert crime, harm, and threat of your choice)? If the zero endpoint (which is never to be reached, but perpetually chased) would arrive, what would we be left with after having 'taken out' all these malicious actors? The current system minus malicious actors? Merely asking such questions reveals the fundamental flaws of these visions—which are already creating a world predicated upon a massive intelligence failure, one that our intelligence services disavow. None of these combat-oriented strategies offer any positive prosocial visions of human flourishing, but it is precisely such visions that we need the most in the current moment.

Funding Statement   This work would not be possible without the generous funding for ground-breaking research by The Research Council of Norway and Ministry of Defence of Norway for the following projects: The Research Council of Norway project no. 313626—*Algorithmic Governance and Cultures of Policing: Comparative Perspectives from Norway, India, Brazil, Russia, and South Africa* (AGOPOL); The Research Council of Norway project no. 313004—*Luxury, Corruption and Global Ethics: Towards a Critical Cultural Theory of the Moral Economy of Fraud* (LUXCORE), the Ministry of Defence of Norway project no. 203480 — *National Security through Private Sector Regulation? Critical Evaluation of Insider Threat Programs and Security Compliance in Current Geopolitical and Regulatory Context (INSIDER)*. Research was conducted in compliance with the research ethics and data protection regulations of OsloMet—Oslo Metropolitan University and in alignment with the NESH *Guidelines for Research Ethics in The Social Sciences, Humanities, Law and Theology*, interview subjects signed informed consent forms.

References

Alvesson, M., & Sköldberg, K. (2018). *Reflexive Methodology: New Vistas for Qualitative Research*. Sage.

Amicelle, A., & Iafolla, V. (2018). Suspicion-in-the-making: Surveillance and Denunciation in Financial Policing. *The British Journal of Criminology, 58*(4), 845–863. https://doi.org/10.1093/bjc/azx051

Amoore, L. (2013). *The Politics of Possibility: Risk and Security Beyond Probability.* Duke University Press. https://doi.org/10.1515/9780822377269

Anderson, E. (2017). *Private Government: How Employers Rule Our Lives (and Why We Don't Talk about It).* Princeton University Press. https://doi.org/10.1515/9781400887781

Arrigo, B., & Sellers, S. (Eds.) (2021). *The Pre-Crime Society: Crime, Culture and Control in the Ultramodern Age.* Bristol University Press. https://doi.org/10.46692/9781529205268

Ball, K. (2010). Workplace Surveillance: An Overview. *Labor History, 51*(1), 87–106. https://doi.org/10.1080/00236561003654776

Barberis, J., Arner, D. W., & Buckley, R. P. (2019). *The RegTech Book: The Financial Technology Handbook for Investors, Entrepreneurs and Visionaries in Regulation.* Willey & Sons Ltd.

Barkan, J. (2013). *Corporate Sovereignty: Law and Government Under Capitalism.* University of Minnesota Press. https://doi.org/10.5749/minnesota/9780816674268.001.0001

Baweja, J., Dunning M. P., & Noonan, C. (2022). Domestic Extremism: How to Counter Threats Posed to Critical Assets. *CITRAP: Counter-Insider Threat Research and Practice, 1*(1), 1–8. https://doi.org/10.2172/1985028

Ben Jaffel, H., & Larsson, S. (Eds.) (2022). *Problematising Intelligence Studies: Towards a New Research Agenda.* Routledge.

Besteman, C., & Gusterson, H. (2019). *Life By Algorithms: How Roboprocesses Are Remaking Our World.* University of Chicago Press. https://doi.org/10.7208/chicago/9780226627731.001.0001

Birch, K., & Muniesa, F. (2020). Introduction: Assetization and Technoscientific Capitalism. In K. Birch & F. Muniesa (Eds.), *Assetization* (pp. 1–41). The MIT Press. https://doi.org/10.7551/mitpress/12075.001.0001

Bishop, M., Engle, S., Frincke, D. A., Gates, C., Greitzer, F. L., Peisert, S., & Whalen, S. (2010). A Risk Management Approach to the 'Insider Threat.' *Advances in Information Security, 49*, 1–24. https://doi.org/10.1007/978-1-4419-7133-3_6

Black, M., Yeung, J., & Yeung, D. (2022). *Insider Threat and White-Collar Crime in Non-Government Organisations and Industries: A Literature Review.* RAND Corporation.

Boels, D., & Verhage, A. (2015). Plural Policing: A State-of-the-Art Review. *Policing: An International Journal of Police Strategies & Management, 39*(1), 2–18. https://doi.org/10.1108/PIJPSM-05-2015-0069

Braithwaite, J. (2008). *Regulatory Capitalism: How it Works, Ideas for Making it Better.* Edward Elgar. https://doi.org/10.4337/9781848441262

Brown, R. A., Yeung, D., Gehlhaus, D., & O'Connor, K. (2020). Corporate Knowledge for Government Decisionmakers: Insights on Screening, Vetting, and Monitoring Processes. *RAND Corporation*. https://doi.org/10.7249/RRA275-1

Busvine, D. (2023). Sanctions Aren't Working: How the West Enables Russia's War on Ukraine. *Politico*, 11 December 2023. https://www.politico.eu/article/russia-sanctions-western-companies-intel-huawei-amd-texas-instruments-ibm/

Buzan, B., Wæver, O., & de Wilde, J. (1998). *Security: A New Framework for Analysis*. Lynne Rienner Publishers. https://doi.org/10.1515/9781685853808

CERT, National Insider Threat Center. (2022). *Common Sense Guide to Mitigating Insider Threats (7th Edition)*. Carnegie Mellon University, Software Engineering Institute.

Chamayou, G. (2012). *Manhunts: A Philosophical History*. Princeton University Press. https://doi.org/10.23943/princeton/9780691151656.001.0001

Chamayou, G. (2015). *Drone Theory*. Penguin.

Chamayou, G. (2021). *The Ungovernable Society: A Genealogy of Authoritarian Liberalism*. Polity.

Christophers, B. (2023). *Our Lives in their Portfolios: Why Asset Managers Own the World*. Verso.

Clarke, G. (2019). The New Global Governors: Globalization, Civil Society, and the Rise of Private Philanthropic Foundations. *Journal of Civil Society, 15*(3), 197–213. https://doi.org/10.1080/17448689.2019.1622760

Cohn, C. (1987). Sex and Death in the Rational World of Defense Intellectuals. *Signs, 12*(4), 687–718. https://doi.org/10.1086/494362

Colwill, C. (2009). Human Factors in Information Security: The Insider Threat—Who Can You Trust These Days? *Information Security Technical Report, 14*, 186–196. https://doi.org/10.1016/j.istr.2010.04.004

Costa, D. L., Collins, M. L., Samuel, J. P., Michael, J. A., Silowash, G. J., & Spooner, D. J. (2014). An Ontology for Insider Threat Indicators. *CEUR Workshop Proceedings*.

Craig, R., Amernic, J., & Tourish, D. (2014). Perverse Audit Culture and Accountability of the Modern Public University. *Financial Accountability & Management, 30*(1), 1–24. https://doi.org/10.1111/faam.12025

Diphoorn, T., & Wiegnick, N. (2021). Corporate Sovereignty: Negotiating Permissive Power for Profit in Southern Africa. *Anthropological Theory*, September 2021, 1–21. https://doi.org/10.1177/14634996211037124

Donovan, K. P. (2018). The Rise of the Randomistas: On the Experimental Turn in International Aid. *Economy and Society, 47*(1), 27–58. https://doi.org/10.1080/03085147.2018.1432153

Drezner, D. W., Farrell, H., & Newman, A. L. (Eds.). (2021). *The Uses and Abuses of Weaponized Interdependence.* Brookings Institution Press.

Edelman, L. B., & Suchman, M. C. (1999). When the 'Haves' Hold Court: Speculations on the Organizational Internalization of Law. *Law & Society Review, 33*(4), 941–991. https://doi.org/10.2307/3115155

Egbert, S. (2019). Predictive Policing and the Platformization of Police Work. *Surveillance & Society, 17*(1/2), 83–88. https://doi.org/10.24908/ss.v17i1/2.12920

Elifoglu, I. H., Abel, I., & Tasseven, Ö. (2018). Minimizing Insider Threat Risk with Behavioral Monitoring. *Review of Business: Interdisciplinary Journal on Risk and Society, 38*(2), 61–73.

Ericson, R. V., & Haggerty, K. D. (1997). *Policing the Risk Society.* University of Toronto Press.

Ferguson, A. G. (2017). *The Rise of Big Data Policing: Surveillance, Race, and the Future of Law Enforcement.* New York University Press. https://doi.org/10.2307/j.ctt1pwtb27

Foucault, M. (1980). The Confession of the Flesh. In C. Gordon (Ed.), *Power/Knowledge: Selected Interviews and Other Writings 1972–1977* (pp. 194–228). Pantheon Books.

Franko, K. (2020). *The Crimmigrant Other: Migration and Penal Power.* Routledge. https://doi.org/10.4324/9781351001441

Frischmann, B., & Selinger, E. (2018). *Re-engineering Humanity.* Cambridge University Press. https://doi.org/10.1017/9781316544846

Fyfe, N., Gundhus, H., & Rønn, K. V. (2018). *Moral Issues in Intelligence-led Policing.* Routledge. https://doi.org/10.4324/9781315231259

Fukuyama, F. (1992). *The End of History and the Last Man.* Free Press.

Gabriel, C. (2018). The Rise of Kleptocracy: Malaysia's Missing Billions. *Journal of Democracy, 29*(1), 69–75. https://doi.org/10.1353/jod.2018.0005

Garland, D. (2001). *The Culture of Control: Crime and Social Order in Contemporary Society.* Chicago University Press. https://doi.org/10.7208/chicago/9780226190174.001.0001

Garrett, B. L. (2014). *Too Big to Jail: How Prosecutors Compromise with Corporations.* The Belknap Press of Harvard University Press. https://doi.org/10.4159/9780674735712

Garsten, C., & de Montoya, M. L. (2008). *Transparency in a New Global Order: Unveiling Organizational Visions*. Edward Elgar. https://doi.org/10.4337/9781848441354

Garsten, C., & Jacobsson, K. (2012). Post-Political Regulation: Soft Power and Post-Political Visions in Global Governance. *Critical Sociology, 39*(3), 421–437. https://doi.org/10.1177/0896920511413942

Garsten, C., & Sörbom, A. (2018). *Discreet Power: How the World Economic Forum Shapes Market Agendas*. Stanford University Press.

Glasbeek, H. (2002). *Wealth by Stealth: Corporate Crime, Corporate Law, and the Perversion of Democracy*. Between the Lines.

Godard, J. (2014). The Psychologisation of Employment Relations? *Human Resource Management Journal, 24*(1), 1–18. https://doi.org/10.1111/1748-8583.12030

Guido, M. D., & Brooks, M. W. (2013). Insider Threat Program Best Practices. *IEEE: 46th International Conference on System Sciences*, 1831–9. https://doi.org/10.1109/HICSS.2013.279

Hall, S. (2012). *Theorizing Crime and Deviance: A New Perspective*. SAGE. https://doi.org/10.4135/9781446251669

Hall, S., & Wilson, D. (2014). New Foundations: Pseudo-Pacification and Special Liberty as Potential Cornerstones for a Multi-level Theory of Homicide and Serial Murder. *European Journal of Criminology, 11*(5), 635–655. https://doi.org/10.1177/1477370814536831

Hamilton, C., & Lippert, R. K. (2020). Governing Through Human Rights in Counter-Terrorism: Proofing, Problematization and Securitization. *Critical Criminology, 28*, 127–145. https://doi.org/10.1007/s10612-020-09496-3

Han, B.-C. (2015). *The Transparency Society*. Stanford University Press.

Hansen, H.K. & Tang-Jensen, M.H. (2015). Making Up Corruption Control: Conducting Due Diligence in a Danish Law Firm. *Ephemera: Theory & Politics in Organization, 15*(2), 365–385.

Hatlebrekke, K., & Smith, M. L. R. (2010). Towards a New Theory of Intelligence Failure? The Impact of Cognitive Closure and Discourse Failure. *Intelligence and National Security, 25*(2), 147–182.

Haugh, T. (2017). The Criminalization of Compliance. *Notre Dame Law Review, 92*(3), 1215–1270.

Head, B. W. (2008). Three Lenses of Evidence-Based Policy. *The Australian Journal of Public Administration, 67*(1), 1–11. https://doi.org/10.1111/j.1467-8500.2007.00564.x

Henninger, D. (2023). Biden's March to State Capitalism. *Wall Street Journal,* 14 June 2023. https://www.wsj.com/articles/bidens-march-to-state-capita lism-white-house-government-election-china-ce22b035

Højer, L., & Bandak, A. (2015). Special Issue: The Power of Example. Anthropological Explorations in Persuasion, Evocation, and Imitation. *Journal of Royal Anthropological Institute, 21*(1), 1–17. https://doi.org/10.1111/1467-9655.12173

Homoliak, I., Toffalini, F., Guarnizo, J., Elovici, Y., & Ochoa, M. (2019). Insight Into Insiders and IT: A Survey of Insider Threat Taxononomies, Analysis, Modeling and Countermeasures. *ACM Computing Surveys, 52*(2), 1–40. https://doi.org/10.1145/3303771

INSA. (2018). *Assessing the Mind of the Malicious Insider: Using a Behavioral Model and Data Analytics to Improve Continuous Evaluation.* Intelligence and National Security Alliance, Security Policy Reform Council, Insider Threat Subcommittee. https://www.nationalinsiderthreatsig.org/itrmresou rces/Assessing%20the%20Mind%20Of%20The%20Malicious%20Insider. pdf

INSA. (2022). *Background Paper: Insider Threat Program Naming Convention.* Intelligence and National Security Alliance. https://www.insaonline.org/ docs/default-source/default-document-library/2022-white-papers/insa_wp_t erminology.pdf?sfvrsn=a5989f28_3

Jacobsen, J. T. (2020). From Neurotic Citizen to Hysteric Security Expert: A Lacanian Reading of the Perpetual Demand for US Cyber Defence. *Critical Studies on Security, 8*(1), 46–58. https://doi.org/10.1080/21624887.2020. 1735830

Jakobi, A. P. (2013). *Common Goods and Evils? The Formation of Global Crime Governance.* Oxford University Press. https://doi.org/10.1093/acprof:oso/ 9780199674602.001.0001

Jeppesen, K. K. (2019). The Role of Auditing in the Fight Against Corruption. *The British Accounting Review, 51*(5), 100798. https://doi.org/10.1016/j.bar. 2018.06.001

Joh, E. E. (2004). The Paradox of Private Policing. *Journal of Criminal Law and Criminology, 95*(1), 49–132. https://doi.org/10.2307/3491382

Joh, E. E. (2017). Artificial Intelligence and Policing: First Questions. *Seattle University Law Review, 41*, 1139–1144.

Johansen, M.-L.E., Warburg, A. B., & Mynster, M. (2021). Frictional Security Governance. *Perspectives on Terrorism, 15*(4), 111–124.

Kaleem, A. (2022). Citizen-Led Intelligence Gathering under UK's Prevent Duty. In H. Ben Jaffel & S. Larsson (Eds.), *Problematising Intelligence*

Studies: Towards a New Research Agenda (pp. 73–95). Routledge.https://doi. org/10.4324/9781003205463-6

Kandias, M., Mylonas, A., Virvillis, N., Theoharidou, M., & Gritzalis, D. (2010). An Insider Threat Prediction Model. In S. Katsikas, J. Lopez, & M. Soriano (Eds.), *TrustBus 2010* (pp. 26–37). Springer. https://doi.org/10. 1007/978-3-642-15152-1_3

Keefe, P. R. (2010). Privatized Spying: The Emerging Intelligence Industry. In L. K. Johnson (Ed.), *The Oxford Handbook of National Security Intelligence* (pp. 297–310). Oxford University Press. https://doi.org/10.1093/oxfordhb/ 9780195375886.003.0018

Klein, E., Mills, C., Achuthan, A., & Hilberg, E. (2021). Human Technologies, Affect and the Global Psy-complex. *Economy and Society, 50*(3), 347–358. https://doi.org/10.1080/03085147.2021.1899658

Koops, B.-J. (2021). The Concept of Function Creep. *Law, Innovation and Technology, 13*(1), 29–56. https://doi.org/10.1080/17579961.2021.189 8299

Kuldova, T. Ø. (2022). *Compliance-Industrial Complex: The Operating System of a Pre-Crime Society*. Palgrave Macmillan. https://doi.org/10.1007/978-3- 031-19224-1

Kuldova, T. Ø., & Nordrik, B. (2023). Workplace Investigations, the Epistemic Power of Managerialism, and the Hollowing Out of the Norwegian Model of Co-determination. *Class and Capital*. https://doi.org/10.1177/030 98168231179971

Kuldova, T. Ø., Østbø, J., & Raymen, T. (2024). *Luxury and Corruption: Challenging the Anti-Corruption Consensus*. Bristol University Press.

Lallerstedt, K. (2021). Rebuilding Total Defense in a Globalized Deregulated Economy: The Case of Sweden. *Prism, 9*(3), 90–105.

Lang, E.L. (2022). Seven (Science-Based) Commandments for Understanding and Countering Insider Threats. *CITRAP: Counter-Insider Threat Research and Practice, 1*(1), 1–14.

Lenzenweger, M. F., & Shaw, E. D. (2022). The Critical Pathway to Insider Risk Model: Brief Overview and Future Directions. *CITRAP: Counter-Insider Threat Research and Practice, 1*(1),1–21.

Levi-Faur, D. (2017). Regulatory Capitalism. In P. Drahos (Ed.), *Regulatory Theory: Foundation and Applications* (pp. 289–302). ANU Press. https:// doi.org/10.22459/RT.02.2017.17

Liss, C., & Sharman, J. C. (2015). Global Corporate Crime-Fighters: Private Transnational Responses to Piracy and Money Laundering. *Review of International Political Economy, 22*(4), 693–718. https://doi.org/10.1080/096 92290.2014.936482

Løkeland-Stai, E. (2023). Fikk nei til jobb og beskjed om at familie og venner kan utsettes for russisk press. *Khrono*, 20 June 2023. https://www.khrono. no/fikk-nei-til-jobb-og-beskjed-om-at-familie-og-venner-kan-utsettes-for-russisk-press/788634

Luckey, D., Stebbins, D., Orrie, R., Rehban, E., Bhatt, S. D., & Beaghley, S. (2019). *Assessing Continuous Evaluation Approaches for Insider Threats: How Can the Security Posture of the U.S. Departments and Agencies Be Improved?* RAND Corporation. https://doi.org/10.7249/RR2684

Lyon, D. (2014). Surveillance, Snowden, and Big Data: Capacities, Consequences, Critique. *Big Data & Society*, July–December, 1–13. https://doi. org/10.1177/2053951714541861

Maasberg, M., Warren, J., & Beebe, N. L. (2015). The Dark Side of the Insider: Detecting the Insider Threat Through Examination of Dark Triad Personality Traits. *48th Hawaii International Conference on System Science*, 3518–26. https://doi.org/10.1109/HICSS.2015.423

Marlin-Bennett, R. (2016). Everyday Rules and Embodied Information: Anti-Money Laundering/Counter-Terrorist Financing Practices and Radio Frequency Identification Tags as Security Politics. *Critical Studies on Security, 4*(2), 169–186. https://doi.org/10.1080/21624887.2016.1160199

Mbadiwe, T. (2018). Algorithmic Injustice. *The New Atlantis: A Journal of Technology & Society Winter*, 3–28.

McCarthy, D. R. (2021). Imagining the Security of Innovation: Technological Innovation, National Security, and the American Way of Life. *Critical Studies on Security, 9*(3), 196–211. https://doi.org/10.1080/216 24887.2021.1934640

Merry, S. E. (2011). Measuring the World: Indicators, Human Rights, and Global Governance. *Current Anthropology, 52*, S83–S95. https://doi.org/10. 1086/657241

Merry, S. E. (2016). *The Seductions of Quantification: Measuring Human Rights, Gender Violence, and Sex Trafficking*. University of Chicago Press.

Moore, A. P., Gardner, C., & Rousseau, D. M. (2022). Reducing Insider Risk Through Positive Deterrence. *CITRAP: Counter-Insider Threat Resarch and Practice, 1*(1),1–11.

Morozov, E. (2013). *To Save Everything, Click Here*. Public Affairs.

Morrow, M. A. R. (2022). Private Sector Intelligence: On the Long Path of Professionalization. *Intelligence and National Security, 37*(3), 402–420. https://doi.org/10.1080/02684527.2022.2029099

Nelson, J. S. (2021). Compliance as Management. In B. van Rooij & D. D. Sokol (Eds.), *The Cambridge Handbook of Compliance* (pp. 104–22). Cambridge University Press. https://doi.org/10.1017/9781108759458.009

Nieto Martín, A. (2022). *Global Criminal Law: Postnational Criminal Justice in the Twenty-First Century.* Palgrave Macmillan. https://doi.org/10.1007/978-3-030-84831-6

Noponen, N., Feschenko, P., Auvinen, T., Luaho-aho, V., & Abrahamsson, P. (2023). Taylorism on Steroids or Enabling Autonomy? A Systematic Review of Algorithmic Management. *Management Review Quarterly*, Online First. https://doi.org/10.1007/s11301-023-00345-5

Notaker, H. (2023). Nasjonal sikkerhet eller økonomisk effektivitet? Norges evne til å avdekke hybride trusler i samtidshistorisk perspektiv. *Internasjonal Politikk, 81*(1), 115–141, https://doi.org/10.23865/intpol.v81.5157

NSM. (2020). *Temarapport: Innsiderisiko.* NSM. The Norwegian National Security Authority. https://nsm.no/getfile.php/133153-1591706148/NSM/Filer/Dokumenter/Rapporter/Temarapport%20innsidere.pdf

NSM. (2023). *Sikkerhetsfaglig råd: Et motstandsdyktig Norge.* NSM. The Norwegian National Security Authority. https://nsm.no/regelverk-og-hjelp/rapporter/sikkerhetsfaglig-rad-et-motstandsdyktig-norge

O'Neil, C. (2016). *Weapons of Math Destruction: How Big Data Increases Inequality and Threatens Democracy.* Crown.

O'Neill, E. (2019). *Gray Day: My Undercover Mission to Expose America's First Cyber Spy.* Crown Publishing Group.

OSEPI. (2022). *Why the European Union Needs Anticorruption Sanctions: A Powerful Tool in the Fight Against Corruption.* Policy Brief March 2022. Open Society European Policy Institute (OSEPI).

Østbø, J. (2017). Securitizing 'Spiritual-Moral Values' in Russia. *Post-Soviet Affairs, 33*(3), 200–216. https://doi.org/10.1080/1060586X.2016.1251023

Petersen, K. L. (2012). *Corporate Risk and National Security Redefined.* Routledge.

Perkowski, N., & Squire, V. (2019). The Anti-policy of European Anti-smuggling as a Site of Contestation in the Mediterranean Migration 'Crisis.' *Journal of Ethnic and Migration Studies, 45*(12), 2167–2184. https://doi.org/10.1080/1369183X.2018.1468315

Postman, N. (1993). *Technopoly: The Surrender of Culture to Technology.* Vintage Books.

Power, M. (1997). *The Audit Society: Rituals of Verification.* Oxford University Press.

Ratcliffe, J. H. (2016). *Intelligence-Led Policing.* Routledge. https://doi.org/10. 4324/9781315717579

Rohde, J. (2013). *Armed with Expertise: The Militarization of American Social Research during the Cold War.* Cornell University Press.

Rohde, J. (2017). Pax Technologica: Computers, International Affairs, and Human Reason in the Cold War. *Isis, 108*(4), 792–813.

Roland, A. (2007). The Military-Industrial Complex: Lobby and Trope. In A. J. Bacevich (Ed.), *The Long War: A New History of U.S. National Security Policy Since World War II* (pp. 355–70). Columbia University Press.

Rongved, G., & Norheim-Martinsen, P. M. (2022). *Totalforsvaret i praksis.* Gyldendal.

Rose, N. (1999). *Governing the Soul: The Shaping of the Private Self.* Free Association Books.

Rosenblat, A. (2018). *Uberland: How Algorithms Are Rewriting the Rules of Work.* University of California Press. https://doi.org/10.1525/978052097 0632

Runciman, D. (2023). *The Handover: How We Gave Control of Our Lives to Corporations.* Profile Books.

Schmidt, R. (2018). *Regulatory Integration Across Borders Public-Private Cooperation in Transnational Regulation.* Cambridge University Press. https://doi. org/10.1017/9781108667692

Schuilenburg, M. (2011). The Securitization of Society: On the Rise of Quasi-Criminal Law and Selective Exclusion. *Social Justice, 38*(1/2), 73–89.

Schulz, T., Knobbe, M., Hesse, M., Book, S., Hage, S., Fahrion, G., Sauga, M., & Traufetter, G. (2022). Prosperity Under Pressure: Germany and the End of Globalization. *Spiegel International.* 27 July 2022. https://www.spi egel.de/international/world/germany-and-the-end-of-globalization-prospe rity-under-pressure-a-4f0b98ce-a2a5-4889-8375-d0dcf64cee2c

Scoles, S. (2022). Your Bosses Could Have a File on You, and They May Misinterpret It. *New York Times.* 15 May 2022. https://www.nytimes.com/2022/ 05/17/science/insider-threat-private-companies.html

Sempill, J. (2001). Under the Lens: Electronic Workplace Surveillance. *Australian Journal of Labour Law, 14*, 1–34.

Shagina, M. (2023). Enforcing Russia's Debt to Ukraine: Constraints and Creativity. *Survival, 65*(2), 27–36. https://doi.org/10.1080/00396338. 2023.2193094

Shore, C., & Wright, S. (2015). Audit Culture Revisited: Rankings, Ratings, and the Reassembling of Society. *Current Anthropology, 56*(3), 421–444. https://doi.org/10.1086/681534

Shore, C., & Wright, S. (2018). How the Big 4 Got Big: Audit Culture and the Metamorphosis of International Accountancy Firms. *Critique of Anthropology, 38*(3), 303–324. https://doi.org/10.1177/0308275X18775815

Simon, J. (2007). *Governing Through Crime: How the War on Crime Transformed American Democracy and Created a Culture of Fear.* Oxford University Press.

Snowden, E. (2019). *Permanent Record.* Henry Holt and Company.

Spira, L. F. (2002). *The Audit Committee: Performing Corporate Governance.* Kluwer Academic Publishers.

Strathern, M. (2000a). *Audit Cultures: Anthropological Studies in Accountability.* Routledge.

Strathern, M. (2000b). The Tyranny of Transparency. *British Educational Research Journal, 26*(3), 309–321. https://doi.org/10.1080/713651562

Suchman, L. (2020). Algorithmic Warfare and the Reinvention of Accuracy. *Critical Studies on Security, 8*(2), 175–187. https://doi.org/10.1080/216 24887.2020.1760587

Sunde, J. Ø. (2023). *1000 år med norsk rettshistorie: ei annleis noregshistorie om rett, kommunikasjonsteknologi, historisk endring og rettsstat.* Dreyer.

Supiot, A. (2017). *Governance by Numbers: The Making of a Legal Model of Allegiance.* Bloomsbury.

The White House, US. (2023). *National Cybersecurity Strategy.* https://www.whitehouse.gov/wp-content/uploads/2023/03/National-Cybersecurity-Strategy-2023.pdf

Todolí-Signes, A. (2019). Algorithms, Artificial Intelligence and Automated Decisions Concerning Workers and the Risks of Discrimination: The Necessary Collective Governance of Data Protection. *Transfer, 25*(4), 465–481. https://doi.org/10.1177/1024258919876416

Toelle, E. (2021). *Microsoft 365 Compliance: A Practical Guide to Managing Risk.* Apress. https://doi.org/10.1007/978-1-4842-5778-4

Tombs, S., & Whyte, D. (2007). Researching Corporate and White-Collar Crime in an Era of Neoliberalism. In G. Geis, & H. N. Pontell (Eds.), *International Handbook of White-Collar and Corporate Crime* (pp. 125–47). Springer. https://doi.org/10.1007/978-0-387-34111-8_6

Tsingou, E. (2018). New Governors on the Block: The Rise of Anti-Money Laundering Professionals. *Crime, Law and Social Change, 69*, 191–205. https://doi.org/10.1007/s10611-017-9751-x

Tuori, K. (2014). Transnational Law: On Legal Hybrids and Perspectivism. In M. Maduro, K. Turoi & S. Sankari (Eds.), *Transnational Law: Rethinking European Law and Legal Thinking* (pp. 11–58). Cambridge University Press. https://doi.org/10.1017/CBO9781139236041.002

Valasik, M., & Torres, J. (2022). Civilizing Space or Criminalizing Place: Using Routine Activities Theory to Better Understand How Legal Hybridity Spatially Regulates "Deviant Populations." *Critical Criminology, 30*, 443–463. https://doi.org/10.1007/s10612-020-09537-x

Valverde, M. (2001). Governing Security, Governing Through Security. In J. Ronald, P. Daniels, P. Macklem, & K. Roach (Eds.), *The Security of Freedom: Essays on Canada's Anti-terrorism Bill*. University of Toronto Press. https://doi.org/10.3138/9781442682337-007

Valverde, M. (2022). *Infrastructure: New Trajectories in Law*. Routledge.

Valverde, M., & Mopas, M. (2004). Insecurity and the Dream of Targeted Governance. In W. Larner & W. Walters (Eds.), *Global Governmentality: Governing International Spaces* (pp. 233–50). Routledge.

Verhage, A. (2011). *The Anti Money Laundering Complex and the Compliance Industry*. Routledge. https://doi.org/10.4324/9780203828489

Wall, D. S. (2013). Enemies Within: Redefining the Insider Threat in Organizational Security Policy. *Security Journal, 26*(2), 107–124. https://doi.org/10.1057/sj.2012.1

Walters, W. (2008). Anti-policy and Anti-politics: Critical Reflections on Certain Schemes to Govern Bad Things. *European Journal of Cultural Studies, 11*(3), 267–288. https://doi.org/10.1177/1367549408091844

Waye, V. (2019). Regtech: New Frontier in Legal Scholarship. *Adelaide Law Review, 40*, 363–386.

Wedel, J. (2014). *Unaccountable: How the Establishment Corrupted Our Finances*. Pegasus Books.

Whyte, D. (2003). Lethal Regulation: State-Corporate Crime and the United Kingdom Government's New Mercenaries. *Journal of Law and Society, 30*(4), 575–600. https://doi.org/10.1111/j.1467-6478.2003.00271.x

Wood, A. J. (2021). Algorithmic Management Consequences for Work Organisation and Working Conditions. In JRC *Working Papers Series on Labour, Education and Technology*, 1–27. European Commission, Joint Research Centre (JRC).

Woodiwiss, M. (2005). *Gangster Capitalism: The United States and the Global Rise of Organized Crime*. Constable.

Yuan, S., & Wu, X. (2021). Deep Learning for Insider Threat Detection: Review, Challenges, and Opportunities. *Computers & Security, 104*, 1–14. https://doi.org/10.1016/j.cose.2021.102221

Zamfir, I. (2023). *Towards an EU Global Sanctions Regime for Corruption.* European Parliament: EPRS European Parliamentary Research Service.

Zegart, A. B. (2016). The Fort Hood Terrorist Attack: An Organizational Postmortem of Army and FBI Deficiencies. In M. Bunn & S. D. Sagan (Eds.), *Insider Threats* (pp. 42–73). Cornell University Press. https://doi.org/10.7591/9781501705946-005

Žižek, S. (1989). *The Sublime Object of Ideology.* Verso.

Zuboff, S. (2019). *The Age of Surveillance Capitalism: The Fight for a Human Future at the New Frontier of Power.* Profile Books.

3

Russian Intelligence-Driven Technopoly: Efficiency, Positivism, Governance by Data in an Authoritarian State

Jardar Østbø (ID)

Introduction: Russian Intelligence Old and New

The full-scale Russian invasion of Ukraine in February 2022 seemed to confirm Western stereotypical views about Russian intelligence. At the time of writing, with the war between Russia and Ukraine having raged for two years and Russia being relatively successful, it is often forgotten that Russia's initial strategy was completely different, envisaging a 'special military operation', or else, a *Blitzkrieg* of sorts to execute regime change, an operation that was supposed to last only days or weeks. The march on Kyiv, however, was a fiasco, and many observers pointed to the apparently highly flawed intelligence on which the decision to invade was

J. Østbø (✉)
Institute for Defence Studies, Norwegian Defence University College, Oslo, Norway
e-mail: jaostbo@mil.no

© The Author(s), under exclusive license to Springer Nature Switzerland AG 2024
T. Ø. Kuldova et al. (eds.), *Policing and Intelligence in the Global Big Data Era, Volume I*, Palgrave's Critical Policing Studies, https://doi.org/10.1007/978-3-031-68326-8_3

based. The blame was put on Russia's allegedly incompetent foreign intelligence as well as Russia's authoritarian personalistic regime structure, which were seen as two sides of the same coin. Hence, the decision to invade has been deemed an *intelligence failure* (Miller & Belton, 2022) typical of authoritarian regimes (Dylan et al., 2022) and the war has been characterised as 'dogged by a cascade of intelligence failures at every level of command' (Davies & Steward, 2022). By contrast, the US and the UK appeared to possess high-quality intelligence about Russian movements and even intentions, and used it, rather successfully, to deprive Russia of the element of surprise.

Therefore, the initial course of events would seem to confirm Western intelligence theoreticians' claim about the difference between Russia's authoritarian intelligence and intelligence in democratic states, with the former inefficient, prejudiced, politicized, and irrational, and the latter efficient, rational, and apolitical in its assessments (Dylan et al., 2022). This corresponds to theoreticians' views of how intelligence in non-democratic states is fundamentally different from intelligence in democracies (Andrew, 2004; Bar-Joseph, 2013; Scott & Jackson, 2004). However, it is important to point out that this pertains to traditional intelligence, defined as 'secret, state activity to understand or influence foreign entities' (Warner, 2002, p. 21), perhaps supplemented with the partially corresponding '"intelligence" is what intelligence agencies do' (Stout & Warner, 2018, p. 517). These definitions were most appropriate during the Cold War.

But in today's postmodern world, such an analytical delimitation of 'intelligence' is less and less relevant. Practices that were formerly associated with state intelligence agencies, tasked with state security in the narrow sense, are spreading to ever-new spheres to the tune of ever-dispersing securitization—in countries normally referred to as liberal democracies as well as in manifestly non-democratic ones. In the period after the Cold War and not least after 11 September 2001, everything has become intelligence and intelligence has become the everyday (Jaffel & Larsson, 2022a). Threats have become fragmented (Rathmell, 2002). Intelligence is everywhere and is by no means limited to geopolitics and state security in the traditional sense. Surveillance, threat assessments, behavioural analysis, and suspicious activity reports are normalized and part of political, economic, and even everyday life rather than reserved for extreme cases. Many of these activities are also privatized or outsourced (Shorrock, 2008). Intelligence-based or intelligence-driven action or policies are presented as ideal, optimized, and apolitical solutions for a complex and increasingly dangerous social reality, regardless of culture and context (Jaffel & Larsson, 2022b). In this securitizing and optimization-focused paradigm, decisions that were previously regarded as political or subject to citizen and social society participation, are regarded as technical issues with one correct solution to be arrived at by data collection and data analysis—essentially intelligence practices, as we knew them from the sphere of state security.

In Russia, the belief in and use of intelligence methods are not delim-ited to the infamous *chekists,* as the KGB/FSB employees and alumni often self-identify (Fedor, 2013; Riehle, 2022; Skak, 2016).[1] Several leading 'technocrats', many of whom were until recently known as 'systemic liberals', practice what we, by way of the heuristics described above, can call 'new intelligence'. In short, they embrace sweeping surveillance to fuel data-driven governance. Thus, Moscow Mayor Sergei Sobianin presides over ever-increasing surveillance of the capital's popula-tion for the purpose of 'optimizing' the policies (Zakharov, 2020). Prime Minister Mikhail Mishustin, another stellar technocrat, while Head of the Federal Tax Service, expanded drastically the economic surveillance of all citizens (Giles, 2019) and has set out to implement his methods in all spheres. German Gref, who is not only the CEO of Sberbank, a flourishing tech giant and simultaneously Russia's biggest bank, but also responsible for the coordination of the implementation of the state's artificial intelligence strategy, sets an example in his own corporation by aggressive data collection and automatized decisionmaking processes, sometimes cooperating with the state, at other times in competition with it (Østbø, 2021). In short, in present-day Russia, the old *chekist* culture and practices meet hybrid surveillance capitalism (Østbø, 2021) and the postmodern, technology-driven diversification, dispersion, and pluralization of intelligence (Jaffel & Larsson, 2022b; Kuldova, 2022).

---

[1] This refers to the first version of the Soviet secret police, the so-called ChK, or Cheka, short for Chrezvychainaia kommissiia (Extraordinary Commision).

Central to this tendency is the widespread conviction that if only one possesses more and 'better' data and cutting-edge technology to analyse and use them, the solutions will appear automatically. These technological solutions are presented as apolitical and optimal, and their use is therefore regarded as a value in itself. In the extreme, this would mean a 'totalitarian technocracy' and 'the submission of all forms of cultural life to the sovereignty of technique and technology', which is how Neil Postman defines *technopoly* (Postman, 2011, pp. 48, 53). In this chapter, I will present how this manifests itself in Russia. I will first show how the emergence of the technopoly was a result of the increasing degree of authoritarianism and dramatically shrinking space for political dissent within the regime as well as outside. Presenting the main shapes that technopoly takes in Russia, I focus on three key figures who arguably are not only leading representatives of intelligence-driven technopoly, but also represent the most important spheres in this respect: The federal level (Mishustin), the capital, a political and economic powerhouse and 'digital sandbox' (Sobianin), and the business/state interface (Gref). Finally, through a critique of intelligence positivism, I will demonstrate how Russian 'new intelligence' is reminiscent of the dominant Western intelligence paradigm in its self-image of the producers of a privileged and absolute truth which therefore is apolitical.

The Rise of Chekists and Technopolists

The Russian intelligence-driven technopoly emerged in the context of the political development and power struggle within the Russian regime and the wider elite, and has thrived as Putin's regime has become increasingly authoritarian and repressive. Russia is often characterized as a 'KGB state' (Belton, 2020; Marten, 2017), a chekist state (Anderson, 2006, 2007), or as 'penetrated' by the KGB or FSB (Walther, 2014). President Vladimir Putin is in fact the first Soviet/Russian ruler to have been a professionally trained intelligence officer with several years in active service. Under his rule, many people who occupy important positions in politics, administration, and business have a KGB past (Bateman, 2014; Kryshtanovskaya, 2005; O. Kryshtanovskaya & White, 2003). In a sense, this is a past only in name, since they tend to continue drawing heavily on connections and resources, not to mention the cultural influence and worldview inculcated in them during their training and formative years in service (Fedor, 2013; Riehle, 2022). KGB and FSB alumni have in common cynicism, conspiratorial mentality, and sense of 'special liberty' vis-à-vis the law (Hall, 2012; Hall & Wilson, 2014). Politically, they are not opposed to the market economy, Western luxury, or European classical culture, but nevertheless, as regards foreign policy, they are highly anti-Western and regard international relations through a Cold War lens. Their increasing influence is well documented and analysed (Bateman, 2016; Belton, 2020; Fel'shtinskii & Pribylovskii, 2010; Knight, 2000; J. M. Waller, 1994; Walther, 2014).

However, in the beginning of Putin's presidential tenure, the composition of his team as well as appointments further down the hierarchy reflected a power balance between former intelligence officials on the one hand and civilian professionals of law, economy, or other sectors on the other (Minchenko Consulting, 2013; Sakwa, 2021; Yakovlev, 2021). The latter were often called 'systemic liberals', as they were within 'the system', but pursued less securitized, more market-oriented, civilian, and Western-oriented policies. For the late Soviet and early post-Soviet Russian context, Gel'man distinguishes between 'democrats' and 'liberals'. The 'democrats' were preoccupied with democratic reform at the expense of economic issues, about which they had only vague ideas. Conversely, the 'liberals' focused on economic reform, regarding democracy as an impediment. They praised the market economy for its efficiency, not for its supposed inherent values. Of the two, it was the liberals who prevailed, as democracy first was moved down on the list of priorities, then sacrificed in exchange for economic modernization, and finally, in the 2010s, dropped altogether (Gel'man, 2020). Though far from an unproblematic term (Matveev, 2024), not least in a country where the nominally Liberal-Democratic Party is manifestly nationalist,[2] 'systemic liberals' has remained in use.

---

[2] The Liberal-Democratic Party of Russia was led by the infamous 'ultranationalist' Vladimir Zhirinovskii from its foundation until his death in 2022.

As time passed, their political influence gradually diminished, with their area of responsibility shrinking drastically (Treisman, 2022; Yakovlev, 2021). Especially after the 2011 Arab Spring that saw many of Putin's fellow autocrats deposed, as well as the mass opposition demonstrations in Russian cities in 2011–12 following the fraudulent parliamentary elections, not to mention the Euromaidan uprising in Ukraine in 2013–14 (leading to the ouster of Russia-leaning president Viktor Yanukovych), the influence of the *chekists* and other security sector officials and hardliners increased substantially (Yakovlev, 2021). From the regime's perspective, the iron fist had to discard the velvet glove. The full-scale invasion of Ukraine and not least its duration has led to the introduction of draconian or even totalitarian measures against any kind of pronounced opposition, still selectively enforced but dramatic for those involved and a strong deterrent for everybody else. The exceedingly brutal treatment of opposition leader Aleksei Naval'nyi (ending with his death in prison in February 2024) and his associates is a case in point. To the extent that the Soviet Union and Putin-era Russia can be compared, some analysts have calculated that more people have been persecuted for political activities under Putin's fourth presidential period (2018–2024) than under Khrushchev or Brezhnev (Reznikova & Korostelev, 2024). Hence, there is, highly likely even behind the closed doors in the Kremlin, practically no room for meaningful political discussion regarding anything even peripherally related to the war, which encompasses ever-more spheres, from economic matters via healthcare, and down to primary education, popular culture, and even the dress code on closed social events.[3]

Whereas the early President Putin was known to listen to opposing views coming from within the system, by 2021, he was relying on a narrow circle, largely of current and former intelligence officers (Galeotti, 2022). Just before the full-scale invasion, with even military commanders largely in the dark about the imminent plans, some top 'systemic liberals' had tried to dissuade Putin from 'escalating' but were instead asked what could be done to alleviate the predicted adverse effects. They

---

[3] For instance, in late 2023, a closed celebrity lingerie party in Moscow was shamed in the media, politicized, and resulted in public excuses from several participants, as well as a prison sentence for one rapper who subsequently was summoned to the army.

reportedly were stupefied by this response and experienced an even more devastating shock when the war started. But after the initial trauma, they seem to have recuperated, as they introduced several daring measures that economic experts have assessed as saving the economy from collapse that could otherwise have happened due to both Western sanctions and the consequences of the war itself (Matveev, 2024; Seddon & Ivanova, 2022). They have become 'apt managers of the war economy' (Matveev, 2024, p. 8). This was, in a sense, the final nail in the coffin of the 'systemic liberals' category, who now appear more than anything as simply *technocrats* who 'do as they are told' (Treisman, 2022). According to Matveev, they have abandoned 'any pretense of a grand ideological vision and focusing on the most efficient ways of reacting to the necessities of the moment' (Matveev, 2024, p. 8). However, this is imprecise, as *technopoly* in itself can be said to have become an ideology of its own. While disagreements certainly remain, such as the year-long dispute concerning the allotment of frequencies for the 5G network (Kluge, 2021) technopoly does not conflict with the *chekists'* ideological convictions.

The 'technocratization' pertains to old acquaintances of Putin's, such as Gref, as well as professionals who have made their reputation and career as 'efficient managers', such as Sobianin or Mishustin. These are undoubtedly to be regarded as part of the so-called *sistema* or system, consisting of patrimonial networks bound together and constrained by informal practices from which they also profit immensely (Ledeneva, 2006, 2013). If need be, some of them, despite their images as conscientious bureaucrats, may even resort to extra-legal measures.[4] At the same time, they do not share the hardliner views against the West typical of former and current intelligence officers. Instead, they have, at least traditionally, cultivated a vision of Russia becoming a well-governed, prosperous 'normal country', with the rule of law and good relations to its neighbours as well as the West. Hence, they have been reluctant to jump on the patriotic bandwagon and endorse the war effort, doing so only under pressure. Nevertheless, their work has been absolutely

---

[4] A recording has been presented in an American court, allegedly proving that Gref, at a meeting in the government building in 2012, was threatening to kill a businessman and politician if he would not agree to a certain deal (Soldatskikh et al., 2023).

crucial to keeping Russia's wheels running during the war (Matveev, 2024; Seddon & Ivanova, 2022). In private conversations, high officials of the Central Bank, for instance, have argued that in so doing, they have prevented an economic catastrophe, even comparing themselves to Hjalmar Schacht, Hitler's onetime economy minister and central banker (1933–1939), who was acquitted of all charges in Nuremberg after the war (Reiter & Liutova, 2022).

Mishustin—Running the Country as the Tax Service

In a surprise move in early 2020 evidently designed to consolidate his own power, Putin proposed sweeping changes to the Constitution, among other things allowing himself to run for two more six-year terms from 2024. Prime Minister Dmitrii Medvedev's government resigned, and Putin appointed Mikhail Mishustin to preside over an 'overwhelmingly technocratic' government (Sakwa, 2021, p. 231). The new head of government came directly from the post of the Director of the Federal Taxation Service, where he had made his name as a highly efficient manager, conducting an ambitious digitalization programme after having waged a war on 'dirty data'.[5] Under his leadership, Russia became one of the world's leaders in VAT collection, with only an estimated 1 per cent of its VAT going uncollected (Sullivan, 2020). This was largely thanks to a massive data collection programme recording *all* legal monetary transactions nationwide through retail establishments' mandatory online cash registers. Hence, Mishustin could proudly present a reporter with the coffee servings that had been purchased in the latter's hotel on the evening before, boasting that the tax service could 'see everything bought everywhere' (Giles, 2019). Knowing this, the political observer Andrei Kolesnikov stated: 'Now, with [Mishustin's] help, Putin is going to build

---

[5] 'FNS ob"iavila god bor'by s "griaznymi" dannymi, zaiavil glava Sluzhby [FNS declared the year of war on "dirty" data, the head of the service declared], https://ria.ru/20110221/336872 455.html.

a country that resembles the Federal Tax Service: with reports and inspections, security assets, and—where necessary—the digitalization of the entire country' (Andrei Kolesnikov, 2020a, 2020b, p. 6).

Unsurprisingly then, since his inauguration, Mishustin has been an ardent proponent of governance by data and the platformization of state governance. Although digitalization of the state administration had long ago been set as a goal by the president and was on the way under previous governments, Mishustin made it a top priority and put a personal imprint on it. In a meeting with officials responsible for the digitalization process, he emphasized the sense of urgency by calling them the 'digital *spetsnaz*' (as a reference to Russia's famed military special forces), lauding them as 'special people with special skills and special experience'.[6] He declared that they were basically tasked with 'reengineering all working processes within the ministries and agencies', and he asked for concrete results in the shortest possible time. The new Prime Minister also claimed that data are 'the oil, the gold, the platinum of the twenty-first century. The only difference is that the former are finite, and the latter infinite'.[7] He added that the more data, the more their value increases, and they further increase in value as they are structured and processed (ibid.).

Mishustin followed up in deed. Among other things, in May 2021, he ordered the creation, by the end of the year, of a Unified Informational Platform of the National System for Data Management. Behind the rather baroque title was the drive to integrate data from several state registers. Its raison d'être and main official task was to 'improve the quality and accessibility of state and municipal services for the citizens'.[8] Hence, it was to systematize state data and automatize processes of data management.[9] Later that year, Mishustin approved a strategic document

---

6 'Mishustin rasskazal, chem zaimetsia "tsifrovoi spetsnaz" pravitel'stva' [Mishustin told what the government's "digital spetsnaz" would do], https://mir24.tv/news/16401446/mishustin-rasskazal-chem-zaimetsya-cifrovoi-specnaz-pravitelstva.

7 'Mishustin rasskazal o "novoi nefti" XXI veka [Mishustin talked about the "new oil" of the twenty-first century] https://ria.ru/20200312/1568492492.html.

8 'Pravitel'stvo utverdilo polozhenie o Edinoi informatsionnoi platforme upravleniia dannymi' [The government confirmed the provision on the Unified Information Platform for Data Administration], http://government.ru/news/41888/.

9 'Korotko o EIP NSUD' [the Unified Information Platform of the National System for Data Administration in brief], https://info.gosuslugi.ru/articles/Коротко_о_ЕИП_НСУД/.

outlining the main directions of the digitalization of the state administration for the next decade.[10] The document stated that AI, big data, and the Internet of Things should be integrated in the processes. The most important aims were to generate social and economic development, by increasing individuals' purchasing power, improving the investment climate, and enhancing national security and personal safety of individuals. The text is permeated by the vision of technological or even automatized governance by data. For instance, the main problems of the present state administration are identified to be the lack of real-time, reliable data upon which decisions could be made, as well as the lack of oversight and control functions, including 'the means of objective control by the management of the employees' performance of their tasks and their goal achievement'.[11] The digitalization and technical optimalization of state administration would, as per the document, help to gradually change the model for control and oversight to 'use new technological means of objective surveillance and implementation of a model of remote control and oversight according to previously established criteria together with analysis in real time of the current situation in all spheres that are subject to state and municipal control'.[12] To do this, the strategy envisions, among other things, the creation of a 'unified automatized system for collection, processing, and analysis of data from the economic and social spheres', as well as 'a unified platform for the fulfillment of state and municipal control', 'a unified system for the control of the realization and achievement of strategic state tasks and goals', and 'a unified system for automatized budget and accounting processes'.[13]

The next step was to clear the path for a transition to a 'data economy'. This took the form of a national project which was to be the successor of the national project on digitalization, which Mishustin had inherited from the preceding government. The assignment was made public

[10] 'Rasporiazhenie ot 22 oktiabria 2021 No. 2998-r' [Order from 22 October 2021 No. 2998-r], http://static.government.ru/media/files/d3uclO4ZFGNKmxCPBXbL4OaMPALluGdQ.pdf.

[11] 'Rasporiazhenie ot 22 oktiabria 2021 No. 2998-r' [Order from 22 October 2021 No. 2998-r], http://static.government.ru/media/files/d3uclO4ZFGNKmxCPBXbL4OaMPALluGdQ.pdf.

[12] 'Rasporiazhenie ot 22 oktiabria 2021 No. 2998-r' [Order from 22 October 2021 No. 2998-r], http://static.government.ru/media/files/d3uclO4ZFGNKmxCPBXbL4OaMPALluGdQ.pdf.

[13] 'Rasporiazhenie ot 22 oktiabria 2021 No. 2998-r' [Order from 22 October 2021 No. 2998-r], http://static.government.ru/media/files/d3uclO4ZFGNKmxCPBXbL4OaMPALluGdQ.pdf.

in July 2023 and formalized in a presidential order in September that year, where the government was given until July the next year for the completion of the plan for the period until 2030.[14] The project was set to apply to many areas, including education, healthcare, security, industry, housing and municipal services, transport, and communications (Kiniakina & Ustinova, 2023). Its official goals were in tune with Mishustin's previously expressed visions that are 'to bring the entire economy, the social sphere, and the authorities to qualitatively new working principles, to implement governance by data [...]'. To achieve this, the project is to focus on the collection of data, where '[t]he main task is to develop the use of highly sensitive sensors, including quantum sensors'.[15]

Mishustin stated that

> [...] Russia should be one of the first countries to develop the needed services for our citizens and businesspeople by conducting a transition to a data economy. That is when decisions, including economic ones, are not based on expert opinions, prognoses, and assessments, but on reliable data.[16]

Earlier that year, Mishustin declared that he had offered Putin a new model for state governance, envisioning a transition from expert decisionmaking to decisionmaking based on 'reliable data'. Such a model, he stated, was necessary in order to ensure an efficient improvement in the quality of life for every individual in the country. The information should come directly from the source, bypassing all intermediaries, and plans and prognoses should be changed on the go. This is the essence of platformized governance, according to Mishustin. 'Earlier, every expert said that his calculations were the most correct ones. But now, there is the possibility to use reliable information. This is the essense of the platform model. It multiplies the quality of expertise and thus the accuracy of the

---

[14] 'Perechen' poruchenii po itogam vstrechi s uchenymi i plenarnogo zasedaniia Foruma budushchikh tekhnologii' [List of orders after the meeting with academics and plenary meeting at the Forum for Future Technologies], http://kremlin.ru/acts/assignments/orders/72190.

[15] 'V Rossii poiavitsia novyi proekt—"Ekonomika dannykh" [A new project is upcoming in Russia – Economy of data], https://digital.gov.ru/ru/events/45686/.

[16] 'Lektsiia Mishustina' [Mishustin's lecture], http://government.ru/news/50333/.

decisions made' (cit. in Dubrovina & Makutina, 2023). Characteristically, Mishustin refers to decisions as 'accurate' and arising directly from the analysis of the data, which is seen as self-evidently good. In this sense, his technocratic language is self-referential.

Sergei Sobianin and Moscow as an Experimental Ground

In Russia, where politics and economy are highly centralized, the position of the Mayor of Moscow is of federal significance. Sergei Sobianin was installed in the post in 2010, when the then-President Dmitrii Medvedev unseated Yurii Luzhkov, who had been governing the capital for eighteen years. Pro-market Sobianin is often considered a systemic liberal or at least semi-liberal (Hahn, 2018). Governing a city that has developed a large, well-educated, and well-travelled middle class, he was, at least initially, preoccupied with pleasing the liberal electorate. Hence, he resigned voluntarily in 2013 in order to conduct early elections, and Aleksei Naval'nyi was allowed to run against him, as a move to boost Sobianin's democratic legitimacy (J. G. Waller, 2013). Whereas Luzhkov had presided over a breakneck construction boom, Sobianin's focus was on making Moscow a 'comfortable' city (Lähteenmäki & Murawski, 2023), tautologically understood as reaching the 'maximally possible high level of comfort' (Trubina, 2020, p. 5). This 'comfortable city' project was reinforced with the change in the political climate following the large-scale opposition demonstrations after the fraudulent State Duma elections in late 2011, as the protest wave had been particularly strong in the capital. The 'tightening of the screws', meaning increased political repression, an ideological turn towards 'traditional values', and an increasingly anti-Western stance from the centre (Østbø, 2017; Sharafutdinova, 2014), went counter to the preferences of the liberal middle class to whom Sobianin catered. In this context, comfort, convenience, and 'livability' became a way of appeasing Muscovites and making them sacrifice public participation in governance (Argenbright et al., 2020).

This combination of ambition for 'liveability' and minimal space for political participation fits the data-driven intelligence technopoly hand-in-glove. Sobianin's expressed vision for Moscow is a city that is in a digital 'permanent dialogue' with its inhabitants, and the most important thing is that the city should be 'comfortable [and] interesting for everyone'.[17] However, in practice, the dialogue consists of the citizens feeding the authorities with data, whether they want it or not. Increasingly, in pace with technological progress and the gradually chilling political climate, Moscow has become entwined in an accelerating spiral of surveillance and authoritarianism that makes up data-driven governance. Immediately after his inauguration, Sobianin ordered his subordinates to give him 'the city in an online mode' and since then, one of his most-posed questions to his advisers is 'what do the data say?' (Zakharov, 2020). He has also stated that it is practically impossible to govern the city without big data:

> This goes for the governance of transport, healthcare including the implementation of artificial intelligence. It is city construction, analysis of the criminogenic situation, and the development of preventive measures, and measures for fighting crime, and a whole range of other solutions without which it is impossible to govern [...] a modern city efficiently.[18]

The data are harvested from an increasing array of sources. Since 2015, Moscow city and Moscow region authorities have been buying geolocation of all individuals from mobile operators, allegedly in anonymized form, and used analysis thereof, for instance, for mundane tasks such as the planning of new transport. To a large extent, these data are replacing both official statistics and, arguably, politics. After having started to use such data, Sobianin became convinced that there were 25 million inhabitants in Moscow instead of the official statistics' 12.6 million. Dividing the city and region into squares of 500 meters times 500 meters, the

---

[17] 'Sobianin rasskazal o proekte "Umnyj gorod" [Sobianin talked about the "Smart City" project], https://www.tvc.ru/news/show/id/219523.

[18] 'Sergei Sobianin: Bez bol'shikh dannykh upravliat' gorodom prakticheski nevozmozhno' [Sergei Sobianin: Without big data it is practically impossible to govern the city], https://gorodskoyportal.ru/moskva/news/official/51017164/.

analytical system operates with its own definitions of demographic categories such as 'home', 'workplace', 'commuter', and so on. In short, the city and region authorities can monitor all citizens' movements. During the pandemic, for instance, the Moscow authorities, referring to the exceptional situation, had neither any moral qualms nor, apparently, any significant technological problems with using these data to target individuals breaking the quarantine regulations (Zakharov, 2020). Sobianin quickly declared that surveillance and facial recognition software were being used against violators of the quarantine.[19] This was felt by, among others, a Muscovite who after a week in isolation at home went out from his building to walk 'five seconds' to the trashcan and was charged with violating the quarantine regulations after having been caught on a surveillance camera (Borodikhin, 2020).

This 'function' creep is typical. Although it is not known to the public in what form the authorities receive the geolocation data, it is likely that they can also be used for political purposes, as has happened with the surveillance of city transport. In October 2020, Moscow city authorities published a tender for modernizing 59 traffic surveillance cars, so that they would be able to detect 63 different kinds of violations, many of which could be classified as minor, including incorrect parking.[20] In 2023, traffic surveillance cameras were even enabled to fine drivers if their passengers did not use the seat belt (Smirnova, 2023). In late October 2020, Moscow city authorities signed a contract with a provider of surveillance cameras with facial recognition for all of the city's more than 500 electric buses as well as in all new trams (Tishina, 2020). At that point, the entire system of video surveillance in the city was using facial recognition software (Zakharov, 2020). In September 2020, a system for biometric recognition in the Moscow metro was launched,

---

[19] 'Sobianin zaiavil o primenenii sistemy raspoznavania lits iz-za koronavirusa' [Sobianin declared that the facial recognition system would be used due to the corona virus], https://www.rbc.ru/society/21/02/2020/5e4f72139a7947aba40d935e.

[20] 'Moskovskaia meriia nauchit fiksiruiushchie narushcheniia PDD mashiny iskat' eshche i narushitelei karantina' [Moscow City Hall will teach the machines that record traffic rules violations to look for those who violate the quarantine, as well], https://openmedia.io/news/n2/moskovskaya-meriya-nauchit-fiksiruyushhie-narusheniya-pdd-mashiny-iskat-eshhyo-i-narushitelej-karantina/.

and by late 2022, it had helped arresting approximately 5000 people,[21] by early February 2023 more than 7700 people.[22] While many of these were undoubtedly 'ordinary criminals', the police have also arrested hundreds of participants in political protests after the end of the events.[23] Some have even been arrested preventively, for instance in connection with public holidays.[24] In November 2020, Moscow city authorities confirmed that they were about to buy 50 mobile biometric kits with facial recognition for use during mass events. This was explained as a necessary measure to 'increase the efficiency of city services in the case of extraordinary situations during mass events',[25] but the possibilities for using it for political surveillance were obvious.

Muscovites' behaviour online is also subject to increasing surveillance. In 2020, it was revealed that Moscow city authorities had, through its seed funds, invested in the local software company Who Is Blogger (WIB) (a subsidiary of Double Data), which collects data from social networks. Officially a marketing tool, its political potential is obvious (Aleksandr Kolesnikov, 2020a, 2020b). By then, Moscow had intelligence systems in place for detecting various risks via social media, centrally as well as in the particular neighbourhoods. For instance, one system monitors mass media and social media for mentions of Sobianin and the members of the city government, as a way to detect 'media risks' and popular discontent. Another 'information-analytical system' (IAS) is more wide-ranging, having access to the common database of the city hall and the police, which contain archival information about millions

---

[21] 'Okolo 5 tys. chelovek zaderzhali' [Approximately 5 thousand people have been detained], https://www.interfax.ru/moscow/878994.

[22] 'V Moskve blagodaria kameram zaderzhali bolee 7,7 tysiach prestupnikov' [In Moscow, 7700 criminals have been arrested thanks to the cameras], https://ria.ru/20230207/prestupniki-185 0288829.html.

[23] 'Kak ispol'zuiut kamery i raspoznavanie lits protiv protestuiushchikh' [How cameras and facial recognition are used against protesters], https://reports.ovd.info/kak-vlasti-ispolzuyut-kam ery-i-raspoznavanie-lic-protiv-protestuyushchih#1.

[24] 'Kak ispol'zuiut kamery i raspoznavanie lits protiv protestuiushchikh' [How cameras and facial recognition are used against protesters], https://reports.ovd.info/kak-vlasti-ispolzuyut-kam ery-i-raspoznavanie-lic-protiv-protestuyushchih#1.

[25] 'Vlasti Moskvy nachnut primeniat 'ustroistva raspoznavaniia lits na massovykh meropriiati-iakh' [Moscow authorities will start using devices for facial recognition on mass events], https://mbk-news.appspot.com/news/bbiswatchingyou/.

of criminal acts. In order to detect 'divergent patterns', the system analyses media coverage, social networks, and even individuals' search history in order to monitor popular opinion about the crime level in the city. Analogically to its American counterpart Palantir, it is tasked with 'identification, monitoring, warning, planning action and making decisions connected with state politics as it relates to local governance' (Zakharov, 2020). This betrays clear parallels with traditional domestic intelligence, whose overarching objective is to detect disturbance.

Under Sobianin's leadership, it has been a priority to make Moscow a 'smart city', reportedly with Singapore as a role model (Zakharov, 2020). An official strategy to this effect was presented in 2018.[26] On 1 July 2020, a new law came into force making Moscow a test site (digital sandbox), enabling the city authorities to decide how AI technology should be put to use in the city.[27] Among the provisions, there are formulations on the use of 'personal data obtained through depersonalization'—with no regard to the possibility of reversing the process (Zelendinova, 2020). The next year, Sobianin proudly presented that Moscow had been awarded two ISO certificates for 'smart cities', one of which—ISO 37122—it was only the tenth city in the world to gain.[28] Further, under his leadership, Moscow topped the 'smartness rating' (literally: IQ of cities) of Russian cities for five years in a row,[29] and the city has won several national and international awards for its digitalization projects.[30]

---

[26] 'Strategiia "Umnyi gorod—2030"' [The "Smart City 2030" strategy], https://storage.strate gy24.ru/files/strategy/201903/724ca9541151bd969b96ed594f37a103.pdf.

[27] 'Federal'nyi zakon ot 24 aprelia 2020 No. 123-F3' [Federal law of 24 April 2020 No. 123-F3], https://rg.ru/2020/04/28/tehnologii-dok.html.

[28] 'Sobianin: Moskva priznana "umnym" gorodom po mezhdunarodnomu standardu ISO' [Moscow is recognized as "smart city" according to the international ISO standard], https://www.mn.ru/smart/sobyanin-moskva-priznana-umnym-gorodom-po-mezhdunarodnomu-standa rtu-iso-chto-eto-znachit.

[29] 'Moskva v piatyi raz stala liderom v indekse tsifrovizatsii "IQ gorodov"' [Moscow for the fifth time became the leader in the digitalization index "IQ of cities"], https://iz.ru/1550478/ 2023-07-27/moskva-v-piatyi-raz-stala-liderom-v-indekse-tcifrovizatcii-iq-gorodov.

[30] 'Tsifrovye proekty Moskvy otmecheny premiei umnyi gorod' [Moscow's digital projects have received a smart city award], https://www.vedomosti.ru/gorod/smartcity/articles/tsifrovie-proekti-moskvi-otmecheni-premiei-umnii-gorod.

The smart city strategy was presented as a way to secure sustainable growth in Muscovites' quality of life through the use of digital technologies. This is to be achieved through '[c]entralized, end-to-end, transparent governance of the city based on big data and the use of artificial intelligence' (Chukarin, 2018). One part of an official presentation of the strategy is particularly telling: A slide headlined 'digital government: a city governed with the help of data and artificial intelligence' consists of a stylized image. At the bottom, there are three sources of data, all feeding into artificial intelligence solutions. First, there is the 'city/street', consisting of lighting, unmanned transport, renovation, and so on'. Then there is the 'house/apartment' segment, stemming from sensors in the buildings, such as electrometers, surveillance cameras, and acoustic sensors measuring noise levels. Finally, there are the inhabitants, who will feed the AI with data from their portable devices, including but not limited to their geolocation, use of services, and their consumption of content. The AI will collect data from all these sources, structure the data, securing 'uncontradictory decisions on governance' for both the city government and businesses.[31]

The Russian State as a Tech Company—German Gref

German Gref has been one of the few idea-driven 'systemic liberals' to know Putin from his St. Petersburg days, to remain on good personal terms with him and to occupy important positions since then. The two met in 1990, and when Putin was on the losing side in 1996 after his boss, St. Petersburg Mayor Anatolii Sobchak, lost the election, Gref was one of the few to continue backing the unemployed bureaucrat (Sobesednik, 2005). Moreover, Gref became the key architect of the post-Yeltsin economic reforms. From his position as board chairman of the Center for Strategic Research, he led the work on a liberal reform plan that aimed to integrate Russia into the global economy. Although the

---

[31] 'Strategiia "Umnyi gorod—2030"' [The "Smart City 2030" strategy], https://storage.strategy24.ru/files/strategy/201903/724ca9541151bd969b96ed594f37a103.pdf.

aims were by far not reached and the plan not even formally adopted, it served as a guide in the beginning of Putin's tenure (Dmitriev & Yurtaev, 2010). From 2000, Gref served as Minister of Economic Development, before being appointed as the CEO of Sberbank, the state's savings bank, in 2007. Apparently a demotion, the transfer to Sberbank would provide him a 'playground' where he would develop and implement his strategic visions and ideals in a much more radical and consequent way than in the government (Østbø, 2021; Vandenko, 2019). More to the point, he has stated openly that he regards Sberbank as a model for Russia's future (Østbø, 2021; Seddon, 2018). As CEO, he has presided over a continuous cascade of reforms, as the old-fashioned and inefficient savings bank where most Russian citizens had their deposits has become an ambitious tech company with an expanding ecology offering a wide array of platform-based services, from traditional banking to fintech, foodtech, city transport, healthcare, online shopping, entertainment, primary education, cloud services, insurance, home entertainment, digital assistants, and GigaChat, the aspiring Russian alternative to ChatGPT, and more, all the while remaining the bank of choice for most Russians and majority owned by the state. From this position, and thanks also to his personal relationship with Putin, Gref led the work on the Russian state's AI strategy ('Natsional'naia strategiia razvitiia iskusstvennogo intellekta na period do 2030 goda', 2019), and Sber (as the umbrella structure is now called, with 'Sberbank' reserved for more traditional banking operations) was given the main responsibility for coordinating its implementation (Markotkin & Chernenko, 2020).

Sber's impressive and growing list of platforms and services testifies to its immense data collection capabilities. Through the acquisition of tech companies and startups, Sber, though a late starter in the surveillance capitalism race, has reached into more and more spheres of the human experience: How people move around, what they eat, what they buy, and what kind of culture and entertainment they consume, what services they use. Although it does not dominate in any of these spheres except banking, it has the potential and doubtlessly the ambition to grow, its status as a bank being a major advantage in the competition with other Russian tech companies. At the end of 2023, Sberbank had 108.5 million active retail clients as well as 3.2 million corporate clients. After the critical year of 2022, business had gone well, with a growth in the number of clients as well as an all-time record net profit of 1.493 billion rubles.[32] The financial data of clients, that is, information about how they actually spend their money, is of course a source of highly valuable data, whose collection Sberbank has pushed forward to speed up. For instance, the company established its own QR payment system, giving access to many kinds of transactions that were previously cash-only. As regards the collection of biometric data, Sberbank has been way ahead of its rivals, not to mention the state. In 2023, when a new law finally required banks to turn the biometric data of individuals over to the state's database, Sberbank had the largest repository of all private businesses, consisting of the facial images of 30 million people (Batyrov, 2023). Since 2017, Sber has its own health platform, Sberzdorov'e, and health-care is a declared priority (Skobelev & Balashova, 2020). This direction got a booster from the Covid-19 pandemic and went hand in hand with the company's smart city initiative. At the time of writing, Sber was even constructing its own ideal, 461 hectares 'smart city' in a Moscow neighbourhood, with residences for approximately 65.000 people and workplaces for 70.000.[33]

Sber has made sure that not even the data of the youngest Russians go to 'waste'. In line with Gref's personal interest in primary education, Sber has invested in an online teaching platform that under the pretext of optimization and personalization of education collects schoolchildren's behavioural and biometric data (Østbø, 2021). Sber has also developed a high-tech monitoring device to be installed in people's homes: Launched in 2020, the SberPortal is a smart display and loudspeaker with integrated virtual assistants and voice, gesture, and facial recognition. It is connected to Sber's other services, so that the owner can use it to make calls, make appointments with a hairdresser or doctor, order food, connect to the state services (*gosuslugi*) or simply as a conversation partner (Sberbank, 2021). Sold under the banner of comfort and

---

[32] SberBank selected RAS results for 12M 2023, https://www.sberbank.com/investor-relations/groupresults/2023.

[33] 'Startoval vtoroi etap prodazh kvartir v SberSiti v Rublevo-Arkhangel'skom' [The second leg of sales of apartments in SberCity in Rublevo-Arkhangel'skoe has started], https://www.kommersant.ru/doc/6531802?erid=4CQwVszH9pWvpC2eE2j&query=сбер.

seamlessness, this device, of course, allows for extensive surveillance of the users (Østbø, 2021). Tellingly, it was developed in cooperation with Speech Technology Center, a company of which Sber owns the majority (Posypkina & Balenko, 2019), and which is the direct descendant of a Soviet acoustic research unit that was run by the KGB as part of the prison system (Soldatov, 2013).

Gref has been preoccupied with organization and governance since his youth, regarding the management model as the key to everything (Vandenko, 2019). Revealingly, in his student days, Gref got fired from his part-time job as a street-sweeper in Omsk, ostensibly for presenting a proposal for the complete reorganization of the street renovation service.[34] According to Gref, Russia's main problem is that it lacks an effective system for state governance (Gereikhanova, 2019). The solution he offers is clear: Governance by data. Back in 2018, Gref declared that it was critically important to implement the concept of 'radical truth' in Sberbank's work, meaning that people should not be afraid to share bad news. He had borrowed that concept from hedge fund manager Ray Dalio, whom he considers his friend (Vandenko, 2020). Gref visited the headquarters of Dalio's fund Bridgewater in 2015, where the CEO showed him the fund's rating system for employees and explained to him the famed 'Principles', a strict set of rules according to which Bridgewater operates (Copeland, 2023, p. 193).

Intrigued, Gref went on to have Dalio's book *Principles* (Dalio, 2017) translated into Russian and published with the support of Sberbank. Gref's panegyrical foreword is worth quoting at length[35]:

> [Ray Dalio] believes that in a sense, we are all machines, and machines work according to laws and principles. Every action is an algorithm. Ray tried to algorithmicize his thinking in order to eliminate risk to the greatest extent possible when making short-term decisions, as well as reaching the main goal—to secure the viability and resilience of the organization when the founding leader decides to withdraw. This is the highest class in leadership and every leader's dream […] [Ray] knows that

---

[34] 'Ot sessii do sessii' [From class to class], https://www.kommersant.ru/gallery/2899960?query=греф&sids=2500087.

[35] See also Østbø (2021).

the rational part of man's brain is small, whereas the emotional, primordial part often prevents the optimal decisions to be taken. Bridgewater is working on a program which makes it possible to completely automatize the running management of the company, including the processes of hiring and firing employees, but also the making of strategically important decisions. (Gref, 2018)

Hence, Gref's AI optimism exceeds even that of Mishustin and Sobianin, who has expressed certain reservations against AI in strategic decisionmaking. In a panel entitled 'State Governance: Between People and Data' at the 2023 St. Petersburg Economic Forum, Sobianin reassured the audience that public governance in Moscow was not entirely automatized and warned against leaving all decisionmaking to AI, as one would risk, at the extreme, that it would, for instance, abolish pensions. Gref responded by distinguishing between emotional and rational decisionmaking, but although he allowed for a space where human decisionmaking is relevant, he emphasized that it all depends on how one will use the AI. If one would ask it simply to minimize budget expenditure, then such things could happen. However, Gref went on to claim that 'if one will task it with doing the most just allocation of the budget, then nobody does that better than AI because [...] there will be honest and even allocation of the budget, so there, human influence, human preferences will not be decent, that's for sure'.[36] AI would, according to Gref, reduce bribery, since it 'doesn't understand where to take bribes from and why, it doesn't know why it should be put under the table'.[37] More to the point, according to Gref, in Sber, a human in the loop is 'automatically regarded as a weak spot, as far as decisionmaking goes. There is a sphere where humans have to remain—well, for the time being, the development of technology is on that level [...] almost all

[36] 'PMEF 2023: Gosupravlenie: mezhdu liud'mi i dannymi. Gref German' [SPIEF 2023: State Governance: between people and data. German Gref] (a), https://www.youtube.com/watch?v=9B2eydNDCxI (06:00).

[37] 'PMEF 2023: Gosupravlenie: mezhdu liud'mi i dannymi. Gref German' [SPIEF 2023: State Governance: between people and data. German Gref](b), https://www.youtube.com/watch?v=DSNNyZHmm1w.

functions can be done by artificial intelligence [...]'.[38] Perhaps the most telling manifestation of Gref's belief in the possibilities of AI came at a meeting in 2023, when Putin asked him, jokingly, if AI would replace Gref as CEO of Sber. Gref responded: 'Vladimir Vladimirovich, I hope it won't happen in my lifetime, but that's the way everything is headed' (Kotova, 2023).

Surveillance, Data, Truth, and Self-Evident Solutions

As we have seen, all three actors who have been discussed in this chapter are proponents of ever-increasing data collection, or surveillance, which would be a less euphemistic term. It is telling that in Moscow's 'smart city strategy', the citizens are put on par with streetlights, watermeters, and 'smart' trash cans, in the sense that their most important purpose is to produce data. Basically, citizens are to trade their personal data for increased 'comfort', 'livability', and safety. It is even a stretch to call them citizens in the traditional sense, as the above-mentioned image vividly illustrates how they most of all are to be considered as *sensors* (among other sensors). Gref's Sberbank has long been setting the example of surveillance in a wide spectrum of areas, while Mishustin prepares the ground for massive surveillance through his strategy to digitalize and create integrated databases. The promised efficiency, optimization, and improved quality of services require 'the ability to identify individuals via the analysis of unique biometric signatures; track their movement through the space of the city; monitor and assess their utterances and other behavior; and predict likely courses of action, including future patterns of movement and association, based on that assessment' (Greenfield, 2013, chapter 11). In this way, 'smart' surveillance provides the authoritarian regime with new possibilities for repression although the initial motivation for installing it might have been different.

---

[38] 'Gref: chelovek v sisteme – slaboe mesto, ego nuzhno ubrat' [Gref: the human in the system is a weak spot, it must be removed], https://youtu.be/V1ZJ_vhZ8zI (00:30).

In addition to an insatiable thirst for data, Russian 'new intelligence' shares Western intelligence's traditional positivism and claims to possess the truth. In its formative period during the early Cold War, the organization and self-image of modern Western intelligence reflected the positivist hegemony in the social sciences. For Sherman Kent, widely considered a founding father of American intelligence, the natural sciences were the highest ideal of intelligence. Kent was firmly convinced that 'for any situation, for every occurrence, there exists a single truth' (Olcott, 2009). Apparently, the only substantial difference Kent acknowledged between the social sciences and the natural sciences was the difficulty of conducting 'controlled and repetitive experiments', and he went on to say that despite this, 'social scientists go on striving for improvements in their method which will afford the exactness of physics and chemistry' (Kent, 1965 [1949], p. 156). With this ideal, also known as 'physics envy', Kent pioneered the 'vocabulary of false precision' in the intelligence profession (Jones & Silberzahn, 2013, pp. 40, 59). This, in turn, betrays an either naïve or idealistic view of intelligence as privileged and objective knowledge that would be foolish or even insane not to follow: in a particularly positivist rhetorical onslaught in the mentioned book, Kent implicitly compares disregarding the scientific 'truth' of intelligence analysis to following the advice of witch doctors or resorting to a Hitler-like 'communion with [one's] intuitive self' (Kent, 1965 [1949], pp. 155–156). This idea of analytic objectivity is derived from an idealized version of science (Marrin, 2020).

Speaking truth onto power is central to the identity of, for instance, British intelligence officers, and 'has been the cornerstone of both the structure and the culture of British intelligence', which traditionally has regarded itself as independent and apolitical, providing 'policy-free' and objective analysis in the best interest of the nation (Scott & Jackson, 2004, p. 150). Arguably, this could be said of most if not all liberal democracies' intelligence services. Indeed, objectivity can be said to represent 'a heroic, idealized myth regarding the role of the intelligence analyst in the policy process' (Marrin, 2020, p. 7). *Politicization* of intelligence can be defined in different ways and take many forms, but the very concept of politicization implies that there is such a thing as pure or nearly pure intelligence, free from politics. But despite all talk of a 'red line' between policymaking and intelligence (Steiner, 2004), intelligence is, at least on one level, inherently political. To appropriate the famous words of Robert Cox on theory (Cox, 1981): Intelligence is always *by* someone *for* some purpose. In Western 'old intelligence', this is acknowledged, as even Kent's textbook (Kent, 1965 [1949]) was entitled 'Strategic Intelligence *for American World Policy*' (my emphasis). Russian 'new intelligence', as it emerges from the visions and practices of Mishustin, Sobianin, and Gref, does not use such caveats, but is explicitly presented as unquestionably true and inalienably good. In this sense, it is its own justification.

In addition, 'new intelligence' claims not only to be the owner of the truth. It also insists on *its* solutions, which 'old' Western intelligence does at times (or lends itself to), but which is much criticized and seen as unforgiveable mistakes, viz. aberrations from the ideal of separation (Bar-Joseph, 1995, 2013; Gentry, 2019). This extreme self-confidence comes from the 'unreconstructed logical positivism' with which the tech industry sells its products, and which presumes that 'the world is perfectly knowable, its contents enumerable and their relations capable of being meaningfully encoded in the state of a technical system, without bias or distortion' (Greenfield, 2017, p. 117). Such a strong conviction that big data and artificial intelligence together are able to deliver optimized and unquestionably good solutions is reminiscent of a religious belief. Even Kent, for all his extreme positivism, was emphatically against leaving analysis to 'the "programmer" and his computer' (Kent, 1964, p. 6). As shown above, in Moscow's smart city strategy, the collected data are to be fed into the AI to provide 'non-contradictory' solutions for the governance of the city, ostensibly for the good of the citizens. In this ideology of 'efficiency' and 'optimization', there is no room for disagreement about which solution is better. In any case, the reliance on these data means that people's preferences and needs are deduced from big data rather than channelled through real democratic participation (Greenfield, 2013).

Conclusions

Before the publication of an unauthorized biography of Ray Dalio, it was not widely known that what Gref describes as the 'friendship' between Dalio and himself was initially a result of the hedge fund manager's infatuation with authoritarian leaders. According to the award-winning journalist Rob Copeland, Dalio reached out to Gref in 2015 in an attempt to get access to Putin, whom he had come to consider a model leader. The original impetus to study Putin's style of leadership had come from Lee Kuan Yew, Singapore's long-time autocrat, whom Dalio knew personally and had long considered 'an iconic hero' (Copeland, 2023, pp. 193, 331). Revealing as this might be, the connection between Russian technopoly and autocracy runs deeper than this anecdote. It is well known that Russian technopolists see their intelligence-driven approach, digital technologies, not least AI, as the solutions to Russia's problems of legal nihilism, widespread informal dealings, and rampant corruption, in short, the problem of 'bad governance' (Gel'man, 2022, pp. 143–144). But it is perhaps more surprising that even Putin, often seen as something of an embodiment of Russian kleptocracy and *chekist* cameradery, methods, and culture (Belton, 2020; Dawisha, 2015; Fedor, 2013), regards AI technologies not only as the key to 'become the ruler the world', as his famous 2017 quote goes,[39] but also as the key to efficiency, transparency, and accountability:

> Artificial intelligence technologies allow for getting rid of the stagnation and sluggishness of the bureaucratic machinery, qualitatively increasing transparency and the efficiency of administrative procedures, which is extremely important for societal resilience. Because only in that case people will see what the authorities are doing. (Putin, cit. in Latukhina, 2019)

But if we take into account the inner logic of Russian politics, this apparent contradiction is revealed as superficial. In a much-cited and highly refined article from 2010, Richard Sakwa conceptualized Russian

---

[39] '"Whoever leads in AI will rule the world": Putin to Russian children on Knowledge Day', https://www.rt.com/news/401731-ai-rule-world-putin/.

politics as 'a struggle between two systems: the formal constitutional order, what we call the *normative state*; and a second world of informal relations, factional conflict, and para-constitutional political practices, termed [...] the *administrative regime*' (Sakwa, 2010, p. 185). Sakwa outlined the complex coexistence and tensions between these orders, accounting for paradoxes such as how 'the infringement of the rule of law is justified not by the logic of the exception but by an appeal to the "dictatorship of law" itself' (Sakwa, 2010, p. 200). Much has happened since then; not least is Russia a full-fledged authoritarian personalistic state that has invaded its neighbour and is in political confrontation with the West. The digitalization has also come a long way. But the basic dynamics of Sakwa's model are arguably still at play, which could be illustrated by the coincidence that on the same day as Aleksei Naval'nyi died in prison,[40] where he, on Putin's orders, was held on trumped-up charges and subjected to continuous mistreatment, Putin presented an updated version of Russia's AI strategy. Here, under the 'fundamental principles' that are 'compulsory in the realization of this Strategy', the first point reads: '[T]he defence of human rights and freedoms: to secure the defence of human rights and freedoms that are guaranteed in the legislation of the Russian Federation, international treaties of the Russian Federation, and generally accepted principles and norms of international law'.[41]

Hence, Russian intelligence-driven technopoly is not only a product of global trends and technological development, but also of the power dynamics of the authoritarian system, with which it lives in a peaceful, even synergetic coexistence. In the historical context of the evolution of the Russian regime and the nearly simultaneous rise of the *chekists* and the technopolists at the expense of the 'systemic liberals' (not to mention the extra-systemic opposition right, left, and centre), it is the logical result of the progressive eradication of democratic residue. As 'new

---

[40] At the time of writing, it was still unclear whether he died of 'natural' causes, but during his entire imprisonment—just after his recovery from poisoning—he was subjected to frequent isolation, denied sufficient amounts of food, big enough clothes, and other amenities, and otherwise punished for minute 'offenses', always with reference to official regulations.

[41] 'Ukaz prezidenta Rossiiskoi Federatsii' [Decree by the President of the Russian Federation], http://publication.pravo.gov.ru/document/0001202402150063, p. 10.

intelligence', Russian intelligence-driven technopoly might not compete with or improve Russia's 'old' foreign intelligence, the politicization and presumed incompetence of which seems to have been among the reasons for Putin's disastrous decision to go to large-scale war against Ukraine. It does, however, bring new possibilities for domestic surveillance and repression that the *chekists* can make 'good' use of in a country where 'discreditation of the army' is a felony and anti-corruption campaigning is considered terrorism.[42] More to the point, despite any noble intentions that some of its proponents theoretically might harbour, intelligence-driven technopoly is a 'greedy' ideological-technological complex that by its very logic has come to take the place that some hoped would be occupied by popular political participation. Hence, not only the seamless integration of this complex in a repressive system, but also its inner logic, should carry important lessons for liberal democracies about the dangers of intelligence-driven, 'smart' solutions for governance, including AI, the uncritical embrace of which arguably epitomizes the highest stage of technopoly.

Funding This work was funded by funded by The Research Council of Norway, grant: 313626, Algorithmic Governance and Cultures of Policing: Comparative Perspectives from Norway, India, Brazil, Russia, and South Africa' (AGOPOL).

References

Anderson, J. (2006). The Chekist Takeover of the Russian State. *International Journal of Intelligence and Counter Intelligence, 19*(2), 237–288. https://doi.org/10.1080/08850600500483699

---

[42] For instance, in 2022, Aleksei Naval'nyi and his top aides were placed on Russia's official list of terrorists, see 'Russia Adds Navalny, Top Aides To 'Terrorists and Extremists' Register', https://www.themoscowtimes.com/2022/01/25/russia-adds-navalny-top-aides-to-terrorists-and-extremists-register-a76144.

Anderson, J. (2007). The HUMINT Offensive from Putin's Chekist State. *International Journal of Intelligence and Counter Intelligence, 20*(2), 258–316. https://doi.org/10.1080/08850600601079958

Andrew, C. (2004). Intelligence, International Relations and 'Under-theorisation.' *Intelligence and National Security, 19*(2), 170–184. https://doi.org/10.1080/0268452042000302949

Argenbright, R., Bityukova, V. R., Kirillov, P. L., Makhrova, A. G., & Nefedova, T. G. (2020). Directed Suburbanization in a Changing Context: "New Moscow" Today. *Eurasian Geography and Economics, 61*(3), 211–239. https://doi.org/10.1080/15387216.2019.1707700

Bar-Joseph, U. (1995). *Intelligence Intervention in the Politics of Democratic States: The United States, Israel, and Britain.* Pennsylvania State University Press.

Bar-Joseph, U. (2013). The Politicization of Intelligence: A Comparative Study. *International Journal of Intelligence and CounterIntelligence, 26*(2), 347–369. https://doi.org/10.1080/08850607.2013.758000

Bateman, A. (2014). The Political Influence of the Russian Security Services. *The Journal of Slavic Military Studies, 27*(3), 380–403. https://doi.org/10.1080/13518046.2014.932626

Bateman, A. (2016). The KGB and Its Enduring Legacy. *The Journal of Slavic Military Studies, 29*(1), 23–47. https://doi.org/10.1080/13518046.2016.1129863

Batyrov, T. (2023). "Sber" nachal uvedomliat' klientov o perenose ikh biometrii v gosudarstvennuiu sistemu ["Sber" Started Informing Clients of the Transfer of Their Biometry to the State's System]. *Forbes*, 26 June 2023. https://www.forbes.ru/tekhnologii/491646-sber-nacal-uvedom lat-klientov-o-perenose-ih-biometrii-v-gosudarstvennuu-sistemu

Belton, C. (2020). *Putin's People: How the KGB Took Back Russia and Then Took on the West.* Farrar, Straus and Giroux.

Borodikhin, A. (2020). Otlov v karantin [Caught in Quarantine]. *Mediazona*, 5 March 2020. https://zona.media/article/2020/03/05/isolation

Chukarin, A. V. (2018). Moskva "Umnyi gorod—2030" [Moscow "Smart City 2030"]. *Global CIO*. https://globalcio.ru/upload/medialibrary/f1e/f1e 31f6d8ea2736e09296b7799c25b18.pdf

Copeland, R. (2023). *The Fund.* MacMillan Business.

Cox, R. W. (1981). Social Forces, States and World Orders: Beyond International Relations Theory. *Millennium: Journal of International Studies, 10*(2), 126–155. https://doi.org/10.1177/03058298810100020501

Dalio, R. (2017). *Principles: Life and Work.* Simon and Shuster.

Davies, P. H. J., & Steward, T. (2022). No War for Old Spies: Putin, the Kremlin and Intelligence. *RUSI.* https://rusi.org/explore-our-research/public ations/commentary/no-war-old-spies-putin-kremlin-and-intelligence

Dawisha, K. (2015). *Putin's Kleptocracy: Who Owns Russia?* Simon and Schuster.

Dmitriev, M., & Yurtaev, A. (2010). Strategiya-2010: plany i rezul'taty [Strategy-2010: Plans and Results]. *Forbes Russia.* 28 May 2010. https://www.forbes.ru/column/50383-strategiya-2010-plany-i-rezultaty

Dubrovina, E., & Makutina, M. (2023). Eksperty otsenili annonsirovan-nuiu Mishustinym novuiu model' gosupravleniia [Experts Assessed the New Model for State Governance Announced by Mishustin]. *Vedomosti,* 26 April 2023. https://www.vedomosti.ru/politics/articles/2023/04/26/972 717-eksperti-otsenili-mishustinim-model-gosupravleniya

Dylan, H., Gioe, D. V., & Grossfeld, E. (2022). The Autocrat's Intelligence Paradox: Vladimir Putin's (Mis) Management of Russian Strategic Assessment in the Ukraine War. *The British Journal of Politics and International Relations, 25*(3), 385–404. https://doi.org/10.1177/13691481221146113

Fedor, J. (2013). *Russia and the Cult of State Security: The Chekist Tradition, from Lenin to Putin.* Routledge. https://doi.org/10.4324/9780203808917

Fel'shtinskii, Y., & Pribylovskii, V. (2010). *Korporatsiia. Rossiia i KGB vo vremena prezidenta Putina.* Terra.

Galeotti, M. (2022). How Vladimir Putin's Shrinking Inner Circle Led to the Invasion of Ukraine. *Daily Telegraph,* 26 February 2022. https://www.telegr aph.co.uk/world-news/2022/02/26/vladimir-putins-shrinking-inner-circle-led-invasion-ukraine/

Gel'man, V. (2020). "Liberals" vs. "Democrats": Ideational Trajectories of Russia's Post-Communist Transformation. *Social Sciences, 51*(2), 4–24. https://doi.org/10.21557/SSC.60231514

Gel'man, V. (2022). *The Politics of Bad Governance in Contemporary Russia.* University of Michigan Press. https://doi.org/10.3998/mpub.11621795

Gentry, J. A. (2019). "Truth" as a Tool of the Politicization of Intelligence. *International Journal of Intelligence and Counter Intelligence, 32*(2), 217–247. https://doi.org/10.1080/08850607.2019.1565265

Gereikhanova, A. (2019). Gref nazval glavnuiu problemu Rossii [Gref Identified Russia's Main Problem]. *Rossiiskaia gazeta,* 14 March 2019. https://rg.ru/2019/03/14/reg-ufo/gref-nazval-glavnuiu-problemu-rossii.html

Giles, C. (2019). Russia's Role in Producing the Taxman of the Future. *Financial Times,* 29 July 2019. https://www.ft.com/content/38967766-aec8-11e9-8030-530adfa879c2

Greenfield, A. (2013). *Against the Smart City.* Do Projects.

Greenfield, A. (2017). *Radical Technologies the Design of Everyday Life.* Verso.

Gref, G. (2018). Predislovie k russkomu izdaniyu [Foreword to the Russian Edition]. In R. Dalio (Ed.), *Printsipy. Zhizn' i rabota [Principles. Life and Work].* Ivanov, Mann i Ferber.

Hall, S. (2012). *Theorizing Crime and Deviance: A New Perspective.* Sage. https://doi.org/10.4135/9781446251669

Hall, S., & Wilson, D. (2014). New Foundations: Pseudo-Pacification and Special Liberty as Potential Cornerstones for a Multi-Level Theory of Homicide and Serial Murder'. *European Journal of Criminology, 11*(5), 635–655. https://doi.org/10.1177/1477370814536831

Hahn, G. (2018). Sobyanin: Putin's Successor? *gordonhahn.com.* https://gordon hahn.com/2018/11/26/sobyanin-putins-successor/

Jaffel, H. B., & Larsson, S. (2022a). Introduction: What's the Problem with Intelligence Studies? Outlining a New Research Agenda on Contemporary Intelligence. In H. B. Jaffel, & S. Larsson (Eds.), *Problematising Intelligence Studies: Towards A New Research Agenda* (pp. 3–29). Routledge. https://doi.org/10.4324/9781003205463-2

Jaffel, H. B., & Larsson, S. (Eds.). (2022b). *Problematising Intelligence Studies: Towards A New Research Agenda.* Routledge.

Jones, M., & Silberzahn, P. (2013). *Constructing Cassandra: Reframing Intelligence Failure at the CIA, 1947–2001.* Standord UP.

Kent, S. (1964). A Crucial Estimate Relived. *CIA.* https://www.cia.gov/readin groom/docs/CIA-RDP80M01009A000300420003-8.pdf

Kent, S. (1965 [1949]). *Strategic Intelligence for American World Policy.* Princeton University Press. https://doi.org/10.1515/9781400879151

Kiniakina, E., & Ustinova, A. (2023). 'Ekonomiku dannykh profinan-siruiut za schet novykh sborov i aktsizov' ['Data Economy' Will Be Funded by Levies and New Taxes']. *Vedomosti,* 27 November 2023. https://www.vedomosti.ru/economics/articles/2023/11/27/1007790-ekonomiku-dannih-profinansiruyut-za-schet-novih-sborov-i-aktsizov

Kluge, J. (2021). The Future Has to Wait: 5G in Russia and the Lack of Elite Consensus. *Post-Soviet Affairs, 37*(5), 489–505. https://doi.org/10.1080/1060586X.2021.1967071

Knight, A. (2000). The Enduring Legacy of the KGB in Russian Politics. *Problems of Post-Communism, 47*(4), 3–15. https://doi.org/10.1080/10758216.2000.11655889

Kolesnikov, A. (2020). Meriia Moskvi investirovala v slezhku za sotssetiami [Moscow City Hall Has Invested in Surveillance of Social Networks].

Oktagon, 8 November. https://octagon.media/istorii/meriya_moskvy_invest irovala_v_slezhku_za_socsetyami.html

Kolesnikov, A. (2020b). Planning for a (Not-So) Post-Putin Russia. *Russian Analytical Digest, 246*, 6–7.

Kotova, E. (2023). Putin v shutku sprosil Grefa, zamenit li ego iskusstvennyi intellekt [Putin Jokingly Asked Gref whether he Would Be Replaced with Artificial Intellect]. *Rossiiskaia gazeta*, 19 July 2023. https://rg.ru/2023/07/19/putin-v-shutku-sprosil-grefa-zamenit-li-ego-iskusstvennyj-intellekt.html

Kryshtanovskaya. (2005). *Anatomiya rossiiskoi elity* [The Anatomy of the Russian Elite]. Zakharov.

Kryshtanovskaya, O., & White, S. (2003). Putin's Militocracy. *Post-Soviet Affairs, 19*(4), 289–306. https://doi.org/10.2747/1060-586X.19.4.289

Kuldova, T. Ø. (2022). *Compliance-Industrial Complex: The Operating System of a Pre-crime Society*. Palgrave Pivot. https://doi.org/10.1007/978-3-031-192 24-1

Lähteenmäki, M., & Murawski, M. (2023). Blagoustroistvo: Infrastructure, Determinism, (Re-)coloniality, and Social Engineering in Moscow, 1917–2022. *Comparative Studies in Society and History, 65*(3), 587–615.

Latukhina, K. (2019). Putin predlozhil sozdat' pravila vzaimodeistviia s iskusstvennym intellektom [Putin Proposed to Introduce Rules for the Interaction with Artificial Intelligence]. *Rossiiskaia gazeta*, 9 November 2019. https://rg.ru/2019/11/09/putin-predlozhil-sozdat-pravila-vzaimodejstviia-s-iskusstvennym-intellektom.html

Ledeneva, A. V. (2006). *How Russia Really Works: The Informal Practices that Shaped Post-Soviet Politics and Business*. Cornell University Press.

Ledeneva, A. V. (2013). *Can Russia Modernise? Sistema, Power Networks and Informal Governance*. Cambridge University Press. https://doi.org/10.1017/CBO9780511978494

Markotkin, N., & Chernenko, E. (2020). Developing Artificial Intelligence in Russia: Objectives and Reality. *Carnegie Moscow Center*. https://carnegie.ru/commentary/82422

Marrin, S. (2020). Analytic Objectivity and Science: Evaluating the US Intelligence Community's Approach to Applied Epistemology. *Intelligence and National Security, 35*(3), 350–366. https://doi.org/10.1080/02684527.2019.1710806

Marten, K. (2017). The 'KGB State' and Russian Political and Foreign Policy Culture. *The Journal of Slavic Military Studies, 30*(2), 131–151. https://doi.org/10.1080/13518046.2017.1270053

Matveev, I. (2024). From the Chicago Boys to Hjalmar Schacht: The Trajectory of the (Neo)liberal Economic Expertise in Russia. *Problems of Post-Communism, 1–10.* https://doi.org/10.1080/10758216.2023.2291359

Miller, G., & Belton, C. (2022). Russia's Spies Misread Ukraine and Misled Kremlin as War Loomed. *Washington Post*, 19 August 2022. https://www.washingtonpost.com/world/interactive/2022/russia-fsb-intelligence-ukraine-war/

Minchenko Consulting. (2013). *Politburo 2.0: Ahead of a Realignment of Elite Groups.* Minchenko Consulting.

Natsional'naia strategiia razvitiia iskusstvennogo intellekta na period do 2030 goda. (2019). http://www.garant.ru/products/ipo/prime/doc/72738946/

Olcott, A. (2009). "Peeling Facts off the Face of the Unknown". *Studies in Intelligence, 53*(2), 21–32.

Østbø, J. (2017). Securitizing "Spiritual-Moral Values" in Russia. *Post-Soviet Affairs, 33*(3), 200–216. https://doi.org/10.1080/1060586X.2016.1251023

Østbø, J. (2021). Hybrid Surveillance Capitalism: Sber's Model for Russia's Modernization. *Post-Soviet Affairs, 37*(5), 435–452. https://doi.org/10.1080/1060586X.2021.1966216

Postman, N. (2011). *Technopoly: The Surrender of Culture to Technology.* Vintage.

Posypkina, A., & Balenko, E. (2019). Sberbank nachal rabotu nad sobstvennoi 'umnoi' kolonkoi [Sberbank Started Working on Its Own Loudspeaker]. *RBK,* 28 August 2019. https://www.rbc.ru/technology_and_media/28/08/2019/5d64fc279a794737ec87e292

Rathmell, A. (2002). Towards Postmodern Intelligence. *Intelligence and National Security, 17*(3), 87–104. https://doi.org/10.1080/02684520412331306560

Reiter, S., & Liutova, M. (2022). Kryshka groba zakryta i kolochena [The Final Nail in the Coffin]. *Meduza,* 27 June 2022. https://meduza.io/feature/2022/06/27/kryshka-groba-zakryta-i-zakolochena

Reznikova, E., & Korostelev, A. (2024). Issledovanie putinskikh repressii [Investigation of Putin's Repression]. *Proekt,* 22 February 2024. https://www.proekt.media/guide/repressii-v-rossii/

Riehle, K. (2022). Post-KGB Lives: Is There Such a Thing as a Former Chekist? *International Journal of Intelligence and CounterIntelligence, Ahead-of-Print, 1–24.* https://doi.org/10.1080/08850607.2022.2064201

Sakwa, R. (2010). The Dual State in Russia. *Post-Soviet Affairs, 26*(3), 185–206. https://doi.org/10.2747/1060-586X.26.3.185

Sakwa, R. (2021). Heterarchy: Russian Politics Between Chaos and Control. *Post-Soviet Affairs, 37*(3), 222–241. https://doi.org/10.1080/1060586X.2020.1871269

Sberbank. (2021). «Saliut, Podai Zaiavlenie V ZAGS!» [«Saliut, Send an Application to the Marriage Registry!». *Sberbank.com,* 7 July 2021. https://www.sberbank.com/ru/news-and-media/press-releases/article?newsID=140 31554-da5d-4648-9a49-bac34ae1ce48&blockID=7&regionID=77&lang=ru&type=NEWS

Scott, L., & Jackson, P. (2004). The Study of Intelligence in Theory and Practice. *Intelligence and National Security, 19*(2), 139–169. https://doi.org/10.1080/0268452042000302930

Seddon, M. (2018). Sberbank: The Bank Trying to Shape Russia's Future. *Financial Times,* 30 September 2018. https://www.ft.com/content/345 0c840-c0a4-11e8-95b1-d36dfef1b89a

Seddon, M., & Ivanova, P. (2022). How Putin's Technocrats Saved the Economy to Fight a War They Opposed. *Financial Times,* 16 December 2022. https://www.ft.com/content/fe5fe0ed-e5d4-474e-bb5a-10c9657285d2

Sharafutdinova, G. (2014). The Pussy Riot Affair and Putin's Démarche from Sovereign Democracy to Sovereign Morality. *Nationalities Papers, 42*(4), 615–621. https://doi.org/10.1080/00905992.2014.917075

Shorrock, T. (2008). *Spies for Hire: The Secret World of Intelligence Outsourcing.* Simon and Schuster.

Skak, M. (2016). Russian Strategic Culture: The Role of Today's Chekisty. *Contemporary Politics, 22*(3), 324–341. https://doi.org/10.1080/13569775.2016.1201317

Skobelev, V., & Balashova, A. (2020). Sberbank zapustil servis postanovko diagnoza s pomoshch'yu neirosetei. *RBK,* 2 December 2020. https://www.rbc.ru/technology_and_media/02/12/2020/5fc632f69a79471e8ce7d8a4

Smirnova, I. (2023). Videofiksatsiia pozvolit shtrafovat' voditelei v Moskva za nepristegnutykh passazhirov [Video Surveillance Makes it Possible to Fine Drivers in Moscow for Passengers Not Using Seat Belts]. *Vedomosti,* 21 September 2023. https://www.vedomosti.ru/gorod/smartcity/articles/videofiksatsiya-pozvolit-shtrafovat-voditelei-v-moskve-za-nepristegnutih-passazhirov

Sobesednik. (2005). Rossiya ne bez Grefa [Russia not without Gref]. *Sobesednik,* 22 June 2005. https://www.lenpravda.ru/today/252758.html

Soldatov, A. (2013). 5 Russian-Made Surveillance Technologies Used in the West. *Wired*, 5 May 2013. https://www.wired.com/2013/05/russian-survei llance-technologies/

Soldatskikh, V., Rubin, M., & Badanin, R. (2023). Nastoiashchie agenty [Real Agents]. *Proekt Media*, 10 January 2023. https://www.proekt.media/ portrait/german-gref/

Steiner, J. E. (2004). *Challenging the Red Line between Intelligence and Policy*. Institute for the Study of Diplomacy, School of Foreign Service, Georgetown University.

Stout, M., & Warner, M. (2018). Intelligence is as Intelligence Does. *Intelligence and National Security, 33*(4), 517–526. https://doi.org/10.1080/026 84527.2018.1452593

Sullivan, J. (2020). Russia's New Prime Minister Augurs Techno-Authoritarianism. *Foreign Policy*, 20 January 2020. https://foreignpo licy.com/2020/01/20/russia-incoming-prime-minister-techno-authoritaria nism/

Tishina, Y. (2020). V elektroavtobusakh zaglianut v litsa [Faces Will be Checked in Electric Buses]. *Kommersant*, 22 October 2020. https://www. kommersant.ru/doc/4540447

Treisman, D. (2022). Putin Unbound: How Repression at Home Presaged Belligerence Abroad. *Foreign Affairs, 101*, 40–53.

Trubina, E. (2020). Sidewalk Fix, Elite Maneuvering and Improvement Sensibilities: The Urban Improvement Campaign in Moscow. *Journal of Transport Geography, 83*, 1–9. https://doi.org/10.1016/j.jtrangeo.2020.102655

Vandenko, A. (2019). German Gref: ne lgi, ne voruy, ne lenis' [German Gref: Don't Lie, Don't Steal, Don't Be Lazy]. *TASS*, 8 February 2019. https://tass. ru/top-officials/6078757

Vandenko, A. (2020). German Gref: ya – igrok vdolguyu [German Gref: I'm in it for the Long Haul]. *TASS*, 29 July 2020. https://tass.ru/business-offici als/8827375

Waller, J. G. (2013). Re-Setting the Game: The Logic and Practice of Official Support for Alexei Navalny's Mayoral Run. *Russian Analytical Digest, 136*, 6–10.

Waller, J. M. (1994). The KGB & Its Successors. *Perspective, 4*(4), 5–9.

Walther, U. (2014). Russia's Failed Transformation: The Power of the KGB/ FSB from Gorbachev to Putin. *International Journal of Intelligence and CounterIntelligence, 27*(4), 666–686. https://doi.org/10.1080/08850607.2014. 924808

Warner, M. (2002). Wanted: A Definition of 'Intelligence.' *Studies in Intelligence, 46*(3), 15–22.

Yakovlev, A. (2021). Composition of the Ruling Elite, Incentives for Productive Usage of Rents, and Prospects for Russia's Limited Access Order. *Post-Soviet Affairs, 37*(5), 417–434. https://doi.org/10.1080/1060586X.2021.1966988

Zakharov, A. (2020). 'Umnyi gorod' ili 'Starshyi brat'? ['Smart City' or 'Big Brother'?]. *BBC Russkaya sluzhba*, 10 April 2020. https://www.bbc.com/russian/features-52219260

Zelendinova, V. (2020). Kontrolery pokhoroshevshei Moskvy [Controllers of Beautified Moscow]. *Octagon*. 23 May 2020. https://octagon.media/politika/kontrolery_poxoroshevshej_moskvy.html

4

Smart Security? Transnational Policing Models and Surveillance Technologies in the City of São Paulo

Alcides Eduardo dos Reis Peron
and Marcos César Alvarez

In recent years, discourses and initiatives labelled as 'intelligent' have gained momentum in São Paulo. At the beginning of his tenure, the then-mayor stated that he would transform São Paulo into a 'Smart City' (Venceslau, 2017). His intention was reiterated by the politicians and other public actors, justified under the premise of purported modernization and with the objective of opening the city up to private capital

This chapter is a translation from Portuguese of an article 'O governo da segurança: Modelos securitários transnacionais e tecnologias de vigilância na cidade de São Paul', published by the periodical *Lua Nova*, in the issue 114, September-December 2021 https://doi.org/10.1590/0102-175212/114 A few stylistic and other changes have been made upon translation. The article has been translated by the authors and with the permission of the journal.

A. E. dos Reis Peron (✉)
FECAP/NEV-USP, São Paulo, Brazil
e-mail: alcides.peron@fecap.br

M. C. Alvarez
NEV-USP/Department of Sociology—USP, São Paulo, Brazil
e-mail: mcalvarez@usp.br

121

T. Ø. Kuldova et al. (eds.), *Policing and Intelligence in the Global Big Data Era, Volume I*, Palgrave's Critical Policing Studies,
https://doi.org/10.1007/978-3-031-68326-8_4

investments in public services. In 2017, a law (16.703/2017) was sanctioned to regulate concessions and public–private partnerships (PPPs) within the Municipal Plan for 'de-statization', encompassing transportation, health, housing, and security projects. Additionally, a video was disseminated by the mayor's cabinet showcasing São Paulo to investors in Dubai as a global city open to foreign capital (Santos, 2017). These notions of modernization and proposals for privatization, coupled with the concept of 'smart cities', have also garnered prominence in forums, expos, and other events related to urban administration and electronic security, spanning various international contexts.

According to Morozov and Bria (2018), the creation of rankings for Smart Cities by various platforms, such as Bright Cities,[1] incorporates a series of criteria, including openness to private capital, transparency, and connectivity, effectively functioning as an investment index closely resembling credit rating agencies. Thus, the term 'smart' conveys an imaginary of connectivity, speed, and technological management of all urban flows, but it also signals extensive agendas of privatizing public services of various kinds.

One of the sectors that have been impacted by this agenda in the city of São Paulo is the public security sector. According to data from the National Federation of Security and Transport of Valuables (Fenavist, 2019), there was a growth of 5.7% in private security companies between 2014 and 2018, particularly in the state of São Paulo. In this context, both national and transnational companies have been offering various 'intelligent' electronic security products, such as cameras, alarm systems, applications, and access controls. Through public–private partnerships (PPPs), these companies have proposed several programs to revitalize public spaces by introducing surveillance and monitoring systems in specific city neighbourhoods.

In the realm of public security, the municipality has created programs and systems aiming to integrate these private sector technologies into government security hubs, through collaboration between the Municipal Secretariat of Urban Security, the Military Police (PMESP, the police

---

[1] https://www.brightcities.city/.

at the state's level), and the Municipal Guard (the police at the municipal level). Some initiatives promoted prior to the current administration have already been fostering the involvement of civilians and even private entities in public security, through community policing and 'Neighbourhood Watch' programs that sought to bring policing closer to local demands and to establish networks of residents and traders involved in security management. Between 2014 and 2017, initiatives like the City Câmeras introduced a cloud-based CCTV system that integrates and shares images from both public and private cameras. These endeavours can be characterized as a multicentric governance of security.

Therefore, these processes cannot be merely described as privatization or the 'smartification' and 'technification' of security, as such labels overlook the multiplicity of effects and articulations that these new models of governance have provoked. For instance, in the 1980s, Mike Davis pointed to the proliferation of monitoring systems throughout Los Angeles and described a form of security administration in which public and private agents intermingled in controlling public spaces in the 'fortress city' (Davis, 2018). In the 1990s, Sassen (2006) highlighted the emergence of 'Global Cities', describing them as crucial nodes for capital reproduction and reflecting on how economic globalization led to the emergence of assemblages (comprising public and private actors and systems) dedicated to governing these spaces. In the early 2000s, Shearing and Wood (2000, 2003) analysed the effects of neoliberal models and techniques of management on the formation of multicentric nodal networks in public security. During the same period, David Garland (2002) and Ericsson and Haggerty (2002) observed that technologies and public–private partnerships stimulated the reorganization of police activity towards 'preventionism', wherein the identification, classification, and management of risk became central methods of security governance. In recent years, Klauser (2010) and Caldeira (2001) explored how new technologies and ideas of 'risk management' led to the amplification of strategies of vigilantism and control, as well as the production of enclosures and tactics of local self-governance by mobilizing various infrastructures (not solely policing-related) for security governance.

Undoubtedly, it is essential to problematize the effects of these identified trends in various countries, particularly in the Global North, and investigate how they interact with tendencies present in the Global South. In dimensions like public and private security, the presence of profound social inequalities, the persistence of violence in society, and the perpetuation of authoritarian state practices significantly reshape the local debate. Historically, public security policies in Brazil have been characterized by top-down direction in their conception, decision-making, and implementation, with their operators often remaining resistant to transparency and to result evaluation, inherent to a democratic environment (Alvarez et al., 2004). The porous boundaries between public and private security and the presence of illegal groups, such as drug traffickers and militias, further complicate the governance spaces in Brazilian metropolises.

Thus, in contexts such as the São Paulo metropolis, it is possible to observe the growing interaction between transnational and local models, systems, and technologies for public and private security. The discourse of Smart Cities, with proposals for opening up to private capital, co-management of public security, and increased civilian engagement in this process, needs to be observed and analysed considering such complexity. Specifically in São Paulo, the introduction of new surveillance technologies, as well as the circulation of security management models with an increasing delegation of responsibilities to non-security professionals highlights this complex interaction between global and local trends in contemporary security governance.

The aim of this chapter is to explore how public–private initiatives impact security in the city of São Paulo, with a critical dialogue regarding three trends already identified in international literature: sphericalization of security, securitized sociability, and the infrastructuring of surveillance. More specifically, we will analyse the effects of the City Câmeras and 'Vigilância Solidária' Program (Neighbourhood Watch), and the São Paulo Inteligente (Smart São Paulo) project, promoted by private companies, associations, and the city administration, to establish security spheres in the Pinheiros and Jardins neighbourhoods. For this purpose, the chapter is divided into two main sections: initially, some theoretical perspectives discussing transnational trends in security are revisited. Subsequently, we review the history and characteristics of the City Câmeras, 'Vigilância Solidária', and 'São Paulo Inteligente', linking each of these projects to the trends identified in the literature. Further, we describe how these trends impact security management in the city and reconfigure the relationship between private and public actors in this process.

Beyond Privatization: Security and Policing in the Twenty-First Century

In recent years, numerous studies have explored how security practices have been influenced by globally diffused trends. Among them, the discussion about the decentralization of policing activities, the formation of collective security management clusters, and the growing vigilantism stand out. In this debate on security, the focus extends beyond policing alone and encompasses a broader scope of actors, instruments, and objectives. For instance, Abrahamsem and Williams (2007) describe contemporary security as an assemblage of practices, discourses, and actors that transcend national boundaries and incorporate techniques and procedures that circulate transnationally. Hence, it becomes evident that an analysis of the transnationalization of security management models necessarily requires approaches that combine elements from criminology, sociology, and international security studies—particularly concerning the increasing mobility of security multinationals—as emphasized by Bigo (2016). Only through this interdisciplinary approach can the breadth and complexity of security debates in a globalized world be fully comprehended.

The analysis proposed here starts from the premise that local security practices are interconnected with transnational ideas, technologies, and models. Policing, therefore, represents one of the elements articulated within this security assemblage.[2] This expression refers to the concepts put forth by Sassen (2006), Abrahamsem and Williams (2007),

---

[2] The concept of assemblage is the English translation of the idea of agencement, as elaborated by Deleuze and Guattari (1993), denoting the notion of a transient arrangement, disposition, or composition of two or more elements. In this context, these assemblages signify, according to Deleuze and Guattari (1993), the coming together and disposition of heterogeneous elements, which do not necessarily form an organic unity but rather a machinic apparatus, a multiplicity

and others, signifying the set of measures, discourses, technologies, theories, actors, and practices that interconnect and mutually influence the production of security effects. On the one hand, it becomes evident that security (or the security realm, referring to security or the intention to produce security) is not something fixed or concrete, but rather a state of affairs that produces effects, such as feelings of security that denote 'being free from concerns' and 'being safe from physical harm', encompassing both the terms security and safety (Rodrigues, 2012). Furthermore, security is not perceived homogeneously by all individuals and groups in a society, implying that acts of security[3] mobilized by one group to construct a security state may, in turn, produce insecurity for others (Bigo & Tsoukala, 2008).

Thanks to the processes of globalization and the intensification of international exchange of ideas and policies, the organization of security and policing has become more susceptible to a series of common trends and practices (Sassen, 2006). This shift took place mainly from the mid-1990s in the United States and European countries, influenced by what some refer to as 'neoliberal rationality', which spread as a principle of state deregulation, impacting the field of security as well (Shearing & Wood, 2000, p. 464). Alongside this, policing underwent reorganizations towards anticipatory and preventive control, resulting in greater decentralization, the privatization of security, and an increasing reliance on new informational and communicational technologies, akin to what Terpstra et al. (2019) discuss in their analysis of police reforms in the Netherlands and Scotland. These reconfigurations can be summarized, according to certain authors, into three security trends: the formation of security sociabilities, the sphericalization of security, and the infrastructuring of surveillance.

---

where the singular elements and their 'essence' are of little relevance to comprehending the array of affects and effects of this multiplicity (Nail, 2017).

[3] The 'Copenhagen School' defined security as the outcome of a 'securitization act' driven by actors capable of articulating discourses that frame individuals, groups, and issues as belonging to the realm of security—and thus subject to emergency and urgent measures for their resolution—(Buzan et al., 1998).

Securitized Sociability

Various studies conducted in the late 1990s in the United States pointed to a dominant trend in the organization of security: the decentralization of its implementation in favour of civilian and private groups, which would promote a kind of 'securitized sociability'. Since the mid-1970s, police forces in cities in the US and England have been implementing community-oriented policing programs, particularly community policing. Skolnick and Bayley (1988), based on an analysis of experiences on four continents, describe how four general principles organize community policing: (1) organizing crime prevention based on community demands and utilizing the community itself as an instrument for surveillance and self-care of property; (2) reorienting patrol activities to prioritize non-emergency services, thereby establishing methods for identifying, preventing, and mitigating risks; (3) increasing the responsibility of local communities for security; (4) finally, the authors highlight the processes of command decentralization, giving greater autonomy for officers and communities to collaborate and produce results in risk management.

In this spirit, various programs were developed, such as the Neighbourhood Watch in England, through which police and the community interact to monitor risks, deviations, and disorders. The common lexicon in interactions between police officers and residents revolves around maintaining security, establishing and upholding rules of behaviour, and fostering self-governance.

Shearing and Wood (2000, 2003) analysed the process of assigning responsibilities to the community and private security companies as a result of the spread of neoliberal ideals around the world. In countries of the Global North, this rationality is described as utilitarian and beneficial to the division of responsibilities among various actors involved in security management, as it bestows a sense of empowerment upon these communities (Shearing & Wood, 2000, p. 460). They generally define this movement as the establishment of a nodal governance of security, characterized by interactions between corporations, the State, and the community in the management of security through networks of relationships. There is no hierarchy among these nodes, nor rigidity; they are established as forms of security governance that are not exclusively state-based (Shearing & Wood, 2003). The authors assess that the immediate outcome of this formation of nodes for a distributed governance of security is the emergence of a type of citizen and citizenship that does not necessarily fully affiliate with the State but draws on principles and organizes their social action based on these multicentric nodes of security governance. The term 'denizen' is used by the authors to denote a type of social affiliation that aligns with one or more spheres of governance and responsibilities, accessing multiple sets of rights and duties (Shearing & Wood, 2003, p. 407).

These developments highlight the issue that practices of decentralization and community policing lead to an increasing allocation of responsibilities to neighbourhood residents for the self-management of security. In this sense, this self-governance does not necessarily exclude the State from security management but coexists with it through distributed forms of governance, where sociability, bonds, and interests among multiple actors are shaped by the semantics of security. For instance, the proposal of projects, the adoption of surveillance mechanisms, the identification and mitigation of risks, and fundamentally, the construction of shared perspectives on security. Within this securitized sociability, terms like self-care, attention, and stewardship become means for creating bonds between residents of specific neighbourhoods and other spaces.

The 'Sphericalization' of Security

Another trend for security governance would be the formation of clusters or, as Tereza Caldeira (2001) described, the formation of fortified enclaves, where the exercise of security is spatialized. According to the author, this process is associated with a contemporary pattern of segregation that, in the case of São Paulo, is established in the city (and has been unfolding since the nineteenth century) and can be defined as the organization of 'privatized spaces, closed and monitored for residence, consumption, leisure and work' that are established due to fear of crime (Caldeira, 2001, p. 211). The author analyses this movement largely as something endogenous, constituted as an unfolding of the process of urban segregation in São Paulo. However, other authors present these enclosures and closures, total or partial, as results of a global security movement.

For example, Shearing and Wood (2003) analyse how nodal networks, in which public and private actors develop dynamics for security management, influence the spatialization of security (formation of security spheres and perimeters), but also evolve as a result of this process, by encouraging the formation of what they describe as 'communal spaces'. These spaces, which are neither private nor public, are similar to what they define as 'mass circulation private properties', such as shopping malls, industrial parks, and recreational spaces, where nodular networks hold a certain management authority, being able to control access or at least limit it (Shearing & Wood, 2003, pp. 410–411).

In analysing itinerant sports mega-events, Klauser (2010) develops an analysis regarding the forms of control and security models that evolve from the strategic organization between space, surveillance, and policing. For this purpose, he delves into the spatial metaphors of spheres—as discussed in the work of Peter Sloterdjik—and the security tendency to circumscribe and delimit spaces for specific actions. The sphere is understood by the author as a socially created and 'self-animated' space, in which a set of communal experiences become possible and where a sense of protection towards the outside world develops (Klauser, 2010, p. 329). The process of sphericalization highlights how security can be understood not only as a set of spatially articulated surveillance practices but also as a force that creates (atmo)spheres. That is, it is not merely about creating securitized spaces—closed or open—but indicates a process through which space and communal perceptions of vulnerability and isolation begin to psychosocially affect individuals.

Therefore, the sphericalization of security is not merely a spatial phenomenon, but also produces effects of regulating relationships and internal perceptions (of risk and security). As the author points out: 'securitization strategies not only separate, differentiate, and articulate distinct physical spaces; they also create and carefully maintain defended atmospheric differences' (Klauser, 2010, p. 336). Despite this influence and the production of common perspectives on security, Klauser makes it clear that these spaces do not necessarily foster solidarity in relationships;

individuals act in pursuit of their self-interest, seeking their own security (Klauser, 2010, p. 337). As he highlights, the pursuit of security and the proliferation of self-governance projects stimulate the formation of these clusters. Within them evolves a sociability that encourages individuals to cooperate in maintaining their security, promoting a continuous vigilantism for the administration of movements and boundaries within these spaces. The boundary that produces this separation, as pointed out by Klauser (2010), manifests as a complex pattern of spatiality anchored in control technologies and physical barriers, indicating that it may not exist as a necessary physical impediment but rather as a set of techniques for controlling and managing movements within these spaces.

Infrastructuring Surveillance

One aspect that permeates all these analysed trends is the massive use of surveillance apparatuses and techniques, aimed at monitoring risks in cities of the Global North. The exercise of a security government of everyday life requires the employment of surveillance, whether for coercion or identification of 'deviations'. Thus, governments have organized security as a risk management process, that is, oriented towards identifying and mitigating future or imminent threats (Amoore & Goede, 2008).

In a series of works on the policing of risk, Ericsson and Haggerty (2002) analyse how policing functions expand beyond the formal boundaries of the police (by incorporating various other institutions) and become oriented towards risk identification and communication. Police activities would thus aim at producing knowledge and data about flows of people, behaviours, and conduct considered suspicious, becoming a hub for reception, analysis, production, and communication of risks with other institutions. When analysing the police institutions in the United States, Britain, and Canada, the authors understand that they become a means for catalysing, calculating, and communicating criminal risk. They clarify that risk is a construct, as 'threats and dangers are recognized, responded to, and made real through human invention and the use of technologies for risk classification' (Ericsson & Haggerty, 2002,

p. 238). As a result, the so-called smart monitoring systems have long been integrated into the arsenal of globally security governance networks. Haggerty and Ericsson (2000, p. 235) point out that policing gradually becomes informational work, centred on the collection and analysis of multi-agency intelligence. The diffusion of surveillance is striking not only as a police instrument but as an element that enables the spatialization of security. The use of surveillance systems establishes an expanded authority of self-governing networks that impose the delimitation of spaces and the consolidation of boundaries, through the interaction between non-state actors and monitoring technologies.

Thus, surveillance manifests itself as a complex grouping of diverse sensors and cameras capable of providing security agents with renewed information. This myriad of apparatuses is understood as a surveillant assemblage (Haggerty & Ericsson, 2000). Such an assemblage is marked by a diffuse collection of data operationalized by different systems and methods, such as cameras and cell phones, which are subsequently aggregated to produce profiles and classifications, not only of individuals but also of situations and spaces. Therefore, surveillance is not exercised from a central core but is based on a set of objects and actors that connect in a unique root, feeding one or multiple spaces (Haggerty & Ericsson, 2000, p. 614).

There is thus a tendency for surveillance to become a central infrastructure for security management. In this case, it instrumentalizes other infrastructures such as surveillance, identification, and risk communication apparatuses. In other words, house facades, lampposts, security guard booths, hospitals, shopping centres, buses, etc., are converted into support infrastructures for maintaining surveillance. This means that the monitoring systems of these infrastructures are mobilized not only for their internal security but also for their surroundings. As Luque-Ayala and Marvin (2016, p. 5) point out, contemporary urban security regimes have been articulated to govern infrastructures and, from there, the mobility and circulation of people.

Several authors thus identify how a series of security reordering trends have interacted and spread worldwide, thanks to global processes. More than just the privatization of security, these processes modulate security as a joint activity between state and non-state actors and convert infrastructures into surveillance systems for controlling communal spaces. The production of similar effects in various cities in the United States and European countries, such as England (Camp & Heatherton, 2016), Scotland, and the Netherlands (Terpstra et al., 2019), evidences the interdependence of these trends. In Brazil, specifically, in São Paulo, due to policy and technology transfer projects initiated by the state and municipality, it is possible to observe that these trends are beginning to circulate locally and produce effects that demand careful analysis.

The Security Tendencies in São Paulo

Over the past five years, various security innovations have been presented as part of a global process of city internationalization, driven by the discourse of Smart Cities. This discourse has supported the adoption of a range of informational systems in various areas of public administration. As Morozov and Bria (2018) explain, Smart Cities discourses and projects require the adoption of technologies that are only available to private companies, leading to increased proximity between public and private entities and the delegation of authority to the latter for management and provision of services—something that had already been on the municipal government's agenda for some time (Franzon, 2018).

In São Paulo, this discourse has facilitated the increasing proliferation of public–private partnerships, particularly in public security, the creation of neighbourhood surveillance projects, and the adoption of various monitoring systems. In our research, between 2018 and 2020, three interviews were conducted with providers of electronic monitoring systems operating in the regions[4] of Pinheiros, Jardins, and Alto de Pinheiros, as well as three members of neighbourhood associations, security councils, and local security project proponents. Additionally, four specific meetings of the Vizinhança Solidária (Neighbourhood Watch)

---

[4] These are neighborhoods that have some adjacency to each other; are of high standard and upper middle class; most are wooded; have extensive integration with public transport systems; and has mostly large mansions or large and well-structured apartment buildings.

program were attended. This material was transcribed, read, and interpreted alongside a larger set of interviews and collected data.[5]

'Vizinhança Solidária' and City Câmeras: Securitization, Spheres, and Atmospheres

Buoyed by the discourse of digitization and smartification of public security, in 2017, the municipal government adopted a program called City Câmeras, which consists of a cloud-based platform for real-time surveillance and monitoring of public spaces, as well as the integration of public and private camera systems, image storage, and even the production of statistics on response and dispatch using the CompStat software. These images could be accessed by both camera owners and private and public security agents and were allegedly intended to serve as both a mechanism to deter crime and a tool for police investigation.

To a large extent, various companies linked to the surveillance and private security sector joined the City Câmeras initiative, entered contracts with the municipality, and obtained authorization to commercialize camera systems and cloud image integration services. These systems are then offered to residential and commercial associations to connect homes and establishments to the municipality's public security apparatus. This procedure has fuelled a market for private security and infrastructure that has spread to various neighbourhoods in the city, with further support from community policing programs such as Vizinhança Solidária (Peron & Alvarez, 2019).

However, City Câmeras is not limited to being a public Closed-Circuit Television (CCTV) system for indoor surveillance, as the cameras connected to the cloud are private, and installed by residents and merchants to monitor public streets in front of their properties and surroundings. In other words, the program utilizes privately owned

---

[5] The interviews, ethnographic incursions, and information surveys are part of a broader research supported by the São Paulo Research Foundation, in which we focus on investigating the use of 'predictive' surveillance and monitoring systems in the state of São Paulo. In this context, approximately 20 interviews were conducted, involving members of associations, residents, researchers, police officers, and business owners.

cameras installed and managed by residents and merchants and shares the videos with both public and private security agents. Furthermore, individuals who contract the system do not do so individually but rather follow guidance from associations, private security companies, and the Military Police of the State of São Paulo (PMESP) regarding camera placement and quantity, to better cover the monitored areas (Fig. 4.1). Thus, by using the camera system for public security purposes, the program instrumentalizes this private property surveillance infrastructure (exercised by residents themselves or contracted companies).

On the one hand, City Câmeras appears to favour a decentralized security model that organizes neighbourhoods and other spaces as true security spheres or 'communal spaces', where various public and private, civilian and police actors overlap in securitization governance. These spaces shape flexible, more or less permeable boundaries managed by barriers (Fig. 4.1), and their informal jurisdiction extends to the visual horizon of the cameras.

Fig. 4.1 City Câmeras and Vizinhança Solidária câmeras and check-points. Images by authors

As an example, a resident who is also the head of security of the Society of Friends of Alto de Pinheiros Neighbourhood (SAAP, in Portuguese), a contracting party of City Câmeras, describes the neighbourhood and the camera layout as a strategic security endeavour and the creation of a securitized sphere based on its access roads, choke points, border limits, and spaces that require more attention, all unveiled with the consultancy of private and public security agents:

> There's a small association near Pôr do Sol square, there in that region they installed [the cameras]. It's within our territory, so, in short, it made complete sense. And then, we mobilized some institutions that also agreed to install them, and they are in strategic locations. So, here [points on the map], the Clube Alto De Pinheiros, they installed two, one here and another here – the Colégio Santa Cruz, which we needed on Botelho Street. So, they acquired a camera and keep both here. And here, on Nazaré Paulista Street, coming down here, Colégio Vera Cruz also acquired one. [...] They are distributed in the main areas. (…) on the axes, so there are cameras on Diógenes and here on Botelho Street. (Interview 8, 2019)

On the other hand, the mere existence and adoption of these camera systems and the delineation of borders do not necessarily constitute these spaces as spheres. Indeed, City Câmeras allows residents, businesses, and police forces to establish a broader form of surveillance over entry points, main routes, enabling the establishment of digital and even physical 'borders' within the neighbourhood. However, as Klauser (2010) points out, the formation of security spheres requires not only the establishment of physical borders but also the formation of a set of common perceptions of security, threats, and vulnerabilities that allow the distinction between 'inside' and 'outside' to become a security nexus that produces a sense of 'being safe' among residents. In this case, the community policing program Vizinhança Solidária played a crucial role in assimilating and organizing security perceptions among the residents of these spaces, where private and public agencies overlap for security management.

The community policing model in São Paulo dates back to 1985 with the creation of the Community Security Councils (Conseg), expanding in 1992 when the PMESP incorporated operational concepts of police action linked to citizenship, adapting 'to the fundamental importance of joining forces with the community to seek common solutions' (Polícia, 2017, p. 5). In 1997, the episode of extortion and police brutality in Favela Naval, Diadema, carried out by military police officers, led to the reformulation of police procedures and the proliferation of community policing models (Godoy, 2017). In 2009, the PMESP initiated a project in the Itaim Bibi neighbourhood together with local residents and workers. Besides distributing leaflets, the project consisted of holding meetings with lectures and debates about security risk factors, in order to capture the demands of these groups. As pointed out by a Military Police officer:

> Initially, we give a primary presentation to the residents, so they avoid unnecessary risks. The inspiration comes from Article 144 of the Federal Constitution, which says that the State is responsible for Public Security, and that people are co-responsible. Thus, as the work progressed, people started to integrate with each other and exchange phone numbers to help watch their neighbour's house [...] People stopped looking from their gate inward and started looking from their gate outward. There was a change in vision and behavior, and they started to exercise citizenship. (Governo, 2017)

This project was called 'Vizinhança Solidária' and became a comprehensive program for the entire city and state. This community policing action places the commitment to security as a determinant of citizenship, as it integrates residents, businesses, and workers as part of the system. As the program's booklet reveals, the community is required to provide a counterpart, as citizens and businesses have a greater responsibility for local security management, namely identifying suspicious conduct and installing camera systems.

In two of the program meetings observed in the Pinheiros neighbourhood, there was a significant interaction between PMESP (Military Police of São Paulo State) and the local community, with their demands being heard, filtered, and worked on by security agents when necessary. In these assemblies, residents and merchants who also act as guardians and caretakers of the neighbourhoods and streets used the opportunity to expose their fears and perceived threats that they considered relevant: electrical network failures, the presence of 'strange' people, and 'overgrown vegetation' in squares were identified as security and deterioration problems that could favour criminal activity.

During a program presentation meeting in a condominium in the Pinheiros neighbourhood, the police were responsible for discussing the main local issues, crime rates, and providing safety tips. At the event, a map registering local occurrences was presented, highlighting a segment of the neighbourhood (in yellow—Fig. 4.2) as the police's area of influence near the Clinique Hospital. These descriptions and classifications familiarize residents with a security jargon, necessary for the formation of security atmospheres. As previously seen, discursive acts are crucial for characterizing and framing problems within the context of security. Discourses about security and the continuous integration and communication among residents in resolving security issues, as encouraged by Vizinhança Solidária and City Câmeras, potentially shape aspects of securitized sociability.

Thus, Vizinhança Solidária enables City Câmeras—as it did with the Detecta system in another context—and the establishment of security spheres by guiding the community in developing social actions centred around security arrangements, such as identifying various threats, maintaining a state of constant suspicion, and establishing a hierarchy of work and surveillance (with street tutors). According to an executive of a company that provides consultancy and services related to electronic security in the Pinheiros and Alto de Pinheiros regions, the introduction of a securitized sociability aims at reducing the supposed 'political influence' within security management in these places. In other words, this political orientation would imply reliance on exclusively public structures and projects for security. Therefore, the decision was made to use private poles (Fig. 4.1), house facades, private internet systems, etc.

According to the executive, by utilizing private infrastructures, the community perceives itself as an active agent in the security management process, gaining access to many other security cameras (Interview 1, 2018). Another businessman clarifies how this sociability, encouraged in communal spaces, results from the integration of residents as part of the surveillance infrastructure. In truth, the sharing of images and the

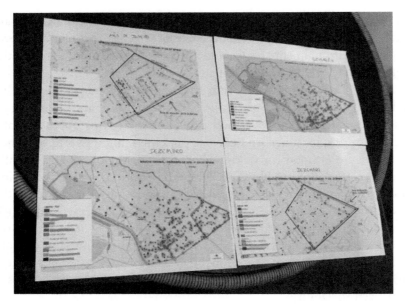

Fig. 4.2 Images with crime spots shown during a Vizinhança Solidária Meeting in Pinheiros Neighbourhood. Photo: authors

potential vigilance appear to shape citizens as agents for classifying and communicating risks, akin to denizens, but now affiliated with a set of local security practices and rules:

> So, you place cameras on public roads, [...] and they [the residents] have access to all the cameras in the neighbourhood [...]. So, with that, you can create solidarity. A neighbour helps monitor another neighbour. So, for example, when you arrive at your residence at night, maybe there, stopped at the traffic light, you can take a look, not only at the camera at your door but also at the corner, the street below, the street behind, to see if there's anyone suspicious around there. If there's any suspicious activity, you either call the police or take a walk around the block, something like that. (Interview 7, 2019)

This denizen and other institutions immersed in securitized sociability—manifested in protection and the distinction between insiders and outsiders, good and bad groups—have collective surveillance as a crucial tool not only for self-protection but also for instrumentalizing their specific demands. It was evident that these demands, as in the case of Alto de Pinheiros, refer to restricting the circulation of non-residents in the area known as 'Pôr do Sol' Square, revealing how the adoption of surveillance apparatuses appears to cater to the interests of local resident groups in limiting or controlling the movement of 'outsiders' in the space. This becomes evident in the interview with the head of security of SAAP, who expresses concerns about drug trafficking and drug use in the neighbourhood:

> Yesterday, we installed a City Câmeras camera in the Pôr do Sol square [...] it's a Dome, donated by a company on the street to the municipality, and that one, we put it in the public City Câmeras. Because it's a square, and, well, people can go there. The police also have access to it because it's a point where, from time to time [...] there's a lot of people gathering. So, that aspect, for residents to have the possibility of having this access for prevention, makes a difference. Then, of course, when something happens, the images are handed over to the Civil Police. [...] We noticed that the flow of people was increasing, especially at night; there's a lot of street vending of drinks there; there are some dealers who sell – because a lot of people consume drugs there. And there was a group that decided to hold a 'rave' party there at night; [...]. So, in this way, some things were done in this process. There were improvements in lighting, it looks like a stadium now. Then, we put this Dome, [...] and integrated it into the City Câmeras for everyone to see. [...] We had no doubt, we put it in the public City Câmeras, everyone can access it, see what's going on, and then everyone settled down. (Interview 8, 2019)

The specific demands for restricting the circulation of 'outsiders' are formulated in the context of a confrontation with drug dealers, drug users, and lawless, deteriorated spaces. This potentially shapes a securitized atmosphere that distinguishes 'good' (internal) and 'bad' (external) forms of circulation and reinforces what Klauser (2010) understands as common perspectives on risks in certain spheres, consequently fostering a solidarity entirely centred on maintaining what is understood as security.

In this same context, due to the COVID-19 pandemic, SAAP, which has long identified the surroundings of 'Pôr do Sol' Square as a high-risk area, managed to obtain authorization from the city authorities to close and fence the square, claiming it was to avoid gatherings. As reported, the speech of the SAAP president collected by the media reveals that the idea behind limiting circulation and claiming exclusive control and use is what motivated this enclosure: 'It's no longer just a neighbourhood square; there's a huge flow of people who go not only to watch the sunset but also stay there all night' (Tamamoto, 2021).

Thus, the formation of these 'spheres' enables the expansion of a perception of security based on the appropriation of public space, its exclusive control, and consequently, the expulsion or management of the circulation of 'outsiders', as a way to solidify this territorial demand for security. This hypothesis gains strength, indicating that the formation of these spheres unfolds a new chapter in the long-standing processes of disputes over public spaces in São Paulo, characterized by removal processes, real estate speculation, and social reorganization (Rolnik, 2017). However, the specificity of this process of spatial segregation lies in its foundation in securitized projects oriented towards self-protection, which may not necessarily manifest as the construction of physical walls or the relocation to remote areas. Instead, it materializes through an authority mediated by monitoring cameras, orientation signs, barriers, and private watchers, all of which constrain the 'foreign' circulation from this virtual 'inside' of the sphere.

The São Paulo Inteligente Program and the Infrastructuring of Surveillance

In the same direction, in 2018, the ABESE (Brazilian Association of Electronic Security Systems Companies), with the support of the municipal government, launched the 'São Paulo Inteligente' (Smart São Paulo) program. The program aimed to create an extensive securitized sphere that would connect the surroundings of Eldorado Shopping (in Jardins Neighbourhood) to the surroundings of the Clinique Hospital (in Pinheiros Neighbourhood) (with a distance of 4 kilometres between them), interlinking internal and external surveillance and monitoring systems of both institutions with those of houses and condominiums within this space, sharing these images and information with law enforcement authorities.

According to the ABESE president, there are risks and problems specific to these neighbourhoods, which could be solved with the employment of an interconnected surveillance apparatus. The president points out that the creation and managing of this digitized enclave happened in a context of knowledge exchange between police forces, residents' demands, and private security agents perspectives:

> This program will be expanded to all other types of establishments, not only the large ones. So, as I mentioned, placing cameras in the surroundings, well-positioned, overlooking public roads, aids public security. They are like eyes; they increase the workforce in an electronic way for them. [...] For example, they presented exactly the points that had no cameras to record and to be able to, when something happened, they... so, for example: Teodoro Sampaio, which has some street vendor points, which are [...] down there. We had no monitoring there. We placed a camera to be able to see what was happening there. [...] We programmed the technology for that. (Interview 12, 2019)

Similarly, the head of security at Clinique Hospital explained that the Military Police delineated the strategic zones in the surroundings of the hospital, indicating bottlenecks and spaces where surveillance and monitoring cameras should be installed, implying the formation of a sphere:

> Because they [PMESP] have a color-coded map where they know where more incidents occur, what type of action, within that map. At the time, it was Colonel [...] from the battalion; she walked around here on foot and said: 'this is an escape route, here is a dangerous intersection, this zone is hotter for cell phone theft,' and she mapped it out. And we will place the cameras, today, exactly where she indicated. Even though she is no longer in command, the police's expertise, the data they have, is very important. [...]. So, when we combine knowledge, and you have someone

in technology willing to do this integration, it's perfect. (Interview 11, 2019)

In this sense, for both interviewed, the delineation of these security spheres and the establishment of surveillance mechanisms seek to restrict informal commerce, begging, and inhibit the effects of intense people flow in these spheres: aggression, theft, and ultimately consolidating the Hospital and the Shopping Mall as centres for monitoring this extensive area:

> For example, the external camera of the shopping mall and mine will be able to see each other, that's going to happen. For example, we have a big one at CESP, which overlooks Dr. Arnaldo [avenue], and I will be able to see here as well. There is one that looks at 'Sumaré subway station' [...] Because my patient, my employee, frequents these places, they walk around there. [...] I managed to block street vendors' access inside the building, due to access control. But what about a shopping mall? It can't control access. How does it control the entry of beggars? (Interview 11, 2019)

We observe that this plan enables both Clinique Hospital and Eldorado Shopping as infrastructures for surveillance, control, and monitoring of their surroundings, reinforcing the ties between private and public actors in the governance of the security in this space. In other words, both structures become devices for identifying and communicating risks that oversee their 'expanded' surroundings, with borders, entry points, and vulnerabilities. The accounts show that these surveillance infrastructures not only assist law enforcement in their blind spots but also take responsibility in this multi-centred arrangement of security governance, identification, and communication of patterns of suspicion. Furthermore, equipped with modern centres, facilities, and specialized personnel, they become significant local command and control centres capable of constant monitoring of deviations in their expanded surroundings, assuming authority to identify, communicate, and sometimes act on these risks.

The conversion of these units into surveillance devices, as well as the transformation of residences into supports for monitoring and risk 'sensors', indicates that security can become the language of relationships and sociability in these communal spaces. The formation of these spheres, therefore, involves constant instrumentalization and modulation of urbanization, infrastructure, and sociability projects in favour of security criteria primarily established by electronic security companies and residents' associations, rather than solely by the public authorities.

In general, the adoption of surveillance and monitoring systems, mobilized by the São Paulo municipality, accelerated the city's adherence to smart city projects, by fostering widely monitored public spaces, and the integration of data between various public administration units. As Morozov and Bria (2018) remind us, not only 'sensorization' and data integration would mark the processes of the city 'smartification', but also the increasing exchange between private and public interests—which in this context would aim to confer agility and 'efficiency' to security management. However, such 'smartification' projects overlook the dynamism of technologies, that is, their capacity to mutually reconfigure and reorder the set of interests in the spaces they are inserted into. Consequently, far from developing more efficient and robust projects, it can be speculated that such transnational security systems and strategies may reinforce spatial disputes and segregative practices in the city, granting extraordinary influence to residents and private agents in the management of the boundaries of the forming spheres.

Final Considerations

The intensification of productive globalization and the circulation of people, ideas, and capital observed in recent years has led to the consideration of security projects, technologies, and trends developed in certain contexts (mostly in the Global North) as relevant solutions in other countries. As pointed out by Peron and Paoliello (2021), there has been a significant growth in the presence of transnational technology and security consulting companies in Latin America and Brazil over the last 15 years. These transnational companies and consultancies engage with the public and private sectors, disseminating locally security models, trends, and policing standards considered 'best international practices'.

The security trends listed at the beginning of this study, including securitization of spheres, modulation of sociability, and infrastructural surveillance, aim to account for part of this set of security models that spreads globally as public–private projects. However, it would be mistaken to assume that these trends remain unchanged when transferred to other social contexts, ignoring local dynamics and hierarchies of power. Shearing and Wood (2003) assert that security nowadays should not be seen solely as a function of the State but as a dimension in which numerous non-state agents are involved in governance matters, challenging the myth of the sovereign State to think and intervene in such issues. Nevertheless, looking at the Brazilian reality makes this diagnosis even more complex due to the problematic nature of constructing the state monopoly of violence in the country (Adorno, 2002). In Brazilian major metropolises, drug trafficking, militias, and other organized groups play a significant role and constitute dynamic protection markets, refracting the decentralization dynamics of security observed in Northern Global countries. Thus, the introduction of Smart Cities programs and decentralization of security models in cities like São Paulo encounters contexts with pre-existing security arrangements, with appropriations of public spaces and the dissemination of various forms of segregation that redefine the contestation for space in the city.

As such, the processes of securitized sociability, sphere-making, and infrastructural surveillance, aligned with 'smartification' projects of security, may become mechanisms that reinforce pre-existing hierarchies and the dominance of certain social groups over specific territories. Analysing Vizinhança Solidária and City Câmeras, on the one hand, reveals how these apparatuses interact, locally disseminating these security trends. On the other hand, it is observed how these initiatives and arrangements seem to intertwine with elitist and patrimonialist forms of public space administration in São Paulo, which have been described by authors like Caldeira (2001) and Rolnik (2017). It is worth noting the potential production of a securitized sociability in the city's neighbourhoods, manifested by the residents' affiliation with particular notions of threat and security and a dichotomous demarcation between inside and outside, with circulations deemed either legitimate or illegitimate. Furthermore, these arrangements between policing practices and technologies redefine the role of the city's infrastructure as devices for information production and risk control.

The discussion we outline indicates that the current technological equipment and operational sophistication implemented in São Paulo, even though oriented to international 'best practices', do not necessarily break away from the conflicted urban design nor surpass the customary spatial and patrimonial disputes in the city. Their implementation seems to reinforce local disputes and introduce new dilemmas, such as private appropriation of public spaces, now under the argument of self-governing security. The fusion of private interests over the territory with public security strategies may dilute the notion of citizenship into one based solely on security semantics.

Undoubtedly, to confirm such suspicions, it would be necessary to go beyond the methodological limitations of this current investigation. The analysis of securitized spheres in high-income neighbourhoods in São Paulo was limited to a group of individuals with relevant purchasing power, capable of hiring moderately priced consultancies and systems, which does not represent the reality of all neighbourhoods in the city. To confirm the hypotheses presented here, further studies will be necessary to determine whether the relationship between income and the acquisition of these products can be an important variable for the pace of expansion of these security models, establishing itself as a general trend. Additionally, the analysed interviews were conducted with individuals connected to associations and organizations, which even limited the contact with residents during ethnographic incursions in the neighbourhoods. Other studies using various methodologies may identify the breadth of these processes and practices, demonstrating changes and adverse experiences resulting from the expansion of these security models in Southern Global metropolises, in order to understand the consolidation of these movements as trends.

Ethics Statement

The authors declare that the research presented in this chapter was conducted with the utmost integrity and adherence to ethical principles. All data collection procedures were carried out in accordance with relevant institutional and national guidelines. Informed consent was obtained from all participants involved in the study. Any potential conflicts of interest have been disclosed. The authors affirm their commitment to transparency and accountability in research practices.

References

Abrahamsem, R., & Williams, M. (2007). Securing the City: Private Security Companies and Non-State Authority in Global Governance. *International Relations, 21*(2), 237–253. https://doi.org/10.1177/0047117807077006

Adorno, S. (2002). O monopólio estatal da violência na sociedade brasileira contemporânea. In: S. MICELI (Ed.), *O que ler na Ciência Social brasileira, 1970–2002* [What to Read in the Brazilian Social Sciences] (1st ed, pp. 1–32). NEV/USP.

Alvarez, M. C., Salla, F., & Souza, L. A. (2004). Políticas de Segurança Pública em São Paulo: uma perspectiva histórica. *Justiça e História, 4*(8), 173–199.

Amoore, L., & Goede, M. (2008). *Risk and the War on Terror.* Routledge. https://doi.org/10.4324/9780203927700

Bigo, D. (2016). Rethinking Security at the Crossroad of International Relations and Criminology. *The British Journal of Criminology, 56*(6), 1068–1086. https://doi.org/10.1093/bjc/azw062

Bigo, D., & Tsoukala, A. (2008). Understanding (In)Security. In D. Bigo, & A. Tsoukala (Eds.), *Terror, Insecurity and Liberty* (pp. 1–9). Routledge. https://doi.org/10.4324/9780203926765-6

Buzan, B., Waever, O., & Wilde, J. (1998). Security: A New Framework for Analysis. *Lynne Rienner Publishers.* https://doi.org/10.1515/9781685853808

Caldeira, T. P. R. (2001). *City of Walls: Crime, Segregation and Citizenship in São Paulo.* University of California Press. https://doi.org/10.1525/978052 0341593

Camp, J., & Heatherton, C. (2016). *Policing the Planet: Why the Policing Crisis Led to Black Lives Matter.* Verso.

Davis, M. (2018). *City of Quartz: Excavating the Future in Los Angeles*. Verso Books.

Deleuze, G., & Guattari, F. (1993). *A Thousand Platos: Capitalism and Schizophrenia*. University of Minnesota Press.

Ericsson, R., & Haggerty, K. (2002). The Policing of Risk. In T. Baker & J. Simon (Eds.), *Embracing Risk: The Changing Culture of Insurance and Responsibility* (pp. 238–272). The University of Chicago Press. https://doi.org/10.7208/chicago/9780226035178.003.0010

Fenavist. (2019). *VI ESSEG: Estudo do Setor de Segurança Privada*. [S. l.]: Editora Gráfica Bernardi Ltda. https://fenavist.org.br/wp-content/uploads/2019/07/ESSEG-19_WEB1.pdf

Franzon, D. J. (2018). *A eleição de João Doria Junior: a ascensão do partido de modelo empresarial?* Dissertação de Mestrado em Ciências Sociais. PUC-SP.

Garland, D. (2002). *The Culture of Control: Crime and Social Order in Contemporary City*. Oxford University Press. https://doi.org/10.1093/acprof:oso/9780199258024.001.0001

Godoy, M. (2017). Após Favela Naval, PM modificou processos. *O Estado de S. Paulo*. 2 September 2017. https://www.estadao.com.br/sao-paulo/apos-favela-naval-pm-modificou-processos/

Governo Do Estado De São Paulo. (2017). Vizinhança Solidária: programa da PM reduz assaltos em residências. https://www.saopaulo.sp.gov.br/spnoticias/vizinhanca-solidaria/

Haggerty, K., & Ericsson, R. (2000). The Surveillant Assemblage. *British Journal of Sociology, 51*(4), 605–622. https://doi.org/10.1080/00071310020015280

Klauser, F. (2010). Splintering Spheres of Security: Peter Sloterdijk and the Contemporary Fortress City. *Society and Space, 28*, 326–340. https://doi.org/10.1068/d14608

Luque-Ayala, A., & Marvin, S. (2016). The Maintenance of Urban Circulation: An Operational Logic of Infrastructural Control. *Society and Space, 1–18*,. https://doi.org/10.1177/0263775815611422

Morozov, E., & Bria, F. (2018). *Rethinking the Smart City: Democratizing Urban Technology*. Rosa Luxemburg Stiftung.

Nail, T. (2017). What is an Assemblage? *SubStance, 46*(1), 21–37. https://doi.org/10.1353/sub.2017.0001

Peron, A., & Alvarez, M. C. (2019). Governing the City: The Detecta Surveillance System in São Paulo and the Role of Private Vigilantism in the Public Security. *Sciences & Actions Sociales, 12*, 33–68. https://doi.org/10.3917/sas.012.0033

Peron, A., & Paoliello, T. (2021). Fear as a Product, Continuum as a Solution: The Role of Private Companies in the Transnational Diffusion of Zero Tolerance Policing to Brazil. *Small Wars & Insurgencies*. https://doi.org/10. 1080/09592318.2021.1904541

Polícia Militar Do Estado De São Paulo. (2017). *Nossa Polícia Comunitária*. Diretoria de Polícia comunitária e de Direitos Humanos.

Rodrigues, T. (2012). Segurança planetária, entre o climático e o humano. *Ecopolítica, 3*, 5–41.

Rolnik, R. (2017). *Territórios em conflito: São Paulo, espaço, história e política*. [Territories Under Conflict: São Paulo, Space, History, and Politics]. Três Estrelas.

Santos, B. (2017). Dória anuncia em vídeo o 'maior programa de privatização de SP'. *Exame*. 14 February 2017. https://exame.com/brasil/doria-anuncia-em-video-o-maior-programa-de-privatizacao-de-sp/

Sassen, S. (2006). *Territory, Authority, Rights: From Medieval to Global Assemblages*. Princeton University Press.

Shearing, C., & Wood, J. (2000). Reflections on the Governance of Security, A Normative Inquiry. *Police Practice, 1*(4), 437–476.

Shearing, C., & Wood, J. (2003). Nodal Governance, Democracy, and the New 'Denizens.' *Journal of Law and Society, 30*(3), 400–419. https://doi.org/10. 1111/1467-6478.00263

Skolnick, J. & Bayley, D. (1988). *Community Policing: Issues and Practices Around the World*. National Institute of Justice.

Tamamoto, V. (2021). Associações pedem e prefeitura acata: Praça do Pôr do Sol começa a ser cercada. *Veja São Paulo*. 11 February 2021. https://vejasp. abril.com.br/cidades/prefeitura-praca-do-por-do-sol-cercada/

Terpstra, J., Fyfe, N., & Salet, R. (2019). The Abstract Police: A Conceptual Exploration of Unintended Changes of Police Organizations. *The Police Journal: Theory, Practice and Principles, 92*(4), 339–359. https://doi.org/10. 1177/0032258X18817999

Venceslau, P. (2017). Vamos transformar SP em 'Smart City', diz Doria. *O Estado de S. Paulo*. 13 April 2017. https://www.estadao.com.br/sao-paulo/vamos-transformar-sp-em-smart-city-diz-doria/

5

Militarized Managerialism and the Bolsonarist Dystopia in Brazil

Bruno Cardoso ⓘ

Focusing on results is the difference between success and commonplace. But what are results? A result is an effect. A result is a consequence. Results are not born when they happen. It is born first, the result of the quality of your decisions, actions and convergence of efforts. Therefore, a positive result comes from the legitimate spirit of leadership within the MO (military organization) at all levels. It is command action. (System of Excellence in the Military Organisation [SEMO], 2008, p. 18)

In this chapter, I analyse the relationship between the rise of the far right in Brazil, culminating in the government of Jair Bolsonaro (2019–2022), and a model of thinking and managing the state that I call *militarized managerialism*. Based on research into the Integrated Command and Control Centre in the city of Rio de Janeiro, from its conception to the first years of operation, I relate two important

B. Cardoso (✉)
Federal University of Rio de Janeiro, Rio de Janeiro, Brazil
e-mail: brunovcardoso@ufrj.br

© The Author(s), under exclusive license to Springer Nature Switzerland AG 2024
T. Ø. Kuldova et al. (eds.), *Policing and Intelligence in the Global Big Data Era, Volume I*, Palgrave's Critical Policing Studies,
https://doi.org/10.1007/978-3-031-68326-8_5

moments in the local public security scenario to Bolsonaro's conception of government: the cycle of mega-events (2013 to 2016) and the Federal Intervention of 2018. The aspects of contemporary politics relating to the Brazilian case, while retaining their peculiarities, illuminate characteristics of the international wave of 'liberal illiberalism' or 'illiberal liberalism' (Furedi, 2022; Laruelle, 2022; Rupnik, 2012) or 'conservative populism' (Johnson, 2022).

Some seldom-explored facts, even in Brazil, presented in this chapter, are helpful to understand the trajectory thus far of what is being called *bolsonarismo*, or bolsonarism. Some other elements have been considered by several Brazilian authors, such as digital communications (Cesarino, 2020); media and judiciary persecution to the Workers' Party (Martins et al., 2019); the electoral weakening of the centre-right (Nicolau, 2020); the Armed Forces' dissatisfaction with the investigation of crimes committed during the 1964–1985 military dictatorship (Leirner, 2020); the economic crisis (Pinheiro Machado & Scalco, 2020); and also the worldwide far-right wave (Da Empoli, 2019). Along with the phenomena just outlined, and a few other factors, I argue that what I term 'militarized-managerialism' is a key piece of the puzzle in the real bolsonarist dystopia.

This chapter is the result of over a decade of research, begun in 2006 and ended in early 2019. Throughout this time, I observed a fast-advancing state militarization process, culminating in the Bolsonaro administration (2019–2022). This chapter seeks to unpack the relationship between neoliberalism, New Public Management (NPM) and the security technology industry, particularly through what is conventionally called 'command and control'. Together, NPM and security technologies shape state agents' action and government models (Cardoso, 2018).

Bolsonarism

Over the course of the 2010s, Jair Bolsonaro went from being an unimportant federal deputy from Rio de Janeiro, with a captive electorate among military personnel, police officers, and their families, to becoming the leading right-wing figure in Brazil and one of the country's most charismatic politicians. Since the 2018 presidential election, in which he was elected, the term *bolsonarismo* has been increasingly used by the press, voters, and analysts (Andrade, 2021; Cesarino, 2019; Cardoso, 2020; Gonçalves & Caldeira Neto, 2022; Pinheiro Machado & Scalco, 2020), and it brings together some of the characteristics of the Brazilian branch of far-right populism (Anderson, 2019).

A standout feature of bolsonarism lies in its connection to the military sphere and the revisionist approach to the historical period of the last dictatorship (1964–1985), characterized by censorship, persecution, torture, and the murder of dissenters. In both his 2018 presidential campaign and his bid for re-election in 2022, Bolsonaro selected two army generals as his vice-presidents and surrounded himself with military personnel among his key advisors and counsellors (Schurster & Silva, 2021). Throughout the Bolsonaro administration, there has been a significant increase in the number of military personnel holding positions of trust within the civilian administrative structure (Nozaki, 2021).

Bolsonarism is also distinctly characterized by an unwavering advocacy for police violence and lethality, a pronounced punitive bias, and a firm rejection of human rights policies (Silva, 2019). Beyond championing the interests of the police and military and endorsing authoritarianism and aggressiveness as governing approaches for the state and the national population, Jair Bolsonaro has implemented several measures to deregulate firearm possession, leading to an increase in the number of armed individuals on the streets. Bolsonaro and his supporters consistently emphasize their virile images, often echoing sexist, homophobic, and violent rhetoric (Brito, 2022; Mendonça & Mendonça, 2021).

Another crucial element of bolsonarism involved advocating for conservative moral agendas, particularly the resistance against 'gender ideology', 'identitarianism', and 'feminism' (Aguiar & Pereira, 2019; Duarte & Cesar, 2021). Bolsonaro successfully gained support from a substantial portion of the conservative Christian electorate, especially evangelicals, based on these agendas (Almeida, 2019; Gracino Jr et al., 2021). Far-right ideologues and influencers consistently underscore the need for constant mobilization and struggle against the perceived omnipresent threat of communism or 'cultural Marxism' (Chagas et al., 2019; Lacerda, 2022). Both Bolsonaro's speeches and those of his followers, as well as his educational and cultural policies, have been characterized by anti-intellectualism (Sinhoretto, 2022).

In the economic realm, Bolsonarism is distinguished by an emphatic advocacy for the tenets of liberalism (Carneiro, 2019), featuring a libertarian inclination akin to the alt-right in the United States (Cooper, 2021). The glorification of business and entrepreneurship as a model, coupled with a disdain for anything associated with political decisions or state intervention, was, in the words of the most outspoken Bolsonarist influencers, intertwined with the fight against the perceived communist threat. Over his four-year presidency, Bolsonaro advanced an economic agenda primarily centred on deregulation, spanning from labour relations to environmental licensing rules, encompassing areas such as weapons and pesticides.

The final aspect I will underscore in this brief overview of bolsonarism is its communication strategy. The WhatsApp messaging app has served as the primary channel for disseminating political (mis)information since well before the 2018 elections, circulating fake news and memes for replication (Bastos Cesarino, 2020; dos Santos et al., 2019; Recuero et al., 2020). WhatsApp and smartphones persist as the most extensively utilized mediums for spreading alternative facts (Tripodi, 2017), and throughout the Bolsonaro administration, this activity was orchestrated from within the government's communication structure, emanating from what became known as the 'Cabinet of Hate' (Mello, 2020; Negreiros, 2022).

A Note on Methodology

This chapter builds upon a research in socio-technical centres managed by the Rio de Janeiro military police.[1] Both ethnographic fieldworks were conducted, six years apart, in two different Command and Control

---

[1] The police structure in Brazil is divided across different realms, each with specific responsibilities: within the states, there is a distinction between the military police (PM) (engaged in ostensible policing and confrontation) and the civil police (PC) (focused on investigative and judicial functions). On a national scale, there is an additional separation between the federal highway police (PRF), responsible for policing roads, and the federal police (PF), handling

systems, where the latter system was presented as an 'evolution' or an expansion of the first. The first ethnography was conducted in 2008, for my doctoral thesis research, where during the 7 months of fieldwork, I spent 8 to 10 weekly hours in two distinct control rooms operated by the Rio de Janeiro military police. In one room, I sat by myself, at the back, in the dark, mostly watching, nearly incognito. I talked to those who came to me and did some interviews. In the other control room, much smaller, where the lights were always on, I sat amidst operators, interacting with them all the time, ending up as a character in my own ethnographic report (Cardoso, 2014).

The second ethnography was rather different. By then, I was already a professor at the Federal University of Rio de Janeiro and my ethnographic visits to the Integrated Command and Control Centre lasted much longer. Over 4 years (2013 to 2017), with irregular frequency, I conducted weekly visits during some months, but sometimes there were more than month-long intervals between visits to the building where I conducted my research. This time, I conducted more interviews, had lunch with managers from the security department, attended meetings where mega-event security operators were instructed about the action and the training for police vehicle dispatch system operators and so on. In addition, this research's empirical content was also built by reading official documents, strategy plans, and reports about purchases made by the government, as well as regular visits to annual security and defence technology fairs in Rio de Janeiro.

Throughout these years, I have followed the implementation of two Command and Control (C2) systems (or the expansion of one system into another), structured in two spaces: the Command and Control Centre (CCC)[2] (Cardoso, 2014) and the Integrated Command and Control Centre (CICC, in Portuguese), a massive building built from the ground up, representing the largest investment ever made in security in the state of Rio de Janeiro and the country's biggest security facility (Cardoso, 2019a). Starting with CICC, the federal government

---

federalized investigations based on factors such as their importance, the jurisdiction involved, or the interstate nature of the case.

[2] Located at the last floor in the city's main train station's tower (Central do Brasil), built in the 1930s.

crafted and implemented an ambitious public security policy, utilizing the Command and Control Integrated System (SICC) as its central component. This system formed the backbone of security preparations for the mega-event cycle in Brazil, with a specific emphasis on Rio de Janeiro. The 2014 World Cup, in particular, stimulated the creation of a security policy that, if not exactly centralized, has in its alleged integration capacity[3] the possibility to centralize or decentralize security, according to the situation (Cardoso, 2013). The project of centralizing, unifying, and integrating was even more daring, considering that public security in Brazil is constitutionally a local responsibility, not a federal one (Fontoura et al., 2009).[4] The optimization of security force actions, guided by situational analyses, involves 'modulating' the integration and coordination among institutional agents based on each specific case. This approach results in varied compositions of actors and institutions, regulated by operational protocols that establish a clear chain of command and obedience (Hirata & Cardoso, 2016).

'Technological Modernization'

'Technological modernization', a native category referring to the purchase of new or replacement technological devices such as computers, cameras, radios, and tablets, was treated by authorities as a public security policy in Rio de Janeiro (Cardoso, 2013). Technologies were presented as capable of solving, in one way or another, historical-structural problems of local police action, in a 'technosolutionist' way (Morozov, 2013), detached most of the time from the objective results it may bring. Certainly, one of the supporting pillars of this drive towards 'technological modernization' is a booming international technology market, where

---

[3] Despite the managers' repeated promises of integrating the different technological systems within the SICC, challenges surfaced right from the start. These challenges involved issues such as institutional distrust among police forces and incompatibility between the computer systems chosen by state governments for their respective police forces.

[4] Additionally, each of the 27 states in the federation possesses two police forces—military and civilian—with distinct functions. In the case of Rio de Janeiro, there is a well-documented history of rivalry between these forces, stemming from disagreements over performance, disputes over financial resources, the use of information, or political influence.

fortunes are flowing and which employs many former public security and defence officials (Bennett & Haggerty, 2012; Bigo, 2006b; Cardoso, 2016; Kuldova, 2022).

I have been treating the security technologies adopted by the police in Rio de Janeiro as socio-technical assemblages (or *agencements*, in French) (Callon, 2003). Briefly, I assume that devices, platforms, and systems are a composition between several heterogeneous elements—or actors— such as people, transmission networks, spaces, documents, algorithms, vehicles, and so on (Latour, 2005). I assume that making a 'techno-logical modernization' work as planned is, in practice, an exception (Akrich, 1993). It takes the intense and uninterrupted articulation of many different actors committed to the task. This does not mean that these technologies do not 'work' in some way, that they do not have effects on public security. They are indeed the object of dispute among interested actors, which frequently leads to uses that are quite different from those that justified their acquisition.

Urban Violence and Inequality in Rio

To understand the promises involved in the implementation of these technologies and their political effects it is necessary to explain the local security context and the problems they sought to eliminate. First, one must not lose sight of the fact that Brazil is a very unequal country, and that the city of Rio de Janeiro, the country's second-largest city, is even more so. For example, in the world ranking based on the Gini index of 167 countries, in increasing order of inequality, Brazil is in 150th. While the Brazilian index is 0.5292, Rio de Janeiro's is even higher: 0.62.[5] However, territorial inequalities within Rio de Janeiro are not limited to the income of its inhabitants. Most important for the dynamics of security are the multiple inequalities that overlap in urban territories, especially in relation to favelas—the poor neighbourhoods often located on the slopes of the many hills that characterize the local

---

[5] In Gini index, 0 is for absolute equality (all economic resources distributed equally to everyone) and 1 is for absolute inequality (all resources belong to a single person).

terrain (Valladares, 2016). In these territories, disadvantages in public services, urban infrastructure, and civil, and human rights accumulate (Machado da Silva, 2008). Life in the favela is marked by precariousness, scarcity, informality, and violence, be it by drug gangs or police forces (Machado da Silva, 2010).

Organized crime in Rio de Janeiro is marked by armed territorial occupation, particularly within favelas and other impoverished neighbourhoods (Misse, 2007). These areas are controlled by four major criminal groups: the *Comando Vermelho* (Red Commmand), *Amigos dos Amigos* (Friends of the Friends), and *Terceiro Comando* (Third Command) factions, and by militias formed mainly by current and former agents of the state. The dispute over these territories—and the many illegal businesses involved—make these criminal groups live in a constant race for heavy weapons, often seized by the police and sold by the same police to other criminal groups. It is not hard to imagine why this scenario makes Rio de Janeiro a city with very high homicide rates, which are, too, very unevenly distributed throughout its territory. In areas under dispute, shootings, executions, curfews, police raids, home invasions, slaughters, and torture are quite common. A different scenario is found in areas where territorial domination is consolidated and, especially, in relation to the neighbourhoods of the city's upper and upper middle classes (GENI, 2021).

The police play a very important role in disputes for territorial domination. First, through what Michel Misse (2018) calls 'political merchandises', referring to the police corruption and its intrinsic relationship with the increasing violence in Rio de Janeiro. Freedom and life are turned into commodities and traded illegally—through threats or violence—by State agents who individually appropriate State prerogatives. These agents negotiate with captured criminals whether they will be arrested, tortured, or killed, with drug dealers whether they will have their weapons and drugs seized.

It is also not for nothing that police forces were first to demonstrate strong support to Jair Bolsonaro in Rio de Janeiro, becoming the future president's most loyal voter base. The combination of violent urban crime, armed territorial dispute and occupation, and the extensive police corruption and violence in the Rio de Janeiro's metropolitan area makes public security one of the region's main concerns, and thus also a highly appealing political agenda (Machado da Silva, 2010; Misse, 2009, 2018).

But there is another reason for Rio to be considered the laboratory for bolsonarism in Brazil, besides being the base for the president's core voters, as well as for two of his politician sons (the third was elected by São Paulo, although he has scarcely lived in the city). In Rio de Janeiro, the militias initially emerged when current and former police officers actively formed criminal organizations. These groups offered protection and security services, adopting a true mafia style. Additionally, they controlled essential services like cable TV and natural gas, while also dominating an illicit real estate market and engaging in drug trafficking (Geni, 2021). Militias operate mainly in low-income areas, where they also have strong influence over voters' choice (Souza Alves, 2008). Bolsonaro's family actively supported militias from their inception, portraying them as an alternative to the armed wing of the illegal drug market that defined local crime since the 1980s. Furthermore, substantial evidence exists linking the Bolsonaro family directly to these criminal organizations (Manso, 2020). Not for nothing, voter turnout for Jair Bolsonaro and his sons has always been most expressive in the state capital's many militia-ruled areas, as well as in military residential neighbourhoods.

Violence statistics in Rio are, indeed, very high. The state homicide rate in 2018, for example, was 37.6 for each 100 thousand citizens, much higher than the already elevated national average, 27.8 (Atlas da Violência, 2023).[6] Within this context of daily violence and crime, strong support exists for discourses that endorse the use of violent police action as a primary security public policy, with a focus on high lethality rates. Concurrently, there is a growing public demand (reflected in newspapers and TV) and population backing (as indicated by opinion polls) for investments to enhance the strength, equipment, and lethality of security forces. Many individuals believe that the armed forces should join police forces in combating urban violence and crime. Although such collaborations have occurred a few times, the outcomes were not significant, and numerous complaints of rights violations arose (Viana, 2021).

---

[6] https://forumseguranca.org.br/atlas-da-violencia/.

Tying this all together, a vague platform about efficiency, management, and technology appears as the horizon to be chased by the state government (Cardoso, 2019a). But to understand how these trends, policies, violence, and fears intersect, we must go back to the mega-event cycle that marked the 2010s in Brazil and, more particularly, in Rio de Janeiro.

Mega-Event's Cycle and SICC

Between 2013 and 2016, Brazil hosted the FIFA Confederations Cup (2013) and the FIFA World Cup (2014), while Rio de Janeiro, specifically, also hosted the World Youth Day (2013) and the Summer Olympic Games (2016). All four events happened entirely in Rio or held their pinnacle (the finals) in the city. When FIFA and the IOC made the decision for Brazil to host three of the world's biggest sporting events in three years, public safety became one of the most recurrent concerns in the press. In addition to the typical problems faced by many of Brazil's large cities—especially the high rates of property crime, crimes against life, and a pattern of violence higher than in most regions of the world where there is no official war—the mega-events also brought concerns about possible terrorist attacks. Similar concerns influenced the preparation of all the mega-events held after the 9/11 2001 attacks on the World Trade Center in New York, as extensively discussed by other authors Giulianotti and Klauser (2010, 2011), significantly impacting the costs of hosting these events.

In all cities and countries that have hosted mega sporting events, those responsible for security have essentially adopted the same solution: the creation or enhancement of command-and-control centres and systems (Bennett & Haggerty, 2012; Samatas, 2011). Brazil followed suit, and in 2012, the federal government released the first version of the Strategic Security Plan for the, 2014 World Cup (2012), announcing the establishment of the SICC. Initially, the SICC comprised 13 integrated command and control centres, helicopters for aerial imaging, trucks functioning as mobile CICCs, among other elements (Cardoso, 2013; Hirata & Cardoso, 2016). Each of the 12 host cities for the World Cup constructed an integrated command and control centre, all interconnected through a network consisting of software, personnel, and digital devices. In Brasilia, the capital, the Ministry of Justice constructed a 13th centre, intended to integrate all local centres and serve as the highest and most comprehensive level for decision-making processes, monitoring, and planning of national actions. Subsequently, CICCs were built and inaugurated in all the country's capitals and some border towns, completing the SICC. In Brasilia, the Federal Police was the primary agency operating the CICC, while in the states, the local military police took prominence, although the involvement of multiple agencies was part of the operational logic of these centres.

The Brazilian government has largely presented the SICC as the main 'security legacy' of the upcoming mega-events (Cardoso, 2013). However, while the SICC played a crucial role, I will argue that the genuine main legacy was the 'militarized managerial logic', which to a large extent both elucidates and has underpinned the Bolsonaro government. This logic revolves around security technologies, and I will elaborate on them here. Both mega-events and command and control centres are acknowledged agents of expansion of the 'new military urbanism' (Graham, 2014). This concept can be summarized, albeit incompletely, as the enduring transformation of urban spaces, both in central and peripheral countries, into territories governed under the premise of war, employing war weapons, and warfare. As mentioned earlier, this transformation has turned Brazil into a fertile ground for the expansion of the international security and defence market, consequently strengthening the influence of the international security technology industry's lobby (Bigo, 2006a, 2006b; Guittet & Jeandesboz, 2010; Hoijtink, 2014).

CICC-RJ

Rio de Janeiro's CICC is the largest and most imposing in Brazil. Despite the planned opening in 2010, it was only in 2013, on the eve of the FIFA Confederations Cup, that Rio de Janeiro's security department inaugurated the building. However, it remained incomplete and notably empty, as witnessed during my various fieldwork visits. The construction costs also surpassed the initial estimate of 36 million reais (Cardoso, 2014), amounting to just over 100 million reais (Hirata & Cardoso, 2016). However, since its planning (in 2009), authorities and managers have repeated that such a significant investment would lead to a paradigm shift in the way security forces act. For the first, CICC would result in a greater integration and coordination of the various Brazilian state security agencies, which would start working together despite their history of rivalry and dispute over resources. For the second, these processes would translate into the production and analysis of criminal data from a cartographic visualization platform. This would lead to police actions based on intelligence and information, thus increasing the efficiency of the police, who would be better prepared to confront criminal groups and liberate territories dominated by them.

The building is structured (literally, in its floor division) to cater to 3 different scenarios: (1) the day-to-day management of public security and urban order, in the first floor; (2); the operational management of different agencies in non-routine situations, in the second floor; (3) crisis management in the third floor. Although CICC was mainly operated by the Rio de Janeiro military police, its main purpose was the integration, or coordinated operation, of various agencies with attributions relating to public security, urban order, or civil defence (Hirata & Cardoso, 2016). Whether daily or on a case-by-case basis, the building was staffed with agents from the four police forces branches (military, civil, federal, and highway patrol), the Brazilian intelligence agency (Abin) and the Armed Forces, as well as representatives from companies providing technological infrastructure. There was even a space set aside on the top floor for the state governor—or even the president—where they could follow, coordinate, or manage big operations or crisis.

Command and Control

Command and control is a 'military doctrine' officially adopted in Brazil—by decree—by the ministry of defence in 2006 (Cardoso, 2013).[7] As explained at the third edition of Doctrine document

---

[7] (Normative Ordinance No. 1888/EMD/MD, of 29 December 2006).

(Normative Ordinance No. 1691/EMCFA/MD, of 5th August 2015), Command and Control is the

> Science and art that deals with the functioning of a chain of command and, in this conception, basically involves three components:
>
> a. legitimately invested authority supported by an organisation from which the decisions that materialise the exercise of command emanate and into which the information necessary for the exercise of control flows;
> b. the system of a decision-making process that allows orders to be formulated, establishes the flow of information and ensures mechanisms designed to guarantee full compliance with orders; and
> c. the structure, including personnel, equipment, doctrine and technology necessary for the authority to monitor the development of operations (Doctrine for the Military Command and Control System, 2015, p. 15).

Command and Control is structured as a unicentric network (in contrast to polycentric networks) with a highly hierarchical, well-defined chain of command and obedience (Walker et al., 2017). In spite of the numerous disparities between the two models, discussions surrounding Command and Control consistently introduced a managerial framework implicitly rooted in the principles of New Public Management (NPM). The central characteristic of NPM involves viewing the state as a company, emphasizing goals, benchmarking techniques, partnerships with the private sector, and accountability, among other factors (Dardot & Laval, 2014; Wathne, 2020).

More precisely, different police officers and security managers from the Rio de Janeiro's government presented the CICC to me as the main way of implementing this managerial logic through an argument I have been calling 'technical overdetermination' (Cardoso, 2014), that is, assuming that a simple acquisition of a technological innovation would have the effect of fulfilling, in itself, the promises and expectations it brings. In the case of CICC, as was often repeated by various managers, this would represent a 'paradigm shift' in the ways of security forces acting, through a process in which machines and software would do everything, and the human beings working with them would amount to little more than cogs in the machine. The ongoing technological modernization seemed to erase or make insignificant the entire history of violence, corruption, and structural inefficiency of Rio de Janeiro's security forces. As I was able to verify on various occasions, as a consequence of this 'technical overdetermination', staff training, and education was sensibly neglected.[8] However, even though the promised paradigm shift did not occur, the Command and Control Integrated Centre had significant effects on state actions. Let us see how this happens in effect, in each CICC scenario.

Different Scenarios

In the first scenario, in the day-to-day management of public safety and urban order, all work is conducted through the mediation of activity management software products, sold by security technology companies, who define, in designing these same software products, the goals, and possibilities of long-distance control (Law, 1984), as well as offering the means for agent inspection and coordination. Thus, the state becomes 'privatized', in that it is increasingly designed by security technology firms (Cardoso, 2018). In this process, important data about the urban landscape and population is produced and shared with these companies, and police work is often lost in achieving goals based on benchmarking strategies embedded in these software products. Responding to evaluation mechanisms becomes the aim of labour activities (Cardoso, 2019b). For instance, as the duration to conclude calls made through the military police hotline (190) stands as a key productivity indicator, police officers handling call responses and dispatching vehicles occasionally, especially in instances of threats or marital violence, strive to persuade callers that the situation could be resolved without police intervention (Cardoso & Hirata, 2017). The objective of this approach is not to create a safer

---

[8] One afternoon in 2014, I observed the training of a new class of video surveillance system operators. The process took around 30 minutes, and only the instructor had access to the single computer used for instruction.

city or safeguard the physical well-being of women seeking police assistance, but rather to diminish the response time and the duration of call responses.

The second scenario consists of non-routine situations, albeit preplanned, either as part of an annual calendar (Carnival, Pride Parade, New Year's Eve) or instigated by political groups (protests and demonstrations). In this scenario, various agencies should collaborate in a coordinated manner. Militarized operations transition into routine, and mega-events, festivals, Carnival, planned raids in favelas, protests, and even the policing of everyday life come to be regarded as a war effort. This entails the deployment of disproportionate force and contingents.

The third scenario envisioned may involve the intensification of one of the previous scenarios, which, for some reason, escalates into a crisis (like a protest turning violent and slipping out of police control), or an unforeseen major event (such as terrorist attacks or a wave of coordinated attacks by armed criminal groups, as witnessed in São Paulo in May 2006; Feltran, 2018). In such instances, a Crisis Cabinet is to be established, under the command of the head of the executive power (state governor or even the president of the republic).

The Constitution of Militarized Managerialism

Treating public security as war and identifying a portion of the population as enemies to be (physically) eliminated is far from new in Rio de Janeiro (Leite, 2012) or in Brazil (Hirata, 2015; Souza, 2015; Viana, 2021). The high rate of police killings did not commence with mega-events, nor was it significantly affected by them. Truth be told, there was no substantial rupture in Rio de Janeiro's public security, nor a genuine paradigm shift in agents' actions. What is new, at least in its twenty-first century version, is the militarization of state action in various fields, such as education and health, both in their management style and in the occupation of various roles by police and military officers, some in retirement. Under the Bolsonaro government, for example, 216 civic-military schools have been created (Alfano, 2023), the entire top echelon of the

Ministry of Health was occupied by military personnel during the Covid-19 pandemic, and in 2020, more than 100 police and military personnel were employed in positions of trust in socio-environmental management (Abraji, 2020).

This movement is supported by a myth of 'military as good managers' (Cardoso, 2019a), stemming from a series of rhetorical 'translations'. The initial translation is the equivalence between authoritarianism and behavioural control. Thus, only through a military-like authority rationale would it be possible to prevent undue behaviour from agents involved in government action. This is the reason, for example, for the Bolsonaro government's creation and rapid expansion of the civic-military schools model, where police officers are integrated into the routine functioning of schools and are responsible for disciplining students' bodies (Foucault, 1975). The second translation associates corruption exclusively with *individual* actions taken by morally reprehensible agents (Kuldova et al., 2024). This leads us to the third translation, where a military-like authority would be capable of 'disciplining and punishing' these bad actors, effectively preventing corruption. Jair Bolsonaro and the generals around him, especially Augusto Heleno and Hamilton Mourão (who also served as his vice-president), frequently mobilized—during the elections and in government—the sophistry that there would be no corruption in the Brazilian Armed Forces, citing the principles of personal honour, military punditry, and class decorum, as laid down in the Brazilian Army's Disciplinary Regulations (R-4).

The fourth translation asserts that command and control (centralized decision-making and technologies ensuring rule and obedience) would be equivalent to management styles associated with NPM, an idea that emerged both in my ethnographic research and in the convergence of the military and neoliberalism in contemporary Brazil (an aspect of bolsonarism) (Andrade, 2021). In my initial research interview, while the CICC building was still in construction, a colonel and a major from the military police, both working in the 'Command and Control Superintendence', presented a PowerPoint they had created. One of the initial slides distinguished between 'bureaucracy' and the 'networked company', referencing Manuel Castells' book *The Rise of the Network Society* (Castells, 2009). As they proceeded with the explanation, I realized that Castells' analysis was regarded as normative, serving as a model to be embraced for achieving efficiency and modernity. The fifth translation, also mirroring the implementation of NPM in Brazil, associates politicians with corruption and private interests, contrasting them with expert technicians who are depicted as efficient and devoted to the public interest. Jair Bolsonaro brought up this issue on multiple occasions, during election campaigns and throughout his administration (Correio Brasiliense, 2018; Estado de Minas, 2018; Graeml, 2023).

The sixth translation involves the depoliticization of military officers, portraying them as 'expert technicians'. It is noteworthy that Brazilian republican history, in all its phases, is marked by actual or attempted military coups and dictatorship, along with other forms of interference. Furthermore, no less than 10 out of the 31 presidents who governed the country were or had been military officers at some point (including Jair Bolsonaro). Additionally, dozens of military or police officers currently serve in Congress, illustrating the profound integration of the military into Brazilian politics.

The seventh translation contrasts technique, truth, and efficiency with ideology, depicting the latter as the origin of moral corruption. A prominent example in Brazil is the far-right 'School without a Party' movement, highly active in the Brazilian political discourse, particularly regarding education and sexuality. This movement advocates for the de-ideologization of Brazilian education in favour of truth and technique (Vaz, 2023). The eighth translation involves equating ideology with the Left/communism, contending that the Right/conservatism safeguards society, primarily through the defence of family and private property, against a significant international conspiracy (Miskolci & Baliero, 2023).

However, these translations alone cannot explain the rise of the militarized-managerial rationale in Brazil, which precedes the Bolsonaro administration. It is precisely here that we must return to the other elements outlined earlier: the mega-events cycle and the CICCs. The aggressive business lobby, along with the concern about public security during the mega-event cycle, propelled the SICC to assume the role of event management's backbone. Simultaneously, the CICCs, with their institutional design, emerged as the primary material security legacy of these events, transitioning the exceptional policing of mega-event seasons into a routine form of everyday policing. These CICCs are increasingly integrated into daily government operations, evolving into 'obligatory passage points' (Latour, 1988) for a growing number of situations. Therefore, they influence state actions, as the most-operative actors in these 'centres of calculation' (Latour, 1987)—police and/or military officers— increase their interference in a wide range of issues. The composition of CICC, thereby, gives shape to the state itself, more and more constituted by technology companies, security software products, and police and military officers (Cardoso, 2016). In addition, a core characteristic of these software products is that, by producing a large number of measurement and control possibilities, they also allow the constant application of benchmarking techniques and the creation of positive results about their own efficiency, even if their relevance is uncertain or doubtful (Cardoso, 2019b). It is, however, enough to create a quite superficial illusion of efficient management since they can choose any performance indicator to 'prove' this 'efficiency'. And—as an important factor in this argument— through its social-technical materiality, CICC facilitates the coupling[9] of militarized urbanism and NPM principles (Cardoso, 2019a).

Federal Military Intervention in Rio de Janeiro

A few months prior to the 2016 Summer Olympics, the financial crisis that hit the state of Rio de Janeiro in 2015, led the local government to declare a state of emergency. The significant reversal of the decline in poverty and inequality over the past decade in Brazil, along with a sharp drop in revenue in the state of Rio de Janeiro,[10] had a considerable impact on local public security. Government security

---

[9] The 'enrolment', per Michel Callon and John Law (1982).

[10] The Brazilian Congress, in 2010, approved a law that modified the allocation of royalties derived from oil exploration. Previously, these royalties were entirely directed to the producing states, with Rio de Janeiro being the primary beneficiary. However, under the new law, the funds were distributed among all 27 Brazilian states. This shift resulted in a significant reduction in revenue for Rio de Janeiro during this period, impacting infrastructure projects, contracted services, assistance to the population, public policies, and the payment of civil service salaries. Revenue declined from 8.235 billion reais in 2012 to 3.5 billion in 2016. (https://portal.faz enda.rj.gov.br/petroleo/receita/2023-2/).

policies, especially the UPP (Pacifying Police Units), an experiment in neighbourhood policing in favelas, were either terminated or subjected to significant budget cuts (Duarte, 2019). This resulted in a marked increase in violent and property crimes, particularly thefts of trucked-in cargo in the metropolitan region of the state capital, Rio de Janeiro (Hirata et al., 2023).

The following year, the situation took a turn for the worse, with the suspension of civil servants' pay and the government's decreasing managing capacity. During that time, the relationship between security forces and state government deteriorated, and the perception of the governor's 'loss of authority' over police forces became commonplace among specialists and the press (Adorno, 2018; Ramiro Junior, 2018; Rodrigues, 2017). In February 2018, per governor's request, a federal intervention in state public security was declared, under the command of the Armed Forces—that period became popularly known as 'military intervention'. General Braga Netto was named intervenor—or the 'intervention commander', taking over governing duties on all things relating to public security, urban order, and civil defence until the end of that year, when a new administration would succeed, after elections to be held in October. The Intervention Cabinet was installed in the CICC itself, redefined as Headquarters, where once again city management was decided. The intervenor became, at that stage, a kind of de facto governor.

Less than a month after the intervention began, Marielle Franco, a young leftist leader, a Black, *LGBTQIA +*, favela-born, very charismatic and eloquent woman, and the driver of her car were both brutally murdered. Even though the executioners were identified and arrested, we still do not know who ordered the crime. It is worth noting, however, that five CCTV cameras in the area where the crime occurred, which transmitted video to the CICC, had been disconnected on the day before the crime (Seara, 2018), interfering with the investigation and pointing towards collaboration inside the centre (the collaborators were probably police officers, since CCTV cameras are managed by the military police). Moreover, it shows the lack of control and the possibility of appropriating technological resources for personal, and even criminal, use.

Studying the Federal Intervention Cabinet Strategic Plan [FICSP] (2018), I found two documents presented as the plan's methodological foundation: the Brazilian Army Excellence in Public Management Model [BAEPMM] and the System of Excellence in the Military Organization [SE-MO] (2008). They were both quite rudimentary and presented a simplified version of some basic New Public Management ideas and strategies. The model presented in these documents, which grounded the federal intervention's planning, was intended to be established as a reference for 'good practices' in public management (not only in the military), even though rudimentary (Cardoso, 2019a; Vasconcelos, 2010). The simplification is notably evident in the 13 principles outlined in the plan: systemic thinking, organizational learning, a culture of innovation, leadership and constancy of purpose, management based on processes and information, a vision of the future, value management, commitment to people, a focus on citizens and society, the development of partnerships, social responsibility, social control, and participatory management (SE-MO, 2008).

In addition, the planning presented by the Intervention Cabinet showed a somewhat overestimated expectation that the military would be able to rearrange the management and command structure of Rio de Janeiro security forces. This assumption rested on two strategies: 'establishing interagency protocols for public security and intelligence actions' and 'strengthening the CICC as the central command and control entity for public security actions' (Ramos et al., 2018, pp. 31–2). This involved creating agreements and documents—protocols—signed by various security agencies and utilizing the CICC's facilities and technological infrastructure, which required updating. The purportedly efficient and technical management skills of the military, along with the excellence model devised by the Brazilian Army, were expected to ensure the success of these strategies.

More important than making the city more orderly or less violent, or influence the population's feeling of insecurity and victimization, the main strategy chosen to consolidate the intervention's image of success and efficiency was creating indicators to corroborate such a claim, despite the lack of material evidence of actual change or improvement. By analysing the figures of the Brazilian Public Security Forum for 2017,

2018 and 2019, we can measure the effect of the intervention and its immediate legacy. Initially, we see a reduction, albeit small (approximately 10%) in violent lethality per 100,000 inhabitants in the state of Rio de Janeiro: 40 (2017), 39 (2018), and 35 (2019) (Atlas da Violência, 2023). In absolute numbers, there has been a reduction from 6749 (2017) to 6714 (2018) and 5980 (2019) victims of intentional violent lethality in the state of Rio de Janeiro. However, to understand what actually happened, we must look elsewhere. First, at the 'deaths resulting from police intervention'—1127 (2017), 1534 (2018) and 1814 (2019)—which indicates an increase of 36% (2017–2018) and then 18% (2018–2019).[11] Police violence was central to the security strategy adopted.[12] The reduction in the number of homicides, which mostly victimize young black men, was achieved through an increase in police killings of young black men. In the balance between homicides committed by state agents and by citizens, very little has changed.

Paradigm Shift

On the other hand, however, a major change has taken place. The emergence and rapid ascent of the militias marked a structural and paradigm shift in violent organized crime in Rio de Janeiro. Currently, these militias constitute the armed group with the greatest territorial control over the metropolitan region of Rio de Janeiro.[13] The distribution of police operations across the urban territory, decided at the CICC, is pointed out as one of the factors in the expansion of militias[14] (GENI, 2021),

---

[11] Deaths as a result of the intervention of state agents reached an all-time high in 2019, but its rise was halted by the Covid-19 pandemic in 2020, and later by an action by social movements, activists, and researchers in the Supreme Court calling for the regulation of police raids (ADPF 635).

[12] On the use of violence by the State under the Federal Intervention, see Viana (2021) and Magalhães (2021).

[13] With this, they supplanted the different drug trafficking factions that for years dominated the news and the criminal imagination of Rio de Janeiro (Machado da Silva, 2010; Misse, 2018).

[14] In 2019, despite the fact that 58.6% of the area under occupation by criminal groups in the city of Rio de Janeiro is controlled by the militia (and 33.9% of the population living in these territories), only 6.5% of police operations took place there (Geni, 2021).

by concentrating in areas under the control of the Comando Vermelho (drug faction) and spanning territories under the control of the militias. In those militia areas, the absence of police raids not only ensures that militia businesses are not disturbed, but also spares the *favelados* from the armed conflicts that victimize them and disrupt their lives. As a result, a *pax miliciana* is being built, which wins the sympathy of many residents, even though it is based on violence, coercion and threats (Araújo Silva, 2017; Geni, 2021; Manso, 2020). It is likely that vested interests in the territorial dispute of criminal groups in Rio de Janeiro are prominent in decisions about police operations, instead of data analysis and processing, hotspot maps and the use of intelligence information. The construction of the 'reduction in violence' that would have been achieved by the Federal Intervention goes hand in hand with the police construction of the territories under militia control as 'safe'. Both arise from the uneven and illicit distribution of police violence across the urban landscape, whether through the execution of individuals and manipulation of statistics or by determining which criminal group to confront and which to support.

Brazil, Bolsonarized

Even though, as previously mentioned, the causes leading to Jair Bolsonaro's victory in the polls in 2018 were many and varied, the Rio de Janeiro federal intervention helped solidify the association between militarism, authoritarianism and efficient, technical management. Even though Jair Bolsonaro was expelled from the Army while still a captain, was a congressman for 27 years, and had managed to elect his three eldest sons for office, he presented himself as a candidate from outside of the world of politics, promising his administration would consist only of capacitated technical experts, ridding the country of political appointment for important offices, of corruption and of (communist) ideology. However, instead of appointing recognized experts or career public officials with technical background, Bolsonaro systematically appointed current or former military and police officers for more and more roles (Nozaki, 2021). In October 2021, there were as much as 6,300 military officers in government offices, occupying a total of 18% of all appointed roles in the executive power structure.

Furthermore, amidst the worst pandemic of the past 100 years in 2020 the president appointed an active-duty general, Eduardo Pazuello, with no previous healthcare background, as the Minister of Health, keeping him in office for over a year, in a decision that, in many people's opinion, aggravated the country's health crises and was directly or indirectly responsible for the death of hundreds of thousands of Brazilian citizens. General Pazuello's only credential was as a logistics expert, although his administration's logistics were highly criticized. In addition to the ministry of health, Bolsonaro appointed another active-duty military general, who was already his Chief of Staff (one of the government's most important roles), as Covid-19 Impact Surveillance and Monitoring Crisis Committee director. The person referred to was General Walter Braga Netto, who had previously served as the federal intervenor in Rio de Janeiro two years earlier. However, he lacked expertise in collective health, epidemiology, or any other specialty essential to address the severe crisis brought on by the pandemic. His shortcomings also extended to public security, as his performance as an intervenor had already proven to be disastrous.

Conclusion

Not intending to exhaust the subject exposed herein, I presented a few usually neglected aspects of the bolsonarist phenomenon, and of the Bolsonaro's administration. Many other points could be incorporated into this analysis. As a conclusion, however, I would like to highlight that the militarized-managerial framework is, above all, an action horizon and not a fulfilled promise. During the Bolsonaro administration, the catastrophic management of the pandemic, leading the country to set records in death and infection rates, did exactly the same as the federal intervention a couple of years before in Rio (with the same actors). In both cases, the managerial aspect of the militarized-managerial rationale became, day by day, more visible as mere militarism, recalling, grossly, and perversely, ideas of efficiency when violently managing the death of a part of the population.

Ethics Statement   This research was conducted in compliance with the code for research ethics and data protection of the Universidade Federal do Rio de Janeiro as well as the American Anthropological Association's (AAA) Statement on Ethics and all participants provided informed consent.

References

Abraji (2020, October 22). Governo Bolsonaro tem 99 militares comissionados na gestão socioambiental. https://www.abraji.org.br/governo-bolsonaro-tem-99-militares-comissionados-na-gestao-socioambiental

Adorno, L. (2018, February 17). Falta de planejamento, facções e crise: como a segurança do Rio chegou ao ponto da intervenção. *Uol*. https://noticias.uol.com.br/cotidiano/ultimas-noticias/2018/02/17/falta-de-planejamento-faccoes-e-crise-como-a-seguranca-do-rio-chegou-ao-ponto-da-intervencao.htm

Aguiar, B. S. de, & Pereira, M. R. (2019). O antifeminismo como backlash nos discursos do governo Bolsonaro. *Revista Agenda Política, 7*(3), Artigo 3. https://doi.org/10.31990/agenda.2019.3.1

Akrich, M. (1993). Essay of Technosociology: A Gasogene in Costa Rica. In P. Lemmonier (Ed.), *Technological Choices: Transformation in Material Cultures since the Neolithic* (pp. 289–337). Routledge.

Alfano, B. (2023). País gastou quase R$ 100 milhões em escolas militares: programa teve uma das 15 maiores verbas da educação básica. *O Globo*. 12 July 2023. https://oglobo.globo.com/brasil/educacao/noticia/2023/07/12/pais-gastou-quase-r-100-milhoes-em-escolas-civico-militares-programa-teve-uma-das-15-maiores-verbas-da-educacao-basica.ghtml

Almeida, R. D. (2019). Bolsonaro Presidente: Conservadorismo, evangelismo e a crise brasileira. *Novos Estudos CEBRAP, 38*, 185–213.

Anderson, P. (2019). *O Brasil De Bolsonaro. Novos Estudos, 113*, 215–254. https://doi.org/10.9771/ccrh.v34i0.44901

Andrade, D. P. (2021). *Neoliberalismo e guerra ao inimigo interno: da Nova República à virada autoritária no Brasil*. *Caderno CRH*, 34. https://doi.org/10.9771/ccrh.v34i0.44901

Araújo Silva, M. de. (2017). Houses, Tranquility and Progress in an área de milícia. *Vibrant. Virtual Brazilian Anthropology*, n. v14n3. https://doi.org/10.1590/1809-43412017v14n3p132

Atlas da Violência (2023). *Fórum Brasileiro de Segurança Pública*. https://for umseguranca.org.br/atlas-da-violencia/

Bastos dos Santos, J. G., Freitas, M., Aldé, A., Santos, K., & Cardozo Cunha, V. C. (2019). WhatsApp, política mobile e desinformação: A hidra nas eleições presidenciais de 2018. *Comunicação & Sociedade, 41*(2), 307. https://doi.org/10.15603/2175-7755/cs.v41n2p307-334

Bennett, C. J., & Haggerty, K. (2012). *Security Games: Surveillance and Control at Mega-events*. Routledge. https://doi.org/10.4324/9780203827475

Bigo, D. (2006a). Security, Exception, Ban and Surveillance. In D. Lyon (Ed.), *Theorizing Surveillance: The Panopticon and Beyond* (pp. 46–68). Willan Publishing.

Bigo, D. (2006b). Internal and External Aspects of Security. *European Security, 15*(4), 385–404. https://doi.org/10.1080/09662830701305831

Brito, L. T. de. (2022). 'Enfrentar o vírus como homem e não como moleque': Quando a masculinidade tóxica se torna genocida. *Revista Docência e Ciberultura, 6*(2), Artigo 2. https://doi.org/10.12957/redoc.2022.62923

Callon, M. (2003). *Quel espace public pour la démocratie technique?* (pp. 197–221). Les Sens Du Public. Publics Politiques.

Callon, M., & Law, J. (1982). On Interests and their Transformation: Enrol-ment and Counter-Enrolment. *Social Studies of Science, 12*(4), 615–625. https://doi.org/10.1177/030631282012004006

Cardoso, A. (2020). *À beira do abismo: Uma sociologia política do bolsonarismo*. Amazon.

Cardoso, B. (2018). Estado, tecnologias de segurança e normatividade neolib-eral. In F. Bruno, B. Cardoso, M. Kanashiro, L. Guilhon E, & L. Melgaço (Eds.), *Tecnopolíticas da vigilância: perspectivas da margem*, pp. 91–105. Boitempo. https://medialabufrj.net/wp-content/uploads/2020/10/Tecnopoli ticas-da-vigilancia_miolo_download.pdf

Cardoso, B. (2019a). Benchmarking et sécurité à Rio de Janeiro. *Statistique Et Société, 7*(1), 25–30.

Cardoso, B. de V. (2019b). A lógica gerencial-militarizada e a segurança pública no Rio de Janeiro: O CICC-RJ e as tecnologias de (re)construção do Estado. *Dilemas, Revista de Estudos de Conflito, Controle Social e Violência, 3*, 22. https://www.redalyc.org/journal/5638/563864592004/563864592004.pdf

Cardoso, B. V. (2013). Megaeventos esportivos e modernização tecnológica: Planos e discursos sobre o legado em segurança pública. *Horizontes Antropológicos, 40*, 30. https://doi.org/10.1590/S0104-718320130 00200005

Cardoso, B. V. (2014). *Todos os olhos: Videovigilâncias, voyeurismos e (re) produção imagética.* EdUFRJ.

Cardoso, B. V. (2016). *Security as a Commodity: Mega Events and Public Security in Brazil.* A Publication of Heinrich Böll Foundation. https://www.boell.de/sites/default/files/cardoso-e-paper-security-en.pdf

Cardoso, B., & Hirata, D. (2017). Dispositivos de inscrição e redes de ordenamento público: Uma aproximação entre a Teoria do Ator-Rede (ANT) e Foucault. *Sociologia & Antropologia, 7*, 77–103. https://doi.org/10.1590/2238-38752017v714

Carneiro, R. (2019). A agenda econômica anacrênica do Governo Bolsonaro. *Brazilian Keynesian Review, 5*(1), Artigo 1. https://doi.org/10.33834/bkr.v5i1.200

Castells, M. (2009). *The Rise of the Network Society.* SD Books. https://doi.org/10.1002/9781444319514

Cesarino, L. (2019). Identidade e representação no bolsonarismo. *Revista de Antropologia, 62*(3), 530–557. https://doi.org/10.11606/2179-0892.ra.2019.165232

Cesarino, L. (2020). Como vencer uma eleição sem sair de casa: A ascensão do populismo digital no Brasil. *Internet & Sociedade, 1*(1), 91–120.

Chagas, V., Modesto, M., & Magalhães, D. (2019). O Brasil vai virar Venezuela: Medo, memes e enquadramentos emocionais no WhatsApp pró-Bolsonaro. *Esferas, 14*, Artigo 14. https://doi.org/10.31501/esf.v0i14.10374

Cooper, M. (2021). The Alt-Right: Neoliberalism, Libertarianism and the Fascist Temptation. *Theory, Culture & Society, 38*(6), 29–50. https://doi.org/10.1177/0263276421999446

Correio Brasiliense (2018, November 24). Critério para preencher ministérios é técnico, não é festa, diz Bolsonaro. https://www.correiobraziliense.com.br/app/noticia/politica/2018/11/24/interna_politica,721333/criterio-para-preencher-ministerios-e-tecnico-nao-e-festa-diz-bolson.shtml

Da Empoli, G. (2019). *Os engenheiros do caos: Como as fake news, as teorias da conspiração e os algoritmos estão sendo utilizados para disseminar ódio, medo e influenciar eleições.* Vestígio Editora.

Dardot, P., & Laval, C. (2014). *The New Way of the World: On Neoliberal Society.* Verso Books.

Doctrine for the Military Command and Control System (2015). https://www.gov.br/defesa/pt-br/arquivos/doutrina_militar/lista_de_publicacoes/md31a_ma_03a_douta_sismca_3a_eda_2015.pdf

Duarte, A. D. M., & César, M. R. D. A. (2021). Corpos, gêneros e sexualidades em disputa no Brasil contemporâneo: Bolsonarismo versus Tropicalismo. *História: Questões & Debates, 69*(2), 75. https://doi.org/10.5380/his.v69i2.80036

Duarte, T. L. (2019). Facções criminais e milícias: Aproximações e distanciamentos propostos pela literatura. *BIB-Revista Brasileira De Informação Bibliográfica Em Ciências Sociais, 90*, 1–16.

Estado de Minas (2018, October 25). Bolsonaro diz que, se eleito, vai nomear ministério "técnico". https://www.em.com.br/app/noticia/politica/2018/10/25/interna_politica,1000038/bolsonaro-diz-que-se-eleito-vai-nomear-ministerio-tecnico.shtml

Federal Intervention Cabinet Strategic Plan [FICSP] (2018). https://gestaodoconhecimento-gifrj.eb.mil.br/bitstream/123456789/1125/1/Plano_Estrat%c3%a9gico_11%20Out%2018_Vers%c3%a3o_Final.pdf

Feltran, G. (2018). *Irmãos: Uma história do PCC*. Editora Companhia das Letras.

Fontoura, N. de O., Rivero, P. S., & Rodrigues, R. I. (2009). Segurança pública na Constituição Federal de 1988: Continuidades e perspectivas. http://www.ipea.gov.br. https://repositorio.ipea.gov.br/handle/11058/4327

Foucault, M. (1975). *Surveiller et punir*. Gallimard.

Furedi, F. (2022). Illiberal Liberalism: A Genealogy. *Journal of Illiberalism Studies, 2*(2), 19–36. https://doi.org/10.53483/WCKT3541

GENI (2021). *A expansão das milícias no Rio de Janeiro. Uso estatal da força, mercado imobiliário e grupos armados*. Rio de Janeiro: Fundação Heinrich Böll. https://br.boell.org/sites/default/files/2021-04/boll_expansao_milicias_RJ_FINAL.pdf

Giulianotti, R., & Klauser, F. (2010). Security Governance and Sport Mega-events: Toward an Interdisciplinary Research Agenda. *Journal of Sport and Social Issues, 34*(1), 49–61. https://doi.org/10.1177/0193723509354042

Giulianotti, R., & Klauser, F. (2011). Introduction: Security and Surveillance at Sport Mega Events. *Urban Studies, 48*(15), 3157–3168. https://doi.org/10.1177/0042098011422400

Gonçalves, L. P., & Neto, O. C. (2022). *Fascism in Brazil: From Integralism to Bolsonarism*. Routledge. https://doi.org/10.4324/9781003224570

Gracino Junior, P., Goulart, M., & Frias, P. (2021). 'Os humilhados serão exaltados': Ressentimento e adesão evangélica ao bolsonarismo. *Cadernos Metrópole, 23*, 547–580. https://doi.org/10.1590/2236-9996.2021-5105

Graeml, C. (2023, March 3). Ministros políticos de Lula e ministros técnicos de Bolsonaro. Tem comparação? *Gazeta do Povo.* https://www.gazetadop ovo.com.br/vozes/cristina-graeml/ministros-politicos-de-lula-e-ministros-tec nicos-de-bolsonaro/

Graham, S. (2014). *Cities under Siege: The New Military Urbanism.* Verso. http://search.ebscohost.com/login.aspx?direct=true&scope=site&db= nlebk&db=nlabk&AN=729928

Guittet, E. P., & Jeandesboz, J. (2010). Security Technologies. In P. Burgess (Ed.), *The Routledge Handbook of New Security Studies* (pp. 229–239). Routledge.

Hirata, D. (2015). Segurança pública e fronteiras: Apontamentos a partir do 'Arco Norte'. *Ciência e Cultura, 67*(2), 30–34. https://doi.org/10.21800/ 2317-66602015000200011

Hirata, D. V., Grillo, C. C., & Telles, V. D. S. (2023). Guerra urbana e expansão de mercados no Rio de Janeiro. *Revista Brasileira De Ciências Sociais, 38*(111), e3811003. https://doi.org/10.1590/3811003/2023

Hirata, D., & Cardoso, B. (2016). Coordenação como tecnologia de governo. *Horizontes Antropológicos, 22*(46), 97–130. https://doi.org/10.1590/S0104-71832016000200004

Hoijtink, M. (2014). Capitalizing on Emergence: The 'New' Civil Security Market in Europe. *Security Dialogue, 45*(5), 458–475. https://doi.org/10. 1177/0967010614544312

Johnson, P. E. (2022). *I the People: The Rhetoric of Conservative Populism in the United States.* University of Alabama Press.

Kuldova, T. Ø. (2022). *Compliance-Industrial Complex: The Operating System of a Pre-Crime Society.* Palgrave. https://doi.org/10.1007/978-3-031-19224-1

Kuldova, T., Østbø, J., & Raymen, T. (2024). *Luxury and Corruption: Challenging the Anti-Corruption Consensus.* Bristol University Press. https://doi.org/10.56687/9781529212426

Lacerda, M. (2022). Contra o comunismo demoníaco: O apoio evangélico ao regime militar brasileiro e seu paralelo com o endosso da direita cristã ao governo Bolsonaro. *Religião & Sociedade, 42*, 153–176. https://doi.org/10. 1590/0100-85872021v42n1cap07

Laruelle, M. (2022). Illiberalism: A Conceptual Introduction. *East European Politics, 38*(2), 303–327. https://doi.org/10.1080/21599165.2022.2037079

Latour, B. (1987). *Science in Action: How to Follow Scientists and Engineers through Society*. Harvard University Press.

Latour, B. (1988). *The Pasteurization of France*. Harvard University Press.

Latour, B. (2005). *Reassembling the Social: An Introduction to Actor-network-theory*. Oxford University Press. https://doi.org/10.1093/oso/978019925 6044.001.0001

Law, J. (1984). On the Methods of Long-distance Control: Vessels, Navigation and the Portuguese Route to India. *The Sociological Review, 32*(1_suppl), 234–263. https://doi.org/10.1111/j.1467-954X.1984.tb0011

Leirner, P. C. (2020). *O Brasil no espectro de uma guerra híbrida: Militares, operações psicológicas e política em uma perspectiva etnográfica*. Alameda.

Leite, M. P. (2012). Da 'metáfora da guerra' ao projeto de 'pacificação': Favelas e políticas de segurança pública no Rio de Janeiro. Rev. bras. segur. pública 6(2), 374–389. https://doi.org/10.31060/rbsp.2012.v6.n2.126

Machado da Silva, L. A. (2008). *Vida sob cerco: Violência e rotina nas favelas do Rio de Janeiro* (pp. 35–76). Nova Fronteira.

Machado da Silva, L. A. (2010). 'Violência urbana', segurança pública e favelas-o caso do Rio de Janeiro atual. *Caderno Crh, 23*(59), 283–300. https://doi.org/10.1590/S0103-49792010000200006

Magalhães, A. (2021). A guerra como modo de governar em favelas do Rio de Janeiro. *Revista Brasileira De Ciências Sociais, 36*(106), e3610600. https://doi.org/10.1590/3610600/2021

Manso, B. P. (2020). *A república das milícias: Dos esquadrões da morte à Era Bolsonaro*. Todavia.

Martins, C. Z., Martins, V. T. Z., & Valim, R. (2019). *Lawfare: Uma introdução*. Editora Contracorrente.

Mello, P. C. (2020). *A máquina do ódio: Notas de uma repórter sobre fake news e violência digital*. Companhia das Letras.

Mendonça, C. M. C., & Mendonça, F. V. K. M. (2021). 'Ô bicharada, toma cuidado: O Bolsonaro vai matar viado!' Cantos homofóbicos de torcidas de futebol como dispositivos discursivos das masculinidades. *Galáxia (são Paulo), 46*, e46768. https://doi.org/10.1590/1982-2553202146768

Miskolci, R., & Balieiro, F. D. F. (2023). The Moralization of Politics in Brazil. *International Sociology, 38*(4), 480–496. https://doi.org/10.1177/026 85809231180879

Misse, M. (2007). Illegal Markets, Protection Rackets and Organized Crime in Rio de Janeiro. *Estudos Avançados, 21*, 139–157. https://doi.org/10.1590/S0103-40142007000300010

Misse, M. (2009). Sobre a acumulação social da violência no Rio de Janeiro. *Civitas—Revista de Ciências Sociais, 8*(3). https://doi.org/10.15448/1984-7289.2008.3.4865

Misse, M. (2018). Violence, Criminal Subjection and Political Merchandise in Brazil: An Overview from Rio. *International Journal of Criminology and Sociology, 7*, 135–148. https://doi.org/10.6000/1929-4409.2018.07.09

Morozov, E. (2013). *To Save Everything: The Folly of Technological Solutionism.* PublicAffairs.

Negreiros, C. R. A. (2022). *Gabinete do ódio e fake news—os métodos da extrema-direita e a corrosão da democracia no Brasil* [Master's Thesis, Universidade Federal da Paraíba]. https://repositorio.ufpb.br/jspui/handle/123456789/26685

Nicolau, J. (2020). *O Brasil dobrou à direita: Uma radiografia da eleição de Bolsonaro em 2018.* Editora Schwarcz-Companhia das Letras.

Nozaki, W. (2021). A Militarização da Administração Pública no Brasil: Projeto de nação ou projeto de poder? *Caderno Da Reforma Administrativa.* https://fpabramo.org.br/observabr/wp-content/uploads/sites/9/2021/05/Cadernos-Reforma-Administrativa-20-V4.pdf

Pinheiro-Machado, R., & Scalco, L. M. (2020). From Hope to Hate: The Rise of Conservative Subjectivity in Brazil. *HAU: Journal of Ethnographic Theory, 10*(1), 21–31. https://doi.org/10.1086/708627

Ramiro Junior, L. C. (2018). A Crise de Segurança Pública do Rio de Janeiro: Um Impasse para o Federalismo Nacional. *Revista da Escola Superior de Guerra, 33*(67), 31–59. https://doi.org/10.47240/revistadaesg.v33i67.904

Ramos, C., OLiveira e Silva, A., & Santos, L. (2018). *Plano estratégico do gabinete de intervenção federal.* Gabinete de Intervenção Federal

Recuero, R., Soares, F., & Vinhas, O. (2020). Discursive Strategies for Disinformation on WhatsApp and Twitter during the 2018 Brazilian Presidential Election. *First Monday.* https://doi.org/10.5210/fm.v26i1.10551

Rodrigues, F. (2017, January 18). Rio de Janeiro está à beira do caos social, apontam especialistas. *Brasil de Fato.* https://www.brasildefato.com.br/2017/01/18/rio-de-janeiro-esta-a-beira-do-caos-social-apontam-especialistas

Rupnik, J. (2012). How Things Went Wrong. *Journal of Democracy, 23*(3), 132–137. https://doi.org/10.1353/jod.2012.0051

Samatas, M. (2011). Surveillance in Athens 2004 and Beijing 2008: A Comparison of the Olympic Surveillance Modalities and Legacies in Two Different Olympic Host Regimes. *Urban Studies, 48*(15), 3347–3366. https://doi.org/10.1177/0042098011422399

Schurster, K., Silva, F. C. T. D. (2021). Militares e bolsonarismo: Um caso da transição falhada e democracia inacabada. *Relaciones internacionales, 30*(60), 167–183. https://doi.org/10.24215/23142766e130

Seara, B. (2018, May 3). Câmera no Estácio foi desligada na véspera das mortes de Marielle e Anderson. *Extra.* https://extra.globo.com/noticias/ extra-extra/camera-no-estacio-foi-desligada-na-vespera-das-mortes-de-mar ielle-anderson-22647648.html

Silva, E. F. (2019). Os direitos humanos no 'bolsonarismo': 'descriminalização de bandidos' e 'punição de policiais'. *Conhecer: Debate entre o Público e o Privado, 9*(22), 133–153. https://doi.org/10.32335/2238-0426.2019.9.22. 1026

Sinhoretto, J. (2022). O governo contra a ciência: Anti-intelectualismo, autoritarismo e universidades públicas. *Áskesis—Revista des discentes do Programa de Pós-Graduação em Sociologia da UFSCar, 11*(1), Artigo 1. https://doi.org/ 10.46269/11EE22.791

Souza Alves, J. C. (2008). Milícias: mudanças na economia política do crime no Rio de Janeiro. *Segurança, tráfico e milícia no Rio de Janeiro* (pp. 33–36). Rio de Janeiro: Fundação Heinrich Böll.

de Souza, L. A. F. (2015). Dispositivo militarizado da segurança pública. Tendências recentes e problemas no Brasil. *Sociedade e Estado, 30*, 207–223. https://doi.org/10.1590/S0102-69922015000100012

Strategic Security Plan for the 2014 World Cup (2012). *Ministério da Justiça, Secretaria Extraordinária de Segurança para Grandes Eventos.* http://memori adasolimpiadas.rb.gov.br/jspui/bitstream/123456789/194/1/SG078%20-% 20MINISTERIO%20DA%20JUSTICA-SESGE_Planejamento%20Estrate gico%20para%20a%20Copa%20do%20Mundo.pdf

System of Excellence in the Military Organisation (2008). *Ministério da Defesa, Gabinete do Comandante do Exército.*

Tripodi, F. (2017). *Searching for Alternative Facts: Analyzing Scriptural Inference in Conservative News Practices* (Data & Society's Media Manipulation Research Initiative). Data & Society. https://datasociety.net/wp-content/upl oads/2018/05/Data_Society_Searching-for-Alternative-Facts.pdf

Valladares, L. do P. (2016). *A invenção da favela: Do mito de origem a favela. com.* editora FGV.

Vasconcelos, G. H. D. D. (2010). *Gestão organizacional: O sistema de excelência no Exército Brasileiro* [Bacharelado em Administração, Universidade de Brasília]. https://doi.org/10.26512/2010.08.TCC.1214

Vaz, A. F. (2023). De uma agenda regressiva: O movimento Escola Sem Partido e o espírito do tempo. *Revista Eletrônica de Educação, 17*, e4551063. https://doi.org/10.14244/198271994551

Viana, N. (2021). *Dano colateral: A intervenção dos militares na segurança pública.* Objetiva.

Walker, G. H., Stanton, N. A., Salmon, P. M., & Jenkins, D. P. (2017). Command and Control: The Sociotechnical Perspective. *CRC Press.* https://doi.org/10.1201/9781315572765

Wathne, C. T. (2020). New Public Management and the Police Profession at Play. *Criminal Justice Ethics, 39*(1), 1–22. https://doi.org/10.1080/0731129X.2020.1746106

6

'For Your Own Safety': The Soft Push of Surveillance by the Private Sector in India

Shivangi Narayan ⓘ

At the 'Trust Summit'[1] at the Indian Institute of Technology in Mumbai in September 2023, I met Sanjay Jain, along with many young and old technologists who have been part of the group that worked on the *Aadhaar* (UID) project in India. Jain was the chief product manager at Unique Identification Authority of India (UIDAI), the organisation that built Aadhaar, India's central biometric identification system which provides a 12-digit number to everyone in exchange of their biometric and demographic information. Some of them were also involved in the Aadhaar enabled payment systems (AEPS) that facilitated payments through point-of-sale machines, in biometrics and 'DigiYatra', a facial recognition system to streamline passenger check in at airports in India. As the event progressed, they congratulated themselves for the heights of

---

[1] https://trustlab.iitb.ac.in/event/trust-summit-2023.

S. Narayan (✉)
Jawaharlal Nehru University, Delhi, India
e-mail: shivangi.narayan@gmail.com

© The Author(s), under exclusive license to Springer Nature Switzerland AG 2024
T. Ø. Kuldova et al. (eds.), *Policing and Intelligence in the Global Big Data Era, Volume I*, Palgrave's Critical Policing Studies, https://doi.org/10.1007/978-3-031-68326-8_6

technological progress they had achieved. When asked about the exclusionary aspect of Aadhaar, AEPS and DigiYatra, they claimed that they had merely constructed the technology and had 'no role in how it was used'. Jain categorically claimed that while Nandan Nilekani, the notorious co-founder and chairman of the board of Infosys, whose pet project Aadhaar was, rallied for a data protection law/system, the government did not pay heed to his request. This was a rather ironic claim after the government agreed to build a billion-dollar identity system based on his idea. Jain also said that UIDAI could not do much in the implementation of the technology it had built because it had no power to enforce anything and could only share best practices, which the government was under no obligation to incorporate. Or as Jain put it, 'We were only interested in the tech, rest everything was up to the government'. This vignette draws us at the heart of the surveillance industry in India.

The Surveillance Industry in India

The surveillance industry in India or those tech companies that provide surveillance hardware and private intelligence services in the country currently roughly account for USD 2.07 billion and is projected to grow to 5.96 billion USD by 2028.[2] A number of small, medium-sized and large companies are all part of this industry[3]; over 120 companies of all ranges showcased their products during the security fair 'IFSEC[4] in the capital city of New Delhi in December 2023'. The products on display were surveillance cameras with night vision, digital video recorders, encoders and decoders, security alarm systems, audio and video door phones, RFID systems, biometric systems, security gates, anti-theft systems and cloud-based video surveillance systems.

---

[2] Mordor intelligence security market research and forecast report: 'India Electronic Security Market Size & Share Analysis—Growth Trends & Forecasts (2024–2029)', https://www.mordor intelligence.com/industry-reports/india-electronic-security-market.

[3] 'The story of ideaForge: From humble beginnings and 26/11 terror attacks to an IPO', *ZeeBiz*, 24 June 2023, https://www.zeebiz.com/companies/news-ideaforge-ipo-subscription-det ails-price-band-issue-price-iit-bombay-drone-26-november-2008-terrorist-attack-taj-hotel-nse-bse-stst-241605.

[4] IFSEC Security exhibition homepage: https://ifsecindia.com/home.

Law enforcement officials from the Delhi Police were among those attending and company representatives were eager to show off their latest tech equipment to the law enforcement agents. This is not a new phenomenon; a number of surveillance companies currently provide surveillance/intelligence services to the police and Delhi government such as facial recognition, drone surveillance, licence plate recognition and more. Police Forces of Delhi, Chennai, Telangana, Punjab, Uttar Pradesh and Haryana have either fully or partially sourced 'face recognition technology' (FRT), a pertinent surveillance system currently being used across the world to monitor people, from private companies. These are a mix of start-ups and established companies from India or even from countries such as Japan (NEC Corporation)[5] and Israel (Cortica)[6] operating in the Indian surveillance market.

Start-ups, however, have a significant share in the FRT ecosystem in India. The three big names in India currently are Staqu[7] that provides FRT to UP and Punjab Police; Hyperverge[8] which is involved with the Telangana police and Innefu labs[9] which provides FRT to Delhi Police. Start-ups are an important part of the security landscape in India as they try to fill a gap left by established IT companies in India who were late in developing the kind of new age surveillance paraphernalia currently in use around the world. They also come with the added cultural expectation of being 'disruptive', more in tune with the latest that the world of surveillance has to offer and more ready to take 'risks'. Their products are also cheaper than those by established companies.

For an ordinary Indian, it is not a common knowledge that the police and the government work with private companies in order to provide high-tech surveillance and security services to its citizens or to control the population. When the Minister of Home Affairs announces in the Lok Sabha that the police have identified 1100 people in the Delhi riots investigation using FRT (Singh, 2020), very few people would have known that it was a private security company, a start-up, that provided

---

[5] Homepage of NEC: https://www.nec.com/.
[6] Homepage of Cortica: https://www.cortica.com/.
[7] Homepage of Staqu Technologies: https://www.staqu.com/.
[8] Homepage of Hyperverge: https://hyperverge.co/.
[9] Homepage of Innefu Labs: https://www.innefu.com/.

Delhi Police with the technology for this exercise. Vipra and Jauhar have also argued that citizens of India only get to know about the involvement of the private sector through media reports, hence there is no option of public scrutiny and accountability of such technology and its use in India (Jauhar and Vipra 2021). I posit that it also enables an unprecedented access and power to the private sector to shape the surveillance and security policies of the government to suit its own sales targets, interests and product design without any accountability, just as authors such as Ball and Snider argued in regard to the surveillance industrial complex in other parts of the world (Ball & Snider, 2013; Ball et al., 2012).

For example, in India, a string of events, such as the Kargil war of 1999 between India and Pakistan, and the terrorist attacks in Mumbai on November 26, 2008, (preceded by several such attacks across the years) necessitated an overhaul of the intelligence wing of the government and streamlining of the information channels of the country resulting in agencies such as the National Grid (NATGRID) (Jain, 2020b) or the National Investigation Agency (NIA)[10] and even Aadhaar or the UID project which facilitate the surveillance of each and every person in the country. The private sector has not only become the foremost technology provider for the government, but it has also influenced and keeps influencing the way Indian authorities envisage its internal security needs and understand the threat landscape. This is clear from reading reports by the Federation of Indian Chambers of Commerce and Industry (FICCI) in the year 2009–2010, immediately after the Mumbai attacks (Task Force Report, 2009). Associated Chambers of Commerce and Industry (ASSOCHAM) in consultation with PricewaterhouseCoopers (PwC) developed the roadmap of 'Smart City/Safe City' projects for Delhi (Sharma & Rajput, 2017; Sharma et al., 2013). This roadmap proposed significant surveillance measures, especially the use of CCTVs in public places, which has now been incorporated by the Delhi Police and government authorities.

These companies function under what has been analysed as the global 'compliance industrial complex' where social problems are converted into policy papers, regulations and moral outrage documents that necessitate

---

[10] Homepage of the National Investigative Agency: https://nia.gov.in/.

risk estimation and threat management with the help of more and more surveillance and data analytics (Kuldova, 2022). Examples of these can be seen in the 'Safe City' project documents (Sharma et al., 2013) where crime prevention is worded in terms of moral outrage regarding the lack of safety of women and children in the city. This, consequently demands, justifies and legitimises more and more granular surveillance, data collection and privacy violations. Moreover, it leads to the overcriminalisation or overpolicing of certain communities designated as 'high-risk', typically the marginalised and those belonging to the minority religion in India. For example, FRT developed by a Delhi-based start-up was used to illegally detain Muslim youth in Delhi riots in the year 2020 (Chander, 2021). Lack of accountability also extends to oversight. For example, companies such as Hikvision and Dahua, restricted in the USA for their apparent proximity to the Chinese government, operate with abandon in India (Jain, 2023).

Why we Must Understand the Role of Private Sector in Shaping Public Security

The influence of the private sector in India's internal security and the overarching effects of resultant surveillance on the citizens make it imperative to understand not just the contours of the rise of industry proper in the security surveillance landscape but also to analyse it culturally. Who are the people behind this industry? What and how do they think? What professional culture are they formed by? Recall the conversation in the introduction of this chapter and the way in which the engineers and other technicians, neck deep in directing policies related to the usage of technology that affects the most marginalised in India, claim to be objective, neutral, culture-free and outside the domain of the social. Most strikingly, the key cultural feature of this industry is precisely the way it insists on not being a product of a certain culture, of not being impacted by culture or society, on not having or being a culture, or else, the way in which it time and again distances itself from the very surroundings in which it works and which it shapes, situating itself outside of culture and within a purely imaginary rational unbiased, neutral and purely technical (and technocratic) world (Forsythe, 2001; Vaghela et al., 2022). However, these very same companies are quick to cash in on an emotionally charged event, such as the terrorist attacks of 9/11 globally or the November 26 Mumbai attacks in India, to promote its products by alluding to their nationalism, self-preservation and the moral quest to combat evil. This chapter seeks to shed light on precisely this paradoxical dynamic as a defining feature of the culture of contemporary private surveillance industry.

Inspired by the study of sales representatives in the pharmaceutical industry and their role in increasing sales and pushing for the usage of their drugs (Oldani, 2004), this chapter aims to study the tangential ways in which surveillance companies push the sales of their products, apart from their usual advertising and marketing efforts. As Oldani argues, sales rep conversations with pharmaceutical companies decide how 'a pharmaceutical product is packaged, used, and thought about' (Oldani, 2004, p. 330). In the same way, I want to understand what *secondary* tactics as well as deeper cultural tropes are employed by surveillance companies to steer the usage of their products. In doing so, how do these companies influence how surveillance is even envisaged in the popular imagination of the country?

Additionally, this chapter joins civil society and academia in criticising the involvement of the private sector in the area of surveillance and security. As Jauhar and Vipra have argued, while surveillance in any form is problematic, it is being handled by a private sector unbound by any responsibility to the people of India, unlike public institutions, can be catastrophic (Jauhar & Vipra, 2021)—and yet, it is precisely the neoliberal policy of the state to both procure and outsource to private actors (see also Kuldova in this volume). The secrecy surrounding private actors makes it impossible for journalists, academics, citizens, or activists to gather evidence, making it difficult for citizens and others to seek recourse in judicial action; this violates the ethos of justice of the Indian constitution (Jauhar & Vipra, 2021). This chapter furthermore argues that the real problem begins with the 'public private partnerships' (PPPs) where lines of ownership and accountability blur even further with no one, from either the government or private sector, being up for taking responsibility for providing recourse to affected people; we therefore witness the massive proliferation of 'unaccountables' (Wedel, 2014).

A Note on Method and Failures of Access

This chapter is grounded in an ethnographic approach which sought to study the tech companies, especially start-ups in Delhi, that provide facial recognition technology to Delhi Police, adapting Laura Nader's approach of 'studying up' to understand how power, the powerful and their institutions shape society (Nader, 1972, 2011). By considering knowledge as situated, ethnography provides a unique way to understand the social, cultural mores that entrepreneurs in the private sector shape and are shaped by. However, access to the private sector is severely limited and this generates a number of issues for 'studying up' in practice. The Covid-19 pandemic has made this even more difficult as in-person meetings were discouraged and it was difficult to travel to meet people. The disastrous second wave of Covid-19 in the summer of 2021 in India left people busy trying to make sense of their own personal affairs, hardly prioritising talking to a researcher. Despite these challenges, I managed to speak to a tech entrepreneur based in Delhi whom I will call Pradeep, who provided security solutions to Delhi Police as of 2017 and till the time of the interview, and his associate, who will be called Himesh, from May 2021 to December 2022. The conversations took place on phone, emails, WhatsApp chats and personal meetings, including driving with Pradeep to his meetings in Delhi as he only had time to talk while driving. Even after many requests, Pradeep did not allow me to attend meetings related to product development as they were confidential and technology proprietary. Since his office was also under renovation during the time of my research and most employees were working from home, I did not get to go to his office or observe him and his employees at work. These are the limitations of this chapter based on these interviews and interactions. These interviews and encounters are therefore read against and along both critical literature on algorithms in the policing and governance of the social, document analysis, reading of policy documents as much as of product websites and promotional materials for these technologies. This being said, I have also managed to attend several trade events and professional conferences, which have served as a unique source of information and ethnographic data—such as the Trust Summit mentioned in the beginning. In this case, I have been inspired by the event-based ethnographic approaches which enable us to study various professionals (Nyquist & Leivestad, 2017).

Video Surveillance and the Use of Facial Recognition Technologies in Delhi

Video surveillance has become the go-to tech for all kinds of 'security' needs in India, be it for tackling crime, disciplining school students or maintaining public order. This can be seen in the proliferation of CCTV cameras across the city. Currently, Delhi is the most CCTV dense city in the world, dethroning the erstwhile king of surveillance, London.[11] Following this surge, a number of companies have started providing hardware and software services related to CCTVs. While hardware services include provision of hi-tech equipment to record video data from all kinds of sources, software services include data analytics of data collected with the use of such devices. One of the analytics that is much in vogue today is the identification and classification of people according to their faces and other markers such as emotions or gait. A large part of the product pie of start-ups that provide security-related products consists of face recognition tech. Delhi Police started using a standalone[12] version of facial recognition tech, sourced from a start-up based in the city, in 2017, when the High Court of Delhi allowed the police to use it to find missing children (Jain, 2020a, 2020b).

---

[11] 'This Indian city has the largest number of CCTVs in the world', *Mint*, 3 December 2021, https://www.livemint.com/news/india/this-indian-city-has-the-highest-number-of-cctvs-in-the-world-beats-london-paris-11638517557065.html.

[12] A standalone FRT tech means that the police have to run the photos of suspects through a software set up on their computers or through a web link in order to identify them. This is in contrast to automated systems that have FRT built into the cameras which automatically identify whoever is in focus.

Lying dormant for a while, this same tech was consequently used to identify suspected perpetrators of riots in North East Delhi following a record number of protests related to the implementation of the National Register of Citizens (NRC) and the announcement of the Citizenship Amendment Act (CAA), which amended the Citizenship Act to provide Indian citizenship only to followers of the Hindu religion, in late 2019 (Shika, 2023). Since then, there has been an uptake in the use of video surveillance using CCTVs and facial recognition in diverse sectors, including schools and airports, in Delhi. All over India as well, the use of CCTVs and ensuing face recognition has seen a marked increase and with that an increase in the number of companies providing this service. As mentioned before, there were around 120 private companies that participated in providing video surveillance and analytics in the IFSEC 2023[13] at Pragati Maidan in Delhi in December 2023.

'We are Safer with Tech'

The existence of private companies who work closely with the government to provide surveillance products (Sachitanand, 2018) indicates the existence of a surveillance industrial complex in India, even when the details around how it works are still hazy. As Ben Hayes argues, those surveillance measures that most closely relate to state coercion, control and power did not just develop ad hoc as societies developed, but were brought to the fore by a mixing of private providers of surveillance with state power (Hayes, 2012, p. 167). It was the private sector along with the power of the state, according to Hayes, that had the means to execute the practical and political steps needed to convert the power of information (embedded in surveillance tech) into state surveillance and control. Historically, private companies such as IBM, Marconi, General Electric and General Dynamics have always been part of war efforts of states such as Britain, Russia and USA. However, they have always been able to maintain a certain distance from death and destruction caused due to

---

[13] IFSEC home page: https://ifsecindia.com/home.

wars and military aggression, posing as mere logistics suppliers instead of being complicit in the agenda of the said war.

While there is no literature documenting how the private sector lobbies for its products in India, from international experience and from the existence of an international 'military industrial complex' and the emergence of national security states (Smith, 2015), it is clear that such a relationship exists. Selling products does not only mean offering them in a market but also implies the creation of a demand for said products. Industry creates this demand in both overt and covert ways by banking on existing ideas, cultural tropes, ruling ideologies, beliefs, anxieties, doubts or even superstitions of its target audience. As we shall see in the next section, this could be done by banking on current resident fears of the minority religion in India, the frustration with the public sector or the notion of saving family or women's honour.

Constructing the Dichotomy of an Inefficient and Corrupt Public Sector vs an Efficient Private Sector with Integrity

The neoliberal turn in governance has led to states replacing and shrinking the public sector, which is deemed inefficient, corrupt and backward, for an efficient, innovative and forward-leaning private sector. This phenomenon has contributed to the boom of the start-up sector which is ready to 'take risks' and 'disrupt' traditional patterns of working for more technology-centric solutions to everyday problems. Start-ups or entrepreneurial ventures in the security market have become the go-to places for providing police with its needed tech solutions. As mentioned, start-ups in cities like Chennai, Gurgaon, Delhi and Bangalore provide these software solutions to a number of public and private agencies in India including Police forces from Delhi, Punjab, Chennai, Uttar Pradesh, Telangana and Uttarakhand. Given that start-ups are associated with efficiency, productivity and affinity to technology and venture capital, the police are also enthusiastic to collaborate with them to develop technological solutions for policing problems.[14] That they come cheaper than established companies is an added advantage,[15] as Pradeep told me that he 'got into law enforcement' by accident because the big corporations, where he was trying to sell his products, wanted a track record of good work which he did not have being a small start-up. According to him, the police back in 2015–16 did not have many funds to rope in international companies or established companies for facial recognition in India, therefore they were more willing to source tech from start-ups.

Pradeep said that one of the biggest reasons for the involvement of the private sector in government surveillance was that the government-based tech companies could not provide the products that the private sector could. This was because, according to him, government employees had no incentive to work due to job security and welfare benefits: 'they have no reason to try new things because their jobs make them comfortable'. He said start-ups, on the other hand, just want to produce great products. He outlined his own achievements with the Delhi Police in the early years of their partnership. According to Pradeep, his products were as good as any established company. About a social media monitoring tool that he developed for the Delhi Police, he said that 'it was so good that the police could not believe that it was from a new company', asserting the quest for excellence that his company follows, despite being small and new. This already reveals how start-ups see themselves and are often seen by others, as active, dynamic, innovative as opposed to the passive, non-evolving and static public sector.

'Start-up' is not just an early-stage company but a *discourse*. It denotes simultaneously a stage of a development of a company and a cultural phenomenon. Start-ups do not just produce tech products but 'attachments to particular kinds of working conditions, and particular kinds of knowledge and ignorance' (Cockayne, 2019, p. 85). As could be seen in the 'gig economy' today, the attachments that start-ups produce

---

[14] 'City police collaborates with startups to provide innovative solutions for problems', *The Times of India*, 9 November 2019, https://timesofindia.indiatimes.com/city/hyderabad/city-pol ice-marshalls-startups-to-find-innovative-solutions-for-problems/articleshow/71976133.cms.

[15] As revealed in interviews with both entrepreneurs and police.

choose efficiency, productivity and individualism over social welfare, solidarity, democratic participation and community living, while displaying an ignorance towards all other modes of work and living except those promoted by Western ideals of efficiency (Dubal, 2020). The public sector is designated as inefficient in the same way as the market is considered to be optimal in terms of providing equal competition to all its participants. As Mancur Olson argued, the public sector is so-called inefficient because it is the only one that has to deal with collective goods, unlike the private sector (Olson, 1973). The checks and balances that make sure that the public sector keeps working for collectivities make it slower and more bureaucratic than the private sector. The myth of the people being lazy because of job security has been broken many times over but persists (Abolade, 2018) and is prevalent in the culture of tech professionals.

India has seen this cultural phenomenon up close and personal where public processes benefiting the poor have been called *leaky* and were to be replaced by more *efficient* processes by introducing technology by the private sector. The program to promote more technology in governance processes, or 'e-governance' was started as the National e-governance program or NeGP[16] started in 2006 with 27 (later increased to 31) mission mode programs which included health, education, welfare delivery, taxes and land records. 'Direct benefits transfer' to citizens was founded on the basis of replacing cash transfers (corrupt) with direct account transfers (non-corrupt). The Unique Identification Project (UID) or *Aadhaar* started in 2009 and aimed to ease the troubles of targeting the right beneficiaries for such transfers. When it was found that majority of the Indian population did not have a bank account, *Aadhaar* was used to ease the identification process to open new bank accounts (Ananth & Raghavan, 2017) and even bring the bank closer to people who lived in remote areas through a concept of the 'banking or the business correspondent' (Goel et al., 2022). The entire ecosystem of financial inclusion was based on including the private sector to achieve

---

[16] National e-governance program https://www.meity.gov.in/divisions/national-e-governance-plan accessed February 26, 2024.

governance goals. The presence of the private sector made the system more profit based than people based (Sriram, 2014).

Aadhaar became the main gateway through which the private sector entered the governance sector, considering it was headed by Nilekani who was co-founder of Infosys (a technology company in India). The project started with the promise to ensure a unique ID to every individual so that (a) the undocumented would have a way to access government services and welfare and (b) it would curtail those who avail more than their share by duplicating their identities through fraud documents. The entire onus of the alleged leakage was put on these fraud beneficiaries who apparently syphon off 85 percent of the government welfare, without mentioning the supply chain frauds where most losses took place (Dreze et al., 2020). It has been 10 years since Aadhaar began and the project has caused more exclusion than before; despite this, government and the private sector have heralded it as a success (Dreze et al., 2020; Khera, 2018, 2019; Rao, 2019).

What Aadhaar really did was to create a behemoth that contains data on all citizens regarding their daily lives or in other words, a large surveillance apparatus that provides data on every aspect of peoples' lives (Khera, 2019; Narayan, 2021; Ramanathan, 2017) which can be tapped by the private sector. The direct outcome of this is iSpirt and India Stack[17] (Dharmakumar, 2017b; Panday, 2023) which has increased the participation of the private sector in India, especially in defence and digital payments in India. As it turned out, the only people to benefit from Aadhaar were not those excluded from the welfare delivery system in India but tech entrepreneurs.

The formation of iSpirt[18] as a group of engineers who volunteer to solve 'India's hard problems' through tech should not be seen as a benevolent organisation committed to India's betterment but as a group of engineers who foresaw the data deluge Aadhaar would bring and saw how it could be harnessed at the earliest. 'India Stack' was born out of a need to provide API (Application Programming Interface) to entrepreneurs in India to aid faster product development and execution, for example,

---

[17] What is India Stack? https://ispirt.in/our-industry/indiastack/.

[18] iSPIRT homepage https://ispirt.in/.

an API to access Aadhaar authentication which aids in faster customer acquisition especially in financial or telecom sectors. However, the people who built the Stack got undue regulatory favours from the government (Dharmakumar, 2017a, 2017b). India Stack holds the keys to Aadhaar data and services without being a government owned or recognised company (Panday, 2023). They can influence policy decisions that help them or the tech startup ecosystem, which I argue further pushes the neoliberal agenda in India by making the private sector a direct partner, without any accountability, in governance in India. Currently, a private company, 'DigiYatra' is in control of managing airport entry and check-ins in India which it does using facial recognition. The company does this without any accountability or oversight of what it would do with people's data or any kind of grievance redressal (Narayan & Chandrasekhar, 2022). The journey of ending corruption in governance has ended in a creation of a parallel private industry that harvests data on people to both increase government's surveillance powers and for profit and pushes its own products and policies for governance. All the while all those who were promised to be more seen and helped by the government continue to be forgotten.

Fear Discourse and Emotional Appeal to Women' and Children's Safety

Every new technology that enables blanket surveillance over people comes with an exaggerated promise of it being beneficial to people, often underpinned by a moral narrative seeking to combat this or that social ill (Kuldova, 2022). Aadhaar, which became a leaky cauldron of data on Indian residents along with a vehicle for their exclusion, was thus promoted as a basic right of the common people (Verma & Kashyap, 2023). The government promoted it and claimed it to become a tool of inclusion of people who did not possess an identification to access welfare benefits in India. 'Safe City' projects, which plan to increase video surveillance manifold in the city are promoted as essential for the safety of women and children (Sharma et al., 2013). In Uttar Pradesh, the Safe City Project claimed to install cameras outside of women's public toilets in order to identify and arrest men loitering near these toilets and thus to increase women's safety in the state (Sur, 2021). Emotional stories of reuniting missing children with their families, which help in keeping the family bond intact, such as the story of a facial recognition system in Chennai, India, that could find missing children through an app (Khatri, 2017), are regular features in media designed to push the appeal of facial recognition systems.

Delhi Police was allowed to use the FRT it currently uses by the Delhi High Court to find missing children way back in 2017 (Tripathi & Jain, 2022). There was never any public consultation on the use of the tech, nor was it followed up by an overarching law or order by the government. Even when researchers argued that the tech was only 2 percent accurate and could not even distinguish boys from girls (Marda, 2019), it was not rolled back; instead, it was used to cull protests and detain marginalised youth in the CAA protests and Delhi riots as mentioned earlier, indicating that the original purpose was never only about finding missing children and pointing to the prevalent function creep of surveillance technologies. When I asked Pradeep how his product could only identify the missing children 2% of the time and could not even distinguish between boys and girls, he said: 'Even if two children were reunited with their families, don't you think that it is great? I could make two families happy, I feel good about it'. The promises of safety or rebuilding lost families are used primarily to gather popular support—this was the main reason in FRT deployment in Delhi (Singh, 2016), Chennai (John, 2017). This is just an entry point for a mass surveillance system that quickly launches into tertiary programs across schools, airports, government organisations and transportation and used to cull democratic rights (Dharmaraj, 2023).

Statistics show that more than 90% of all sexual harassment takes place in the private sphere and overwhelmingly high numbers of corporate sexual harassment or rape are not even reported (Dev, 2014). Yet, in India, the government does not criminalise marital rape (Banerjee & Rao, 2022) but instead spends disproportionate amount of money to surveil public places, which has not been proven to aid the safety of women.

Land use in developing countries relies on fear and property protection (Firmino et al., 2013), and hence is ripe for the use of security systems such as CCTV cameras and analytics systems such as facial recognition. Fear of the Other—in terms of religion, caste or gender, encourages people to accept more and more surveillance systems in their lives. I have argued elsewhere that even those who have borne the brunt of police action due to CCTV surveillance advocate for the tech as a promise for better safety and security. In North East Delhi in India, residents see the increased CCTV installation in their areas as a mark of progress, even an indicator of the government being finally interested in a marginalised area such as theirs (Narayan, 2023). During fieldwork, I found that people from North East Delhi expected the government to provide CCTV cameras only in elite neighbourhoods in the city, because they saw the cameras as a sign of a government that cared for the well-being of its people. Murakami Wood agrees that the phenomenon of the world's elite turning to surveillance (mostly furthered by technology products such as CCTV) for a predictable living experience (such as those in gated communities) has pushed the demand for surveillance from the population (Wood, 2012, p. 340).

Surveillance industry is only happy to oblige to the growing fear of the people by providing them increasingly more advanced surveillance tech to secure their properties, while manufacturing more fear. As my conversation with Pradeep went, he was quick to agree with the current religious insecurities hyped by the ruling Bharatiya Janata Party. Or as he put it, 'Islam is an inherently violent religion and cannot be allowed to rule India', continuing that only the current Prime Minister Modi, with his record of presiding over Hindu Muslim riots,[19] could stop an imminent Islamic rule in India. 'Would you want to walk around with a hijab all the time? No. Only Modi can save us from that', he said.

Pradeep further said that no one in India understands information warfare like the current Prime Minister, Narendra Modi. Information

---

[19] Pradeep believed that by orchestrating the Gujarat riots of 2002, which like him, many believe was the mastermind of then CM of Gujarat and now CM of India, Narendra Modi, Modi put an end to all riots in India. This was because of the scale and brutality of the riots which sent a message to all Indians and declared Modi as the 'boss' who claimed authority over all kinds of communal violence in India.

warfare, according to him, is the bots from neighbouring countries who keep creating mischief on social media and pitting Hindus against Muslims. He said that while the BJP has a thriving IT cell,[20] India does not have one of its own that can neutralise attacks of such information warfare. Though Modi understood this, he was unable to do anything about it. Pradeep did not give any reasons as to why it was so. For our purposes, it was interesting to see that (a) Pradeep conflated the entire government with the Prime Minister and (b) while Pradeep attributed strength and decisiveness to the PM, at the same time he considered him an ordinary helpless man who needed all the help he could get (preferably from the private sector).

Pradeep considered that it was the job of technology providers like him to help the PM achieve this goal, but it was not easy. This was because, according to him, 'Indians are slow to accept technology to bring changes in their life'. He said that he had a tough time making people understand that tech is a viable way to solve their problems at work. 'Indians are happy with their legacy systems and people in the government are in no mood to change or make themselves more efficient'. Pradeep spoke of a meeting with the Delhi Police officials regarding a new project he aimed to sell to them and said (of the twelve people who were in the room): 'There are 12 people in the room, which means that there are twelve egos to massage. It is very difficult to massage those many egos'. He said this because according to him, law enforcement agents were reluctant to adopt newer, more tech friendly methods to make their work easy and efficient.

That tech makes life better is not a new argument from technocrats (see also Østbø in this volume). Eugenics was supposed to suppress the deviant and inferior genes in society and push the superior genes, all for the betterment of society. However, as Molly Lad-Taylor argued, when seen from a social welfare lens, 'it appears less like a deliberate plan for genetic improvement than a mundane and all-too-modern tale of fiscal politics, troubled families, and deeply felt cultural attitudes about disability, welfare dependency, sexuality, and gender' (Lad-Taylor, 2017,

---

[20] What Pradeep calls 'thriving', is known as an abusive organisation by many who have suffered because of incessant online trolling by the BJP IT Cell (Safi, 2016).

p. 2). The push and use of video surveillance, along with other technologies of policing that Pradeep encourages people to use, all come with the promise of making life better (and assuage the fear of the Other). But in reality, they are technologies of control that are being merely sold as promises of safety and security—which they, more often than not, fail to deliver.

Eager Sales Departments

The expectations placed by sales departments on what science and technology can achieve are wild and out of this world, to say the least. Companies, like Microsoft, working to develop 'artificial general intelligence' (AGI) claim that AGI can achieve transhumanism, extropianism, singularity, cosmism, rationalism, effective altruism and longtermism—now shortened to the more manageable 'TESCREAL' (Torres, 2023a, 2023b, 2023c). In all, a number of -isms that promise human beings a better life, even after their current life is over. This claim to fame of AGI has largely created two sets of people, those who want this technology to progress and those who want to stop it. Alas, few focus on the much more immediate wrongs that generative AI and machine learning have been associated with, such as cases of bias and criminalisation and marginalised of the already oppressed (Benjamin, 2021; Buolamwini & Gebru, 2018; Marda & Narayan, 2020; Noble, 2018; Raji et al., 2020) but with the promises (or warnings) of an unidentified future.

Similarly, during my fieldwork I found that expectations from video surveillance were immense; customers, in this case the police, expected it to be a one stop solution for all their security needs. While it is difficult to understand whether it is the police whose demand fuels these expectations or the ways in which these technologies are marketed, the hype is definitely real. In my interviews with Himesh, Pradeep's colleague in the department of 'pre-sales' that acts as a bridge between the customers and the product developers (engineers) so that clients and companies could be on the same page about product requirements and expectations, he told me that the limitations of these technologies are communicated to potential customers very clearly in the early meetings. But that does not stop them from, as Himesh put it, 'expecting the Moon out of them'. Himesh narrated an incident in which a senior officer from the Delhi Police asked him to identify a man caught speeding on CCTV camera. The said man was on his motorbike at 120 kmph while wearing a helmet. The camera was installed at least 15–20 feet above on a pole and was facing the road sideways, so that it only caught a glimpse of the biker. Himesh asked me if people do not employ their 'common sense when making such demands out of a technology'.

According to Himesh, these expectations were not just there with video surveillance tech (along with facial recognition tech), but all other technologies. In another incident, he said that once a Deputy Inspector General of Police (DIG) said that he would only accept that the video surveillance and analytics solutions that Himesh's company was offering were worth using if they could predict when and where an attack would take place in a housing complex during a riot. '*Tab to baat hai*', said the DIG. This is a Hindi phrase that implies that if the tech can achieve this feat, then only it is of some use or has some 'real' capabilities. Himesh said that he made this request without even providing him with granular data of the housing complex (which the police did not even have), which would be a basic requirement.

As with the TESCREAL scenario, these heightened expectations are creations of the companies themselves that seek to make their technologies popular and irresistible to the users. According to Himesh, such inflation of expectations is done by sales and marketing departments who have no idea of the product they are selling and are only interested in closing a deal. The 'tech guys' or the engineers who are the product developers then have to create something to deliver the product promised by the sales department. Himesh said that there were constant disagreements between sales and tech teams in security companies such as theirs; however, the international hype around AI and surveillance technologies makes it difficult for them to lower their offerings or it would be impossible to make a deal. The hype cycle thus creates a simulacrum (Baudrillard, 1994) of expectations that have nothing to do with the reality of the products. I argue that this simulacrum defines further usage of these products, in a sort of a simulation (Baudrillard, 1994) such as the use of facial recognition to identify criminals, which have profound impact on the society, especially its marginalised populations.

Surveillance Tech Industry Defining the Problem of Security

Kate Crawford, while expanding on the multiple meanings of the phrase 'artificial intelligence', argued that technical systems built to detect race through skin colour, or cranial measurements are done, because they *can* be done.

> The affordances of tools become the horizon of truth. The capacity to deploy cranial measurements and digital epidermalization at scale drives a desire to find meaning in these approaches, even if this method has nothing to do with culture, heritage or diversity (...) Technical claims about accuracy and performance are commonly shot through with political choices about categories and norms but are rarely acknowledged as such. (Crawford, 2021, p. 132)

While Crawford is talking about the use of artificial intelligence systems to detect such categories as race or gender, her theory about a social issue being defined by tech is accurate. In the security and safety debate, this is a cascade of what comes to define what. In the first place, safety and security are defined mostly in terms of the property or person which we need to be protected from, typically the marginalised who are historically considered to be 'unsafe' or 'criminal'. This 'issue' becomes defined as a matter of identifying such 'unsafe' bodies, which can be resolved through surveillance. This is how video surveillance comes to be such a sought-after tech for safety and security across the world, in spite of warnings by critics (Sachitanand, 2018). Problems with policing and the police are also categorised as *resource* problems—without looking at the racist, casteist, or classist attitudes of the police force or problems connected to lacking social welfare and more—and thus as issues that can be resolved through effectivization. Entrepreneurs like Pradeep latch on to these definitions. Pradeep told me that even if leftist JNU students[21] wanted to stop technological progress, they would be unable to do so 'for an under-resourced organisation like the Police, tech is an inevitability', he said.

Pradeep said that tech would make policing more efficient as they are short on resources and are overworked. According to Pradeep, an investigating officer (IO) at the police station, generally at the SI (Sub Inspector) or ASI (Assistant Sub Inspector) level, has more than a thousand cases to his name at any given time. He asked me if I believed that the IO actually investigated any of those cases and if they had the time to write the lengthy and detailed chargesheets that they submitted to court. Before I could say anything, Pradeep informed me that the police outsources the job of writing the chargesheets to some writer or lawyer who writes the charge sheet according to a template that has been followed for thousands of cases in the past. 'The chargesheet goes to court and is immediately cancelled because the judge realises that he has seen it before (a million times). The case is closed. Just like that. The only cases that get attention are where the defendants personally know the police or have money or are in any other way influential', said Pradeep.

Pradeep asked me if I could think of ways in which tech could help improve this situation. As was his plan, he wanted to make a body camera such that when the IO goes to a place for investigation, it could record the footage. A voice to text software could put whatever he said into a text file, and it could be automatically submitted to the court. According to him, it would end the complication of filing a chargesheet. 'The police would not have to lie. This is how (and how much) tech helps and can help', he said.

Situating the body worn cameras in the larger assemblage of state surveillance that disproportionately discriminates against the poor, Michael Katell has argued that the data produced by such cameras is inherently biased against some members of the society by the nature

---

[21] JNU or Jawaharlal Nehru University in India's capital New Delhi is a well-known space of left leaning ideology. In its race towards becoming a right-wing and Hindu nation, students and professors from JNU, who have often come out as critical of the government and its policies, are derided to be communists/socialists and generally portrayed as against the idea of India's progress (Subramanian, 2020).

of police work and the 'social construction of suspicion' (Katell, 2018, p. 101). He contends that this adds to 'adverse detection' which is a 'potentially marginalising byproduct' of being recorded/observed in public (in this case by the police cameras but it is true of any other kind of video surveillance) (Katell, 2018). Katell also points to the disparaging effects of creation of such data on people's reputation (who, again by the nature of police work, are inclined to be the marginalised), which has increasingly taken quantitative forms such as in credit scores or rental scores. Kalle and Hammock have observed that 'camera perspective bias' adds to the perception of guilt (Kalle & Hammock, 2019, p. 120). Guilt is more often ascribed to an accused if the camera is facing towards them in a video footage. This can significantly alter reading of the body worn camera footage and the assessments made from it. Jones et al. have argued that the information about an incident (as transmitted by the police officers) can alter the ways in which people perceive an incident (Jones et al., 2017).

Tech industry resorts to cameras in any situation that necessitates truth seeking because visuality is the only aspect, as opposed to perception or the power differentials in society, that could be codified and for which a machine could be used. Video is pushed as the answer because video recording is the only thing that fits its capabilities.

The Perceived Rationality of the Tech Business

Let us return to the quote at the beginning of this chapter. Even after a decade of reported exclusions by India's national biometric ID, UID or Aadhaar, the developers of this technology refused to be associated with its problematic issues and detrimental social consequences. As seen in the conversation, all of them argued that they were *merely* there to create the technology. How the technology was used, or its politics, was the job and responsibility of the government. However, a number of these developers maintained that they work as 'volunteers' to develop the unique biometric ID and that they were driven by the need to do good for the country (in stark contrast to what they are now proposing); the good was thus equated with technological progress and notions of technological neutrality (despite all the evidence to the contrary).

Pradeep, too, saw himself as a mere businessman trying to survive in a competitive industry and provide products for which there was demand. His colleague, Himesh evoked the popular argument that 'guns don't kill people, people kill people' to advocate for the rights of businesses to work independently of the social world. Tech entrepreneurs/developers argue that they simply provide the governments with technology so that it could do its job better and that they have nothing to do with how it is eventually used. At the same time, they rely on and leverage popular emotions and cultural sentiments, cultural ideas of safety and even prevalent discriminatory practices in society to market and sell their products.

Tech companies create a veneer of objectivity and neutrality of their products by banking on the established notions of technology being inherently unbiased and beyond the social (Vaghela et al., 2022). Forsythe also argued that while the AI labs construct the myth of being outside of the social and cultural domain, they are a product of the given cultural and social environment where they are used (Forsythe, 2002). No tech production can exist outside of culture. As Pfaffenberger argued,

> To construct a technology is not merely to deploy materials and techniques; it is also to construct social and economic alliances, to invent new legal principles for social relations, and to provide powerful new vehicles for culturally-provided myths. (Pfaffenberger, 1992, p. 249)

Conclusion

While to a naïve observer it could look like the private sector is merely fulfilling a pre-existing demand of the state, when it comes to surveillance, a closer look at the many ways in which surveillance is normalised and even pushed by the industry, reveals a more complex picture. In states where a recorded surveillance industrial complex exists, the private sector is known to contribute to the policies regarding use of surveillance products and their expansion.

We have seen that there is a thriving private sector in security and surveillance products in India, with the market looking to be close to 2.98 billion US dollars by the year 2028. However, the scale of its involvement with public security policies, or the dynamics, nature and principles binding the public–private partnerships are so far opaque and access to information is difficult. This chapter has advocated for the need to open up the Indian surveillance industry and its ties to the states to scrutiny, opening this investigation through an interrogation of the ways in which the private sector invokes social and cultural beliefs, myths, tropes and principles to normalise and push the use of surveillance products. The most interesting part of this research, and something that led me to pursue it, is the way the private sector remains outside the purview of or shields itself from the consequences of the use of the products manufactured and promoted by them. When inquiring about their roles in the increased exclusion/violence brought about by their products, the industry hides behind the perceived neutrality of technology and association of tech products with progress and efficiency, claiming that they are *merely* fulfilling a *pre-existing* demand in the market (strategically undercommunicating the ways in which they actively fuel this demand). At the same time, they are quick to use the tropes of national security, women and child safety and internal and external security to push the sales of their products, thus legitimising them through the very moral, social and cultural narratives that they otherwise disavow. There are a number of ways, as mentioned above, how this is done not only to increase sales but also normalise and valorise the use of surveillance products. As this happens, the private sector merely watches from the side-lines as these products exacerbate discriminatory practices in the society, marginalise the already marginalised, and feed the appetite for more and more information and data by the government.

Funding and Ethics Statement   This work was funded by The Research Council of Norway under project no. 313626—*Algorithmic Governance and Cultures of Policing: Comparative Perspectives from Norway, India, Brazil, Russia, and South Africa* (AGOPOL). Informed consent has been secured from all research participants and the study was conducted in accordance with the

Jawaharlal Nehru University ethical and data protection guidelines and in compliance with AAA Code of Ethics.

References

Abolade, D. A. (2018). Impact of Employees' Job Insecurity and Employee Turnover on Organisational Performance in Private and Public Sector Organisations. *Studies in Business and Economics, 13*(2), 5–19. https://doi.org/10.2478/sbe-2018-0016

Ananth, B., & Raghavan, M. (2017). Aadhaar's Potential for Financial Inclusion. *Mint.* https://www.livemint.com/Opinion/aBWhaTbvYtXfVLK zTj9o8L/Aadhaars-potential-for-financial-inclusion.html

Ball, K., Haggerty, K. D., & Lyon, D. (2012). *Routledge Handbook of Surveillance Studies.* Routledge. https://doi.org/10.4324/9780203814949

Ball, K., & Snider, L. (Eds.). (2013). *The Surveillance-Industrial Complex: A Political Economy of Surveillance.* Routledge.

Banerjee, D., & Rao, T. S. (2022). The Dark Shadow of Marital Rape: Need to Change the Narrative. *Journal of Psychosexual Health, 4*(1), 11–13. https://doi.org/10.1177/26318318221083709

Baudrillard, J. (1994). Simulacra and Simulation. *University of Michigan Press.* https://doi.org/10.3998/mpub.9904

Benjamin, R. (2021). *Race after Technology: Abolitionist Tools for the New Jim Code.* Polity Press.

Buolamwini, J., & Gebru, T. (2018). Gender Shades: Intersectional Accuracy Disparities in Commercial Gender Classification. In S. A. Friedler & C. Wilson (Eds.), *Proceedings of the 1st Conference on Fairness, Accountability and Transparency* (Vol. 81, pp. 77–91). PMLR. https://proceedings.mlr.press/v81/buolamwini18a.html

Chander, M. (2021, September 13). 11 Ways The Delhi Police Have Muddied The Delhi-Riots Investigation, *Article 14.* https://article-14.com/post/11-ways-the-delhi-police-have-muddied-the-delhi-riots-investigation-613ebb 8c99769

Cockayne, D. (2019). What is a Startup Firm? A Methodological and Epistemological Investigation into Research Objects in Economic Geography. *Geoforum, 107*, 77–87. https://doi.org/10.1016/j.geoforum.2019.10.009

Crawford, K. (2021). *The Atlas of AI*. Yale University Press. https://doi.org/10.2307/j.ctv1ghv45t

Dev, A. (2014, February 14). Women Most Vulnerable Where They Feel Safe, *The Times of India*. https://timesofindia.indiatimes.com/city/bengaluru/women-most-vulnerable-where-they-feel-safe/articleshow/30364855.cms

Dharmakumar, R. (2017a, September 21). Platform Ambitions: The Story of How Ispirt Lost Its True North. *The Ken*. https://the-ken.com/story/platform-ambitions-story-ispirt-lost-true-north/

Dharmakumar, R. (2017b, September 22). For Whom Does the India Stack Bell Toll? *The Ken*. https://the-ken.com/story/india-stack-bell-toll/

Dharmaraj, N. (2023, May 26). The Dangers of Facial-Recognition Technology in Indian Policing, *The Caravan*. https://caravanmagazine.in/technology/dangers-of-facial-recognition-technology-in-indian-policing

Dreze, J., Khera, R., & Somanchi, A. (2020, September 28). Balancing Corruption and Exclusion: A Rejoinder, *Ideas For India* (blog). http://www.ideasforindia.in/topics/poverty-inequality/balancing-corruption-and-exclusion-a-rejoinder.html

Dubal, V. (2020, May 4). A Brief History of the Gig, *Logic(s) Magazine, 10*. https://logicmag.io/security/a-brief-history-of-the-gig/

FICCI. (2009). *Task Force Report on National Security and Terrorism*. Delhi, India: Federation of Indian Chambers of Commerce and Industry. https://aldeilis.net/mumbai/0812.pdf

Firmino, R., Kanashiro, M., Bruno, F., Evangelista, R. & Nascimento, L. (2013). Fear, Security, and the Spread of CCTV in Brazilian Cities: Legislation, Debate, and the Market, *Journal of Urban Technology, 20*(October), 65–84. https://doi.org/10.1080/10630732.2013.809221

Forsythe, D. (2001). *Studying Those Who Study Us: An Anthropologist in the World of Artificial Intelligence*. Stanford University Press. https://doi.org/10.1515/9781503619371

Goel, K., Bandara, W., & Gable, G. (2023). Banking the Unbanked: Conceptualizing Success of the Business Correspondent Model. *Information Systems Frontiers, 25*(5), 1953–1984. https://doi.org/10.1007/s10796-022-10345-7

Hayes, B. (2012). The Surveillance-Industrial Complex. In *Routledge Handbook of Surveillance Studies*. Routledge.

Jain, A. (2020a, February 17). Introduction to Facial Recognition Projects in India. *Panoptic Tracker*. https://panoptic.in/case-study/introduction-to-facial-recognition-projects-in-india

Jain, A. (2020b, September 2). Watch the Watchmen Series Part 1: The National Intelligence Grid. *Internet Freedom Foundation* (blog). https://int ernetfreedom.in/watch-the-watchmen-part-1-the-national-intelligence-grid/

Jain, A. (2023, February 24). Sanctioned Globally, Chinese CCTV Firms Are Entrenched in the Indian Market. *The Ken.* https://the-ken.com/story/san ctioned-globally-chinese-cctv-firms-are-entrenched-in-the-indian-market/

Jain, A. & Bhandari, V. (2022, April 7). The Development of Surveillance Technology in India: Beyond judicial review or oversight, *Verfassungsblog.* https://doi.org/10.17176/20220407-131426-0

Jauhar, A., & Vipra, J. (2021). *Procurement of Facial Recognition Technology for Law Enforcement in India: Legal and Social Implications of the Private Sector's Involvement.* Working Paper. Vidhi Centre for Legal Policy. https:// vidhilegalpolicy.in/research/procurement-of-facial-recognition-technology-for-law-enforcement-in-india-legal-and-social-implications-of-the-private-sectors-involvement/

John, E. A. (2017, July 8). An App That Helps Track Missing Children. *The Times of India.* https://timesofindia.indiatimes.com/city/chennai/an-app-that-helps-track-missing-children/articleshow/59496498.cms

Jones, K. A., Crozier, W. E., & Strange, D. (2017). Believing is Seeing: Biased Viewing of Body-Worn Camera Footage. *Journal of Applied Research in Memory and Cognition, 6*(4), 460–474. https://doi.org/10.1016/j.jarmac. 2017.07.007

Kalle, A., & Hammock, G. (2019). Bias in Video Evidence: Implications for Police Body Cameras. *Applied Psychology in Criminal Justice, 15*(2), 118–140.

Katell, M. A. 2018. 'Adverse Detection: The Promise and Peril of Body-Worn Cameras'. In B. C. Newell, T. Timan, & B. Koops (Eds.), *Surveillance, Privacy and Public Space* (pp. 99–118). Routledge. https://doi.org/10.4324/ 9781315200811-6

Khatri, M. (2017, July 15). To Reunite Hundreds Of Families, This Man Has Created A Missing Children Tracking App. *Indian Women BlogStories of Indian Women* (blog). https://www.indianwomenblog.org/to-reunite-hun dreds-of-families-this-man-has-created-a-missing-children-tracking-app/

Khera, R. (2018). The Aadhaar debate: Where are the sociologists? *Contributions to Indian Sociology, 52*(3), 336–342. https://doi.org/10.1177/006996 6718787029

Khera, R. (2019, April 6). Aadhaar Failures: A Tragedy of Errors, *Epw Engage.* https://www.epw.in/engage/article/aadhaar-failures-food-services-welfare

Kuldova, T. Ø. (2022). *Compliance-Industrial Complex.* Palgrave Macmillan. https://doi.org/10.1007/978-3-031-19224-1

Ladd-Taylor, M. (2017). *Fixing the Poor: Eugenic Sterilization and Child Welfare in the Twentieth Century.* Johns Hopkins University Press.

Marda, V. (2019, July 21). Facial Recognition Is an Invasive and Inefficient Tool. *The Hindu.* https://www.thehindu.com/opinion/op-ed/facial-recognition-is-an-invasive-and-inefficient-tool/article62109426.ece

Marda, V. & Narayan, S. (2020). Data in New Delhi's Predictive Policing System. In *Proceedings of the 2020 Conference on Fairness, Accountability, and Transparency,* pp. 317–24. FAT* '20. New York, NY, USA: Association for Computing Machinery. https://doi.org/10.1145/3351095.3372865

Nader, L. (1972). Up the Anthropologist: Perspectives Gained from Studying Up. In D. Hymes (Ed.), *Reinventing Anthropology* (pp. 284–311). Random House.

Nader, L. (2011). Ethnography as Theory. *HAU: Journal of Ethnographic Theory, 1*(1), 211–219. https://doi.org/10.14318/hau1.1.008

Narayan, S. (2021). Guilty Until Proven Guilty: Policing Caste Through Preventive Policing Registers in India. *Journal of Extreme Anthropology, 5*(1), Article 1. https://doi.org/10.5617/jea.8797

Narayan, S. (2023). CCTVs and the Criminal City. *Surveillance & Society, 21*(4), 363–374. https://doi.org/10.24908/ss.v21i4.15779

Narayan, S., & Chandrasekhar, R. (2022). *Niti Aayog Discussion Paper, November 2022- Adopting the Responsible AI Principles: A Use Case Approach on Facial Recognition Technology* (SSRN Scholarly Paper 4476124). https://doi.org/10.2139/ssrn.4476124

Noble, S. U. (2018). *Algorithms of Oppression: How Search Engines Reinforce Racism* (Illustrated edition). New York University Press.

Nyquist, A., & Leivestad, H. (2017). *Ethnographies of Conferences and Trade Fairs: Shaping Industries.* Palgrave Macmillan.

Oldani, M. J. (2004). Thick Prescriptions: Toward an Interpretation of Pharmaceutical Sales Practices. *Medical Anthropology Quarterly, 18*(3), 325–356. https://doi.org/10.1525/maq.2004.18.3.325

Olson, M. (1973). Evaluating Performance in the Public Sector. In *The Measurement of Economic and Social Performance,* pp. 355–409. NBER. https://www.nber.org/system/files/chapters/c3618/c3618.pdf

Panday, J. (2023). *India Stack: Public-Private Roads to Data Sovereignty.* Internet Governance Project. https://www.internetgovernance.org/research/india-stack-public-private-roads-to-data-sovereignty/

Paul, D. B., & Spencer, H. G. (1995). The Hidden Science of Eugenics. *Nature, 374*, 302–304. https://doi.org/10.1038/374302a0

Pfaffenberger, B. (1992). Social Anthropology of Technology. *Annual Review of Anthropology, 21*, 491–516. https://doi.org/10.1146/annurev.an.21.100192.002423

Raji, I. D., Gebru, T., Mitchell, M., Buolamwini, J., Lee, J., & Denton, E. (2020). Saving Face: Investigating the Ethical Concerns of Facial Recognition Auditing. In *Proceedings of the AAAI/ACM Conference on AI, Ethics, and Society* (pp. 145–151). Association for Computing Machinery. https://doi.org/10.1145/3375627.3375820

Ramanathan, U. (2017, April 12). Blundering along, dangerously. *Frontline.* https://frontline.thehindu.com/cover-story/blundering-along-dangerously/article9629188.ece

Rao, U. (2019). Response to 'The Aadhaar Debate: Where are the Sociologists?' *Contributions to Indian Sociology, 53*(3), 431–440. https://doi.org/10.1177/0069966719861759

Sachitanand, R. (2018, October 30). Sales of Surveillance Cameras Are Soaring, Raising Questions about Privacy. *The Economic Times.* https://economictimes.indiatimes.com/news/politics-and-nation/sales-of-surveillance-cameras-are-soaring-raising-questions-about-privacy-regulation/articleshow/66195866.cms?from=mdr

Safi, M. (2016, December 27). India's Ruling Party Ordered Online Abuse of Opponents, Claims Book. *The Guardian.* https://www.theguardian.com/world/2016/dec/27/india-bjp-party-ordering-online-abuse-opponents-actors-modi-claims-book

Sharma, A., Singh, A., Singh, D., Bansal, K., Chowdhary, R., & Jain, V. (2013). 'Safe Cities: The India Story'. *PwC.* https://www.pwc.com/gx/en/psrc/assets/pwc-psrc-safe-cities-the-india-story.pdf

Sharma, P. & Rajput, S. eds. (2017). *Sustainable Smart Cities in India: Challenges and Future Perspectives.* Springer International.

Shika, S. (2023, February 24). Delhi Burning: A Timeline of CAA Protests and North East Delhi Violence. *Outlook India.* https://www.outlookindia.com/national/delhi-burning-a-timeline-of-caa-protests-and-northeast-delhi-violence-news-265077

Singh, S. R. (2016, October 29). Missing Kids: Govt Looks for Developer to Make Facial Recognition Software, *Hindustan Times.* https://www.hindustantimes.com/delhi/missing-kids-govt-looks-for-developer-to-make-facial-recognition-software/story-cG8ggrabtkaaJICiMv7ieL.html

Smith, D. T. (2015). From the Military-industrial Complex to the National Security State. *Australian Journal of Political Science, 50*(3), 576–590. https://doi.org/10.1080/10361146.2015.1067761

Sriram, M. S. (2014). Identity for Inclusion: Moving beyond Aadhaar. *Economic and Political Weekly, 49*(28), 148–154. JSTOR.

Subramanian, S. (2020, February 20). How Hindu Supremacists are Tearing India Apart. *The Guardian.* https://www.theguardian.com/world/2020/feb/20/hindu-supremacists-nationalism-tearing-india-apart-modi-bjp-rss-jnu-attacks

Sur, A. (2021, Auust 19). Lucknow Safe City Project: Uttar Pradesh to Deploy Facial Recognition, "label" Faces. *MediaNama.* https://www.medianama.com/2021/08/223-lucknow-safe-city-project-uttar-pradesh-facial-recognition/

Torres, É. P. (2023a, October 14). The "TESCREAL Conspiracy Theory" Conspiracy Theory. *Medium* (blog). https://xriskology.medium.com/the-tescreal-conspiracy-theory-conspiracy-theory-34f20bb8ecb9

Torres, É. P. (2023b, June 11). AI and the Threat of "Human Extinction": What Are the Tech-Bros Worried about? It's Not You and Me. *Salon.* https://www.salon.com/2023/06/11/ai-and-the-of-human-extinction-what-are-the-tech-bros-worried-about-its-not-you-and-me/

Torres, É. P. (2023c, June 15). TESCREALism: The Acronym Behind Our Wildest AI Dreams and Nightmares. *Truthdig.* https://www.truthdig.com/articles/the-acronym-behind-our-wildest-ai-dreams-and-nightmares/

Tripathi, G. P., & Jain, A. (2022, August 21). Explained | Delhi Police's Use of Facial Recognition Technology. *The Hindu.* https://www.thehindu.com/sci-tech/technology/explained-delhi-polices-use-of-facial-recognition-technology/article65793897.ece

Vaghela, P., Jackson, S. J., & Sengers, P. (2022). Interrupting Merit, Subverting Legibility: Navigating Caste In 'Casteless' Worlds of Computing. *Proceedings of the 2022 CHI Conference on Human Factors in Computing Systems.* https://doi.org/10.1145/3491102.3502059

Verma, M., & Kashyap, P. (2023, April 23). In Widening Scope of Aadhaar, Government Is Crossing Red Lines Set by Supreme Court. *The Indian Express.* https://indianexpress.com/article/opinion/columns/in-widening-scope-of-aadhaar-government-is-crossing-red-lines-set-by-supreme-court-8571764/

Wedel, J. (2014). *Unaccountable: How the Establishment Corrupted Our Finances.* Pegasus Books.

Wood, D. M. (2012). Globalization and Surveillance. In K. Ball, K. Haggerty & D. Lyon (Eds.), *Routledge Handbook of Surveillance Studies* (pp. 333–342). Routledge. https://doi.org/10.4324/9780203814949.ch3_5_a

7

E-Governance and Smart Policing in Kerala, India: Towards a Kerala Model of Algorithmic Governance?

Ashwin Varghese ⓘ

In 2019, Kerala Police became the first police force in India to launch/recruit a humanoid police robot, called 'KP Bot' at the Sub-Inspector (SI) rank to serve in the Kerala Police headquarters. While the primary tasks of the humanoid robot were to perform duties at the front office of the police headquarters, it was an initiative aimed at the introduction of technology into policing (Unnithan, 2019). This initiative must be seen in the context of other technology-related initiatives and policies of the Kerala state government. Kerala was the first state in India to recognize the right to the internet as a basic human right in 2017 (TNN, 2017). Through numerous initiatives, Kerala has been attempting to integrate the use of technology in its various government schemes. In 2021, the state government laid out elaborate plans for 'e-governance' integrating existing state service with Information Communication Technology

A. Varghese (✉)
O.P. Jindal Global University, Sonipat, India
e-mail: ashwin.varghese@jgu.edu.in

213

T. Ø. Kuldova et al. (eds.), *Policing and Intelligence in the Global Big Data Era, Volume I*, Palgrave's Critical Policing Studies, https://doi.org/10.1007/978-3-031-68326-8_7

(ICT) for 'better governance' (Administrative Reforms Commission, 2021).

Digitization of policing practices, the integration of everyday policing with ICT, and more recently with AI, are all parts of these initiatives. In this regard, in 2022 the Kerala Police and the Digital University of Kerala launched a special training programme for 'capacity building in responsible AI and data analytics for the police department' (Staff Reporter, 2022). The police are also reported to have been working on introducing a new software, iCoPS, to leverage the extensive volume of data available on the Crime and Criminal Tracking Network and System (CCTNS)[1] for everyday policing. Cited as next-generation policing, it is visualized as part of the e-governance initiative, laying down the path to transition from 'conventional policing' to 'intelligent policing' (Staff Reporter, 2022).

While the previous decade focused on digitization of existing policing infrastructure, or else equipping police stations with computers, using in-house software to coordinate filing systems and internal communication and so on, the current decade—as per the *Kerala Police Vision Document 2030* (Vision 2030 Kerala Police, 2021) is to focus on incorporating technology for crime and criminal information management for better decision-making through AI, big data repository, cyber-surveillance technologies and so on. This attempt at modernization is aimed at introducing predictive policing and new modes of crime prevention and pre-emption.

Some measures in this regard are already under way at the time of writing (December 2023). The motor vehicle department has installed 726 AI-enabled cameras across the state of Kerala to track minor traffic violations and report them automatically to the state control unit, to be processed into penalties/fines (George, 2023). In this case, the officials have argued that the aim is to create a mechanism that seeks compliance from the citizens rather than increasing surveillance. The transition to e-governance and adoption of technology for governance received a renewed impetus during the Covid-19 pandemic governance-induced

---

[1] CCTNS is a National online platform for the recording of police data related to crimes and cases across police stations in India.

lockdowns. Digital infrastructure in state services, till the era of Covid-19, was an additional component of civic infrastructure, accessed by the select few. Post-Covid-19, digital infrastructure became incorporated into public imagination as part of the *essential* or even critical infrastructure of the state, necessitating a need to transform and 'modernize' this state infrastructure.

For both e-Governance and policing in Kerala, the incorporation of modern technology (Big Data, AI, ICT and algorithmic infrastructures) is envisioned as a response to the need of 'modernization'. In this context, the perceived merits of e-governance are, according to the Administrative Reforms Commission.

> providing various government services with transparency, effective inter-action between the government and the public, people empowerment by enabling information dissemination, alleviation of corruption, reduced expenditure on governance and, overcoming delay in providing various government services. (Administrative Reforms Commission, 2021, p. 7)

The need for reform, articulated in the governance and policy circles as much as the police itself, emerges from the perception that existing modes of policing and governance are outdated, outmoded and inefficient and the perception of the state as incapable of addressing the contemporary needs of the people. In effect, the rhetoric of 'efficiency' guides the transformation towards e-governance and smart policing.

Contextualizing 'Efficiency' in the Indian Bureaucracy

Given that 'efficiency' is the main legitimizing framework for the introduction of these technologies and that the concept has conventionally guided reform of state institutions, it is important to contextualize and unpack it here. The rhetoric of efficiency has conventionally been used to enable neoliberal transformations of the state. In the context of the police in India, the 'misuse' of police for partisan interests emerged as a reason for advocating police reforms in the 1970s; this was most prominent during the period of national emergency from 1975–1977 when under the aegis of the then central government, the emergency provisions of the Indian Constitution were invoked to suspend civil liberties and impose central executive control over the democratic machinery of the nation. During this period several reports emerged of central government's 'misuse' of police to suppress dissent and criticism (for more see Prakash, 2018). Following the period of emergency, the new central government appointed the National Police Commission to enquire into excesses committed during the emergency to look into the entire policing administration and suggest changes, 'to make the institution more democratic and in tune with the wishes of the voter' (Verma, 2011). The demands for insulation of police from political interference and functional autonomy emerged prominently in the Second Report of the National Police Commission (1979). With the advent of neoliberalism in the 1980s and 1990s in India, the police reform agenda picked up pace. Setting commissions to advocate reforms became progressively more rapid in the neoliberal phase, these included the Ribeiro Committee (1998), Padmanabaiah Committee (2000), Malimath Committee (2001–03), Soli Sorabjee Committee (2005) and the landmark Supreme Court Judgment in the *Prakash Singh and Ors. vs. Union of India and Ors. (2006)* case. Through these commissions 'insulation' and 'functional autonomy for efficient policing' increasingly became the rhetoric of demanding transformation of policing systems. As is evident from the *Prakash Singh and Ors. vs. Union of India and Ors. (2006)* case, the police reform agenda in the 1990s became more and more a subject of judicial activism, where hopes of police reform were pinned on judicial orders from the Supreme Court. While in the 1970s police reform had been a political debate, in the 1990s under neoliberalism it became a matter of technocratic transformation (Das Gupta, 2016; Varghese, 2023).

Neoliberal states, as Harvey (2007) argues, persistently seek internal reorganization, with a profound preference for executive and judicial orders and strong distrust for democratic decision-making. Neoliberals, pace Harvey, prefer to insulate key institutions of the state from democratic pressures; this creates a paradox of intense state interventions by elites and 'experts' by a state which is not supposed to be interventionist. The adoption of algorithmic infrastructures is perhaps the latest wave of 'internal reorganization' of the state that allows the state institutions to be further insulated from democratic pressures and ever more dependent on the rule of experts, knowledge and data brokers and intermediaries (Kuldova, 2022). While on the one hand, judicial and legislative responses to demands of police reforms owing to 'misuse' of police for partisan interests have led to the advocacy of functional autonomy and insulation from political interference, on the other hand, actual executive-led reforms have led to further centralization and militarization of an already paramilitary policing system. Verma (2005) has highlighted the phenomenal growth of armed police and paramilitary forces in post-colonial India, on the grounds of escalating violent conflicts, terrorism and threats to stability; to the extent that today central and provincial level armed police units far outnumber those engaged in crime control tasks.

Technological transformation of state institutions has been the dream of technocratic, neoliberal reforms, whereby technology is perceived to be bias free, objective, non-partisan and driven by expertise, thereby making state institutions more 'efficient'. Echoing the same arguments elsewhere, technological transformation of the state under the promise of 'efficiency' has been extensively debated in the West through concepts like the 'network state' (Castells, 2005), 'algorithmic governance' (Katzenbach & Ulbricht, 2019) 'digital veillance' (Lupton, 2015) and 'hyperconnectivity' (Brubaker, 2023). It appears therefore that algorithmic governance under the promise of 'efficiency' also offers the possibility of reform via expertise insulated from democratic pressures. Here it becomes doubly important to unpack why the state of Kerala, which has been famous for the propagation of an alternate development strategy, popularly known as the Kerala Model, and vociferous in its opposition to neoliberalism, is spearheading the transition towards algorithmic governance in India.

Kerala Model and Technology

What is the Kerala Model?

The Kerala model of development has received international critical attention and has been a source of political debate and deliberation, predominantly associated with its sustainability. This model is seen to be a humanitarian model, with primary focus on improving human development indicators through consistently high social sector spending on sectors like primary health, education, food and so on, rather than unmitigated growth. The model is premised on a dedication to egalitarian redistribution of available resources (Varghese, 2021).

Owing to the quasi-federal structure of Indian polity, the fiscal autonomy of the State has been significantly conditioned by national policies. The period of 1980s and 1990s characterized as Neoliberalism in India (Das Gupta, 2016) also brought challenges for the Kerala model. A period of virtual economic stagnation for two decades and declining employment opportunities in the 1980s forced a revision in the Kerala model. This period of stagnation was seen as a crisis wherein consistently high social sector spending, coupled with low growth and a declining capacity to meet the state's expenditures led to discussions on the long-term sustainability of the Kerala model (Varghese, 2021). This spurred a revision in the Kerala model, as a 'transition within capitalism' (Heller, 1999), wherein strategic concessions to capital were provided to stimulate productive investment, with a strong impetus for small private cooperative enterprises rather than despotic forms of capitalist production.

While this transition was able to overcome the economic stagnation in the 1980s, the increasing adoption of neoliberal policies, globally and nationally, has resulted in the shrinking of the relative autonomy of the state (Poulantzas, 2000 [1978]) necessitating a revision in the Kerala model. To mitigate these effects, the Kerala government had launched an ambitious programme of democratic decentralization, popularly known as the People's Planning Campaign (PPC), first in 1980s and then in the late 1990s. While decentralization itself was a neoliberal policy of the World Bank and IMF, Kerala attempted to adapt the same as a strategy of resistance to the structural adjustment policies by emphasizing its democratic element. In this experiment, the focus was on devolution of decision-making powers to the grass root level from parliament to local self-government units. The stated aim here was to create a possibility for direct participation of the masses in day-to-day governance (Isaac & Franke, 2004). This campaign was subsequently abandoned owing to severe opposition, as well as perceived failure of the project in instances where decentralization of power also led to decentralization of corruption.

In this context of the shrinking of the relative autonomy of the state under neoliberal policies, Kerala has consistently been attempting to adapt modern technology as a means to democratize governance, often attempting to adapt policies spearheaded by neoliberal states. The adoption of an e-governance framework and spearheading algorithmic transformation of state practices including policing today thus follows the rhetoric of efficiency, with the aim of democratization understood as citizen's direct participation in governance and state processes. Since the project of e-governance is still in its initial stages, it remains to be seen how this will play out.

The Rhetoric of AI and Big Data in Kerala—'To Serve a Pluralist Democracy'

The vision for algorithmic governance becomes clearer in the 11th Administrative Reforms Committee Report of the government of Kerala (Administrative Reforms Commission, 2021), which sees 'e-governance' as a paradigm shift in governance systems, for which adoption of AI, Big Data, Data Analytics and so on, is necessary. However, it also imbues the State government with a responsibility to include vulnerable and marginalized sections of society while adopting ICT technologies.

After the experiment with decentralization, and increased instances of corruption, e-governance, that is access to government services through online services in public service delivery, is seen to improve transparency and accountability while reducing the cost-of-service delivery. As noted above, the ARC report states that.

the merits of e-Governance are – providing various government services with transparency, effective interaction between the government and the public, people empowerment by enabling information dissemination, alleviation of corruption, reduced expenditure on governance and, over-coming delay in providing various government services. (Administrative Reforms Commission, 2021, p. 7)

In this way, online services are seen as a way of decentralizing and democratizing state services. In this vision, existing mechanisms are seen as outdated and in need of modernization; therefore, a larger chunk of these initiatives included the transition from physical record, to computer-based systems.

The transition towards algorithmic governance is advocated as a progressive development, implemented through two phases. Here, the policymakes a distinction between 'e-government' and 'e-governance', with the former being a transformation of government services through the incorporation of ICT, while the latter is associated with a further transformation in government-people relationship premised on people-centricity, choice, consultation, engagement and empowerment, with the aim of digital transformation.

The adoption of algorithmic infrastructures in policing in Kerala can be seen in this framework of e-government vs. e-governance as well. Algorithmic transformation in policing is envisioned as a requirement to serve the policing needs of a transforming society in Kerala. In addition to demographic changes, migration patterns and other factors, the need for modernization of policing is seen to emerge from the growing penetration of modern technology in everyday lives—or else, the effects of digital hyperconnectivity on the transformation of self and social life (Brubaker, 2023). Thereby the first impetus emerges from the need to keep pace with the changing mode of social life. In this regard, as mentioned above, the previous decade focused on digitization of current infrastructure, and the current decade focuses on the incorporation of AI, Big Data, machine learning, cyber-surveillance and other rapidly evolving technologies.

This second phase may be seen as the transition towards e-governance which in the context of policing is seen to offer the capacity to improve information collection, preservation and analysis through AI-based platforms, and hence improve decision-making, thereby making the policing system more efficient through automation, as well as through surveillance and algorithmic infrastructures, creating the capacity to predict crime which will be beneficial for society and state alike (Kerala Police, 2021).

The rhetoric of e-governance and algorithmic transformation of existing cultures of policing are thus aimed at modernizing the state and its services to serve the needs of a 'pluralistic democracy', by making it efficient, bias-free and corruption free. So far, I have outlined the rhetoric as it appears in state reports and publications. To contextualize this, it is important to unpack how state functionaries and the general public perceive these transitions as well.

AI and Big Data: General Perception

In the official rhetoric, there appears to be no differentiation between the two phases—incorporation of computers, and adoption of frameworks of algorithmic governance/e-governance as outlined in the Kerala Police Vision Document 2030 and the 11th Administrative Reforms Committee Report. They are seen as logical extensions in the path of modernization. However, in the perception of the general public, as is evident from media reports, advocacy groups and civil society debates, a crucial difference can be seen in the two phases. While digitization as incorporation of modern technology (computers, phones and other digital devices) is not viewed as threatening privacy and increasing surveillance, the adoption of algorithmic infrastructures is increasingly seen to have the possibility of violating privacy, furthering discrimination and marginalization (Benny, 2023; Manorama, 2023). The Kerala Police Vision Document 2030 acknowledges this as well, wherein having laid out the merits of algorithm-driven policing, it notes that 'although modern surveillance through Data Science, Big-data and algorithm-driven policing has already been projected as a threat to personal security, privacy and constitutional rights of citizens' (Kerala Police, 2021, p. 44). However, while there is an acknowledgement of these possible harms in the vision document, there is no mechanism presented through which the Police in its adoption of algorithmic infrastructures would ensure the mitigation of these threats and harms. For the police, the stated primary purpose is to protect the integrity of the Union of India, and internal security 'while' protecting life, liberty and dignity of every person. Therefore, in the logic of policing, it appears that the 'threats' to privacy, personal security and constitutional rights are secondary to the threats to the integrity of the Union and internal security.

The framework of policing itself cannot be seen to address these threats, as accountability of the policing infrastructure emerges from the executive structure that the police are a part of. One may state that the e-governance framework imbues the responsibility of democratic accountability and 'people-centric' implementation of digital transformation of social life into the governance framework. Since the adoption of algorithmic infrastructure is currently in its nascent stages, whether this interface of e-governance and algorithm-driven policing will create people-centric digital transformation of the state remains to be seen.

In practice, the roll-out of algorithmic infrastructures in policing, during the writing of this chapter in summer 2023, had been done on three fronts: (1) AI cameras for road safety, to monitor traffic violations, (2) AI-enabled Facial Recognition System and AI for data management through iCoPS, a software to record and analyse police data and (3) Drone X—a state wide drone surveillance mechanism with district units. Reports of 'teething' troubles have already emerged where the AI cameras for road safety have detected images which are not violations: for instance, a driver in black shirt is detected as driving without a seat belt, thereby mandating a further manual monitoring (Kallungal, 2023). However, it is expected that with time the system would learn to make more accurate detections.

In other instances, Kerala Police reported having successfully identified suspects in theft cases using FRS in the iCoPS software allowing personnel to instantaneously compare images of suspects through a database of 1.5 lakh 'criminals'. Similarly, they reported identification of unidentified deceased persons with the use of FRS (AS, 2023; Mathrubhumi, 2023). However, this comes against the backdrop of other reports of misidentification and wrongful prosecution of individuals as suspects through CCTV footage (although not through AI) (Padanna, 2023). Potential misrecognition and wrongful prosecution through AI-enabled FRS has been discussed by various scholars and commentators (Jaswal, 2023).

Kerala has been proactively incorporating algorithmic infrastructure in its arsenal of policing and surveillance tools. It has become the first state in India to implement drone surveillance in all districts and launch an indigenously developed anti-drone software to identify and immobilize malicious drones. The stated purpose here has been law-and-order and disaster management, especially in difficult and hard-to-reach terrain (Press Trust of India, 2023).

In all these instances, it is important to note, that algorithmic infrastructures do not replace existing mechanisms, but increase the speed or rate through which decisions could be made, alas not necessarily accurately. Speed is therefore equated with efficiency. For instance, in the case of FRS the earlier mechanism would have been of personnel manually scanning the database of 1.5 lakh criminals to find a match with the image of the suspect, which the AI-enabled FRS does instantaneously, thereby providing 'evidence' for instant police action.

Policing today is seen to be outdated also because it is perceived as slow. Algorithmic infrastructures allow for fast policing, fast decision-making, thereby improving 'efficiency'. However, inaccuracy in instances of misrecognition and wrongful prosecution may have devastating consequences for individuals, such as wrongful imprisonment as in the case of misidentification through CCTV footage mentioned above.

The adoption of algorithmic infrastructures in policing, given the primary purpose, framework and mechanism of policing in India, is driven by two perspectives—first, a perception that social life is transforming and becoming high-tech, owing to which crime and criminal activity have also become high-tech and therefore policing mechanisms 'need' to modernize to keep pace with the changing nature of society and crime, to be able to perform its basic functions. The ingress of Chat GPT in everyday life is frequently cited as an example of this. The first perspective is therefore derived from a perceived need of modernizing to perform basic functions (Kerala Police Officers Association 33rd

State Conference, 2023b). Second, a perspective that algorithmic infrastructures provide quick 'evidence' for prosecution and therefore allow for swift action, leading to swift justice (Kerala Police Officers Association 33rd State Conference, 2023a). This perspective is derived from improving the speed at which policing tasks are done. AI is seen to offer faster detection, faster and wider analysis of data, 'objective' evidence and therefore faster disposal of cases. Efficiency in policing, and in bureaucracy in general, is marked by the rate at which cases are cleared. Pendency is indicative of inefficiency, and therefore mechanisms that allow for swift disposal of cases are viewed to increase efficiency.

The internal logic of bureaucracy and policing thus prioritizes internal functions and discipline over democratic accountability. This responsibility rests on the democratically elected executive that is the State government, which must implement e-governance from a people-centric perspective. Therefore, under the current mechanism, democratic accountability rests on the interface of e-governance and algorithmic infrastructures and is not embedded in the infrastructures themselves, which also means that the actual practice of algorithmic infrastructures would be heavily dependent on the dominant political will of the State.

Democratization and Cultures of Policing

The ARC report indicates the political will of the state in its rhetoric, wherein it notes that the adoption of e-governance to spearhead the digital transformation towards a 'digital Kerala' is premised on the idea of 'people-centricity', i.e., 'looking at service delivery from the eyes of the people rather than the process or operational perspective of government' (Administrative Reforms Commission, 2021, p. 136). This is to be operationalized through the creation of new value, using three lenses— 'cashless, presence-less, and paperless' (Administrative Reforms Commission, 2021, p. 127). People-centricity is thus derived from infrastructures that are burdensome for those accessing state services, which through these three lenses could be streamlined and speeded up. The agenda behind becomes clearer when government functionaries refer to how e-governance has transformed state services. The key stated effect of this infrastructural transformation has been in the reduction of corruption. Government functionaries claim that e-governance has reduced corruption, because the system has created an infrastructure wherein people can access and avail state services, without relying on human interface which may lead to corruption (Kerala Police Officers Association 33rd State Conference, 2023a). In this way, one may note that the emphasis on the three lenses—cashless, presence-less, paperless—is to highlight the absence of an infrastructure where availing state service is dependent on a paper application being processed by state functionaries through a paper trail, wherein the state functionary becomes an always potentially either corruptible or corrupted intermediary and hence a potential site of abuse of power through the demand or taking of bribes.

Automation here is seen as a means to bypass the face-to-face mechanisms of corruption, while making state services accessible to the public. One may speculate that this has been designed through the experience of the people's planning campaign, where decentralization of decision-making operated by creating multiple nodes of decision-making centres in local self-government institutions, reportedly leading to decentralization of corruption, allegations of related malpractices and misappropriation of funds (Chathukulam & John, 2002; Varghese, 2021). E-governance infrastructures and automation of decision-making are viewed here as having a democratic potential.

The blame of abuse of state power and authority is placed on *individual* functionaries and the fallible and corruptible *human*, wherein democratization is seen as a consequence of *machinistic* automation since automation is also leading to automatic and timely access to state services. Human fallibility in the face of technology and automation operates by embedding Promethean shame (van Dijk, 2000) within the human actors, wherein convinced of their inherent fallibility and obsolescence, trust and responsibility are transferred to and vested on what are perceived to be 'technologically advanced' (albeit obscure and unreliable) frameworks, willingly by human actors to create mechanisms bereft of human error. This promotes a technocratic vision of state services, where human participants are viewed as potential sites of corruption and abuse, thereby creating a logic where automation is equated with democratization and good governance (Kuldova et al., 2024). In this framework, biases of the algorithmic infrastructure are not seen as having serious consequences, but are rather errors that can be fixed through software upgrades. This application of automated solutions to problems of the bureaucracy is premised on an inherent technocratic imagination of bureaucratic functioning, where human agents are required to function in the design of automation, as mechanical workers, in providing state services.

A similar transformation in policing practices however may have different effects. Since the purpose of policing is social order, operationalized through a monopoly over legitimate use of violence, 'errors' in automation have far more devastating consequences.

Legacy of Policing—Discipline and Control

Everyday practices of policing in India still follow a colonial legacy. Scholars (Arnold, 1986; Baxi, 1982; Bayley, 1971; Raghavan, 1986) have noted how everyday practices today are reminiscent of a colonial past, where the police were established to serve the interests and needs of the government in power, rather than the population. These practices were established by the Police Act of 1861, the Indian Penal Code 1860 and the Criminal Procedure Code 1862. While the Police Act 1861 and Criminal Procedure Code 1862 are not in force today, many of the practices established in these still hold sway.

Following Independence, the police in India were not radically overhauled, but rather adapted to serve the needs of a parliamentary democracy. Many of the internal structures and practices were retained as they were, with one important change being that the police had been made accountable to a democratically elected state executives. In this way, while several states have passed laws to constitute and regulate the police forces in the state, like the Kerala Police Act of 2011 or the Delhi Police Act of 1978, in its organizational framework they still owe allegiance to the 1861 Police Act.

Drawing on its legacy and continuity from the colonial model, I have argued that the everyday practices of police work predate its regulation by laws of independent India, as remnants of a system where the task of the police was dictated by executive orders rather than by constitutional law. These practices viewed policing as primarily a mechanism to impose social order through internal disciplinary control (Varghese, 2023).

Disciplinary control within the internal functioning of the police is paramount. Discipline is conceptualized as fundamental to the functioning of the police, wherein discipline is seen to be necessary to ensure the proper functioning of police duties and responsibilities. Effectively the police, within the framework of *governmentality*, is a technology of the state (Foucault, 2007) operationalized to control its population and fabricate a social order that aligns with the dominant mode of production (Neocleous, 2000). To achieve this, however, I argue, that the police force, that is police personnel themselves, have to be subjected to disciplinary control first. In this case, discipline exists as a mechanism of internal control, so as to execute social reordering.

While the political framework of the state has today transformed from colonial to postcolonial, the importance of discipline in policing has remained intact. The Kerala Police Vision Document 2030 states that

> it is necessary that the Police are subject to disciplinary control with the objective of ensuring that they do not abuse the lawful authority vested in them. Simultaneously, it is necessary that the Police are protected from unwarranted influences to enable them to function impartially as required by the Constitution. (Kerala Police, 2021, p. 11)

The framework of discipline in the colonial state was necessary to ensure that subordinate personnel do not collude with the colonial subjects and turn against the state (Arnold, 1986). Discipline was necessary to control the indigenous subordinate personnel who were perceived with distrust by the colonial state. This mechanism has morphed in postcolonial state into distrust of personnel and the potential to abuse lawful authority.

Discipline in policing aims to achieve what I have called elsewhere 'automatic docility' (Varghese, 2022). Automatic docility may be seen as an expression of power relations which do not attract conscious reflection or engagement. This is primarily expressed in manners of the body as 'automatic' gestures, ways of talking, perceiving, etc. The disciplinary apparatus in police organizations is primarily aimed at creating, as Foucault terms it, 'docile bodies' (Foucault, 1991, p. 138). Automatic docility represents the embodiment of discipline in a manner that potentially translates into automatic execution of orders.

To understand what algorithmic governance transforms in everyday practice, we need to first unpack the competing interests that condition everyday practices. While in rhetoric, e-governance, algorithmic infrastructures, AI and so on are seen as offering avenues for swift and automatic service delivery, I argue that they offer avenues and renewed possibility to achieve automatic docility.

Algorithmic Infrastructures and Automatic Docility

The operationalization of state power is contingent on the everyday practices of the state personnel. State practices that are contingent on decision-making of these personnel, represent multiple sites of power relations, wherein some instances may represent 'abuse of power', such as bribery, corruption or disproportionate targeting of minorities. Human participation in state practices are sites of complex power relations and thus also potential sites of contestations. Algorithmic infrastructures sanitize the decision-making frameworks of these sites of contestations by attempting to automate decision-making. In general parlance, this automation is what leads to the guise of automated decision-making as bias free, objective and non-partisan—as apolitical because technical. Automation of decision-making, however, does not make those frameworks democratic or just.

Automation aims to rid the decision-making process of discretion and bias. This can potentially lead to unmitigated social control and discipline. Discipline within policing strives for the subjection of the personnel to the automatic execution of orders. Automatic docility operationalizes the subjection of the 'person' in personnel, in such a manner that the execution of an order is performed by a 'rank' and not a 'person'. The personal and the human of the personnel are stripped of personality through automatic docility and reduced to the function of the rank. For instance, in the case of traffic violations, police personnel deployed at traffic intersections and police stations based on their discretion would assess whether particular instances of non-adherence of traffic rules qualify as an offence for which fines need to be issued. In these situations, personnel would often ignore certain instances of non-adherence based on their own self-estimation. The schema of discipline however demands that these tasks be performed by specific ranks in the subordinate police, irrespective of their personal intent, wherein the personnel's role is conceptualized as objective interpretation and application of legal norms. This is a dehumanizing function of discipline, which views discretionary acts as biased and prone to error. AI-enabled cameras function by stripping the subordinate personnel of their discretionary role and replacing it with the AI infrastructure, which both assesses the perceived non-adherence of rules and issues fines automatically, thereby leaving the personnel to act only as operators to execute the decisions that the AI framework has made.

Algorithmic infrastructures, through automated decision-making, provide a renewed impetus to automatic docility, wherein personnel may be further potentially reduced to executing/implementing decisions that the algorithmic infrastructure has made. Since abuse of power and misuse of authority is visualized only at the level of the subordinate personnel, that is the personnel who interact with the general public, algorithmic infrastructures in effect strip these positions of decision-making powers, while by default positioning the top echelons as beyond doubt and suspicion; both suspicion and discipline are targeted at those below (Kuldova, 2022). A crucial achievement in this regard is that these algorithmic infrastructures, by incorporating roboprocesses free themselves of accountability and responsibility while exerting new forms of discipline and control over human participants (Besteman & Gusterson, 2019). These processes potentially develop into 'out of control systems' of algorithmic governance, where personnel have little to no control to take autonomous decisions over algorithmically generated 'recommendations' (Katzenbach & Ulbricht, 2019). In effect, algorithmic infrastructures retain the decision-making capacity for upper administration. Especially in the police, with its hierarchy of disciplinary control, automated decision-making provides renewed possibilities for automatic docility, which may potentially exert a stronger control over subordinate, potentially 'corruptible' personnel, by reserving decision-making powers for algorithms and upper administration.

Kerala Model of Algorithmic Governance?

Algorithmic infrastructures in state service, especially predictive policing systems, have been subject to considerable criticisms for their potential lack of accountability. The black box problem has frequently been seen as potentially undermining autonomy, understandability, accountability in state services which are fundamental democratic concepts (Leese, 2023). Algorithmic governance functions as an algorithmic Leviathan which yields optimization and coordination when individuals give up their autonomy thereby producing a fundamentally apolitical mode of governance (König, 2020). We may further expand on the potential of algorithmic governance to undermine democratic principles by directing our focus on the question 'whose behaviours are algorithmic infrastructures designed to control?' since they may be directed towards the behaviours of the citizens or of police officers (Katzenbach & Ulbricht, 2019). In the previous section, I discussed the potential for algorithmic structures to reinforce existing tendencies of automatic docility in the police.

However, this does not apply to the policing institution and other state institutions in their entirety. Algorithmic infrastructures, especially those developed through private sector technology are also viewed as opaque and threatening to the digital sovereignty of the state (Leese, 2023). This is especially true in Kerala. The ARC report highlighted how different departments in the state had been uncomfortable with the model of TSP (Total Solution Provider) where technology was developed and maintained by external agencies. This mechanism is viewed to be inefficient and dysfunctional. The ARC recommends a reformulation in the procurement mechanism in line with the people-centricity focus of the e-governance policy.

In practice, this has transformed to a framework where the state is investing and focusing on capacity building of existing functionaries and departments, rather than relying on external agencies for tech-solutions. In this regard, as mentioned earlier, in 2022 Kerala Police and the Digital University of Kerala launched a special training programme for 'capacity building in responsible AI and data analytics for the police department', where a team of 15 police officers attended a 45-day workshop on responsible AI and how it may be integrated in routine police work. Similarly, the anti-drone software and the AI camera monitoring software all rely on in-house capacity and software development through capacity building of state functionaries, bypassing the dependence on private tech companies. This also aligns with the Kerala model of development, where the model relies on the creation of infrastructures that are not dependent on despotic forms of capitalism and privatization.

State institutions and especially the police in their adoption of technological tools thus often consider concerns about their own role in/ vis-à-vis society, owing to democratic discussions and concerns around digital sovereignty (Leese, 2023). Kerala's experiment with algorithmic governance is a case in point. However, while replacing third-party tools with in-house development might resolve issues around black box, accountability, data sharing and similar, it still does not resolve concerns around technologically-mediated policing (Leese, 2023).

To understand how states in their particularistic contexts engage with and manage the concerns around technology in state services, and especially technology-mediated policing, we need a framework that considers the actual practices of how technology is integrated in everyday state practices. Often these practices reveal that state functionaries themselves express concern over the practical effects of automation (Leese, 2021). In this framework, we must also consider how the state keeps revising its rhetoric to manage the application of technology. For state functionaries, automation offers a solution from a design perspective as a relief from dull, monotonous and time-consuming tasks such as handling and analysing large data-sets (Parasuraman et al., 2000). This however does not undo the biases that may be embedded in data-sets, which eventually leads to distrust of algorithms.

In the context of Kerala, to manage this issue of distrust, while retaining the 'positive' aspect of automation of monotonous tasks, the concept of 'Responsible AI' has been invoked. This however is not unique to Kerala, 'Responsible AI' emerged from the discussion on AI ethics in the west in the late 1900s. These discussions were taking place in the tech industry in the west as well, with tech giants like Google, Facebook, Amazon, IBM and Microsoft forming a 'partnership on AI' to conduct research and recommend best practices on ethics, fairness, trust and accountability among other things (Hern, 2016). With the growing penetration of AI in industry use, ethics and trust became incorporated in regulation and governance frameworks in the west as well. The European Union's forthcoming AI Act (EU Parliament, 2023) has been one such regulation framework in a sea of governance measures that attempt to regulate the use of AI. These concepts are often uncritically adopted in developing nations like India, wherein the adoption of a western regulatory phenomenon itself is deemed to be enough to build trust.

Responsible AI: Building 'Trust' in AI

In general, public discourse and perceptions among police personnel/ state functionaries in Kerala see the adoption of AI and algorithmic infrastructures in state services as part of the modernization process. Or else, the incorporation of AI is seen as a natural extension of digitization of state services. Since the algorithmic infrastructures incorporating AI in Kerala are still being formulated and rolled out on a pilot basis, public discourse has not yet viewed AI as a radical departure from everyday practices.

This however is not the view of technology experts, who are instrumental in designing these frameworks. As mentioned above, Digital University of Kerala ran a capacity building workshop for Kerala Police on responsible AI and data analytics, organized and designed by a team of technology scholars and practitioners at the University. Expanding upon the nature, focus and scope of the capacity building programme, one of the scholars (Interviewee 1) noted that the workshop was part of a government-sponsored programme focusing on capacity building of state departments and functionaries for training in e-governance. Herein the design of the workshop follows a common overall structure;

however, each workshop is catered to the specific needs of the depart-ment. Other institutions that have participated in similar workshops include the Departments of Statistics, and plans were under way for the training of Department of Animal Husbandry.

It is in the context of governance and service delivery that the notion of responsible AI emerges. Interviewee 1 explained that the concept of 'responsible AI' is linked to e-governance and noted that since AI was earlier confined to research alone and has only recently come to real-world applications through commercial usage, the practical effects of AI application are only now becoming apparent. Since AI itself is superficial and artificial, trust in AI has to be built through concerted effort. She noted that this is where responsible AI comes into the picture, noting that those using it, have to build trust in the model that it would be used for the general welfare of the public (Interviewee 1, 2023).

Responsible AI is thus not a concept related to algorithmic modelling, but rather pertaining to everyday practice and real-world applications, where through political action trust has to be first built in AI analysis. These frameworks touch upon AI ethics, which includes questions of how data is generated, stored and used, to routinely counter concerns of legitimacy (*see* also Paulsen in this volume).

Contrary to the general perception however, Interviewee 1 noted that with respect to AI application, data scarcity is a big challenge. One of the stated aims of AI incorporation in policing in Kerala, through the iCoPS software, had been that AI would be able to scan through years of crime data that is available in the state and national crime record database, since the colonial era, to analyse patterns, and accurately predict crime. However, this data lacks the necessary parameters that are required for AI models. Interviewee 1 noted that the accuracy of AI predictions is dependent on the data set, if the data set is flawed the prediction would also be flawed, AI itself of course lacks cognition, and therefore accuracy and usefulness of AI prediction remains a matter of human cognition and application. For AI predictions to really be accurate there is a need for a large amount of data, with relevant parameters that could be used for AI predictive modelling. All data therefore is not relevant.

Incorporation of AI is therefore also dependent on transformation of everyday practices of data collection, for which contemporary practices will not suffice. It remains to be seen whether these practices would be incorporated or not, as often large-scale changes are also resisted by state functionaries in bureaucratic institutions.

In the era of surveillance thus, security is morphing into a new enterprise, wherein discipline and security are connected (Bauman & Lyon, 2013) through digital technology and statistical reasoning that functions under a new epistemology of control. To really understand how this plays out, we have to consider the context. The view that technology leads to 'social control' in the 'big brother' fashion lays 'stress on tools and tyrants and ignores the spirit that animates surveillance, the ideologies that drive it forward, the events that give it its chance and the ordinary people who comply with it, question it' (Bauman & Lyon, 2013, p. 12).

The Kerala model and its relation to algorithmic governance is thus one way of framing the question of how digitization and e-governance transforming the state. It helps us look at the context in which algorithmic governance is perceived, adapted and implemented, while understanding the operational power relations that guide these transformations.

Elective Affinities and the Evolution of Algorithmic Governance

The emphasis on responsible AI, AI ethics, people-centricity and e-governance, through the development of in-house capacity, bypassing private and third-party technology, are adaptations of discourses on algorithmic infrastructures that are emerging from the Kerala model of development and governance. While this is unique in the adoption of algorithmic infrastructures in India, similar attempts have been documented in other parts of the world. For instance Leese (2023; see also Leese in this volume) shows how Swiss Police departments internally bypass and delegitimize private technology owing to 'democratic considerations' while accommodating considerations of their own role in/ vis-à-vis society in their everyday practices. Bypassing private enterprise alone does not automatically make algorithmic infrastructures democratic. What is interesting in the context of Kerala however is how the state is incorporating such rhetoric into its own unique context of the Kerala model and its associated gains.

Owing to the dynamic character of this field, it remains to be seen how this will play out. While in the political rhetoric and practice, algorithmic governance is being imbued with democratic responsibilities, it is also functioning through a contradictory potential of automatic docility. With the potential of automation to restrict decision-making authority among subordinate personnel, the degree of automation and transparency with respect to normative implications for accountability and democracy will be the key elements in the evaluations of different forms of algorithmic governance (Katzenbach & Ulbricht, 2019). The degree matters, since AI is largely perceived to be artificial and superficial, and therefore legitimacy of the system in real-world application still depends on a certain amount of decision-making resting on 'legitimate' human participants in their role as professional experts and ethical subjects (Katzenbach & Ulbricht, 2019; see also Paulsen in this volume). In the disciplinary hierarchical framework of policing institutions in India, this 'legitimate' authority is likely to be senior administration.

Since algorithmic governance is not universal, it is heavily contingent on context, and therefore it is possible to view multiple forms of algorithmic governance. The Kerala model of algorithmic governance may potentially offer a new model that perhaps is built by bypassing private technology and big capital if it is able to continue its tradition of radical redistribution of available resources premised on public participation. This transformation is shaped by dominant interests, powers and modes of resistance and is a largely dynamic field.

The literature on science and technology studies has noted how technological frameworks are socially constructed artefacts (Pinch & Bijker, 2012). In the context of India, modern (western) science arrived as a technology of colonialism and flourished through a common ground between British scientists, colonial imperatives and interests of the indigenous elites. To understand the application of science and technology in any society, the key task is a sociohistorical examination of 'elective affinities' between social structures and the worldviews of science, technology and nature (Baber, 1996). These elective affinities shape, on the one hand, how science and technology are adopted and promoted, and on the other how science and technology are made instrumental to specific kinds of economic-political systems, capitalist or otherwise.

In the context of algorithmic governance in Kerala, this chapter has tried to outline the framework through which we may be able to perceive these elective affinities. Since algorithmic transitions are still taking place, it is difficult to ascertain the nature of these affinities at this stage. However, one can easily trace and locate the ongoing transformation in Kerala in relation to global trends. In its political rhetoric a Kerala model of algorithmic governance is capable of offering an alternative framework to neoliberal models. However, it remains to be seen how its everyday implementation is sufficiently distinct from neoliberal models that gave rise to the algorithmic infrastructures in the first place. The ongoing transformations are heavily dependent on how elective affinities that shape the economy and politics of the state would evolve. If Kerala is able to develop a Kerala model of algorithmic governance—staying true to its core principles of radical redistribution of available resources and democratic participation—it would be an unprecedented achievement. Whether the Kerala model of algorithmic governance is an oxymoron or a real possibility, only time will tell.

Funding and Ethics Statement   This work was funded by The Research Council of Norway under project no. 313626—*Algorithmic Governance and Cultures of Policing: Comparative Perspectives from Norway, India, Brazil, Russia, and South Africa* (AGOPOL). Informed consent has been secured from all research participants and the study was conducted in accordance with the O.P. Jindal Global University ethical guidelines and the British Sociological Association Guidelines on Ethical Research. The author would like to thank Tereza Østbø Kuldova, Christin Thea Wathne and Helene Oppen Ingebrigtsen Gundhus for their invaluable comments and suggestions on this chapter.

References

Administrative Reforms Commission. (2021). *Eleventh Report*. Government of Kerala. https://arc.kerala.gov.in/sites/default/files/inline-files/11thReport-e-Governance-Part1%262-Forprinting.pdf

Arnold, D. (1986). *Police Power and Colonial Rule: Madras 1859–1947*. Oxford University Press.

AS, S. (2023, April 03). Police Go High-Tech, Use AI to Fill 'Gallery' of 1.5 lakh criminals. *The New Indian Express*. https://www.newindianexpress.com/states/kerala/2023/apr/03/police-go-high-tech-use-ai-to-fill-gallery-of-15-lakh-criminals-2562107.html

Baber, Z. (1996). Conclusions: Science, Technology and Ecological Limits. In Z. Baber, *The Science of Empire: Scientific Knowledge, Civilization and Colonial Rule in India* (pp. 246–256). State University of New York Press.

Bauman , Z., & Lyon, D. (2013). *Liquid Surveillance: A Conversation*. Polity.

Baxi, U. (1982). The Indian Police: A Colonial Minority? In U. Baxi (Ed.), *The Crisis of the Indian Legal System* (pp. 84–120). Vikas Publishing House.

Bayley, D. H. (1971). The Police in India. *Economic and Political Weekly, 6*(45), 2287–2291. http://www.jstor.org/stable/4382720

Benny, N. (2023, September 7). AI Cameras Don't Violate Citizens' Privacy; All Data Encrypted and no Question of Leakage: State Defends 'Safe Kerala Project' in High Court. *Live Law*. https://www.livelaw.in/high-court/kerala-high-court/kerala-high-court-ai-cameras-on-roads-privacy-safe-kerala-project-motor-accidents-237280?infinitescroll=1

Besteman, C., & Gusterson, H. (2019). *Life by Algorithms: How Roboprocesses Are Remaking Our World*. University of Chicago Press. https://doi.org/10.7208/chicago/9780226627731.001.0001

Brubaker, R. (2023). *Hyperconnectivity and Its Discontents*. Polity Press.

Castells, M. (2005). Global Governance and Global Politics. *PS: Political Science and Politics, 38*(1), 9–16. https://doi.org/10.1017/S104909650505 5678

Chathukulam, J., & John, M. S. (2002). Five Years of Participatory Planning in Kerala: Rhetoric and Reality. *Economic and Political Weekly, 37*(49), 4917–426. https://www.epw.in/journal/2002/49/special-articles/five-years-participatory-planning-kerala.html

Das Gupta, C. (2016). *State and Capital in Independent India: Institutions and Accumulation*. Cambridge University Press. https://doi.org/10.1017/CBO 9781316182505

EU Parliament. (2023, December 19). EU AI Act: First Regulation on Artificial Intelligence. *European Parliament News.* https://www.europarl.eur opa.eu/news/en/headlines/society/20230601STO93804/eu-ai-act-first-reg ulation-on-artificial-intelligence

Foucault, M. (1991). *Discipline and Punish: The Birth of the Prison.* (A. Sheridan, Trans.) Penguin Books.

Foucault, M. (2007). *Security, Territory, Population: Lectures at the Collège de France, 1977–78.* (M. Senellart, Ed., & G. Burchell, Trans.) Picador.

George, S. B. (2023, April 23). Explained I How AI-powered Cameras can Rein in Traffic Violations. *The Hindu.* https://www.thehindu.com/news/ national/kerala/explained-how-ai-powered-cameras-can-rein-in-traffic-violat ions/article66766712.ece

Harvey, D. (2007). *A Brief History of Neoliberalism.* Oxford University Press.

Heller, P. (1999). *The Labour of Development: Workers and the Transformation of Capitalism in Kerala.* Cornell University Press. https://doi.org/10.7591/978 1501720734

Hern, A. (2016, September 28). 'Partnership on AI' formed by Google, Facebook, Amazon, IBM and Microsoft. *The Guardian.* https://www.the guardian.com/technology/2016/sep/28/google-facebook-amazon-ibm-mic rosoft-partnership-on-ai-tech-firms

Interviewee 1. (2023). *AI, Data Analytics and E-Governance in Kerala.* 23 July 2023. (A. Varghese, Interviewer).

Isaac, T. T., & Franke, R. W. (2004). *Local Democracy and Development: People's Campaign for Decentralized Planning in Kerala.* Leftword Books.

Jaswal, R. T. (2023, June 19). Automated Facial Recognition Systems: Not the Win we were Rooting For. *The Leaflet.* https://theleaflet.in/automated-fac ial-recognition-systems-not-the-win-we-were-rooting-for/

Kallungal, D. (2023, June 13). Teething Troubles Mark First Week of AI-camera Operations. *The Hindu.* https://www.thehindu.com/news/nat ional/kerala/teething-troubles-mark-first-week-of-ai-camera-operations/art icle66965083.ece

Katzenbach, C., & Ulbricht, L. (2019). Algorithmic Governance. *Internet Policy Review, 8*(4). https://doi.org/10.14763/2019.4.1424

Kerala Police Officers Association 33rd State Conference. (2023a, May 25). Samshuddha Keralam Samshuddha Police സംശുദ്ധ കേരളം സംശുദ്ധ പോലീസ്. Ernakulam, Kerala, India.

Kerala Police Officers Association 33rd State Conference. (2023b, May 18). Seminar: The Police of New Kerala. Thiruvananthapuram, Kerala, India. https://www.facebook.com/KPOAStateCommittee/videos

Kerala Police. (2021). *Vision 2030 Kerala Police.* Thiruvananthapuram: Shri. Loknath Behera IPS, DGP and State Police Chief.

König, P. D. (2019). Dissecting the Algorithmic Leviathan: On the Socio-Political Anatomy of Algorithmic Governance. *Philos. Technol., 33,* 467–485. https://doi.org/10.1007/s13347-019-00363-w

Kuldova, T. Ø. (2022). *Compliance-Industrial Complex: The Operating System of a Pre-Crime Society.* Palgrave Macmillan. https://doi.org/10.1007/978-3-031-19224-1

Kuldova, T. Ø., Østbø, J. & Raymen, T. (2024). *Luxury and Corruption: Challenging the Anti-Corruption Consensus.* Bristol University Press. https://doi.org/10.56687/9781529212426

Leese, M. (2021). Security as Socio-Technical Practice: Predictive. *Swiss Political Science Review, 27*(1), 150–157. https://doi.org/10.1111/spsr.12432

Leese, M. (2023). Staying in Control of Technology: Predictive. *Democratization.* https://doi.org/10.1080/13510347.2023.2197217

Lupton, D. (2015). *Digital Sociology.* Routledge. https://doi.org/10.4324/9781315776880

Manorama. (2023, April 24). AI Cameras Violate Privacy Laws, say Legal Experts. *Manorama Online.* https://www.onmanorama.com/news/kerala/2023/04/24/ai-cameras-violate-privacy-laws-say-legal-experts.html

Mathrubhumi. (2023, July 24). Kerala Police's new AI-Enabled Face Recognition System Identifies Suspect in Theft Case, Dead Body. *Mathrubhumi.com.* https://english.mathrubhumi.com/news/kerala/kerala-police-unveils-ai-enabled-face-recognition-system-for-criminal-identification-1.8757830

Ministry of Home Affairs, Government of India. (1979). *Second Report of the National Police Commission.*

Neocleous, M. (2000). *The Fabrication of Social Order: A Critical Theory of Police Power.* Pluto Press.

Padanna, A. (2023, May 25). Kerala: Man Wrongly Accused due to CCTV Image Speaks Out. *BBC.* https://www.bbc.com/news/world-asia-india-65668099

Parasuraman, R., Sheridan, T. B., & Wickens, C. D. (2000). A Model for Types and Levels of Human Interaction With Automation. *IEEE Transactions on Systems, Man, and Cybernetics - Part a: Systems and Humans, 30*(3), 286–297. https://doi.org/10.1109/3468.844354

Pinch, T. J., & Bijker, W. E. (2012). The Social Construction of Facts and Artifacts: Or How the Sociology of Science and the Sociology of Technology Might Benefit Each Other. In W. E. Bijker, T. P. Hughes, & T. Pinch (Eds.), *The Social Construction of Technological Systems: New Directions in the Sociology and History of Technology* (pp. 11–44). The MIT Press.

Poulantzas, N. (2000[1978]). *State, Power, Socialism.* Verso.

Prakash Singh & Ors vs Union Of India And Ors. (2006). Writ Petition (civil) 310 of 1996. Supreme Court of India.

Prakash, G. (2018). *Emergency Chronicles: Indira Gandhi and Democracy's Turning Point.* Penguin.

Press Trust of India. (2023, May 11). Kerala 1st Indian State To Have Drone Surveillance In All Police Districts. *NDTV.* https://www.ndtv.com/kerala-news/kerala-1st-indian-state-to-have-drone-surveillance-in-all-police-distri cts-4024341

Raghavan, R. K. (1986). An Anatomy of the Indian Police. *The Indian Journal of Political Science, 47*(3), 399–412. http://www.jstor.org/stable/41855254

Staff Reporter. (2022, March 4). Next-gen Policing with Digital Varsity's Help. *The Hindu.* https://www.thehindu.com/news/national/kerala/next-gen-pol icing-with-digital-varsitys-help/article65190436.ece

TNN. (2017, March 4). Kerala budget 2017: Internet Access a Basic Right, Says TM Thomas Isaac. *The Times of India.* https://timesofindia.indiatimes. com/city/thiruvananthapuram/kerala-budget-2017-internet-access-a-basic-right-tm-thomas-isaac/articleshow/57459111.cms

Unnithan, P. S. (2019, February 20). India's first RoboCop: Kerala Police Inducts Robot, gives it SI rank. *India Today.* https://www.indiatoday.in/tre nding-news/story/india-first-robocop-kerala-police-inducts-robot-gives-si-rank-1460371-2019-02-20

Van Dijk, P. (2000). Anthropology in the Age of Technology: The Philosophical Contribution of Günther Anders. *Brill.* https://doi.org/10.1163/978 9004495708

Varghese, A. (2021). Combating Capitalism: A Case Study of Left Polity in Kerala. *International Critical Thought, 11*(2), 303–320. https://doi.org/10. 1080/21598282.2021.1886593

Varghese, A. (2022). Police Interactions in Post-colonial India: How Particularistic Accountability, Legitimacy and Tolerated Illegality Condition Everyday Policing in Delhi and Kerala. *Journal of Organizational Ethnography, 11*(2), 162–180. https://doi.org/10.1108/JOE-12-2020-0057

Varghese, A. (2023). *Police and Power: Understanding Power Relations in the Political Economy and Everyday of Police Stations*. Dr. B.R. Ambedkar University Delhi.

Verma, A. (2005). *The Indian Police: A Critical Evaluation*. Regency Publications.

Verma, A. (2011). *The New Khaki: The Evolving Nature of Policing in India*. CRC Press. https://doi.org/10.4324/9781482296013

8

Musical Policing in Today's Brazil: A Study of Jingles in the Bolsonaro Movement

Kjetil Klette-Bøhler(iD)

How are music and jingles used to recruit voters during election campaigns? And, to what extent can this be understood as specific forms of *musical policing* as people are exposed to political arguments and moral visions as catchy melodies take hold in their bodies? More importantly, to what extent are such forms of musical policing shaped by broader changes towards 'algorithmic governance' (Kalpokas, 2019; Kuldova et al., 2021) as jingles operate as political earworms on social media by releasing dopamine, oxytocin, and serotonin in voters during elections thus reconfiguring people's sense of logos, ethos, and pathos, musically? This chapter explores these questions through a study of how Jair Messiah Bolsonaro used music to recruit voters in Brazil during the 2018 and 2022 elections. In doing so I also describe the broader historical context of jingles in Brazil and combine historical research together with music analysis and ethnography, with a focus on the latter. My

K. Klette-Bøhler (✉)
University of South-Eastern Norway, Notodden, Norway
e-mail: kjetil.k.bohler@usn.no

© The Author(s), under exclusive license to Springer Nature Switzerland AG 2024
T. Ø. Kuldova et al. (eds.), *Policing and Intelligence in the Global Big Data Era, Volume I*, Palgrave's Critical Policing Studies,
https://doi.org/10.1007/978-3-031-68326-8_8

ethnographic data includes field notes, sound recordings, images, and video recordings, as well as 86 semi-structured qualitative interviews, each lasting between one and two hours, carried out during two years of fieldwork between 2016 and 2023 where I examined jingles in Brazilian politics. My fieldwork was carried out in the regions of São Paulo, Rio de Janeiro, Bahia, Pernambuco, Ceará, Amazonas, and Maranhão, with most of my ethnography carried out in São Paulo. Most of my informants were either Bolsonaro or Lula supporters, and I focus particularly on eight interviews (six men and two women) that illuminate how jingles work politically during elections. Five of these are anonymized to protect the identity of my informants while three of them are represented with full name as they are famous jingle composers and public figures in Brazil including Hilton Acioli, Jader Finamore, and João Augusto Neves.[1] All three wanted to participate with full name in the study.

Before I analyse my ethnographic data, I develop *musical policing* as a new concept. In doing so I draw on Rancière's broad notion of 'the police' as a particular 'distribution of the sensible [that shapes] what is common to the community' (Rancière, 2004, p. 12) by establishing social divisions, in dialog with Foucault's work on 'governmentality', and Aristotle's emphasis on the interplay between 'logos', 'ethos', and 'pathos' in political rhetoric together with studies on music and politics. By reading these humanistic theories in light of recent developments in music psychology and media studies I propose that musical policing, today, is social, biological, and algorithmic, as successful political songs may take hold in our bodies by both releasing physical pleasure (e.g., through dopamine) (Montag, 2019), *and* by taking on a new social life as songs spread through 'algorithmic governance' (Boler & Davis, 2018; Flannery et al., 2024; Kalpokas, 2019; Kuldova et al., 2021) on social media by connecting people across platforms, smartphones, and contexts. *Musical policing* complements existing theories related to

---

[1] Hilton Acioli is one of Brazil's most famous jingle composers, the author of 'Lula la, Sem Medo de ser feliz' (1989), one of the most played jingles of all times, while Jader Finamore belongs to a younger generation of jingle composers and have been among the most used jingle producers in the North-East part of Brazil the last decade. João Augusto Neves is a Brazilian historian, working on music and politics, who recently defended his PhD in history at the University of Campinas, and who was worked extensively on jingles and music and politics more broadly.

the politics of music that often privilege music's emancipatory potential (Monson, 2007; Street, 2003; Walser, 1995) by instead focusing on how music's contagious qualities build identities and ways of being together, across the political spectrum, as musical sounds shape political ideologies. This case study thus relies on an investigation of musical policing online and offline, in public spaces and through ethnographic, musical as well as cinematic methods,[2] combined with a review of existing research. However, before we approach jingles in Brazilian politics, let us first turn to the concept of musical policing.

Conceptualizing Musical Policing

I propose *musical policing* as a concept to study how the contagious qualities of music shape subjectivities and communities in the making by restructuring established divisions of *logos, ethos,* and *pathos,* as musical sounds breathe new life into political ideologies. My understanding of policing, in this sense, has little to do with police forces, law enforcement or security agencies. Instead, it is better understood in light of Jacques Rancière's notion of 'the police' (Rancière et al., 2001), which he defines as a particular 'distribution of the sensible [that shapes] what is common to the community' (Rancière, 2004, p. 12) as social hierarchies

---

[2] In 2024, the author has directed and produced, together with João Neves, Gabi Perissinotto, and Marcel Vecchia, the ethnographic film *Jingles as Affective Politics in Brazil's 2022 Election* which explores how political candidates used jingles to recruit voters in Brazil's 2022 election. The film has a particular focus on Bolsonaro and Lula's use of jingles, and how music created political awareness and affective mobilization among voter groups. It features in-depth interviews with influential jingle producers such as Hilton Acioli and Juliano Maderada, as well as with scholars working in the field of music and politics in Brazil. It also contains interviews with voters and volunteers that worked for different political campaigns. The film draws on material gathered throughout the 2022 election campaign, including film of political events, movements, street protests and other political events.

and political imaginaries gain force through music and arts.[3] Following Rancière,

> the police are not primarily a strong-arm repressive force, but a form of intervention which prescribes what can be seen and what cannot be seen, what can be said and what cannot be said. (Rancière, 1998, p. 28)

Hence, when for instance songs are used to disseminate a particular sentiment, politics, or way of seeing the world, they can be interpreted as modes of musical policing because they define 'which bodies are in the right place and which [are] in the wrong' (Rancière, 2007, p. 561) as social divisions, and political visions, gain affective force musically. Rancière's concept of the police is perhaps best understood in light of Foucault's notions of 'bio-politics' (Foucault, 1978b, pp. 137–139) and 'governmentality' (Foucault, 1978a, p. 186). Both concepts draw attention to how specific forms of power and social hierarchies are reproduced, often in tacit ways and subconsciously, through bodily and discursive practices as particular modes of control (Foucault, 1991; Neuman, 2011, pp. 41–55). Jocelyne Guilbault offers an excellent study of how these ideas operate through music in her book *Governing Sound* (2007), by developing 'governing sound' as a concept to study how calypso has been 'implicated in the articulation of the nation-state, national belonging, politics of representation and power relations' (Guilbault, 2007, p. 1) in Trinidad and Tobago. One way in which governing sound works in practice, according to Guilbault, is through musical pleasures which operate as 'vital forces in community formation and also as forces of production'

---

[3] While Rancière usually defines 'the police' as how specific ways of seeing the world, and being together are modelled on established social divisions, and reproduced through aesthetic, sensory and discursive techniques, and 'politics' as ruptures against such 'police orders' by claiming the emergence of a new subject (Bøhler, 2020; Rancière et al., 2001), he sometimes uses 'police' and 'politics' interchangeably (e.g., Rancière, 2010, p. 152, 2004, pp. 7–15, Samuel, 2013, pp. 38–88). More importantly, most articulations of 'politics' as rupture can develop into new police orders by safeguarding their marginalized subjects at the expense of others who feel excluded by that new political order. However, in this paper I draw on Rancière's mentioned understanding of 'police' as the reproduction of communities with inherent social divisions, to theorize musical policing outside the realm law enforcement and shed new light on the political work that music does.

(Guilbault, 2007, p. 274) in calypso and related music. Similar arguments have been pointed out by others (Austerlitz, 1997; Boehler, 2016; Bøhler, 2018), and a number of scholars have described the complex ways in which music operates as affective propaganda in different political ideologies (Buch et al., 2016; Kater, 1999; Levi, 1996; Street, 2013, pp. 140–160).

However, prior to these considerations, almost 2500 years ago, Plato had already described how changes in musical taste following the Persian wars fuelled social unrest and critiques of authorities, while nurturing new political imaginations (Plato, 2019, pp. 700a-701b). This insight prompted Plato to argue that music should be strictly regulated by those in power because it could influence political life and matters of governing (Plato, 1966, pp. 4.424b-d; Plato, 2019, pp. 2.660a-b). Plato believed that musical properties, such as the shape of a rhythm and the organization of a melody, could have a direct impact on public sentiment and people's visions as 'rhythm and harmony permeate the inner part of the soul more than anything else' (Plato in Bourgault, 2012, p. 70). Plato's recognition of the political force of music, and his aim to control it, in a sense, anticipates the mentioned concept of musical policing. Aristotle held a related, but more positive, view on music's social and political affordances as he believed that specific scales could give rise to particular affects within groups of people and influence social formations (Schneider, 2010, p. 77).

More importantly, he believed that these musical pleasures could inspire good judgments and noble actions, and thereby improve the *polis* (Aristotle, 1995, p. 1340a). These ideas were linked to Aristotle's broader theory on *Rhetoric*, and his argument that to convince the public, the speaker should combine his moral character (*êthos*), the affective state of the listener (*pathos*), and the argument itself (*logos*) (Aristotle, 1991, pp. 1403b, 1410). Aristotle claimed pathos to be particularly powerful because people who are emotionally engaged are more devoted to a specific cause (Aristotle, 1991, pp. 1378a, 1320). While Aristotle recognized the social and political force of musical pleasures his arguments came under critique during the middle ages as new Christian ideas aimed to control bodies and affects (Kobialka, 2009; Newhauser, 2023). In contrast to the Ancient Greek's focus on bodily pleasures this new

Christian regime aimed to regulate music, affects, and above all, hedonic pleasures, which were associated with the devil, by introducing a moral order modelled on sin and guilt (Snyder, 1965; Tentler, 2015). These arguments gained force during the renaissance (Wegman, 2002, 2003), after the reformation, and throughout the 'Age of Enlightenment', as a new 'Doctrine of Affections' (Affektenlehre) enhanced specific forms of musical beauty, linked to God, while hedonic pleasures in music were suppressed (Bartel, 1997; Kivy, 1993; Wessel, 1955). However, it was Kant's critique of pleasure as anti-aesthetic (Kant, pp. 70–93), and Hegel's argument that pleasure represented a barbaric underdeveloped art form as opposed to 'Great Art' (Hegel, 1997, pp. 136–151), which he argued should be modelled on Christian values, philosophy, rational principles, and ideas of progress (Hegel, 1979), that had the strongest impact in separating musical pleasure from arts and aesthetics. Inspired by these ideas, and the growing influence of avant-garde, expressionism, and marxism at the birth of the twentieth century, Adorno developed a strong critique of musical pleasure in popular music by arguing that these affects were pre-fabricated modes of capitalist manipulation that could weaken critical thinking (Adorno & Simpson, 1941). In doing so Adorno recalls Platonic modes of musical policing by calling for a sense of indirect musical censorship that targets the pleasures of popular music. While these views had a strong impact on how music was later taught at universities and conservatories, and within the field of cultural sociology, one of Adorno's colleagues, Walter Benjamin, developed a more positive view on pleasure, technological development, and popular culture through his research on film. Benjamin envisioned that film, as a new art form, could play a central role in developing a more equal, harmonic, and enlightened society modelled on Marxist ideas paraphrasing Berthold Brecht. Benjamin argued that

> The first technology really sought to master nature, whereas the second aims rather at an interplay between nature and humanity. The primary social function of art today is to rehearse that interplay. This applies especially to film. The function of film is to train human beings in the apperception and reactions needed to deal with a vast apparatus whose

role in their lives is expanding almost daily. Dealing with this apparatus also teaches them that technology will release them from their enslavement to the powers of the apparatus only when humanity's whole constitution has adapted itself to the new productive forces which the second technology has set free. (Benjamin et al., 1996, pp. 107–108)

For Benjamin, film had a unique potential to educate 'the people' and free man from 'the slavery' of capitalist exploitation and thereby create a more just society. And he was intrigued by the popular appeal of cinematic pleasures and the film's integration of different art forms (visual arts, drama and narrative, the use of sounds and music, etc.). However, at the same time, related but different ideas were picked up by researchers working in advertising and marketing (Lebergott, 2014), as well as by totalitarian regimes (Levi, 1996; O'Brien, 2004; Potter, 2017), and both music and film soon started playing important roles in commercials and propaganda as technological innovations, such as the radio and TV, brought musical pleasures and engaging film narratives directly to citizens (Cox, 2008). A turning point was the release of the first jingle in the U.S., 'Try Wheaties',[4] by a vocal quartet, on American radio, as its joyful melody and soft harmonies, spread the words:

Have you tried Wheaties? They're whole wheat with all of the bran. Won't you try Wheaties? For wheat is the best food of man. They're crispy and crunchy the whole year through. The kiddies never tire of them and neither will you. So just buy Wheaties, the best breakfast food in the land. (Cox, 2008, p. 156)

Jingles became a commercial success that turned the advertisement industry upside down (Cox, 2008; Shapiro, 2004; Taylor, 2015). Quickly, jingles started playing an important role in presidential elections in the United States (Rodman, 2022; Schoening & Kasper, 2011), and elsewhere (Charles, 2006; Manhanelli, 2011; Omidiora et al., 2020). During the 50 s music in general, and jingles in particular, were already an integrated part of American election campaigns (Christiansen, 2017,

---

[4] Have You Tried Wheaties? (1926 Radio Jingle), Channel: Jake, The Air Warden, *YouTube*, 3 October 2020, https://www.youtube.com/watch?v=CJpeR6GvpC8.

pp. 31–56; Schoening & Kasper, 2011, pp. 121–139) and increasingly used by larger corporations as illustrated in the growing influence of Muzak, which used music to manipulate behaviour and enhance profit (Allen Anderson, 2015; Lanza, 2004; Radano, 1989).

Around the same time, the psychologist Theodor Reik published the book *The Haunting Melody* where he described how some melodies and rhythms have a unique ability to stick in our brains and bodies as we remember songs (Reik, 1953). Almost half a century later, music psychologists started exploring Reik's ideas through systematic empirical research on how our bodies remember melodies and rhythms (Dawkins, 2016, pp. 250–258; Krumhansl, 2000; Snyder, 2009; Wallace, 1994). During the last decade, scholars working at the intersection of neuroscience and music have showed how the musical pleasures that Adorno and Plato were so afraid of are in fact both social *and* biological: experiences of musical pleasure are associated with the convergence of neurotransmitters such as serotonin, oxytocin, and dopamine (Harvey, 2020; Zatorre, 2015, 2023; Zatorre & Salimpoor, 2013). Inspired by this work, and extensive qualitative research on music's contagious character, scholars soon started developing a new concept of *earworms*, inspired by the German word *Ohrwurm*, as in Daniel Levitin's *This is Your Brain on Music: Understanding a Human Obsession*. The book became a bestseller affecting both the scholarly community and the larger public. Here Levitin describes earworms as 'the neural circuits representing the song get stuck in a "playback mode"' (Levitin, 2006, p. 155). Subsequent studies have described earworms as 'unwanted catchy tunes that repeat' (Beaman & Williams, 2010, p. 637) and that usually consist of shorter musical phrases with lyrics (Beaman & Williams, 2010, p. 639). Soon important qualitative research followed, and in a study from 2014 Williamson and Jilka argue that

> The ubiquity of music means that we are surrounded by it as we go about our everyday life [...] The music does not necessarily stop in silence either; nearly 90% of people report experiencing the mental phenomenon of involuntary musical imagery (INMI) at least once per week [...] This everyday phenomenon, also known as "earworms," is characterized by experiencing sections of music in the absence of an external source that

goes on to repeat outside of conscious control. (Williamson & Jilka, 2014, p. 653)

Throughout the article they present qualitative evidence that illustrates music's contagious character and ability to take hold of people's bodies. The following quote by one of their informants may illustrate:

> it's almost as though the earworms come in and they just take me, they just manage to certainly calm me down a bit, without me triggering them. Without me calling on them. They seem to just arrive. (Williamson & Jilka, 2014, 662)

The growth of social media and of new forms of 'algorithmic governance' (Kalpokas, 2019; Katzenbach & Ulbricht, 2019; Kuldova et al., 2021) in politics, marketing and branding (Carah & Angus, 2018), and the shaping of musical taste (Karakayali et al., 2018), suggest that earworms today, probably, enact musical policing across contexts as we are exposed to different political narratives musically on multiple digital platforms. A number of studies have already showed how music and jingles are distributed on TikTok, YouTube, and WhatsApp during election campaigns together with visual symbols and political arguments (Cervi et al., 2023; Patch, 2023; Saffle, 2015). Related studies have elaborated on how social media usage activates the mentioned neurotransmitters associated to pleasure as we participate in audio-visual narratives with our bodies (Doheny & Lighthall, 2023; Flannery et al., 2024; Montag, 2019; Sherman et al., 2018). More importantly, affects in general, and pleasure in particular, are now regarded as key features of algorithmic governance as developments in social media aim to take hold of our emotions (Boler & Davis, 2018; Kalpokas, 2019; Michel & Gandon, 2024).

The presented arguments from research in psychology, musicology, philosophy, sociology, and media studies suggest that complex forms of musical policing, potentially, operate through both social *and* biological forces as jingles gain force through social media by operating as musical forms of algorithmic governance. Below, I draw on the presented arguments by using *musical policing* as a conceptual frame to analyse the role of jingles in Brazilian politics.

Jingles in Brazilian Politics

Jingles are integrated parts of Brazilian politics and election campaigns; candidates use them to market their policies to gain voters as they are trying to become majors, governors, senators, or presidents (Bøhler, 2021b; de Andrade, 1996; Manhanelli, 2011; Panke, 2015; Panke & Couto, 2006). According to Carlos Manhanelli (2011), jingles aim to create an affective presence for respective candidates by repeating key slogans, crucial metaphors, and central arguments. Ideally, they should be repetitive, short, catchy, and contagious so that they 'reach the heart of the [voter], even before [they] reach his head' (Mendonça, 2001, p. 91; translation mine). Wolney Ramos elaborates by suggesting that good jingles have 'engaging rhythms, which have the advantage of reaching the voters "emotions"' (Ramos, 2004; translation mine). Others have pointed out the importance of engaging melodies that can stick in people's heads and bodies (Albin, 2006; Manhanelli, 2011, pp. 636–639). A closer look at Jânio Quadros' classic jingle 'Varre, Varre Vassourinha' (Sweep and Wash up with the Broom), from the election in 1960, illustrates this. Quadros was a right-wing politician who used the broom as a political metaphor to clean up corruption and enhance morality and conservative values. His jingle became incredibly popular, as it blasted out of radio stations and loudspeakers across the country (Hoffmann & Santos, 2017). Close listening to the jingle,[5] coupled with a quick look at the lyrics, may illustrate how it mobilized voters (Fig. 8.1).

The lyrics tell the story of a disillusioned and abandoned Brazilian people as the jingle makes an implicit reference to several corruption scandals in the 1950s and deep social inequalities (Maram, 1992;

---

[5] 'Varre varre vassourinha! Jânio Quadros', *YouTube*, channel Gabriel Wermelinger, 2 September 2010, https://www.youtube.com/watch?v=m0QfM_IJsBw.

Sweep, sweep, sweep, sweep, sweep up, with the broom	*Varre, varre, varre, varre, varre, varre, vassourinha*
Sweep, sweep up the [political] mess	*Varre, varre a bandalheira*
The people are already tired	*Que o povo já está cansado*
of suffering like this	*De sofrer dessa maneira*
Jânio Quadros is the hope of this abandoned people	*Jânio Quadros é a esperança desse povo abandonado*
Jânio Quadros is the evidence of a moralized Brazil	*Jânio Quadros é a certeza de um Brasil moralizado*
Alert, my brother	*Alerta, meu irmão*
Broom, fellow countryman	*Vassoura, conterrâneo*
Let's win with Jânio	*Vamos vencer com Jânio*
(In the entire history of Brazil)	*(Em toda história do Brasil)*
(It's never been easier to choose the best) (For President	*(Nunca foi tão fácil escolher o melhor)*
of the Republic)	*(Para Presidente da República)*
(Vote for Jânio Quadros)	*(Vote em Jânio Quadros)*

Fig. 8.1 Lyrics from the jingle 'Varre varre vassourinha'

McCann, 2003; Smallman, 1997; Young, 1963). As we follow the jingle's narrative, Jânio Quadros' right-wing policies are proposed as the solution to the crisis as they represent 'hope for the abandoned people', and the restoration of morality and national values, which were key values in his campaign (Loureiro, 2017; Queler, 2014). However, these words did not reach voters as written or spoken words but as a sung political narrative that gained affective and musical meanings through catchy phrases as they developed into a coherent melody following a classical verse-refrain structure. More importantly, these musical structures made the words danceable, and easy to sing along and remember. This is further enhanced by the big band arrangement, and the strong brass section, which reflected popular music taste in Brazil at the time. Taken together these musical features invest the political message with a contagious force that, potentially, allowed the jingle to reach millions of voters. When I asked the music historian João Augusto Neves about the jingle, he elaborated on its political importance, and argued:

Jânio Quadros [...] had fight against corruption as his main slogan and decided to use the broom, an aesthetic element from everyday life, as a key symbol in his political campaign. That is why they are singing 'wash, wash, wash, with the broom'. [Neves sings to illustrate the catchiness of the phrase] as if they are cleaning up state corruption in the country. [...] The broom is used as a political symbol to engage the public [..] During the campaign, the song was often used in combination with other visual symbols and posters, that featured a broom, which also visualized

Jânio Quadros' physical appearance as a slender man with a mustache. (Interview, Campinas, 17 February 2023)

After the interview Neves gave me examples of some of the pictures that were used in tandem with the jingle as part of Quadros' campaign by pointing me to YouTube videos and films. In one of them, we see people smiling as they are holding up brooms and political posters, while we are participating in the jingle's melodic narrative as listeners.[6] The visual symbols, and the song, are clearly affective and illustrate how the broom and the jingle invited to new forms of political participation as voters carried brooms to political rallies to support Quadros in his fight against corruption. These arguments illustrate how jingles are part of a larger political network, where different communication strategies are combined and mutually influence each other, such as visual symbols, sounds, songs, jingles, slogans, and catch phrases. More importantly, the analysis of Quadros' broom-jingle suggests that this mode of political communication also engages voters through humour, laughter, and irony, together with the contagious melody, and a number of studies have elaborated on how both humour, pleasure, and music have a long history in Brazilian politics (Brito et al., 2019; Carneiro & Jalalzai, 2021; Panke, 2013, 2015) and elsewhere (Jones, 2010; Kuipers, 2011; Pels & Corner, 2003; Van Zoonen, 2005). Such forms of political communication are particularly important in Brazil, due to strong carnival traditions and important *festas populares*, both of which have a long history of addressing social inequalities and political commentary through humour, pleasure, beauty, and irony (Branford & Kucinski, 1995; Drury & DaMatta, 2020; Snyder, 2022; Taylor, 1982).

While 'Varre, Varre Vassourinha' is one of Brazil's most famous jingles, it was not the first. Instead, 'Seu Julinho Vem',[7] used by the socialist candidate Julio Prestes in 1929, is often considered the first jingle used

---

[6] Varre Varre, Vassourinha, Jingle, Eleições 1960 (Brazilian Presidential Elections)' *YouTube*, from the film *Jingle's as Affective Politics*, (05:55–06:05), https://www.youtube.com/watch?v=Wnx3_j_d3zU.

[7] 'Seu Julinho Vem—Jingle Júlio Prestes—Eleições 1929 (Brazilian Presidential Elections)', *YouTube*, channel. História Resumida, 3 July 2020, https://www.youtube.com/watch?v=y_aoqBN202A.

during presidential elections. It was sung at different rallies and political events by Francisco Alves, who was already an established figure on the popular music scene. However, it was only after jingles were formally allowed on the radio, in 1932, that they became an indispensable tool of mass communication in Brazilian politics and elections and their importance gradually increased the subsequent decades (Manhanelli, 2011, pp. 48–59). Prior to this, similar songs and melodies had long time been used in marketing as new propaganda agencies emerged at the birth of the twentieth century (Martins, 1999, pp. 23–26). Before this, the *pregão*, which was a form of popular music sung by merchants and street vendors to attract customers during the eighteenth and nineteenth centuries, had done similar work (Simões, 1990; Tinhorão, 1976, 1998). Musically speaking, *pregões* were characterized by short and catchy melodies and syncopated contagious rhythms, that helped disseminate catch phrases among street vendors (Garcia, 2013, pp. 19–24), and research suggests that *pregões* were integrated parts of commercial life since the birth of the colonial period (Garcia, 2013, pp. 27–33; Simões, 1990, p. 171). Both *pregões* and jingles have, historically, been particularly influential among non-literate and semi-literate citizens (Ramos, 2004, p. 3) as they are deeply rooted in Brazilian oral culture. However, jingles can also influence literate citizens and anybody who struggle to get melodies out of their head (Ramos, 2004), as illustrated in the review on earworms in my prior discussion on musical policing, as contagious music that repeats non-stop in "playback mode'" (Levitin, 2006, p. 155), have a unique ability to expose citizens to political candidates and visions, as well as commercial brands such as Wheaties' cereals.

From Jingles to Hymns? 'Lula la'—'That Phrase Made Lula a National Symbol'

'Ricardo', who was a Bolsonaro supporter from São Paulo, and who deeply hated Lula and the workers party, blamed Lula's iconic jingle 'Lula la: Sem medo de ser feliz',[8] from the 1989 election, for turning Lula into a national figure, when we talked about jingles during an interview:

> Kjetil: 'Tell me more about that jingle, 'Lula La', why was it so important?'
> Ricardo: 'It was that jingle that, that 'Lula la' phrase, that made Lula a national symbol for the leftist. That song made him known across the country. From Acre to Porto Alegre. Before that jingle, he was popular, but only among some groups, I think that jingle made him a national figure.'

Throughout my fieldwork most informants started talking about 'Lula La' after I asked them about jingles, and the refrain of the song seemed to constitute a national earworm, as many just sang part of the refrain as a first reply. In an interview on YouTube and national television in 2022, Brazil's current president, Luiz Inácio Lula da Silva (hence Lula), elaborates on the jingle's importance in his political career:

> I don't believe that anybody would ever be able to make a song that communicate the sentiment, and the language of the people, during that time, like that song. It was my first participation in presidential election of this country, and this music, this music, allowed, us to create the most emotional campaign throughout history. Because this music shakes the hearts of the people, and it engages the mind of the Brazilian people. Now it is almost 35 years ago, but I am still getting emotional when I hear this song. I get the same feeling, as I got then, back in 1989.[9]

---

[8] 'Lula La!!.', YouTube, channel: webjingles, 29 July 2010, https://www.youtube.com/watch?v=jSOVyhaymvg.

[9] 'Especial Hilton Acioli—Programa 02 A História do Hino Lula Lá—Conexão Cultural Pós TV DHnet', *YouTube*, channel: Pós TV DHnet Direitos Humanos, 24 October 2021, https://www.youtube.com/watch?v=ni2boYr3G3I.

At the end of the interview, Brazil's current president starts crying as he embraces Hilton Acioli, the composer of 'Lula la: Sem medo de ser Feliz', underscoring the jingle's affective and political importance. The title of the TV program 'História do Hino Lula Lá', illustrates how the song, for many, is no longer a jingle, but a hymn and cultural symbol associated with Lula and the spreading of 'Lulismo', that is, Lula politics, in the twenty-first century (Singer, 2012). When I asked the composer of the song, Hilton Acioli, about how the song developed, he replied:

Acioli: 'Well, first I was contacted by Paulo de Tarso da Cunha Santos, he was a good friend of mine. He worked in a propaganda agency for the workers party back then in the late 80s. I had already created some successful jingles for other candidates, at the municipality level, and he liked my music. So, he called me and said: "Hilton, what do you think about this? 'Lula la' [Lula there, as president]?" I first found that phrase boring. What he said [Lula la] meant nothing to me. But then I started making the jingle [...] First, I created a samba ["Vai lá e vê"[10]] because we believed the following; Lula is a man of the workers, right? But in order to give him an image that was not restricted to that group, the workers in the fabric and people like that, I believed that it need to be something more general, bigger. Something that represent all of Brazil. So that is why I had the idea of [samba] as a sense of nobility. Popular nobility [nobreza popular]. At that point, I was already convinced about Lula la" [...] I liked the samba jingle, and the other people in the campaign also liked it [...]. But the day before I was supposed to present the jingle for Lula I suddenly felt, "no, this is not the right song". Then, this other melody came into my head: "Lula la, brilha uma estrelha , lula la, nosso esperanca, lula la...". (Lula there [as president], a star is shining, Lula there [as president], our hope is reborn, Lula there [as president...]). I immediately knew that this was the right song. Next day I sang it for them, accompanying myself on the guitar, and they all loved it. [...] That jingle became part of popular culture, people sang it at public events, even the political marketers of the opposition came to me and said, that "Lula la" was a strong song. It became extremely popular. I think it gave people a

---

[10] 'Vai Lá E Vê - Lula lá', *YouTube*, channel: Claudemir Vasconcelos, 25 May 2014, https://www.youtube.com/watch?v=V1FB3HsDR8c.

sense of hope after almost two decades of dictatorship and chaotic politics in the late 80s.' (Interview with Acioli, Natal, 18 March 2023)

Even though Lula lost the election in 89, 'Lula la: Sem medo de ser Feliz' went viral and became so popular that it became the soundtrack to all the following elections. That is why established artists on the Brazilian left decided to make a new version of 'Lula La' during the elections in 2022, only this time they changed the name of the song to 'Sem medo de ser Feliz' (Don't be afraid to be happy).[11] Just like with 'Lula la' in 1989, 'Sem medo de ser Feliz' was everywhere, blasting out of loudspeakers *and* from singing individuals at public events. It got vital support from other jingles such as Juliano Maderada's 'Tá Na Hora do Jair Já Ir Embora' (It is time for Jair [Bolsonaro] to leave [office]) which was the most played song on Spotify in Brazil during the election period (Facina, 2023).[12] While 'Lula La' from 1989 did important work in spreading the catch-phrase 'Lula la', it also gave birth to a new catch phrase, 'Sem medo ser feliz', the title of the 2022 jingle. That phrase is now an emblematic worker's party phrase that is often on banners, social media campaigns, and T-shirts. Acioli explained me how that phrase just 'came to him', organically, as he composed the song:

Acioli: 'While "Lula la" helped to spread Cunha Santos's phrase "Lula la" it also gave birth to a new catch phrase, *sem medo de ser feliz*. That phrase was not defined by Cunha Santos or others in the workers party, it just came to me as I was working on the lyrics and placed it at the end of the refrain of "Lula la".'

Kjetil: 'What does it mean, politically? Not afraid to be happy?'

Acioli: 'It means that Brazilians should not be afraid of democracy, of developing social welfare, and all these different policies that the workers party and the left try to create. That is at least how I understand it. Instead, we should embrace happiness. Political happiness. Political hope, of creating a better and more equal Brazil. I used it in response to

---

[11] 'Sem Medo de Ser Feliz', YouTube, channel: PT - Partido dos Trabalhadores, 26 October 2022, https://www.youtube.com/watch?v=x3HpJuXn7y0.

[12] "'Tá na hora do Jair já ir embora' chega ao 1º lugar do Spotify no Brasil com vitória de Lula", Rodrigo Ortega, 31/10, 2022, *Globo* https://g1.globo.com/pop-arte/musica/noticia/2022/10/31/ta-na-hora-do-jair-ja-ir-embora-chega-ao-1o-lugar-do-spotify-no-brasil-com-vitoria-de-lula.ghtml.

critiques by right-wing parties that always describe anything on the left as a dangerous communist threat [...] the phrase is actually from a football commentator named Fernando Vannucci who used to say "he is not afraid to be happy" (*sem medo de ser feliz*) when he commented on goals scored by football players who sacrificed everything to win the ball and get it in the net. I liked that phrase, so I used it.' (Interview with Acioli, Natal, 18 March 2023)

Acioli's arguments illustrate how jingles are not only passive instruments to disseminate pre-fabricated political slogans like 'Lula la'. Jingles can also actively shape political discourse as in the case of '*sem medo de ser feliz*' (don't be afraid to be happy). Today, that phrase is one of Lula's most iconic catch phrases and a quick Google search on 'sem medo de ser feliz Lula' reveals more than one million results, including links to hundreds of Lula jingles that have been composed since 1989 that further elaborates on the phrase, including the main jingle of the 2022 election. The phrase translated political visions on the left to a sense of happiness and fearlessness that communicated more directly, and affectively, to Brazilian citizens than complex Marxist arguments and bureaucratic theories on social welfare. As a populist leftist, with a unique ability to address the people's concern and articulate complex politics in simple terms, Lula always made several references to happiness when he talked to the electorate, as the following example from an interview in the newspaper *Correio Braziliense*[13] illustrates: 'People have to go back to eating barbecue, picanha and having a beer' (O povo tem que voltar a comer um churrasquinho, a comer uma picanha e tomar uma cervejinha).[14] The phrase was a critique of the increase in poverty and hunger under Bolsonaro's presidency and part of a broader argument where Lula aimed to increase the purchasing power of the Brazilian working class (Ferreira & Green, 2023; Jannuzzi & Sátyro, 2023). But Acioli's reflections also illuminate how jingles play with established imaginations in

---

[13] 'Lula no JN: O povo tem que voltar a comer churrasquinho e picanha', *Correio Braziliense*, 25 August 2022, https://www.correiobraziliense.com.br/politica/2022/08/5032120-lula-no-jn-o-povo-tem-que-voltar-a-comer-churrasquinho-e-picanha.html.

[14] For more work on Lula as a populist leftist, see, for example Coutinho et al. (2017), de Barros an Lago (2022), Ronderos and Glynos (2023).

popular culture, such as catch phrases from football commentators. As shown so far, this is not new but part of a longer musical political tradition where jingles, and precursors such as *pregões* and political songs, have used intertextual references, irony, satire, and metaphors, deeply rooted in popular culture, together with musical pleasure to shape public opinion, voice critique and attract supporters. Similar rhetorical strategies were also used by leftist musicians during the military dictatorship as they played a key role in disseminating hopes that Brazil one day could become a truly democracy country through popular songs (Napolitano, 2013; Ridenti, 2005, 2016).

Music of the Right

While 'Lula la' illustrates how the Brazilian left used music politically right-wing movements also worked musically to get their visions across (Bøhler, 2021b; Manhanelli, 2011, pp. 164–235). I witnessed this during a meeting at the University of Campinas organized by the right-wing organization *Movimento Brasil Livre* (hence MBL),[15] in 2017, as I heard the following speech by one of its upcoming leaders, Kim Kataguiri:

> We have to take the music! We have to make our own music. So that the Brazilian people can hear us. To show the Brazilian people why we need to change and to end the corrupt labor party government [*governo petista*]. To give people the freedom they deserve. All the musicians are communists and leftists. Because the Brazilian people love music, it is time that we made our voice heard through music. We have to make our own songs to get our message across. Songs about freedom and democracy to disseminate the pride of being Brazilian, which they [the labor party] have destroyed. (Summary based on field notes from the event, November 2017)

Kataguiri's speech was not about music but politics. Still, he was interested in music's popularity, and its ability to move people and create new

---

communities, as that musical force could help get MBL's message across and convince Brazilians that were fed up with corrupt politics that a change was needed. As the movement writes on their Facebook page, that new political community should be structured around the following values:

> The MBL, Movimento Brasil Livre, is a movement without commercial interest that aims to bring citizens together in a shared fight for justice, prosperity, and freedom. We defend democracy, the [Brazilian] republic, freedom of expression and a free press, and the free market, the dismantlement of the state, and the reduction of bureaucracy.[16]

The emphasis on justice, prosperity, and freedom—as well as on the importance of defending Brazilian democracy against corrupt politics; the autonomy of the republic; and, above all, freeing the market through massive privatization—were key parts of Kataguiri's speech that aligned themselves with the messaging power of music. More importantly, these words linked Kataguiri and MBL's political visions to a Bolsonaro movement that was on the rise in 2017 as the impeachment against Dilma Rouseff one year earlier, and massive corruption scandals in the workers party had placed Brazil in a political limbo (Buch et al., 2016; Clemente, 2022). In this context, right-wing candidate Jair Messias Bolsonaro emerged as a classic populist leader as he fused 'authoritarianism [with] charismatic leadership' (Laclau, 2005, p. 4) by arguing for massive privatization, more collaboration with the military, and a strengthening of Christian values (Mezzanotti & Løland, 2023; Nobre, 2022; Wink, 2021, 2023) as he aimed to shut down social welfare (Fleury et al., 2023).

Kataguiri was a great performer and situated himself within the broader Bolsonarismo movement at the time (see also Cardoso in this volume).[17] All of the attendees at the meeting, including me, were

---

[16] Original: O MBL—Movimento Brasil Livre—é uma entidade sem fins lucrativos que visa mobilizar cidadãos em favor de uma sociedade mais livre, justa e próspera. Defendemos a Democracia, a República, a Liberdade de Expressão e de Imprensa, o Livre Mercado, a Redução do Estado, Redução da Burocracia. https://www.facebook.com/mblivre/.

[17] For more research on the Bolsonaro movement, see, for example, Almeida (2019), Avritzer, L. (2020). Manso (2020), Todavia and Rennó (2020).

readily engaged, and almost hypnotized.[18] Through his 'aura' (Benjamin, 1969, pp. 4–7), he was bringing about a new political community opposed to the Brazilian labor party, *lulismo* (Singer, 2012), and the various leftist movements that, according to Kataguiri, threatened to create a communist dictatorship similar to Venezuela that undermined national independence. Most in the audience were young men—probably students at the University of Campinas—but there were also some older men in their fifties and sixties. According to my fieldnotes, there were about eighty people in total, closely grouped together in one of the bigger auditoriums at the university. Additional followers listened from the corridor outside the open door. As I listened to him, I was more and more puzzled by Kataguiri's emphasis on music. After all, this meeting was about politics—promoted weeks in advance through social media to recruit participants and supporters of the MBL movement to mobilize for the election next year. Yet, Kataguiri would not abandon his conviction that Brazilian music was a political force that could be used by the movement and a force that could police public opinion.

Spreading Jingles Through Sound Cars in the *Periferia*

As I was reflecting upon my fieldnotes from Kataguiri's speech, I realized that I had witnessed part of the musical force he talked about when I did fieldwork on jingles, one year earlier, during the 2016 municipal election in Campo Grande, outside Campinas. Back then, 'Thiago', the owner of a sound car (cars with massive loudspeakers that drive around in neighbourhoods with jingles or commercials on repeat), who worked for a conservative party, had articulated the importance of jingles in election campaigns to disseminate candidates. When I asked him about why he, and others, focused so much on jingles, he replied:

---

[18] An American fellowship enabled Kataguiri to study in the United States.

These jingles are very powerful, you know, because they get into the people's head [*ficar na cabeza*]. I think this is much more important than flyers and other forms of marketing, because when we give people flyers, we see the flyers afterward in the trash can. But good music gets into the people's head. Music kind of gets into your body, whether you like it or not. For our candidate [a right-wing politician], *sertanjeo* music [Brazilian country music] is the best, because that is the music of our people. [. . .] And you have to remember that it is mandatory to vote in Brazil—I don't know how this is in your country, but here, people have to vote; if not, they lose social welfare benefits and other things. That is why it is so important to play the jingles here in the *periferia* [suburbs with working-class Brazilians], because these people cannot afford to lose these benefits, and they have low levels of education, so if a jingle can get into the people's head, I believe it can influence their voting.

When I asked him to tell me more about how jingles work in practice, he continued:

Recently, we have developed a new strategy, which I think works very well. Because we know that many people here don't care about politics and that they try to close their ears to these jingles we are thinking about new methods. So, in this election, we have started making jingles that also communicate well with children because we know we have many mothers who live alone with several children here. So, if these children like the jingle, and memorize it and sing along the jingle, and maybe even after the sound car has passed, then the mother will hear the jingle many times from her own kids, which she loves [.... We] drive around with our sound car in the neighborhood during the forty-three days of the final round of the election from 8 AM to 5 PM each day, and that is what we do. We drive our routes, playing the same jingle, which last around fifty seconds, every day from 8 to 5. [...] After the election, I use my sound car for other types of work, selling different commodities. Driving that car is my work. (Interview carried out in Campo Grande, Campinas, 15 September 2016) (Fig. 8.2).

In the context of Thiago's arguments, Kataguiri's speech made more sense. Poor Brazilians had to vote, even if all the candidates were

Fig. 8.2 Sound car playing jingles in Campo Grande, Photo by author, 15 September 2016

corrupt.[19] If not, they had to pay a fine and could risk losing important social welfare benefits. In such conditions, a catchy jingle could do vital political work in *helping people to pick a certain candidate on voting day. For example, if the jingle would succeed in* operating as an 'earworm' a citizen could, in theory, be exposed to a political candidate multiple times on a daily basis because 'the neural circuits representing the song [could] get stuck in a "playback mode"' (Levitin, 2006, p. 155). More importantly, these processes could have social and biological ramifications if the candidate heard her children singing the same song as specific forms of *musical* policing could operate sonically as 'brand love' (Batra

---

[19] While it is possible to vote 'blank' in Brazil, studies show that this is infrequent. People tend to go ahead and vote for someone, even when they dislike them all and have no faith in the political system—the clown Tiririca, for example, received a massive number of votes in 2010 and was elected to the parliament despite lacking either political background or platform (Aires & Câmara, 2017; Saraiva & Silva, 2012).

et al., 2012), which refers to how consumers 'fall in love' in particular brands as they create affective, familiar, and intimate relationships with people and products. Because mothers usually love their children, they also tend to love their songs and musical performances. A rich body scholarship has already documented how different marketing techniques, such as jingles, aim to create such affective relationships by making consumers, or voters, 'fall in love', as these forms of emotional engagement can shape behaviour (Belk et al., 2003; Fournier, 1998; Grisaffe & Nguyen, 2011; Langner et al., 2016). In addition, Thiago seemed convince that these modes of musical policing were more powerful than flyers, as he had seen too many of those in the trash cane afterwards (Fig. 8.3).

Fig. 8.3 Massive soundcars, and trio electrico, broadcasting jingles for Bolsonaro, at Avenida Paulista, 17 October 2018. Photo by author

Bolsonaro Jingles at Avenida Paulista During the Second Round of the 2018 Election

As I did on fieldwork during the second round of the 2018 election in São Paulo at Avenida Paulista, I heard Bolsonaro jingles of different kinds blasting out of sound cars and trailers. Music was everywhere. Large trailers filled with massive loudspeakers, similar to the so-called 'trio electrico' that are used in carnival in Bahia (Baran, 2007), were placed at key spots and decorated in green and yellow, the colours of the Brazilian flag. The following picture illustrates this.

The banners focused more on anti-labour party sentiment than on exactly what change Bolsonaro would bring about (see, for example, PT Não [no to the labour party] and Fora PT [out with the labour party]). The jingle '[Military] Captain, Raise Up' (Capitão levanta-te) by el Veneceo was played several times. It is a pop song with a sparse and engaging beat and pronounced autotuning in the sung melody. The refrain of Capitão levanta-te by El Veneceo and Vhero[20] compares Bolsonaro to a military captain who should rise to the occasion (Fig. 8.4).

This jingle recalled Bolsonaro's emphasis on increased collaboration with the military and reminded potential voters that Bolsonaro used to work for the military.[21] He insisted that thirty-eight years of corrupt democracy had proven that collaboration with the military was necessary to bring forth the 'Ordem e Progreso' that was written on the Brazilian flag (from 1964 to 1985, Brazil had been governed by the military). A number of Brazilians agreed, and this Bolsonaro jingle mobilized Brazilians to participate in a shared fight about the very future of the

Captain get up	*Capitão levanta-te*
Because the Brazilian people need you	*Porque o povo brasileiro precisa de você*
Captain get up	*Capitão levanta-te*

Fig. 8.4 Lyrics from the Bolsonaro jingle Capitão levanta-te

---

[20] 'Capitão levanta te - El Veneco Feat Vhero', *YouTube*. channel: Cobra Fumante BR, 7 September 2018, https://www.youtube.com/watch?v=BNIUhz24WoM.

[21] Bolsonaro was kicked out of the military for failing certain tests and exams, so the initial allusion was in fact a bit more complicated.

Call 1: Right-wing São Paulo, what is your mission? Response 1: Elect Bolsonaro as president for this nation	Direita São Paulo qual e seu missão Elige Bolsonaro presidente de nação
Call 2: Right wing São Paulo, what are you doing? Response 2: I fight for my fatherland, no more to communism.	Direita São Paulo, o que você faz? Eu luto pela pátria, comunismo nunca mais
Call 3: Right-wing São Paulo, see who just arrived! Response 3: Bolsonaro has just arrived and he makes the leftist afraid.	Direita São Paulo olha quem chegou! Chegou o Bolsonaro pra Esquerda um temor
Refrain (everybody sing together) Ohhh, the military captain has arrived, the military captain has arrived, the military captain has arrived,	Ohhh, o capitão chegou, o capitão chegou, o capitão chegou,

Fig. 8.5 Lyrics from the Bolsonaro supporters singing and dancing together in the street, while accompanying each other on percussion

nation. Roughly 100 meters down at Avenida Paulista, young Bolsonaro supporters, dressed in Neymar's football T-shirts, had made their own carnivalesque street song, as they sang the following words together in the fashion of call and response (Fig. 8.5).

Each call was played in rhythmic unison by accompanying snare drums and other improvised percussion instruments and participants where dancing along, as they waved the Brazilian flag and called for the arrival of their military captain. A certain climax was reached at the refrain, as they sang the words 'Ahhh, the military captain has arrived' over a chant that everybody knew as it is commonly heard at football games. The refrain invited to further participation as fellow citizens started singing and dancing along as the social community expanded.[22]

As I walked deeper into the crowd and passed other sound cars, a jingle by *sertanejo* artist Cowboy Reaça (*sertanejo* is a type of country music), was boosting the following words out of massive loudspeakers: 'The country looks like a brother, and against all these criminals we shall fight, we will reconstruct our pride in being Brazilian, we will make the communist hide forever, and they have to respect the family'.[23] Some

---

[22] A film of the event can be found here: Youtube: Channel: TV Formiga Discussões Públicas de Filmes (33:33–33:55). https://www.youtube.com/watch?v=7SS7fufw-8A&t=1009s.

[23] 'Cowboy Reaça - Bolsonaro Presidente 17 / INSCREVA-SE NO CANAL', *YouTube*, channel: Paródia REAÇA, 4 September 2018, https://www.youtube.com/watch?v=cyYnhbQrJaM.

Bolsonaro supporters were singing along while waving the Brazilian flag. Both the soundscape, and the visual landscape, were articulating Bolsonarismo politics as his supporters had conquered Avenida Paulista. Again, pathos seemed to do more political work than logos and ethos in this Bolsonaro soundscape, at least in my ears. More importantly, the power of these musical pleasures almost reminded us that the present election was about the very survival of the Brazilian nation and that it was time to choose between good and evil. Corruption or God. These pleasures were engaging, sensory, powerful, and everywhere, at Avenida Paulista, during the 2018 election.

Musicking Bolsonarismo and Classed Musical Policing Online and Offline

When I met 'Maria', who was affiliated to the workers party, and lived in Diadema, a *periferia* in the outskirts of São Paulo, and asked her about Bolsonaro's musical presence during the 2018 election, she recalled a number of large sound cars and trailers that usually boosted jingles close to her house, but she talked particularly about the importance of new jingles on TikTok and WhatsApp through so-called Do-It-Yourself technologies (DIY). She elaborated:

> I remember that a number of new music videos, made by Bolsonaro supporters, went completely viral on social media. Many of them were made based upon existing popular tunes, such as 'Baile the favela' [a popular funk song], and one of them, was sung by a little girl, probably only 8 years old or something. She, or her parents, I don't know, had created their own lyrics where the girl was singing: 'Haddad is gay, Bolsonaro is our captain, and on the 18th of October he will win our election'. [Haddad, Bolsonoaro's opponent in 2018, was not gay, but a defender of LGBTQ rights].[24] That song went completely viral. I remember hearing it everywhere, on all the smartphones, and through loudspeakers. [...] Bolsonaro had many such music videos that went viral

---

[24] 'Menina canta a musica do capitão jair Bolsonaro ficou massa', *YouTube*, channel: LBBC DØGMAL, 18 January 2019, https://www.youtube.com/watch?v=y6PP1ScUfjo.

on TikTok, WhatsApp and Instagram, for example that famous Bolsonaro dance from Fortaleza, which had millions of views in just a couple of days.[25] I think social media, has become incredibly important to spread political campaigns. And music is crucial there, people make their own music, just like that, and release it on TikTok, WhatsApp, Instagram and Facebook. It is dangerous. (interview with Maria)

Even though I had witnessed both municipality elections and presidential elections in rich neighbourhoods, like Ipanema in Rio De Janeiro and Jardims in São Paulo, as well as Barão Geraldo, outside Campinas, I heard few jingles there. However, as I did fieldwork at the *periferia* in Campo Grande, at the outskirts of Campinas, as well as in Diadema in São Paulo, and Rocinha and Cantagalo in Rio, I heard jingles boosting non-stop out of massive trailers and soundcards. When I asked 'Ricardo', a Bolsonaro supporter about this difference, he explained:

You will never hear these jingles in the richer neighbourhoods, because it is illegal, it is sonic pollution, so if they come, the residents just call the police, and the driver of the sound car has to leave. It is the law. But the law doesn't apply in the *periferia*, so even though it is not allowed, nobody cares, and many are also accustomed to a different culture of noise and music.

'Gabriela' who had lived most of her life in a favela in Rio, elaborated on Ricardo's arguments, and argued:

In the favela where I grew up, we have this sound system, so that if something happens, for example rain, or the police is coming or anything, then they can announce it on the sound system so that everybody hear it. It is very loud and efficient. During elections, there are always some candidates that are allowed to play their songs on this sound system, it is usually some repetitions during lunch, and particularly after work, around 5, when people are back from work. Then these jingles are very intense and played loud. I think they [the politicians] pay for it, and that they often promise to do something for the favela in return.

---

[25] 'Em Fortaleza, apoiadores de Bolsonaro fazem coreografia para o candidato' *YouTube*, channel: Poder360, 9 September 2018, https://www.youtube.com/watch?v=m7P34mAtPLc.

Both Ricardo and Gabriela's arguments illustrate an important classed aspect of musical policing, and about legislation and politics in general, in Brazil. While Brazil have one of the most progressive constitutions in terms of participatory democracy and citizenship rights these rights are not enforced equally throughout the country and as a common saying goes 'the law exists to protect the rich' (do Valle, 2020; Friendly, 2013; Hagopian, 2011; Holston, 2011; Miki, 2018). These inequalities have deep roots in the country's colonial history, the distribution of wealth, and racialized policies that have marginalized blacks and indigenous groups for centuries (Bailey, 2009; McNamee, 2020; Weinstein, 2015) and widespread clientilism (Epstein, 2009). A number of studies have documented how access to legal protection, social welfare, public transport, and various public policies, vary substantially throughout the country, and particularly between the centre of the city, where the rich lives, and so-called favelas and poorer neighbourhoods, often located in the outskirts (Fischer, 2008; Holston, 2011; Marques & Arretche, 2022). In these latter areas, alternative 'rules of law' operate as drug traffickers and criminal gangs' control specific areas.

One example is how PCC [Primeiro Comando da Capital[26]] controls large parts of Sao Paulo (Cohen, 2022; Seigel, 2020). However, despite low education, unemployment, and high poverty rates in these marginalized neighbourhoods smartphones are common and people here are high consumers of social media, particularly WhatsApp, which, Maria explained me, allow people in Brazil to receive and download data, even though they have no credit on the phone. These factors allowed jingles on WhatsApp, produced on TikTok and YouTube, to spread rapidly across the country. And as I interviewed residents in marginalized neighbourhoods in Rio de Janeiro, São Paulo, Recife and Salvador, they all reported of having clear memories of jingles going viral on social media during elections, and, of boosting out loudly from sound cars. More importantly, many of these jingles were made by people living in these areas, as illustrated in Maria's quote, through different Do-it-Yourself-Technologies, which allowed them to first spread locally (Arora, 2019;

---

[26] PCC is Latin America's largest criminal organization, according to *The Economist*, 2023. https://www.economist.com/the-americas/2023/11/23/brazils-biggest-drug-gang-has-gone-global.

Bøhler, 2021b). Recently such technologies have gained force due to development in artificial intelligence (de Jesus & de Holanda, 2020; Ferreira & Green, 2023; Risse, 2022; Salazar, 2020), and the spread of TikTok (Cervi et al., 2023; Grandinetti & Bruinsma, 2023; Zamora-Medina et al., 2023), and these developments may further amplify musical policing, by disseminating political earworms, in marginalized neighbourhoods.

Musicking Bolsonarismo in the 2022 Election

During the 2022 election, both Lula and Bolsonaro intensified their jingle production. While social media campaigns were crucial so was TV and Radio and to get the most out of their limited time candidates hired jingle producers, as part of their political team, that recorded jingles on a daily basis, often several jingles each day. Jingle producer and musician, Jader Finamore, explained how he often worked non-stop during such periods, as each of these daily jingles should be aligned with the political debate and talks at that time, for example, the day before. So, it all needed to be very dynamic, if Lula talked about public health on Thursday, the 15 seconds jingle on Friday morning should be related to public health, and sometimes he only had a couple of hours to make the song, he explained:

> Jingles are crucial to get your message across on TV and radio and here in Brazil. Different parties get different time on TV and radio. So, if for example, Lula has 5 minutes on television each day, he can do two jingles of 15-30 seconds each day. To engage the citizen, you cannot talk all the time, you also need jingles. These very short jingles are often constructed around a catchy refrain and sung in call and response. (interview with Jader Finamore)

As mentioned above part of this work was amplified by developments in artificial intelligence and a number of Bolsonaro and Lula supporters created topical jingles, on a weekly basis, that circulated mainly on TikTok, Instagram and WhatsApp. Through the production and distribution of these jingles new modes of musical policing spread that both tried to shake the hearts and soul of Lula supporters, and among Bolonaro-supporters. These sounds often merged with political arguments and symbols of different kind that added further weight to logos, ethos, and above all the pathos dimension, of Bolsonaro and Lula's political visions. However, while artificial intelligence and DIY technologies were important, so was traditional jingles made by musicians in studios, and of them, 'The Captain of the People' (*É o capitão do povo*),[27] had a ubiquitous position in the Brazilian soundscape while I did fieldwork during the second round of the 2022 election. The jingle starts with a variation of the national anthem, and images of people raising the Brazilian flag, before they started singing the following words (Fig. 8.6).

The refrain is catchy and easy to memorize and sing along, I even found myself singing along it subconsciously. The music video presents several pictures of Bolsonaro in a military uniform, and a central part of his 2022 campaigns was to increase governmental collaboration with the military and privatize the public sector to bring 'freedom, liberty and prosperity' to the Brazilian people (Bedê et al., 2023; de Lima, 2023; Søndergaard, 2023). The music also features his most popular phrase

Refrain:	Refrain:
He is the captain of the people	É o capitão do povo
Who will win again	Que vai vencer de novo
He is a man of God, you can trust him	Ele é de Deus, 'cê pode confiar
He defend your family, and won't deceive you	Defende a família e não vai te enganar
He is the captain of the people	É o capitão do povo
Who will win again	Que vai vencer de novo
There has never been anybody like him	Igual a ele nunca existiu
He is the salvation of our Brazil	É a salvação do nosso Brasil
Verse	**Verse**
Hey, he is our hero, I put my faith	Ei, no mito eu boto fé
He is the one who defends the nation	É ele quem defende a nação
And he has our flag in his heart	E tem nossa bandeira no seu coração
Hey, it's in our hands	Ei, está em nossas mãos
We have the chance again	Temos a chance de novo
To take care of our people	De cuidar do nosso povo
And shout, 'Brazil above all and God above all'	E gritar, Brasil acima de tudo e Deus acima de todos

Fig. 8.6 Lyrics from the Bolsonaro jingle O capitão do povo

---

[27] ' Capitão do Povo', YouTube, channel: Capitão do Povo—emne, 6 September 2022, https://www.youtube.com/watch?v=N0kye6ZBi9E.

'Brazil above all and God above all', which elaborates on the image of Bolsonaro as a military captain as it is both used in the military, and in religious contexts. 'Joao', a Bolsonaro supporter, elaborated on the importance of that phrase in Bolsonaro's campaign during an interview and argued:

> Catch phrases are crucial in Brazilian politics, so people remember your values, and jingles are very important to communicate these phrases. That phrase from Bolsonaro, 'Brazil above all and God above all', is brilliant because first he is honouring Brazil, and then he describes himself as a man of God, that Bolsonaro is with God [...] and he knows the bible, and uses strong phrases from the bible as well, such as the phrase 'You will know the truth, and the truth will set you free' (*E conhecereis a verdade, e a verdade vos libertará*).[28]

Throughout the second round of his election campaign Bolsonaro aimed to consolidate his position among Christian Brazilians and the idea that he was a man of God. As I participated in Bolsonaro's election campaign at Igreja Mundial do Poder de Deus, in Santana, São Paulo, I saw clearly how his political rhetoric mobilized the Church community. He shared the scene with the charismatic pastor Valdemiro Santiago, who is the leader of the World Church of God's Power, a pentecoastal church organization with more than 6000 churches in 24 countries, which focus particularly on faith healing and miracles which are performed live on its TV channel Rede Mundial (Gonçalves, 2019). Bolsonaro's vice candidate, Tarcísio Gomes de Freitas, the current governor of São Paulo, was also present and demonstrated his deep understanding of the Bible by interpreting the current election in light of the sacred book, while underscoring that it is time to choose between good or evil, God or corruption. On stage Bolsonaro gave several biblical phrases, including the one above mentioned above 'You will know the truth, and the truth will set you free' (*E conhecereis a verdade, e a verdade vos libertará*) to communicate with his voters that he was a man of God evidenced by the bible in his hand.

---

[28] 'Bolsonaro cita João 8:32 e afirma que revelará 'a verdade' sobre a Amazônia', *Estado de minas*, 26 August 2019, https://www.em.com.br/app/noticia/politica/2019/08/26/interna_politica,1080106/bolsonaro-cita-joao-8-32-afirma-revelara-verdade-sobre-amazonia.shtml.

Igreja Mundial do Poder de Deus was full, and probably had around 10.000 participants, many of which saw Bolsonaro on large screens that were placed in different parts of the church as they were far from the centre stage. The crowd waved their hands and applauded Bolsonaro for his talks. However, the deepest and strongest sense of political participation was created musically as the whole community sang the following words of the national anthem, while lightening a candle as the light was turned off. Everybody were placing a hand on their chest to dignify the Brazilian fatherland while singing together, in full voice (Fig. 8.7).

The musical moment was sacred and deeply political. The upward melodic development, which starts with an arpeggiated dominant chord to build musical tension during the singing of the phrase from the introduction 'O beloved country, worshiped. Hail! Hail', gave me goose bumps. These political affects were amplified by the sound of piano and choir that provided melodic guidelines, if some in the audience should fall out of tune melodically speaking and loose the melody.

Intro	**Intro**
O beloved country, worshiped. Hail! Hail	Ó Pátria amada, Idolatrada, Salve! Salve!
Verse	**Verse**
Brazil, be a symbol of eternal love	Brasil, de amor eterno seja símbolo
The banner that you bear with stars	O lábaro que ostentas estrelado,
And let the green of your streamer proclaim	E diga o verde-louro dessa flâmula
- Peace in the future and glory in the past.	- Paz no futuro e glória no passado.
Variation	**Variation**
But if you raise the strong gavel of justice,	Mas se ergues da justiça a clava forte,
You will see that your son does not run away from the fight,	Verás que um filho teu não foge à luta,
Nor do they fear, those who adore you, their own death.	Nem teme, quem te adora, à própria morte.
Bridge	**Bridge**
Beloved land	Terra adorada
Amongst a thousand others	Entre outras mil
It's you, Brazil,	És tu, Brasil,
beloved homeland!	Pátria amada,
Coda	**Coda**
Of the children of this soil	Dos filhos deste solo
You are a kind mother,	És mãe gentil,
Beloved homeland,	Pátria amada,
Brazil!	Brasil!

Fig. 8.7 Lyrics from Brazil's national anthem. I want to thank Dr. Juan Diego Diaz Meneses for helping me with parts of this translation

Interestingly, the organizers of the event only sang the second verse of the anthem. However, hearing the sung words, and particularly the bridge, which sing the following words with a galloping rhythm that invited to embodied engagement, 'peace in the future and glory in the past'; 'beloved homeland'; 'you are our kind mother, we the children of your soil'—clearly echoed Bolsonaro's emphasis on family values, nation-building, and national pride. The final strophe of the variation captured Bolsonaro's combativeness towards what he called corrupt labour party communism as they were all singing, together, in the church: 'You will see that your son does not run away from the fight, nor do they fear, those who adore you, their own death'. Sharing these words, in a church that was famous for Valdemir Santiago's miracles and faith healings, was deeply moving. After they had sung the anthem I saw many Bolsonaro supporters with tears in their eyes, while other were waving the Brazilian flag. Bolsonaro, Tarcisio and Valdemir Santiago kept silence for roughly a minute after the performance of the anthem, as if the lack of sound, after hearing thousands of voices singing together, was further dignifying the nation, and echoing with Bolsonaro's catch phrase, which was written on posters: 'Brazil above everything, God above everyone' (Brasil Acima de Tudo, Deus Acima de Todos). Some Bolsonaro supporters started shouting 'Mito, mito' (Saviour, Saviour). Soon other joined in. The sound was loud. More importantly, the sound directed attention towards Bolsonaro's middle name, Messiah, among ten thousand Brazilian voters in one of São Paulo's biggest churches.

Conclusion

The aim of this chapter was to develop a new concept of musical policing to explore how music and jingles are used to recruit voters during presidential elections, with a focus on Bolsonaro's campaigns in 2018 and 2022, inspired by research in philosophy, musicology, psychology, sociology, and media studies. I developed musical policing conceptually inspired by Rancière's broad notion of 'the police', Foucault's work on 'governmentality' and Aristotle's work on the interplay between logos, ethos, and pathos in political rhetoric, together with studies in music and politics. By interpreting these theories considering recent developments in music psychology and media studies I showed how musical policing, today, is social, biological, and algorithmic as successful political songs take hold in our bodies by both releasing physical pleasure *and* by taking on a new social life as songs spread through 'algorithmic governance' on social media by connecting people across platforms, smartphones, and contexts. I showed how these modes of musical policing have a long history in Brazilian politics, dating all the way back to the birth of the colonial period, as *pregões* were precursors to modern jingles and used by street vendors. I described how *pregões* developed into professional jingles in the early twentieth-century thanks to technological developments as radio and TV turned upside down on Brazilian marketing, politics, and election campaigns. I showed how iconic jingles such as 'Lulla la: Sem medo de ser feliz' (Acioli) turned Lula into a national figure and how politicians on the right started developing new strategies to boost their musical presence during election campaigns. By looking closely at how Bolsonaro mobilized voters musically during the last two elections my findings indicate that right-wing politicians have a particularly strong presence on social media, and important competence in techniques of 'algorithmic governance', that allow them to create and use jingles in powerful ways to get their arguments across. Similar findings have been shown by others (Brito et al., 2019; Huszár et al., 2022; Khosravinik, 2017; Lim, 2017; Wahlström & Törnberg, 2021). Considering recent developments in artificial intelligence it is likely that the political force, and use, of such jingles will intensify the coming years and that we will hear, and see, a number of jingles 'without authors' going viral on social media platforms that can have a huge impact on elections if they manage to stick 'like bubble-gum music' (Manhanelli, 2011, p. 83) in people's bodies (Carnovalini & Rodà, 2020; Civit et al., 2022; Miranda, 2021). Even before the advent of these technologies, and the ground-breaking research on earworms in music psychology (Arthur, 2023; Scullin et al., 2021; Starcke et al., 2023), Brazilian scholars showed a deep sensitivity to music's contagious and visceral character and its social and political affordances (Manhanelli, 2011, pp. 80–85; Ramos, 2004, pp. 73–77; Teixeira, 2000, p. 91).

The ways in which musical policing sheds new light on the affective dimensions of 'algorithmic governance' during elections invite us to critically examine how participatory democracy works today as the increasing role 'affective governance' (Maxwell & Greenaway, 2022; Xu & Weninger, 2022) on TikTok and WhatsApp, and related forms of 'affective politics' (Boler & Davis, 2018, 2020; Grigoryan, 2024; Lünenborg & Röttger-Rössler, 2024), suggest that emotional manipulation may challenge pre-existing ideas of how democracy works that traditionally privilege deliberation and rational arguments (Bohman, 2000; Habermas, 1985, 1989). While such a recognition of musical policing may, of course, be dangerous as it speaks about the dark side of music's political power, it is important to account for as artificial intelligence and affects are shaping the future of politics, including democratic elections (Bakir & McStay, 2020; Jungherr, 2023; König & Wenzelburger, 2020; Manheim & Kaplan, 2019). More importantly, musical policing should, in one sense, be understood as a technique that can be used for 'the good', as well as 'the bad', and that a key point in democratic theory is to acknowledge the diversity of moral viewpoints and to account for disagreements as people believe in different political systems. In that sense, musical policing is first and foremost a descriptive term that aims to identify some of the political work that music does in election campaigns.

The conceptual definition of musical policing, and its link to neuroscience and music psychology, as well as the analysis of its operation in Brazilian politics, challenge dominant views that the politics of music cannot be found in 'the music itself' (Frith, 1996; Negus, 1997) and the corresponding growth of constructivist sociological and anthropological music research the last decades. Musical policing suggests that the music itself, indeed, matter, as catchy melodies can transform into earworms that, potentially, expose us to political imaginations beyond our own will as melodies play on repeat in our own bodies. As I have argued elsewhere, this is perhaps better understood as "the political force of musical actants" (Bøhler, 2021a), which refers to how the music itself has a sense of political agency that can do vital work in specific contexts. More importantly, the political agency of the earworm may, potentially, interact with other material agencies that operate through social media and that, together, give rise to new subjectivities, social divisions, and ways of being together. Of course, these agencies are also shaped by individual choice and our sense of 'active agency' (Giddens & Pierson, 1998, p. 22), as well as broader social structures, such as Bolsonaro's evocation of 'olvaism'[29] (Wink, 2021, pp. 191–245; Wink, 2023) and Lula's inspiration from the UN and Marxist theory (French, 2009, 2022). Still, an understanding of how these broader social structures work does not preclude inter-acting agencies of the music itself (Bøhler, 2017), the image itself, TikTok itself, WhatsApp itself, YouTube itself, and other forms of algorithmic and aesthetic governance, that constantly shape our sense of politics by reconfiguring our perceptions of logos, ethos, and pathos. While political theory, political science, and political sociology long time have privileged logos and ethos over pathos (Nussbaum, 2013), the present study of musical policing in Brazil suggest that pathos play a vital role, musically, in politics. More importantly, this importance is likely to intensify as use of social media and artificial intelligence accelerates the coming years. Whether this is good, or bad, is another question, and depends on contexts, and the political theory we apply. My aim of developing musical policing was to offer some steppingstones to understand its modus operandi when it interacts with music, and, to use this to provide a deeper understanding of the interplay between music, elections, and politics in Brazil. But more research is needed.

Funding and Ethics Statement   This work was funded by The Research Council of Norway under project no. 313626—*Algorithmic Governance and Cultures of Policing: Comparative Perspectives from Norway, India, Brazil, Russia, and South Africa* (AGOPOL). Research was conducted in compliance with the research ethics regulations of University of South-Eastern Norway, all informants supplied either written or oral consent depending on circumstances and in alignment with the NESH *Guidelines for Research Ethics in The Social Sciences, Humanities, Law and Theology.*

---

[29] Olavism refers to Bolsonaro's use of ideas developed by the Brazilian philosopher Olavo de Carvalho, the intellectual father of the new right in Brazil, which are characterized by their focus on conservative Christian values and a general fear of communism (dos Reis Cruz, 2023; Wink, 2021, 2023).

References

Adorno, T. W., & Simpson, G. (1941). *On Popular Music. Zeitschrift Für Sozialforschung, 9*(1), 17–48. https://doi.org/10.5840/zfs1941913

Aires, J., & Câmara, C. (2017). A mídia e os limites do personalismo na política brasileira: uma análise dos mandatos de Tiririca, Jean Willys e Celso Russomanno. *Compolítica, 7*(2), 153–180.

Albin, R. C. (2006). *Dicionário Houaiss ilustrado: música popular brasileira.* Paracatu Editora.

Allen Anderson, P. (2015). Neo-Muzak and the Business of Mood. *Critical Inquiry, 41*(4), 811–840. https://doi.org/10.1086/681787

Almeida, R., & d. (2019). Bolsonaro presidente: Conservadorismo, evangelismo e a crise brasileira. *Novos Estudos CEBRAP, 38*, 185–213.

Aristotle, O. R. (1991). *On Rhetoric.* trans. George A. Kennedy. Oxford University Press.

Aristotle, P. (1995). *Politics.* trans. Ernest Barker. Oxford University Press. https://doi.org/10.1093/oseo/instance.00259304

Arora, P. (2019). *The Next Billion Users: Digital Life Beyond the West.* Harvard University Press. https://doi.org/10.4159/9780674238879

Arthur, C. (2023). Why do Songs get "Stuck in Our Heads"? Towards a Theory for Explaining Earworms. *Music & Science, 6.* https://doi.org/10.1177/205 92043231164581

Austerlitz, P. (1997). *Merengue: Dominican Music and Dominican Identity.* Temple University Press.

Avritzer, L. (2020). *Política e antipolítica: a crise do governo Bolsonaro.* Todavia.

Bailey, S. (2009). *Legacies of Race: Identities, Attitudes, and Politics in Brazil.* Stanford University Press. https://doi.org/10.1515/9780804776264

Bakir, V., & McStay, A. (2020). Empathic Media, Emotional AI, and the Optimization of Disinformation. In *Affective Politics of Digital Media* (pp. 263–279). Routledge. https://doi.org/10.4324/9781003052272-13

Baran, M. D. (2007). "Girl, You Are Not Morena. We Are Negras!": Questioning the Concept of "Race" in Southern Bahia, Brazil. *Ethos, 35*(3), 383–409.

Bartel, D. (1997). *Musica Poetica: Musical-Rhetorical Figures in German Baroque Music.* University of Nebraska Press.

Batra, R., Ahuvia, A., & Bagozzi, R. P. (2012). Brand Love. *Journal of Marketing, 76*(2), 1–16. https://doi.org/10.1509/jm.09.0339

Beaman, C. P., & Williams, T. I. (2010). Earworms (stuck song syndrome): Towards a Natural History of Intrusive Thoughts. *British Journal of Psychology, 101*(4), 637–653. https://doi.org/10.1348/000712609X479636

Bedê, F., Domingues, J. M., Herz, M., Gonçalves, G. L., & Rodríguez, M. E. (2023). *Capital and Politics: Links and Distance During the Bolsonaro Government*. WITS University Press.

Belk, R. W., Ger, G., & Askegaard, S. (2003). The fire of desire: A multisited Inquiry into Consumer Passion. *Journal of Consumer Research, 30*(3), 326–351. https://doi.org/10.1086/378613

Benjamin, W. (1969). *The Work of Art in the Age of Mechanical Reproduction*. Illuminations/Schocken Books.

Benjamin, W., Eiland, H., & Smith, G. (1996). *Selected Writings: 1935–1938* (Vol. 3). Harvard University Press.

Boehler, K. K. (2016). "Somos la mezcla perfecta, la combinación más pura, cubanos, la más grande creación": Grooves, Pleasures, and Politics in Today's Cuba. *Latin American Music Review, 37*(2), 165–207. https://doi.org/10.7560/LAMR37202

Bøhler, K. K. (2017). Theorizing Musical Politics through Case Studies: Feminist Grooves against the Temer Government in Today's Brazil. *International Journal of Gender, Science and Technology, 9*(2), 118–140.

Bøhler, K. K. (2018). The Political Aesthetics of Musicking during Carnival in Santiago de Cuba. In *The Routledge Companion to the Study of Local Musicking* (pp. 443–457). Routledge. https://doi.org/10.4324/9781315687353-39

Bøhler, K. K. (2020). Musical Politics in the Cuban Police Order. *Rancière and Music* (pp 177–206). Edinburgh University Press. https://doi.org/10.3366/edinburgh/9781474440226.003.0009

Bøhler, K. K. (2021a). The Political Force of Musical Actants: Grooves, Pleasures, and Politics in Havana D'Primera's 'Pasaporte' Live in Havana. *Twentieth-Century Music, 18*(2), 185–222. https://doi.org/10.1017/S1478572220000614

Bøhler, K. K. (2021b). Rhythm Politics in a Changing Brazil: A Study of the Musical Mobilization of Voters by Bolsonaro and Haddad in the 2018 Election. *Qualitative Studies, 6*(2) https://doi.org/10.7146/qs.v6i2.127312

Bohman, J. (2000). *Public Deliberation: Pluralism, Complexity, and Democracy*. MIT press.

Boler, M., & Davis, E. (2018). The Affective Politics of the "Post-truth" era: Feeling Rules and Networked Subjectivity. *Emotion, Space and Society, 27*, 75–85. https://doi.org/10.1016/j.emospa.2018.03.002

Boler, M., & Davis, E. (2020). *Affective Politics of Digital Media*. Routledge. https://doi.org/10.4324/9781003052272

Bourgault, S. (2012). Music and Pedagogy in the Platonic City. *Journal of Aesthetic Education, 46*(1), 59–72. https://doi.org/10.5406/jaesteduc.46.1.0059

Branford, S., & Kucinski, B. (1995). *Brazil: Carnival of the Oppressed*. Latin American Bureau London. https://doi.org/10.3362/9781909013551

Brito, K., Paula, N., Fernandes, M., & Meira, S. (2019). *Social Media and Presidential Campaigns–Preliminary Results of the 2018 Brazilian Presidential Election*. Proceedings of the 20th Annual International Conference on Digital Government Research. https://doi.org/10.1145/3325112.3325252

Buch, E., Zubillaga, I. C., & Silva, M. D. (2016). *Composing for the State: Music in Twentieth-Century Dictatorships*. Routledge. https://doi.org/10.4324/9781315573236

Carah, N., & Angus, D. (2018). Algorithmic Brand Culture: Participatory Labour, Machine Learning and Branding on Social Media. *Media, Culture & Society, 40*(2), 178–194. https://doi.org/10.1177/0163443718754648

Carneiro, A., & Jalalzai, F. (2021). Gender Tensions: The Humorous Character of Dilma Bolada. *International Journal of Media & Cultural Politics, 17*(3), 263–289. https://doi.org/10.1386/macp_00052_1

Carnovalini, F., & Rodà, A. (2020). Computational Creativity and Music Generation Systems: An Introduction to the State of the Art. *Frontiers in Artificial Intelligence, 3*, 14. https://doi.org/10.3389/frai.2020.00014

Cervi, L., Tejedor, S., & Blesa, F. G. (2023). TikTok and Political Communication: The Latest Frontier of Politainment? A Case Study. *Media and communication, 11*(2), 203–217. https://doi.org/10.17645/mac.v11i2.6390

Charles, C. A. (2006). The Psychology of Music and Electioneering in the 2002 Jamaican Election. *Social and Economic Studies*, 133–166.

Christiansen, P. (2017). *Orchestrating Public Opinion: How Music Persuades in Television Political ads for US Presidential Campaigns, 1952–2016*. Amsterdam University Press. https://doi.org/10.5117/9789462981881

Civit, M., Civit-Masot, J., Cuadrado, F., & Escalona, M. J. (2022). A Systematic Review of Artificial Intelligence-based Music Generation: Scope, Applications, and Future Trends. *Expert Systems with Applications, 209*, 118190. https://doi.org/10.1016/j.eswa.2022.118190

Clemente, D. (2022). From Lula to Bolsonaro: The Crisis of Neodevelopmentalism in Brazil. *Latin American Perspectives, 49*(2), 87–103. https://doi.org/10.1177/0094582X211058172

Cohen, C. (2022). The 'Debate' and the Politics of the PCC's Informal Justice in São Paulo. *Contemporary Social Science, 17*(3), 235–247. https://doi.org/10.1080/21582041.2021.1998588

Coutinho, B., Lopes, A. C., & do Nascimento, D. (2017). Populism and the People in Lula's Political Discourse: Bridging Linguistic and Social Theory. *Revista de Estudos da linguagem, 25*(2), 681–710. https://doi.org/10.17851/2237-2083.25.2.681-710

Cox, J. (2008). *Sold on Radio: Advertisers in the Golden Age of Broadcasting.* McFarland.

Dawkins, R. (2016). *The Selfish Gene.* Oxford University Press. https://doi.org/10.4324/9781912281251

de Andrade, S. A. (1996). *Como vencer eleições usando TV e rádio.* NBL Editora.

de Barros, T. Z., & Lago, M. (2022). *Do que falamos quando falamos de populismo.* Companhia das Letras.

de Jesus, D. S. V., & de Holanda, A. F. B. (2020). Artificial Intelligence and the 2020 municipal elections in Brazil. *International Journal of Business Administration, 11*(5). https://doi.org/10.5430/ijba.v11n5p1

de Lima, R. S. (2023). Bolsonaro's Brazil: National Populism and the Role of the Police. In *Right-Wing Populism in Latin America and Beyond* (pp. 196–222). Routledge. https://doi.org/10.4324/9781003311676-14

do Valle, V. R. L. (2020). The Brazilian Constitution: Context, Structure and Current Challenges. *British Journal of American Legal Studies, 9*(3), 423–440. https://doi.org/10.2478/bjals-2020-0009

Doheny, M. M., & Lighthall, N. R. (2023). Social Cognitive Neuroscience in the Digital age. *Frontiers in Human Neuroscience, 17*, 1168788. https://doi.org/10.3389/fnhum.2023.1168788

dos Reis Cruz, N. (2023). O Pensamento Olavista sobre a Nova Ordem Internacional. *Revista Tempo e Argumento, 15*(39). https://doi.org/10.5965/2175180315392023e0201

Drury, J., & DaMatta, R. (2020). *Carnivals, Rogues, and Heroes: An Interpretation of the Brazilian Dilemma.* University of Notre Dame Press. https://doi.org/10.2307/j.ctv19m64wh

Epstein, D. J. (2009). Clientelism Versus Ideology: Problems of Party Development in Brazil. *Party Politics, 15*(3), 335–355.

Facina, A. (2023). Brasil da Esperança: Uma análise da campanha presidencial de 2022. *Mana, 29*, e2023042. https://doi.org/10.1590/1678-49442023v29n3e2023042.pt

Ferreira, T., & Green, J. N. (2023). Introduction: Brazil under Bolsonaro. *Latin American Perspectives, 50*(1), 3–13. https://doi.org/10.1177/0094582X2311 57700

Fischer, B. M. (2008). *A Poverty of Rights: Citizenship and Inequality in Twentieth-Century Rio de Janeiro.* Stanford University Press. https://doi.org/10.1515/9781503625631

Flannery, J. S., Burnell, K., Kwon, S.-J., Jorgensen, N. A., Prinstein, M. J., Lindquist, K. A., & Telzer, E. H. (2024). Developmental Changes in Brain Function Linked with Addiction-like Social Media use Two Years Later. *Social Cognitive and Affective Neuroscience, 19*(1), nsae008. https://doi.org/10.1093/scan/nsae008

Fleury, S., Lanzara, A., Pinho, C., Pernasetti, F., Lobato, L., Burlandy, L., Senna, M., & Teodoro, R. (2023). Authoritarian Populism, De-democratization, and Social Policy Dismantling: Lessons from Brazil. In *Social Policy Dismantling and De-democratization in Brazil: Citizenship in Danger* (pp. 217–240). Springer. https://doi.org/10.1007/978-3-031-351 10-5

Foucault, M. (1978a). *The History of Sexuality, Volume 1: An introduction* (R. Hurley, Trans.). Vintage.

Foucault, M. (1978b). *The Birth of Biopolitics. Lectures at the Collège de France, 1979.* Palgrave Macmillan.

Foucault, M. (1991). *The Foucault Effect: Studies in Governmentality.* University of Chicago Press.

Fournier, S. (1998). Consumers and Their Brands: Developing Relationship Theory in Consumer Research. *Journal of Consumer Research, 24*(4), 343–373. https://doi.org/10.1086/209515

French, J. D. (2009). Understanding the Politics of Latin America's Plural Lefts (Chavez/Lula): Social Democracy, Populism and Convergence on the Path to a Post-neoliberal World. *Third World Quarterly, 30*(2), 349–370. https://doi.org/10.1080/01436590802681090

French, J. D. (2022). Charisma's Birth from the Bottom Up: Lula, ABC's Metalworkers' Strikes and the Social History of Brazilian Politics. *Journal of Latin American Studies, 54*(4), 705–729. https://doi.org/10.1017/S00222 16X22000694

Friendly, A. (2013). The Right to the City: Theory and Practice in Brazil. *Planning Theory & Practice, 14*(2), 158–179. https://doi.org/10.1080/146 49357.2013.783098

Frith, S. (1996). *Performing Rites: On the Value of Popular Music.* Harvard University Press. https://doi.org/10.1093/oso/9780198163329.001.0001

Garcia, W. (2013). *Melancolias, mercadorias: Dorival Caymmi, Chico Buarque o Pregão de Rua e a canção popular-comercial no Brasil*. Ateliê Editorial.

Giddens, A., & Pierson, C. (1998). *Conversations with Anthony Giddens: Making Sense of Modernity*. Stanford University Press.

Gonçalves, C. A. V. (2019). A crença nas palavras: (des) construções lexicais em antropônimos de líderes religiosos. *Estudos Linguísticos (São Paulo. 1978), 48*(2), 899–918. https://doi.org/10.21165/el.v48i2.2446

Grandinetti, J., & Bruinsma, J. (2023). The Affective Algorithms of Conspiracy TikTok. *Journal of Broadcasting & Electronic Media, 67*(3), 274–293. https://doi.org/10.1080/08838151.2022.2140806

Grigoryan, N. (2024). The Politically Engaged: Gen Z's Use of TikTok and Instagram in the 2020 Presidential Elections. In *Social Media Politics* (pp. 213–236). Routledge. https://doi.org/10.4324/9781003409427-11

Grisaffe, D. B., & Nguyen, H. P. (2011). Antecedents of Emotional Attachment to Brands. *Journal of Business Research, 64*(10), 1052–1059.

Guilbault, J. (2007). *Governing Sound: The Cultural Politics of Trinidad's Carnival Musics*. University of Chicago Press.

Habermas, J. (1985). *The Theory of Communicative Action: Volume 2: Lifeword and System: A Critique of Functionalist Reason* (Vol. 2). Beacon Press.

Habermas, J. (1989). *The Structural Transformation of the Public Sphere, trans*. MIT Press.

Hagopian, F. (2011). Paradoxes of Democracy and Citizenship in Brazil. *Latin American Research Review, 46*(3), 216–227. https://doi.org/10.1353/lar.2011.0056

Harvey, A. R. (2020). Links between the Neurobiology of Oxytocin and Human Musicality. *Frontiers in Human Neuroscience, 14*, 350. https://doi.org/10.3389/fnhum.2020.00350

Hegel, G. W. F. (1979). *Hegel's Introduction to Aesthetics, trans*. TM Knox, with an interpretative essay by Charles Karelis. Oxford University Press.

Hegel, G. W. F. (1997). *Forelæsninger over historiens filosofi*. Samlerens Bogklub.

Hoffmann, F., & Santos, E. R. (2017). Os jingles como formas simbólicas estratégicas de persuasão político-eleitoral. *Cadernos do Tempo Presente, 8*(04), 27–38. https://doi.org/10.33662/ctp.v8i04.9888

Holston, J. (2011). Contesting Privilege with Right: The Transformation of Differentiated Citizenship in Brazil. *Citizenship Studies, 15*(3–4), 335–352. https://doi.org/10.1080/13621025.2011.565157

Hunter, W., & Power, T. J. (2019). Bolsonaro and Brazil's Illiberal Backlash. *Journal of Democracy, 30*(1), 68–82. https://doi.org/10.1353/jod.2019.0005

Huszár, F., Ktena, S. I., O'Brien, C., Belli, L., Schlaikjer, A., & Hardt, M. (2022). Algorithmic Amplification of Politics on Twitter. *Proceedings of the National Academy of Sciences, 119*(1), e2025334119. https://doi.org/10. 1073/pnas.2025334119

Jannuzzi, P., & Sátyro, N. (2023). Social Policies, Poverty, and Hunger in Brazil: The Social and Institutional lLegacy of the Lula/Dilma governments. In *Brazil after Bolsonaro* (pp. 67–79). Routledge. https://doi.org/10.4324/ 9781003407546-8

Jones, J. P. (2010). *Entertaining Politics: Satiric Television and Political Engagement*. Rowman & Littlefield Publishers.

Jungherr, A. (2023). Artificial Intelligence and Democracy: A Conceptual Framework. *Social Media+ Society, 9*(3), 20563051231186353. https://doi. org/10.1177/20563051231186353

Kalpokas, I. (2019). *Algorithmic Governance: Politics and Law in the Post-Human Era*. Palgrave Macmillan. https://doi.org/10.1007/978-3-030-319 22-9

Kant, I. (2008). *The Critique of Judgment*. The University of Adelaide Press.

Karakayali, N., Kostem, B., & Galip, I. (2018). Recommendation Systems as Technologies of the Self: Algorithmic Control and the Formation of Music Taste. *Theory, Culture & Society, 35*(2), 3–24. https://doi.org/10.1177/026 3276417722391

Kater, M. H. (1999). *The Twisted Muse: Musicians and their Music in the Third Reich*. Oxford University Press.

Katzenbach, C., & Ulbricht, L. (2019). Algorithmic Governance. *Internet Policy Review, 8*(4), 1–18. https://doi.org/10.14763/2019.4.1424

Khosravinik, M. (2017). Right wing Populism in the West: Social Media Discourse and Echo Chambers. *Insight Turkey, 19*(3), 53–68. https://doi. org/10.25253/99.2017193.04

Kivy, P. (1993). Kant and the Affektenlehre: What he said, and what I wish he had said. *The Fine Art of Repetition: Essays in the Philosophy of Music*, 250–264.

Kobialka, M. A. (2009). *This Is My Body: Representational Practices in the Early Middle Ages*. University of Michigan Press.

König, P. D., & Wenzelburger, G. (2020). Opportunity for Renewal or Disruptive Force? How Artificial Intelligence Alters Democratic Politics. *Government Information Quarterly, 37*(3), 101489. https://doi.org/10.1016/ j.giq.2020.101489

Krumhansl, C. L. (2000). Rhythm and Pitch in Music Cognition. *Psychological Bulletin, 126*(1), 159. https://doi.org/10.1037/0033-2909.126.1.159

Kuipers, G. (2011). The Politics of Humour in the Public Sphere: Cartoons, Power and Modernity in the First Transnational Humour Scandal. *European Journal of Cultural Studies, 14*(1), 63–80. https://doi.org/10.1177/136754 9410370072

Kuldova, T. Ø., Wathne, C. T., & Nordrik, B. (2021). Editorial: Algorithmic Governance: Fantasies of Social Control. *Journal of Extreme Anthropology, 5*(1), i–v. https://doi.org/10.5617/jea.9038

Laclau, E. (2005). *On Populist Reason.* Verso.

Langner, T., Bruns, D., Fischer, A., & Rossiter, J. R. (2016). Falling in Love with Brands: A Dynamic Analysis of the Trajectories of Brand Love. *Marketing Letters, 27*, 15–26.

Lanza, J. (2004). *Elevator Music: A Surreal History of Muzak, Easy-listening, and Other Moodsong.* University of Michigan Press.

Lebergott, S. (2014). *Pursuing Happiness: American Consumers in the Twentieth Century.* Princeton University Press.

Levi, E. (1996). *Music in the Third Reich.* Springer.

Levitin, D. J. (2006). *This is Your Brain on Music: The Science of a Human Obsession.* Penguin.

Lim, M. (2017). Freedom to Hate: Social Media, Algorithmic Enclaves, and the Rise of Tribal Nationalism in Indonesia. *Critical Asian Studies, 49*(3), 411–427. https://doi.org/10.1080/14672715.2017.1341188

Loureiro, F. P. (2017). *Empresários, trabalhadores e grupos de interesse: a política econômica nos governos Jânio Quadros e João Goulart, 1961–1964.* SciELO-Editora UNESP.

Lünenborg, M., & Röttger-Rössler, B. (2024). *Affective Formation of Publics: Places, Networks, and Media.* Routledge.

Manhanelli, C. A. (2011). *Jingles eleitorais e marketing político: uma dupla do barulho.* Summus Editorial.

Manheim, K., & Kaplan, L. (2019). Artificial Intelligence: Risks to Privacy and Democracy. *Yale JL & Tech., 21*, 106. https://doi.org/10.3390/bdcc3020021

Manso, B. P. (2020). *A república das milícias: Dos esquadrões da morte à era Bolsonaro.* Todavia.

Maram, S. (1992). Juscelino Kubitschek and the 1960 Presidential Election. *Journal of Latin American Studies, 24*(1), 123–145. https://doi.org/10.1017/S0022216X00022975

Marques, E., & Arretche, M. (2022). 25. Social Policies and Security in Favelas and Urban Peripheries of Brazilian Cities. *Handbook on Urban Social Policies: International Perspectives on Multilevel Governance and Local Welfare, 384.* https://doi.org/10.4337/9781788116152.00036

Martins, F. (1999). *Senhores ouvintes, no ar--: a cidade eo rádio*. Editora C/Arte.

Maxwell, K., & Greenaway, J. (2022). Understanding "Flow": A Multimodal Reading of Political Economy and Capitalist Erotics in Hip Hop. *Multimodality & Society, 2*(4), 410–433. https://doi.org/10.1177/263497952211 36859

McCann, B. (2003). Carlos Lacerda: The Rise and Fall of a Middle-class Populist in 1950s Brazil. *Hispanic American Historical Review, 83*(4), 661–696. https://doi.org/10.1215/00182168-83-4-661

McNamee, L. (2020). Colonial Legacies and Comparative Racial Identification in the Americas. *American Journal of Sociology, 126*(2), 318–353. https://doi.org/10.1086/711063

Mendonça, D. (2001). *Casos & coisas*. Globo São Paulo.

Mezzanotti, G., & Løland, O. J. (2023). From Religious Populism to Civil Religion: A Discourse Analysis of Bolsonaro's and Lula's Inaugural and Victory Speeches. *International Journal of Latin American Religions, 1–26*. https://doi.org/10.1007/s41603-023-00214-9

Michel, F., & Gandon, F. (2024). *Pay Attention: a Call to Regulate the Attention Market and Prevent Algorithmic Emotional Governance*. arXiv preprint arXiv: 2402.16670

Miki, Y. (2018). *Frontiers of Citizenship: A Black and Indigenous History of Postcolonial Brazil*. Cambridge University Press. https://doi.org/10.1017/978 1108277778

Miranda, E. R. (2021). *Handbook of Artificial Intelligence for Music*. Springer. https://doi.org/10.1007/978-3-030-72116-9

Monson, I. (2007). *Freedom Sounds: Civil Rights Call Out to Jazz and Africa*. Oxford University Press. https://doi.org/10.1093/acprof:oso/978019 5128253.001.0001

Montag, C. (2019). The Neuroscience of Smartphone/Social Media Usage and the Growing need to Include Methods from 'Psychoinformatics.' *Information Systems and Neuroscience: Neurois Retreat, 2018*. https://doi.org/10. 1007/978-3-030-01087-4_32

Napolitano, M. (2013). *História & música*. Autêntica.

Negus, K. (1997). *Popular Music in Theory: An Introduction*. Wesleyan University Press.

Neuman, I. (2011). *Tilbake til Durkheim*. Universitetsforlaget.

Newhauser, R. (2023). *Sin: Essays on the Moral Tradition in the Western Middle Ages*. Taylor & Francis.

Nobre, M. (2022). *Limits of Democracy: From the June 2013 Uprisings in Brazil to the Bolsonaro Government*. Springer Nature. https://doi.org/10.1007/978-3-031-16392-0

Nussbaum, M. C. (2013). *Political Emotions*. Harvard University Press. https://doi.org/10.2307/j.ctt6wpqm7

O'Brien, M.-E. (2004). *Nazi Cinema as Enchantment: The Politics of Entertainment in the Third Reich*. Camden House. https://doi.org/10.1017/978157 1136336

Omidiora, O., Ajiboye, E., & Abioye, T. (2020). Political Communication And Popular Literature: An Analysis of Political Jingles in Nigerian Electoral Discourse. *Journal of Creative Communications, 15*(2), 194–208. https://doi.org/10.1177/0973258619886161

Panke, L. (2013). Polintertainment: The Use of Humour in Political Communication. *Sphera Pública, 1*(13), 2–18.

Panke, L. (2015). Uma proposta de tipologia para os jingles. *Rádio-Leituras, 6*(2).

Panke, L., & Couto, E. (2006). *O jingle na publicidade e propaganda*. In BRAGA, Davi. Comunicação e marketing.

Patch, J. (2023). The Changing Political Economy of Music in Presidential Campaigns. *Journal of Popular Music Studies, 35*(1), 67–84. https://doi.org/10.1525/jpms.2023.35.1.67

Pels, D., & Corner, J. (2003). Media and the Restyling of Politics: Consumerism, Celebrity and Cynicism. *Media and the Restyling of Politics, 1–224*. https://doi.org/10.4135/9781446216804.n1

Plato, B. (1966). *Plato's Republic*. Cambridge University Press.

Plato, P. (2019). *Laws*. BoD–Books on Demand.

Potter, P. M. (2017). What is "Nazi music"? In *Music and Ideology* (pp. 235–262). Routledge. https://doi.org/10.4324/9781315090979-11

Queler, J. J. (2014). Jânio Quadros, o pai dos pobres: Tradição e paternalismo na projeção do líder (1959–1960). *Revista Brasileira De Ciências Sociais, 29*, 119–133. https://doi.org/10.1590/S0102-69092014000100008

Radano, R. M. (1989). Interpreting Muzak: Speculations on Musical Experience in Everyday Life. *American Music, 448–460*. https://doi.org/10.2307/3051915

Ramos, W. (2004). *Manual das eleições 2004 para vereadores*. São Paulo: CMP Editora.

Rancière, J. (1998). The Cause of the Other. *Parallax, 4*(2), 25–33. https://doi.org/10.1080/135346498250217

Rancière, J. (2004). *The Politics of Aesthetics*. Continuum.

Rancière, J. (2007). What Does it Mean to Be Un? *Continuum, 21*(4), 559–569. https://doi.org/10.1080/10304310701629961

Rancière, J. (2010). *Dissensus: On Politics and Aesthetics*. Continuum. https://doi.org/10.5040/9781472547378.ch-001

Rancière, J., Panagia, D., & Bowlby, R. (2001). Ten theses on Politics. *Theory & event, 5*(3). https://doi.org/10.1353/tae.2001.0028

Reik, T. (1953). *The Haunting Melody; Psychoanalytic Experiences in Life and Music*. Farrar, Straus & Young.

Rennó, L. R. (2020). The Bolsonaro Voter: Issue Positions and Vote Choice in the 2018 Brazilian Presidential Elections. *Latin American Politics and Society, 62*(4), 1–23. https://doi.org/10.1017/lap.2020.13

Ridenti, M. (2005). Artistas e intelectuais no Brasil pós-1960. *Tempo Social, 17*, 81–110.

Ridenti, M. (2016). *Em busca do povo brasileiro*. Editora Unesp.

Risse, M. (2022). Artificial Intelligence and the Past, Present, and Future of Democracy. *Carr Center for Human Rights Policy: Harvard Kennedy School*. https://doi.org/10.1017/9781009207898.009

Rodman, R. (2022). Orchestrating Public Opinion: How Music Persuades in Television Political Ads for US Presidential Campaigns, 1952–2016 by Paul Christiansen. *Music, Sound, and the Moving Image, 16*(2), 179–183.

Ronderos, S., & Glynos, J. (2023). Anti-populist Fantasies: Interrogating Veja's Discursive Constructions, from Lula to Bolsonaro. *Critical Discourse Studies, 20*(6), 618–642. https://doi.org/10.1080/17405904.2022.2156567

Saffle, M. (2015). User-generated Campaign Music and the 2012 US Presidential Election. *Music and Politics, 9*(2). https://doi.org/10.3998/mp.946 0447.0009.204

Salazar, G. (2020). *Dangerous Dice: Playing with Artificial Intelligence and Populism during Brazil's 2018 Election*. Master Thesis, University of San Fransisco.

Samuel, C. (2013). *The Lessons of Rancière*. Oxford University Press.

Saraiva, C. L. C., & Silva, M. D. B. (2012). Da transgressão e ethos forjado à câmara dos deputados: uma análise do discurso utilizado na campanha eleitoral de Tiririca 2010. *Revele: Revista Virtual dos Estudantes de Letras, 4*, 50–68.

Schneider, A. (2010). Music and Gestures: A Historical Introduction and Survey of Earlier Research. In *Musical Gestures* (pp. 81–112). Routledge.

Schoening, B. S., & Kasper, E. T. (2011). *Don't Stop Thinking About the Music: The Politics of Songs and Musicians in Presidential Campaigns*. Lexington Books.

Scullin, M. K., Gao, C., & Fillmore, P. (2021). Bedtime Music, Involuntary Musical Imagery, and Sleep. *Psychological Science, 32*(7), 985–997. https://doi.org/10.1177/0956797621989724

Seigel, M. (2020). Places Without Police: Brazilian Visions. *Radical History Review, 2020*(137), 177–192. https://doi.org/10.1215/01636545-8092846

Shapiro, L. (2004). And here she is... your Betty Crocker! *The American Scholar, 73*(2), 87–99.

Sherman, L. E., Hernandez, L. M., Greenfield, P. M., & Dapretto, M. (2018). What the Brain 'Likes': Neural Correlates of Providing Feedback on Social Media. *Social Cognitive and Affective Neuroscience, 13*(7), 699–707. https://doi.org/10.1093/scan/nsy051

Simões, R. (1990). Do pregão ao jingle. *História da propaganda no Brasil. São Paulo: T. A Queiroz Editor*, 447–460.

Singer, A. (2012). *Os sentidos do lulismo: reforma gradual e pacto conservador.* Editora Companhia das Letras.

Smallman, S. C. (1997). Shady business: Corruption in the Brazilian Army before 1954. *Latin American Research Review, 32*(3), 39–62. https://doi.org/10.1017/S0023879100038036

Snyder, A. G. (2022). *Critical Brass.* Wesleyan University Press.

Snyder, B. (2009). Memory for Music. *The Oxford Handbook of Music Psychology* (pp. 107–117). Oxford University Press.

Snyder, S. (1965). The Left Hand of God: Despair in Medieval and Renaissance Tradition. *Studies in the Renaissance, 12*, 18–59. https://doi.org/10.2307/2857068

Søndergaard, N. (2023). Between Markets and Barracks: The Economic Policy Narrative of Brazilian Authoritarianism. *Latin American Perspectives, 50*(1), 64–79. https://doi.org/10.1177/0094582X231154226

Starcke, K., Lüders, F. G., & von Georgi, R. (2023). Craving for Music Increases After Music listening and is Related to Earworms and Personality. *Psychology of Music.* https://doi.org/10.1177/03057356231212401

Street, J. (2003). 'Fight the power': The Politics of Music and the Music of Politics. *Government and Opposition, 38*(1), 113–130. https://doi.org/10.1111/1477-7053.00007

Street, J. (2013). *Music and Politics.* John Wiley & Sons.

Taylor, J. M. (1982). The Politics of Aesthetic Debate: The Case of Brazilian Carnival. *Ethnology, 21*(4), 301–311. https://doi.org/10.2307/3773761

Taylor, T. D. (2015). Music in Advertising in the US: History and Issues. *The SAGE Handbook of Popular Music, 154–167.* https://doi.org/10.4135/9781473910362.n9

Teixeira, S. (2000). *Sobras de campanhas: marketing eleitoral: o que candidatos e eleitores podem aprender com eleições passadas.* Editora Esfera.

Tentler, T. N. (2015). Sin and Confession on the Eve of the Reformation. *Princeton University Press.* https://doi.org/10.1515/9781400871407

Tinhorão, J. R. (1976). *Música Popular: os sons que vêm da rua.* Edições Tinhorão.

Tinhorão, J. R. (1998). *História social da música popular brasileira.* Editora 34.

Van Zoonen, L. (2005). *Entertaining the Citizen: When Politics and Popular Culture Converge.* Rowman & Littlefield.

Wahlström, M., & Törnberg, A. (2021). Social Media Mechanisms for Right-wing Political Violence in the 21st Century: Discursive Opportunities, Group dynamics, and Co-ordination. *Terrorism and Political Violence, 33*(4), 766–787. https://doi.org/10.1080/09546553.2019.1586676

Wallace, W. T. (1994). Memory for Music: Effect of Melody on Recall of Text. *Journal of Experimental Psychology: Learning, Memory, and Cognition, 20*(6), 1471. https://doi.org/10.1037/0278-7393.20.6.1471

Walser, R. (1995). Rhythm, Rhyme, and Rhetoric in the Music of Public Enemy. *Ethnomusicology, 39*(2), 193–217. https://doi.org/10.2307/924425

Wegman, R. C. (2002). Musical Understanding in the 15th Century. *Early Music, 30*(1), 47–66. https://doi.org/10.1093/em/30.1.46

Wegman, R. C. (2003). Johannes Tinctoris and the 'New Art.' *Music and Letters, 84*(2), 171–188. https://doi.org/10.1093/ml/84.2.171

Weinstein, B. (2015). *The Color of Modernity: São Paulo and the Making of Race and Nation in Brazil.* Duke University Press. https://doi.org/10.1215/9780822376156

Wessel, F. T. (1955). *The Affektenlehre in the Eighteenth Century.* Indiana University Press.

Williamson, V. J., & Jilka, S. R. (2014). Experiencing Earworms: An Interview Study of Involuntary Musical Imagery. *Psychology of Music, 42*(5), 653–670. https://doi.org/10.1177/0305735613483848

Wink, G. (2021). *Brazil, Land of the Past: The Ideological Roots of the New Right.* Bibliotopía.

Wink, G. (2023). Angels at the Top, Rocks at the Bottom: Naturalized Inequality in Brazilian Conservative Thought. *Social Sciences, 12*(12), 692. https://doi.org/10.3390/socsci12120692

Xu, H., & Weninger, C. (2022). Affective Governance as Multimodal Discursive Practice in Singapore'COVID-19 Vaccination Video. *Multimodality & Society, 2*(2), 174–196. https://doi.org/10.1177/26349795221096626

Young, J. M. (1963). The Brazilian Congressional Elections. *Journal of Inter-American Studies, 5*(1), 123–132. https://doi.org/10.2307/165289

Zamora-Medina, R., Suminas, A., & Fahmy, S. S. (2023). Securing the Youth Vote: A Comparative Analysis of Digital Persuasion on TikTok among Political Actors. *Media and communication, 11*(2), 218–231. https://doi.org/10.17645/mac.v11i2.6348

Zatorre, R. (2023). *From Perception to Pleasure: The Neuroscience of Music and Why We Love it.* Oxford University Press. https://doi.org/10.1093/oso/9780197558287.001.0001

Zatorre, R. J. (2015). Musical Pleasure and Reward: Mechanisms and Dysfunction. *Annals of the New York Academy of Sciences, 1337*(1), 202–211. https://doi.org/10.1111/nyas.12677

Zatorre, R. J., & Salimpoor, V. N. (2013). From Perception to Pleasure: Music and Its Neural Substrates. *Proceedings of the National Academy of Sciences, 110*(supplement_2), 10430–10437. https://doi.org/10.1073/pnas.1301228110

9

A Historical Perspective on Civil Society Activism and the Campaign to Ban Digital Facial Recognition Technologies in Public Security in Brazil

Paulo Cruz Terra ⓘ

This chapter seeks to contribute to the debate on cultures of policing in the age of big data and algorithms by highlighting the significance of addressing the perspectives and activism of civil society on this subject. I argue that it is essential to analyse not only the effects of technology on policing but also the forms of resistance encountered, and the alternatives formulated. To this effect, this chapter proposes an analysis of the Brazilian context and, more specifically, of the recent movement of civil society entities to ban digital facial recognition technologies (FRT) in Brazilian Public Security. First, it provides an overview of the literature concerning the perspective and activism of civil society in relation to transformations in the age of big data, with a focus on policing and FRT. It aims also to outline the historiographical methodological perspective used in the analysis. Subsequently, through interviews with activists and policymakers and analysis of materials produced by civil

P. C. Terra (✉)
Federal Fluminense University, Niterói, Brazil
e-mail: paulocruzterra@id.uff.br

293

T. Ø. Kuldova et al. (eds.), *Policing and Intelligence in the Global Big Data Era,*
Volume I, Palgrave's Critical Policing Studies,
https://doi.org/10.1007/978-3-031-68326-8_9

society organizations, the chapter explores the perspectives, strategies, and demands presented in the campaign to ban FRT in public security in Brazil. Among the points addressed and explored are the national and international context of the campaign; the police's use of FRT and its connections to Brazil's history; and, finally, the new developments and challenges in advocating for the banning of FRT use by security forces.

The argument put forward is that the case analysed allows us to see that civil society mobilization about the FRT has grown and strengthened, and that although it is recent, it makes sense when placed in a historical perspective, especially in relation to other social movements. Furthermore, although the investigation is centred on a case study in Brazil, the global connections are explored.

Academic Debate on Civil Society Activism and the Facial Recognition Technology

Since the goal of this text is to explore the perspective and activism of civil society regarding FRT, a first step is to attempt to provide a basic definition of what civil society is. While the concept of civil society is a subject of much debate (Chambers & Kopstein, 2006), the definition used here is that of Becky Kazansky and Stefania Milan, who state that the.

> umbrella term "civil society" identifies the realm of human action beyond the state and the market: a diverse group where distinct visions and values coexist, not without frictions. It includes non-governmental organizations, informal coalitions and groupings, and concerned individuals. (Kazansky & Milan, 2021, p. 377)

FRT, similarly, needs to be defined. A useful definition here is that by Kelly Gates, who sees FRT as the effort 'to teach computers to "see" the human face—to develop automated systems for identifying human faces and distinguishing them from one another, and for recognizing human facial expressions' (Gates, 2011, p. 3). Although research on the possibilities of this technology began in the 1960s in the United States, it gained momentum in the 1990s, 'along with commercialization and the integration of prototypes into existing real-world identification systems'

(Gates, 2004, p. 9). Among the different purposes of FRT, security has received significant prominence.

Regarding the literature that deals with the relationship between civil society and digital surveillance in general, which includes FRT, Becky Kazansky and Stefania Milan, for example, analysed, through practitioner interviews, participant observation in digital rights events, and surveying projects, how civil society actors try to transform dominant algorithmic imaginaries, contributing to an understanding of 'how individuals and social groups make sense of the challenges of datafication from the bottom-up' (Kazansky & Milan, 2021, p. 363). They specifically investigated three software projects as a means to observe civil society counter-imaginaries. The authors point out that these projects sought to increase agency, protect autonomy, and provide an investigation 'into new ways of being and doing amid the threats of pervasive datafication' (Kazansky & Milan, 2021, p. 376).

The different actors and responses to algorithmic harms are also the subject of analysis by Maya Ganesh and Emanuel Moss. They propose a categorization of response types based on 'a critical reflection on expert and epistemic communities', with resistance to algorithmic systems being the foremost category. Algorithmic 'harms like bias or unfairness have become the subject of resistance that Big Tech is now also part of' (Ganesh & Moss, 2022, p. 90). They also identified modes of refusal.

> that recognize the limits of Big Tech's resistance; built on practices of feminist organizing, decoloniality, and New-Luddism, they encourage a rethinking of the place and value of technologies in mediating human social and personal life; and not just how they can deterministically 'improve' social relations. (Ganesh & Moss, 2022, p. 90)

Although they do not focus on civil society organizations, Adelaide Bragias, Kelly Hine, and Robert Fleet analysed the public perceptions of police use of FRT. The authors indicated that the literature dedicated to this topic generally focused on legislation for policing practices and highlighted issues related to the citizens' legal rights, such as the right to privacy and human rights. Another approach has focused precisely on the public perceptions of its uses, primarily utilizing survey data as a means of analysis. The research undertaken by the aforementioned authors specifically aimed to investigate public commentary on YouTube postings about police use of FRT (Bragias et al., 2021).

Texts that specifically explore the relationship between organized civil society and FRT are still relatively rare, according to Peter Dauvergne, who has himself contributed to this discussion with a book published in 2022, entitled *Identified, Tracked, and Profiled: The Politics of Resisting Facial Recognition Technology*. This book on the transnational social movement of resistance is a crucial contribution. Brazil is included in the 'developing world', and the author notes that in places like Brazil, civil society resistance to surveillance technology is growing, 'although more slowly than in Europe and North America' (Dauvergne, 2022, p. 55). Dauvergne mentions some initiatives in this direction, but not the one that will be addressed in the present text. Even though opposition to FRT has grown in developing countries, Dauvergne states that 'few, if any, regulatory controls exist over facial recognition surveillance in the developing world', and, in fact, governments have supported the expansion of FRT usage to increase the state's power over civil society (Dauvergne, 2022, p. 57). This text will try to show that Brazilian civil society activism has become much stronger and more relevant, questioning the assertion that mobilizations in the central countries are necessarily more robust.

In the case of studies produced in Brazil, civil society movements are mentioned in articles that address the issues of FRT usage in the country (Melo & Serra, 2022; Vargas, 2022). The study that provided a deeper analysis of forms of resistance was conducted by Michel Souza and Rafael Zanatta, in an article published in 2021. From a perspective primarily concerned with the relationship with legislation, the authors identified three forms of action by civil society organizations: '(i) production of knowledge and alert to the population; (ii) monitoring of cases of injustice linked to facial recognition; (iii) judicial and administrative sanction cases' (Souza & Zanatta, 2021, p. 24).

The present text aims to contribute to the debate by analysing a specific initiative of civil society in Brazil that has not been adequately explored, thereby engaging in a dialogue with texts that address resistance movements in other contexts. In distinction from the previously mentioned analyses, the perspective adopted here is historical. This implies, on the one hand, investigating how participants in civil society organizations perceive the continuities and ruptures that FRT has brought to the history of policing in the country, and how the contestation of the technology use by the police has a past in the country. On the other hand, the research was conducted through the analysis of press and documents produced by organizations, but primarily through interviews, where 'oral history' techniques (Alberti, 2004; Delgado, 2003) were employed. Besides, this text is related to the micro-spatial perspective by focusing on analysing a specific case in a particular place, Brazil, and yet being attentive to global connections. According to Christian De Vito, this aims to bring together 'the epistemological perspective of microhistory and the spatially sensitive methodology of global history' (De Vito, 2019, p. 349). Micro-spatial history differs from other analyses that bring the two together, 'which are based on the assumed associations of micro with local, and macro with global' (De Vito, 2019, p. 349), as well as moving away from perspectives that place the micro as the sphere of agency and the macro as the sphere of structures.

Opposition to Facial Recognition Technology in Brazil

The concern of civil society with digital surveillance has increased significantly in the last decade. Kazansky and Milan indicated that concerns 'peaked in 2013 following the Snowden leaks, which exposed the blanket monitoring of citizens by national security agencies and industry collaborators' (Kazansky & Milan, 2021, p. 367). In the following years, civil society has engaged in mobilizations against 'data exploitation', for the right to encryption, privacy, and around the just application of automated systems.

Specific opposition to FRT in a global context is also growing. Dauvergne pointed out that 2019 was a 'turn point in the global campaign to stop police, intelligence services, schools, and private businesses from deploying face surveillance technology' (Dauvergne, 2022, p. 51). That year, more than 100 civil society organizations issued the Albania Declaration, which calls on all 'countries to suspend the further deployment of facial recognition technology for mass surveillance' (Dauvergne, 2022, p. 51).[1] The Covid-19 pandemic negatively impacted the global campaign against this technology in the first half of 2020. However, the murder of George Floyd in May 2020 in the USA, rekindled the commitment, with activists from around the world 'pointing to facial recognition technology as an example of racism as a policing tool' (Dauvergne, 2022, p. 51).

In Brazil, at least since 2018, mobilizations have challenged the use of FRT. In 2018, the Brazilian Institute for Consumer Defense (Idec) organized a public civil action against the use of facial recognition technologies by the São Paulo subway. Souza and Zanatta indicated that in 2019, 'during the Internet Governance Forum in Berlin, the *Coalizão Direitos na Rede* (CDR) published an open letter from representatives of Brazilian civil society facing threats to the democratic, free, and open internet in Brazil', mentioning specifically the use of automated facial recognition systems by the police (Souza & Zanatta, 2021, p. 9). In 2020, the same NGO coalition (CDR) published an open letter about the rise of techno-authoritarianism (see also Duarte in this volume).[2]

Souza and Zanatta stated that, in Brazil, 'the main critical reactions to the use of facial recognition technologies started after notorious cases of arrests of black people' in 2019 (Souza & Zanatta, 2021, p. 12). Resistance in Brazil is growing, according to Dauvergne, partly because of the arrival of Jair Bolsonaro as president in 2019. Bolsonaro was reportedly moving quickly to integrate FRT into policing and security services, claiming that high-tech surveillance is essential to prevent assassinations and gang violence (Dauvergne, 2022, p. 56). The interviews I conducted

---

[1] *Declaration: A Moratorium on Facial Recognition Technology for Mass Surveillance*, October 2019, Tirana, Albania https://thepublicvoice.org/ban-facial-recognition/.

[2] *Open letter from Brazilian civil society on the occasion of the 15th edition of the United Nations Internet Governance Forum*, November 2020, https://direitosnarede.org.br/2020/11/17/open-letter-from-brazilian-civil-society-on-the-occasion-of-the-15th-edition-of-the-united-nations-internet-governance-forum/.

show that activists see the rapid expansion of the use of FRT as an element of concern but also as a trigger for mobilization.

Among the different initiatives of the civil society in Brazil, this text focuses on #TireMeuRostoDaSuaMira.[3] I chose this campaign because it is not merely a one-off reaction but because it proposes a set of actions, and it comprises the whole country. The campaign initiated in 2022 is led by the CDR, which is a network of entities that brings together more than 50 academic and civil society organizations advocating for digital rights. It calls for a total ban on the use of facial recognition technology in public security in the country, a topic that has not been extensively analysed in other academic texts. It is important to mention initially, therefore, that it is situated within the context of other mobilizations in Brazil and the global context.

The #TireMeuRostoDaSuaMira campaign has issued an open letter dated March 8, 2022, signed by 52 civil society organizations, some of which are already involved in other actions, such as the Brazilian Institute for Consumer Defense (Idec). The document points out that this technology can 'follow, individually highlighting and tracking people everywhere they go, potentially violating rights such as: privacy, data protection, freedom of assembly and association, equality and non-discrimination' (Carta aberta pelo banimento, 2022).

It is further alleged that 'the use of facial recognition technologies in public security would exacerbate racist practices within the Brazilian penal system'. It also points out that, in addition to racism, 'classism, misogyny and LGBTQIA + phobia impact how people, in their diversity, have their bodies perceived, interpreted, approached and even discriminated against and repressed', and may interfere, therefore, in FRT (Carta aberta pelo banimento, 2022). The document proposes that even if corrections are made and the creation of an 'alleged and supposedly 'error-free' technology, this constant, massive, and indiscriminate surveillance is, in itself, a violation of the rights and freedoms of people' (Carta aberta pelo banimento, 2022). Therefore, they demand a total ban.

---

[3] https://tiremeurostodasuamira.org.br.

The proposal for the ban represents a shift in the attitude of civil society organizations towards the issue. Not only in Brazil, according to Souza and Zanatta, civil entities are transitioning from a corrective discourse to an oppositional one (Souza & Zanatta, 2021). Until recently, the primary criticism of technologies in Brazil was 'of a corrective nature: these cannot continue to operate in this way, with this type of consequence for the black population, due to false positives and problems of system accuracy' (Souza & Zanatta, 2021, p. 28). The #TireMeuRostoDaSuaMira campaign changes this perspective, as the primary demand is to ban the use of this technology in public safety. Within the campaign, there is also the specific initiative #SaiDaMinhaCara. On June 21, 2022, more than 50 parliamentarians from different political parties presented bills to ban facial recognition in public spaces.[4] Twelve states and the Federal District had bills presented in Brazil at the state or municipal level.

As mentioned earlier, the research was conducted through the analysis of materials produced by the campaign, but primarily through interviews with individuals involved in the process of its construction and development. In total, ten people were interviewed, and all of them agreed to be named. Pablo Nunes is one of them and is the coordinator of Panóptico,[5] which 'is a project of the Centro de Estudos de Segurança e Cidadania – CESeC – that monitors the adoption of facial recognition technology by public security institutions in Brazil' (Pablo Nunes, personal interview, 12 January 2022).[6] Assistant coordinator of the Panóptico, Thalita Lima, is a PhD student in International Relations at the Pontifical Catholic University of Rio de Janeiro and also a researcher in the DATAS research group—Research Network on Data, Technocontrol, Authority, and Subjectivity, at PUC-Rio (Thalita Lima, personal interview, 5 April 2023). Horrara Moreira is the coordinator of the #TireMeuRostoDaSuaMira campaign, has a degree in Law, and

---

[4] https://medium.com/codingrights/parlamentares-de-todas-as-regiões-do-brasil-apresentam-pro jetos-de-lei-pelo-banimento-do-ad33a8e6552e.

[5] https://www.opanoptico.com.br.

[6] All the interviews collected will be made available to the public through the website of the Oral History and Image Laboratory of the Fluminense Federal University: http://www.labhoi. uff.br.

is also a researcher at the Data Privacy Brazil Association[7] (Horrara Moreira, personal interview, 18 April 2023). Debora Pio, researcher at O MediaLab.UFRJ, which is a laboratory at the Federal University of Rio de Janeiro (UFRJ) focused on the intersections between technopolitics, subjectivities, and visibilities[8] (Debora Pio, personal interview, 18 January 2022). In addition to representatives from civil society organizations, an interview was conducted with Dani Monteiro, a member of the Rio de Janeiro State Assembly, who is responsible for introducing one of the bills as part of the #SaiDaMinhaCara initiative (Dani Monteiro, personal interview, 13 December 2022). Other interviewees included Fernanda Campagnucci, who is the executive director of Open Knowledge Brazil, a civil society organization dedicated to promoting open knowledge; Raquel Rachid is a lawyer and researcher at the Public Policy and Internet Laboratory (LAPIN), currently a PhD candidate in Social Change and Political Participation at the University of São Paulo (USP); Paulo Rená da Silva Santarém has a master's degree in Law from Brasília University (UnB). He is co-founder of the Pirate Party, AqualtuneLAB and IBIDEM, a CDR NGO; Natalia Viana is a master's student in Education at the State University of Rio de Janeiro (UERJ), a researcher at the Favelas Observatory and took part in the 'What intelligence?' platform; Mariah Rafaela Silva has a PhD in communication from the Fluminense Federal University (UFF) and is a visiting professor at the Federal University of Pará (UFPA). She was part of Panoptico. Next, the main issues present in the analysis of the interviews and materials are explored.

National and International Relations of the Campaign

The Open Letter of the #TireMeuRostoDaSuaMira campaign has one of its argumentative strategies aimed at demonstrating that FRT is already widely used in the country and the risks it poses. It is indicated that

---

[7] https://dataprivacy.com.br.
[8] https://medialabufrj.net.

this technology is present in most Brazilian states, and the specific case of Bahia is mentioned, where since 2018, 'facial recognition cameras have been installed for the official purpose of combating crime, but without evidence of having effectively achieved that goal' (Carta aberta pelo banimento, 2022).

In the bill for the ban on facial recognition technology in the São Paulo State Legislature, as part of the #SaiDaMinhaCara initiative, the case of Bahia is revisited. On the one hand, the initiative in that state is mentioned, expanding the facial recognition system to over 70 municipalities in the interior, with an expenditure of 665 million reais, while some of these cities lack hospitals, schools, access to justice services, among others. On the other hand, it is noted that in 2019, during the four days of carnival in the city of Feira de Santana, in the same state, 'the video monitoring system captured the faces of more than 1.3 million people, generating 903 alerts, which resulted in the execution of 18 warrants and the arrest of 15 people; in other words, out of all the alerts issued, more than 96% did not lead to any meaningful outcomes' (Projeto de lei nº 385/2022).

The bill in the state of Rio de Janeiro presented that, since January 2019, various police forces and private companies have been working together to deploy facial recognition technology in the streets of cities in the state. The case of testing this technology for policing by the Military Police Department of Rio de Janeiro (SEPM) in some neighbourhoods of the state capital is mentioned. According to the document, the test did not show a reduction in key crime indicators, 'besides the project not being transparent in terms of the security of the collected information and the error rates of the algorithms' (Projeto de lei nº 5240/2021). A report that exposed the flaws in the state's Military Police system is also mentioned. One of the failures pointed to was the case of a woman who was mistakenly taken to a police station and identified as a murderer. The person who had actually been convicted of murder was no longer a fugitive and was already in custody at that time (Projeto de lei nº 5240/2021). Within the argumentative strategy of the campaign, it is observed that importance is given to demonstrating, primarily, that FRT was already being implemented in the country and that it was flawed. Additionally, it was presented that substantial public resources were being invested in this problematic technology in areas lacking basic public services.

Despite the #TireMeuRostoDaSuaMira campaign being focused on the national scenario, its international relation can be observed. In the bills for the ban on FRT, the connection with the global movement in this direction was explicitly stated. In the bill presented in the state of Rio de Janeiro by Deputy Dani Monteiro, it was informed that various international perspectives were gathered for its preparation, 'considering that there is already a trend towards banning the use of facial recognition technologies' (Projeto de lei n° 5240/2021).

In the mentioned project, the case of the ban in the city of San Francisco, United States, is referenced with the justification of 'the high potential for abusive use and the establishment of an oppressive and massive surveillance state' (Projeto de lei n° 5240/2021). Other examples of bans in cities in the USA were cited, such as Portland, Minneapolis, Cambridge, Oakland, and New Orleans, considering 'that technologies can create or perpetuate existing oppressions in society and that facial recognition technologies have shown little accuracy in identifying Black individuals and women' (Projeto de lei n° 5240/2021). The project also references Europe, in the sense that entities like the European Commission and Data Protection Authorities recommend the general prohibition of using facial recognition technologies in public spaces. It was also mentioned that in March 2021, the European Data Protection Authority issued an opinion in favour of banning facial recognition technologies throughout the European Union, and that 'more recently, Italy has prohibited the use of facial recognition in public and publicly accessible spaces' (Projeto de lei n° 5240/2021).

Sara Solarova et al. pointed out that California was the first state of the USA to ban FRT in law enforcement in 2019 (Solarova et al., 2023). The following year, Illinois created a law restricting the collection and use of its residents' biometric data. In 2019, cities in California, such as Berkeley and San Francisco, banned facial recognition technology. Regarding the EU, the discussion of FRT regulation is present in the General Data Protection Regulation (GDPR) and the Law Enforcement Directive (LED) (Solarova et al., 2023).

The presence in the bill of FRT bans and regulatory inspiration and cases from the USA and Europe points to policy translation. According to Farhad Mukhtarov, policy translation 'can be defined as the process of modification of policy ideas and creation of new meanings and designs in the process of the cross-jurisdictional travel of policy ideas' (Mukhtarov, 2014, p. 76). Translation allows the analyses of the connections between the 'global' and 'local' (Mukhtarov, 2014). Thus, the authors of the Rio de Janeiro law made it clear what their inspirations were, but they also undertook translation processes in the formulation of local measures.

Pablo Nunes, one of the authors of the bill, stated that during the development of the campaign, the CDR organized a meeting with local politicians from Oregon precisely to exchange experiences on how they managed to get the ban on FRT approved. He also indicated how contact with international cases was important to highlight how Brazil was lagging behind in terms of discussion, regulation, and the ban on this technology. Furthermore, Nunes pointed out that mentioning international examples is crucial in the process of attempting to convince the public, including authorities such as judges (Pablo Nunes, personal interview, 12 January 2022). The search for legitimacy therefore involved not only evoking international examples, but also specific examples from the Global North. It can thus be seen that in the circulation and production of knowledge geopolitics, there is a hierarchy between the centre and the periphery, in a context that can be read as part of 'intellectual imperialism' (Pinheiro, 2020).

The Open Letter of the #TireMeuRostoDaSuaMira campaign also refers to the ReclaimYourFace initiative (n.d.), which is a movement led by civil society organizations across Europe to ban FRT (Carta aberta pelo banimento, 2022). It is important to note that all the references and connections are from central countries, which aligns with what Peter Dauvergne mentioned about the absence of regulatory controls over facial recognition surveillance in the developing world.

On the campaign's website, however, two Latin American mobilizations are presented that are supported by #TireMeuRostoDaSuaMira. The first one is #ConMiCaraNo (n.d.) organized by the Argentine entity Asociación por los Derechos Civiles (ADC), which discusses the weaknesses of FRT and promotes a debate on the advancement of surveillance and population control in Buenos Aires. One of the measures taken was an action filed with the Superior Court of Justice in Buenos Aires to declare the facial recognition system unconstitutional. The other one is promoted by La Red en Defensa de los Derechos Digitales (R3D) from Mexico and is titled #NoNosVeanLaCara (n.d.).

The initiative #TireMeuRostoDaSuaMira highlights the increasing interest of the country's governments in surveilling citizens with facial recognition technologies and educates about the problems of FRT in a didactic manner. Rachel Rachid, one of the organizers of the campaign, stated that it is just as important to understand the international connections as it is to recognize the specific aspects of peripheral contexts such as Brazil. According to her, it is essential to relate the use of FRT by security forces to the fact that Brazil is the third country in the world in terms of its incarcerated population (Rachel Rachid, personal interview, 14 January 2022).

A similar perspective was also presented by Paulo Rená from AqualtuneLab,[9] a legal collective with multidisciplinary support for studies, proposals, and analysis of the interrelationships between Law, Technology, and Race. For him, the exchange with international experience is important, but in terms of convincing, the specificities of Brazil are more relevant to the campaign. Thus, in our country, the connection to the origins of the police with the slave past prevails, which 'inclines it to reproduce racism, in addition to all the prison-related issues' (Paulo Rená, personal interview, 14 January 2022).

The activists, therefore, do not deny the importance of the connection with the international context in terms of FRT regulation and the mobilization of civil society. However, they reinforce the importance of the local context, pointing out that even though Brazil is a peripheral country, it is essential not to see it as simply receiving and copying global perspectives, which in many cases represent perspectives from central countries. In this sense, they point out the importance of thinking about the role of the Global South in the circulation of knowledge, including in terms of mobilizing civil society about FRT, not as an adjunct but as an active agent in the process. The next section precisely explores the

---

[9] https://aqualtunelab.com.br.

perception of those involved in the campaign, and, in the campaign itself, regarding the relationship between the use of FRT by security forces in Brazil and the country's history.

The Use of FRT by the Police and Continuities with Brazil's History

Analysing the #SaiDaMinhaCara initiative allows us to reflect on the activists' conceptions of the continuities brought about by the use of FRT in policing. A prevalent argument revolves around the possibility of racism associated with the use of these technologies. According to the bill presented in the State of Rio de Janeiro, the implementation of FRT implies 'significant differences regarding the (lack of) accuracy of facial recognition systems in evaluating the faces of non-white people', highlighting 'that solutions in facial recognition technologies are not neutral and reflect pre-existing racism in society' (Projeto de lei n⁰ 5240/2021). Additionally, the 'application in security contexts that refer to criminal selectivism and the improvement of criminal policies with harmfully racialized effects is a serious risk and has already been observed in several situations that represent security for some people and repression for others' (Projeto de lei n⁰ 5240/2021). The justification for the bill presents the diagnosis regarding the uses of these technologies in the country, produced by the Network of Security Observatories.[10] They raised 151 cases of unjust arrests involving the use of facial recognition, in which 90% of the cases involved black people who were arrested for crimes with a low potential for harm, such as trafficking in small amounts of drugs and theft (Projeto de lei n⁰ 5240/2021).

Debora Pio, one of the drafters of the bill, indicated that the debate on the introduction of new technologies in policing is directly related to racism because the police in Brazil 'has been racist since its inception'. Technology is yet another tool for public security forces to continue the work of criminalizing the black population that they have always done, and it even enhances this process further. In addition, the technology

---

[10] http://observatorioseguranca.com.br.

could also bring the effect of removing responsibility for those involved in the security forces for their actions 'because they can say that the identification error was the machine's fault', outsourcing the problem (Debora Pio, personal interview, 18 January 2022). According to Pio's argument, which is shared by some of the interviewed activists, facial recognition technology would represent a continuity in terms of the structural racism present in police work. In Pio's words, the police forces 'would continue to do what they have always done'. But the change could also increase the potentiality of the racist offensive by the security forces. The idea of 'neutrality' attributed to this technology would also mask the responsibility of security agents in perpetuating racism (Debora Pio, personal interview, 18 January 2022).

According to Souza and Zanatta, the Brazilian debate became *racialized* after the global protests following George Floyd's death and the retreat of technology companies from offering facial recognition technologies (Souza & Zanatta, 2021). I agree with the impact of global protests after the murder of George Floyd. However, it is important to consider another aspect present in activism related to public safety in the country. According to Pio, the activists' struggle to debate artificial intelligence technology spreads more easily in the field of public security precisely because there has long been a battle of activism in Brazil surrounding unjust arrests due to photographic recognition (Debora Pio, personal interview, 18 January 2022). This also highlights the racist facet of police work in the country. In Brazil, the recognition of suspects is admitted by exposing witnesses to a database of photographs of alleged criminals already existing in the public security databases (Nunes et al., 2016).

The Deputy of the Legislative Assembly of Rio de Janeiro, Dani Monteiro, stated that civil society organizations approached her to introduce the bill to ban facial recognition as part of the Campaign precisely because of her activism regarding photographic recognition arrests (Dani Monteiro, personal interview, 13 December 2022). Monteiro is the president of the Commission for the Defense of Human Rights and Citizenship of the Legislative Assembly of Rio de Janeiro, which works, among other things, to defend people who are unjustly arrested through photographic recognition. The Commission's report indicates that out of 90 people unfairly arrested based on photographic recognition in Rio de Janeiro state between 2012 and 2020, 86% were Black (*Comissão dos direitos humanos e cidadania da ALERJ*, 2021). According to Lívia Ruback, Sandra Avila, and Lucia Cantero, the ongoing failures in photographic recognition arrests perpetuate racism and exacerbate the mass incarceration of the Black population (Ruback et al., 2021).

Monteiro pointed out the parallel between photographic recognition, which represents the past in terms of police work, and FRT, which represents the future, lies precisely in the reproduction of social errors in Brazil, 'such as the idea of the racialization of bodies, the hierarchy of races, and the assumption that the commission of crimes is linked to a moral issue and not a class issue' (Dani Monteiro, personal interview, 13 December 2022). As the justification of the bill presented by her indicates:

> Any research and analysis of how policing has historically been conducted shows that the experimental use of surveillance technologies commonly criminalizes low-income and marginalized communities, the same communities that have traditionally faced structural racism and discrimination. The use of facial recognition is no exception to this, and for that reason, it must be halted before an even more dangerous surveillance infrastructure is created or becomes permanently operational. (Projeto de lei nº 5240/2021)

It is possible to perceive the proposition that, in the Brazilian case, the use of FRT by the police should be directly related to the structural racism present in the country (concerning the structural racism in Brazil see Almeida, 2018), and consequently, to the racism present in the history of law enforcement agencies. In this sense, it is important to emphasize the relevance of Brazilian Black movements in denouncing the use of photographic recognition as one of the State's strategies for the mass incarceration of the Black population (Neves, 2023).

Thus, another layer of the relevance of the historical perspective on the mobilization of civil society organizations regarding FRT is evident. Despite the technology being new and bringing new challenges, the campaign members emphasized the importance of anchoring their arguments and criticisms in the history of law enforcement actions, whose racism has already been strongly denounced by Black movements in the country (for the history of black movements in Brazil see Alberti & Pereira, 2007; Terra & Giacomoni, 2014). Thus, mobilizations around FRT should, at least in the Brazilian case, be related to existing social movements.

The connections with the past, however, go further. Civil society's opposition to the use of technology in policing also has a historical basis in Brazil. In January 1900, in Rio de Janeiro, Brazil's capital, a strike began by transport workers that paralyzed the city's streets. One of the main points of the strike was the supposed obligation for workers to be photographed by the police (Terra, 2013). Why was being photographed by the police considered a bad thing by workers? All the newspapers indicated that this was a procedure that, until then, had been given to thieves. The heads of the Judicial Identification Service, Renato Carmil and Souza Gomes, writing to a newspaper on the occasion of the strike, declared that some people wanted to evade identification because 'it will be better for them to appear with the name of Paulo, sometimes with any other name that' occurs to them (*Jornal do Brasil*, 16/01/1900, 1).

Faced with the possibility of being forced to take portraits, transport workers saw themselves compared to thieves. The workers' demand for the end of the photography requirement was linked to the symbolic aspect that it represented, given that this was a new technology implemented by the police precisely to identify criminals. If it was just an unfounded proposal for the authorities—as it was not included in the regulation's text—the workers claimed that the companies and the vehicle inspectorate required the procedure.

The aforementioned Judicial Identification Service of Rio de Janeiro was created in 1899 and established 'the mandatory anthropometric identification of arrested defendants, according to Alphonse Bertillon's system' (Galeno, 2012, p. 735). French police officer Alphonse Bertillon was an essential inventor of police techniques in the late nineteenth century, such as anthropometry and metric photography. Introducing these techniques in Brazil was seen as a way to modernize the police, although it also encountered resistance from politicians and identification specialists, who claimed the superiority of the fingerprint method.

Also, in the letter from the heads of the Identification Service, they explained that the photograph was being used as a means of general identification, and not just of criminals, in other countries, in the case of people who had 'an interest in being recognized with absolute precision' (*Jornal do Brasil*, 16/01/1900, 1). However, it is possible to verify that resistance to this technology also occurred in other spaces.

In 1909, the Municipality of Buenos Aires sanctioned a law of penalties that included the intention of instituting the 'neighbourhood card' among workers, which consisted of a document with a photo and fingerprint to facilitate the identification of the most tumultuous, especially the vehicle drivers, in order to impose punishments and sanctions on them. This measure and the wage drop in 1909 served as the basis for the general strike in early May of that year and was known as the Red Week (Quinterno, 2011).

The questioning of the police use of technology by civil society has thus existed in Brazil for a long time. However, in the next section, I will explore the challenges of the activism for the ban on the use of FRT by security forces.

Novelties and Challenges of Activism for the FRT Ban

A public persuasion strategy present in the #TireMeuRostoDaSuaMira campaign was precisely to relate the use of FRT to the history of racism in the actions of public security forces in Brazil. Emphasis was placed on the extensive questioning of photographic recognition. However, those involved in the campaign pointed out that the representations associated with the technology posed a challenge for mobilization. Horrara Moreira, the coordinator of the campaign, indicated that when trying to present the topic of banning FRT, there is constantly the reaction that this technology is something of the future, very distant, almost science fiction, and not something that is already present in the daily life of many Brazilian cities (Horrara Moreira, personal interview, 18 April 2023).

Thalita Lima, who is part of the Panóptico, stated that all discourse surrounding technology 'is anchored in an idea of science as something that will bring justice or something more impartial, neutral'. The image of neutrality and efficiency, and of future, associated with new technologies takes on even greater significance when related to policing. Lima cited the example of photographic recognition in the country. She indicated that if there are many questions about the errors and subjectivity present in this practice, FRT is presented as a *solution* that passes through neutrality and objectivity (Thalita Lima, personal interview, 5 April 2023).

Nunes also pointed out the connection between the resistance presented in the debate about the risks of algorithmizing policing and photographic recognition. There was indeed a correspondence between the neutrality and objectivity of FRT against the racism present in the country's police institution. He pointed out that it took a while for colleagues who were critical of public security to realize that algorithms 'do not come from the world of ideas' and that they 'are not only constructed by society but are also fed by information that we historically produce' (Pablo Nunes, personal interview, 5 April 2023). Convincing other social movements in the country about the relevance of the fight for the banning of FRT is an important challenge that unfolds for the campaign. Faced with the historical struggles of Brazilian social movements, such as those for education and housing, Moreira pointed out that the fight against FRT is often seen as less urgent. In this sense, she indicates that it becomes urgent to show that everything is interconnected:

> How are we going to go to the square, show our faces, make a demonstration, create a movement demanding a right, if our faces are being filmed, and from that footage, there's a whole possibility of data crossing that will know where I've been, what I do, what my political stance is, all of this in the hands of the police? 'Do we trust the police for this kind of activity, to have this kind of power, processing, intelligence?'. (Horrara Moreira, personal interview, 18 April 2023)

It is possible to perceive that the campaign seeks to reinforce that the use of FRT by security forces impacts not only on the historical racism present in the police but also brings new violations in terms of human rights. The justification for the bill presented by Dani Monteiro, as part of the #SaiDaMinhaCara initiative, indicates that the ban is necessary because 'the technical improvements of these systems will not prevent the threat they pose to our human rights'. Among the forms of threats to rights related to this technology would be.

> The training data – the database of faces against which the input data is compared and the biometric data handled by these systems – is generally obtained without the knowledge, consent or (…) free choice of those who are included in them, which means that these technologies encourage mass and discriminatory surveillance from their inception.
> Second, if people in publicly accessible spaces can be instantly identified, highlighted, or tracked, their human rights will be undermined. Even the idea that these technologies could operate in publicly accessible spaces creates an inhibitory effect that undermines people's ability to exercise their rights. (Projeto de lei n° 5240/2021)

Among the action strategies of the Campaign, which are linked to initiatives in other countries, is what Lima defines as 'raising awareness, sensitizing people, civil society' about what FRT is. According to her, the proposal has been to conduct pedagogical workshops, as well as to explore other formats such as a makeup contest titled # MeuRostoNao, which awarded makeups that promoted the debate about the threats of facial recognition systems in Brazilian public security (Thalita Lima, personal interview, 5 April 2023). There is a current debate about how makeup can thwart FRT.[11] One of the main challenges faced by the #TireMeuRostoDaSuaMira campaign lies precisely in the cultural representation of technological neutrality and efficiency. In this regard, it is important to convince society at large and other social movements of the issues related to FRT.

---

[11] See: https://www.vice.com/en/article/k78v9m/researchers-defeated-advanced-facial-recognition-tech-using-makeup.

Final Considerations

The #TireMeuRostoDaSuaMira campaign in Brazil, led by civil society organizations, is part of the global context of the anti-FRT movement, which was analysed by Dauvergne, who indicated that it 'is generating a groundswell of local resistance' (Dauvergne, 2022, p. 90). It was even presented how the Brazilian experience made a point of mentioning those of other countries. The campaign is a turning point in Brazilian anti-FRT activism because it calls for the ban and brings together various forms of mobilization, such as the multiple bills submitted in different parts of the country. The scope and actions of the campaign can make us reconsider Dauvergne's definition that the layers of resistance are necessarily thinnest in Latin America.

In the relationship between the local and the global, some of the activists interviewed pointed out the importance of the specific context in building the mobilization that questions the use of FRT in public security. In this sense, in a global context of the anti-FRT movement, peripheral countries such as Brazil should not be seen as simple recipients and replicators of ideas from central countries. What becomes essential is precisely an understanding of the process as translation, while trying to perceive the connections not only from North Global to South but in multiple directions.

The present text sought to contribute to the debate on civil society activism and FRT not only by exploring a recent and important initiative in Brazil but also by proposing the possibilities of a historical perspective. As much as mobilizations like #TireMeuRostoDaSuaMira are quite recent, we emphasized the importance of placing them within a historical context. On the one hand, we sought to investigate how activists perceive the continuities of FRT in relation to the history of policing in Brazil. In this sense, the racism present in the history of public security in the country represents the connection between past and present, configuring a continuum, including the discourse of neutrality and efficiency associated with technology. On the other hand, I showed that civil society mobilizations questioning the use of technology by the police are not new in the country and presented the case of a strike in 1900 in which workers questioned the supposed obligation to be photographed by the police.

If there is a historical background to the anti-FRT mobilizations, one of the challenges faced by activists in the present is precisely in convincing the general society and other social movements of the inherent risks of using FRT, including the mystification surrounding the technology. A strategy, also present in the educational efforts of the campaign, was to demonstrate how various human rights are affected by the use of FRT in policing. Throughout the chapter, I sought to demonstrate the importance of addressing the perspectives and activism of civil society in the debate on cultures of policing in the age of big data and algorithms. In dialogue with other authors who deal with the subject in multiple contexts, I argue that this perspective is essential to analyse not only the effects of technology on policing but also the perceptions by the civil society and forms of resistance encountered. A fundamental reminder from the activists is that technologies in policing should not be seen as fatalistic and that other alternatives and futures could be imagined and constructed.

Funding and Ethics Statement   This work was funded by The Research Council of Norway under project no. 313626—*Algorithmic Governance and Cultures of Policing: Comparative Perspectives from Norway, India, Brazil, Russia, and South Africa* (AGOPOL). Informed consent has been secured from all research participants, and the study was conducted in accordance with the Federal Fluminense University ethical and data protection guidelines.

References

#ConMiCaraNo (n.d.). https://conmicarano.adc.org.ar

#NoNosVeanLaCara (n.d.).https://nonosveanlacara.r3d.mx

Alberti, V. (2004). *Manual de história oral*. FGV.

Alberti, V. & Pereira, A. (Eds.) (2007). *História do movimento negro no Brasil*: depoimentos ao CPDOC. FGV/Pallas.

Almeida, S. L. de (2018). *O que é racismo estrutural?* Letramento.

Bragias, A., Hine, K., & Fleet, R. (2021). "Only in Our Best Interest, Right?" Public Perceptions of Police Use of Facial Recognition Technology. *Police Practice and Research, 22*(6), 1637–1654. https://doi.org/10.1080/156 14263.2021.1942873

Carta aberta pelo banimento (2022, March 8). https://tiremeurostodasuamira. org.br/carta-aberta/

Chambers, S.; Kopstein, J. (2006). Civil Society and the State In J. Dryzek, B. Honig & A. Phillips (Eds.), *The Oxford Handbook of Political Theory* (pp. 363–381). Oxford University Press. https://doi.org/10.1093/oxfordhb/ 9780199548439.003.0020

Dauvergne, P. (2022). Identified, Tracked, and Profiled: The Politics of Resisting Facial Recognition Technology. *Edward Elgar*. https://doi.org/10. 4337/9781803925899

De Vito, C. G. (2019). History Without Scale: The Micro-spatial Perspective. *Past & Present, 242*, 348–372. https://doi.org/10.1093/pastj/gtz048

Delgado, L. de A. N. (2003). História oral e narrativa: tempo, memória e identidades. *História Oral, 6*, 9–25. https://doi.org/10.51880/ho.v6i0.62

Galeano, D. (2012). Identidade cifrada no corpo: O bertillonage e o gabinete antropométrico na polícia do Rio de Janeiro, 1894–1903. *Boletim Do Museu Paraense Emílio Goeldi, 7*(3), 721–742. https://doi.org/10.1590/S1981-812 2201200030000

Ganesh, M. I., & Moss, E. (2022). Resistance and Refusal to Algorithmic Harms: Varieties of 'Knowledge Projects.' *Media International Australia, 183*(1), 90–106. https://doi.org/10.1177/1329878X221076288

Gates, K. (2004). *The Past Perfect Promise of Facial Recognition Technology.* ACDIS.

Gates, K. (2011). *Our Biometric Future: Facial Recognition Technology and the Culture of Surveillance.* NYU Press.

Kazansky, B., & Milan, S. (2021). "Bodies not Templates": Contesting Dominant Algorithmic Imaginaries. *New Media & Society, 23*(2), 363–381. https://doi.org/10.1177/1461444820929316

Melo, P. V. & Serra, P. (2022). Tecnologia de Reconhecimento Facial e Segurança Pública nas capitais brasileiras: apontamentos e problematizações. *Comunicação e sociedade, 42*, 205–220. https://doi.org/10.17231/comsoc. 42(2022).3984

Mukhtarov, F. (2014). Rethinking the Travel of Ideas: Policy Translation in the Water Sector. *Policy and Politics: An International Journal, 42*(1), 71–88. https://doi.org/10.1332/030557312X655459

Neves, F. V. dos S. (2023). Política Antirracista no Sistema de Justiça: a experiência da Coordenadoria de Promoção da Equidade Racial da Defensoria Pública do Estado do Rio de Janeiro. *Revista de Ciências Sociais, 54*(2), 21–60. https://doi.org/10.36517/rcs.54.2.d02

Nunes, F. T. et al. (2016). Um estudo sobre técnicas de biometria baseadas em padrões faciais e sua utilização In J. F. SPANHOL (Ed.). *Tecnologia e Informação na Segurança Pública e Direitos Humanos* (pp.113–129). Editora Edgar Blucher. https://doi.org/10.5151/9788580391763-08

Projeto de lei nº 385 /2022 (2022). https://www.al.sp.gov.br/propositura/?id=1000448817

Projeto de lei nº 5240/2021 (2021). http://www3.alerj.rj.gov.br/lotus_notes/default.asp?id=144&url=L3NjcHJvMTkyMy5uc2YvMThjMWRkNjhmOTZiZTNlNzgzMjU2NmVjMDAxOGQ4MzMvYTdkYTU1NGFiZWUzMTBhYTAzMjU4N2E1MDA1YmNmmMDE%2FT3BlbkRvY3VtZW50W50&s=09

Pinheiro, J. A. P. (2020). A geopolítica da produção e da circulação do conhecimento. *Conexão Política, 9*(1), 221–233.

Quinterno, Hugo (2011). 'Padres de la patria' contra 'hijos del pueblo'. Discursos y praticas Del régimen político argentino ante lãs huelgas y conflictos sociales en la Buenos Aires de 1909". *Anais do I Coloquio Internacional Greves e conflitos sociais no século XX.* https://sinteseeventos.com/site/index.php/acervo/anais/anaisiassc

ReclaimYourFace (n.d.). https://reclaimyourface.eu

Ruback, L., Avila, S., & Cantero, L. (2021). *Vieses No Aprendizado De Máquina e Suas Implicações Sociais: Um Estudo De Caso No Reconhecimento Facial in Anais Do Workshop Sobre as Implicações Da Computação Na Sociedade (WICS).* https://doi.org/10.5753/wics.2021.15967

Solarova, S., et al. (2023). Reconsidering the Regulation of Facial Recognition in Public Spaces. *AI Ethics, 3*(2), 625–635. https://doi.org/10.1007/s43681-022-00194-0

Souza, M. R. O., & Zanatta, R. A. F. (2021). The Problem of Automated Facial Recognition Technologies in Brazil: Social Countermovements and the New Frontiers of Fundamental Rights. *Latin American Human Rights Studies, 1,* 1–34.

Terra, P. C. & Giacomini, S. M. (2014). Participação e movimento negro: os desafios do "racismo institucional" In J. S. L. Lopes & B. Heredia (Eds.), *Movimentos sociais e esfera pública* (pp. 187–209). CBAE.

Terra, P. C. (2013). *Cidadania e trabalhadores: cocheiros e carroceiros no Rio de Janeiro (1870–1906)*. Arquivo Geral da Cidade do Rio de Janeiro.

Vargas, É. N. P. (2022). *O uso da tecnologia de reconhecimento facial como política de segurança pública no Estado da Bahia* [Master's thesis, UNIFACS].

10

Algorithmic Police Reform: 'Reading' a Police Early Intervention Algorithm

Matthew Nesvet[ID]

Reflections on 'Automatic' Governance

On June 19, 1802, the American President, Thomas Jefferson, residing in Washington, D.C., wrote a letter to the English chemist and liberal theologian Joseph Priestley. Priestley, who had arrived in America to great fanfare after a mob in Birmingham, England set his house alight, driving him into exile, wrote to Jefferson to praise the American constitution and the protections it afforded him. Jefferson replied to Priestley that he did not have as much influence over the drafting of the constitution as Priestley's letter implied. 'I was in Europe when the constitution was planned & established,' Jefferson wrote, 'and never saw it till after it was established' (Jefferson, 1802). Jefferson then goes on to turn his

M. Nesvet (✉)
Indiana University, Bloomington, IN, USA
e-mail: nesvet@iu.edu
URL: https://www.mattnesvet.com

University of South Florida, Miami Dade College, Miami, FL, USA

© The Author(s), under exclusive license to Springer Nature
Switzerland AG 2024
T. Ø. Kuldova et al. (eds.), *Policing and Intelligence in the Global Big Data Era, Volume I*, Palgrave's Critical Policing Studies,
https://doi.org/10.1007/978-3-031-68326-8_10

modesty into a humble brag, writing that, after returning to America, he suggested to his friend James Madison that the first Congress amend the constitution to include ten rights the original document left out. Congress went on to pass these bills into law, now called *The Bill of Rights*, though they neither extended to enslaved African Americans nor seemed to make much difference for Native American nations who white settlers were encroaching upon and displacing.

Jefferson in his letter set out to not only win him credit for the constitutional protections that the exile Priestley cherished so much, but also explain the genius, as he saw it, of a written constitution. People can easily violate written constitutions, Jefferson wrote, just like other laws can be broken or go unenforced. But because written constitutions are impervious to at least fleeting expressions of public will, even if this means there is little cause to enforce their provisions, the documents can 'lock' their written codes and the norms these contain into governing practice. 'Tho' written constitutions may be violated in moments of passion or delusion,' Jefferson wrote, 'yet they furnish a text to which those who are watchful may again rally and recall the people: they fix too for the people principles for their political creed' (Jefferson, 1802). Constitutions, in other words, restrain publics over time, assuring that neither passion nor delusion can permanently erase a citizenry's original governing will, even if the promises constitutions make are frequently broken and the documents themselves tend to neither endure nor ever fully fulfill their promises (Colley, 2021). Like written language itself, constitutions persist as discursive objects that influence publics and government officials long after their authors have stopped writing. This is especially true for constitutions that, like James Madison's and Thomas Jefferson's, were made to resist a public's changing appetites.

Constitutions, though long celebrated legal technologies, are not unique in their abilities to preserve a long-term vision of a nation-state's founders by constraining popular change. Certain treaties and contracts; the architecture of a de-politicized civil service bureaucracy that can survive across different governing regimes; lifetime judicial and political appointments; and limits on the state's intervention into families and corporations, which restrict popular power under liberal conceptions of the state, family, and market, all aim to steady fluctuations in popular will by at least partly locking in decisions from long ago.

Such governance, which tethers popular will to an original moment when a constitution is written and ratified, civil service law passed, or judicial appointment confirmed, or at least makes these moments' meanings and the intent of authors relevant to how rules and practices are read and reenacted, might be called 'automatic' governance. In automatic governance, like any automated process, labor and will are required to govern, but its dogma is that of a labor-less, unchanging, and automatic reality that does not seem to require the constant ascent of the governed and replaces what framers like Jefferson and Madison feared—democratic fervor—with the slow, stable grind of an inertial politics that promises stability by requiring great energy to be overcome.

The algorithms that this chapter delves into—rules devised by police reformers and police department leaders working together to advance accountability and increase popular legitimacy—are powerful examples of automatic, and automated, governance. They are employed to govern, reign in, and reform police long after the moment of their making, without a federal court, court monitor, federal government official, or police leader or supervisor present to constantly oversee individual officers as they go about the everyday work of policing the public.

This chapter reads the semiotics of contemporary police reform programs and police reform dogma through the algorithms that the police reform industry, agency leaders, and federal court-appointed monitors overseeing troubled police departments create and implement in officer accountability software and agency processes. By analyzing the meaning and operation of one type of police reform and accountability algorithm, which is encoded in an early warning/early intervention system a Canadian government contractor makes and sells to some of the largest police departments in the United States and elsewhere, I contend that the algorithms police accountability and reform systems use to flag problem officers for intervention deflect problems from agencies, policies, and leaders to individual officers, normalizing violence in police agencies, creating myopic understandings of organizational problems, and foreclosing real change to police practices that police officers and publics might deliberate, enact, and support if given the chance (see also

Kuldova in this volume for a similar argument in regard to the insider threat management systems in the context of national security).

Consent Decrees and Algorithmic Police Reform

Police compliance software, like the firms that develop and sell these to police departments, is global in reach, rooted in a network of government buyers and private makers and sellers who form a revolving door of police officialdom and the industries that supply them with technological prowess. The software is also rooted in a multiplicity of founding moments and stories. 1994 was one of the most significant of these moments, which catalyzed algorithmic governance as central to the enacting of police reform and oversight. That year, in the United States, Congress passed the *Violent Crime and Law Enforcement Act of 1994*.[1] This legislation authorized the federal government to provide approximately three billion dollars to states to construct 50,000 new prison beds, reflecting both the expansion of prison populations in the 1980's and early 1990's and the government's fealty to the carceral governance that the reactionary turn in American politics in the 1970's and 1980's inscribed into law and policy (by the time Congress passed the 1994 crime bill, prison populations had been expanding annually by approximately 7% for more than a decade; in 1994, the rate had continued to grow, but slowed to less than 3% annually) (Sabol & Johnson, 2020). The 1994 bill also provided federal grant funding to expand the number of police officers state and local governments hired, among other tough-on-crime policies it enacted (see Christie, 2017 for a history of police funding in late twentieth-century America).

Congress passed this bill two years after Los Angeles Police Department (LAPD) officers were filmed beating Rodney King and then acquitted in a jury trial (*see* King, 2012 for Rodney King's account of his beating and its aftermath). The beating of a Black man on the streets of Los Angeles and subsequent acquittal at trial set off a violent

---

[1] https://www.govinfo.gov/content/pkg/COMPS-10824/pdf/COMPS-10824.pdf.

public uprising the likes of which no city in the United States had seen since the urban riots that followed Dr. Martin Luther King's assassination. Subsequently, some democratic Members of Congress, especially those belonging to the Congressional Black Caucus, advocated for federal police reform legislation, which they achieved two years later.

To win support for the 1994 crime bill and address police abuse amidst the dramatic federal expansion of local and state police budgets, Congress included a provision in the legislation, Sect. 14,141 (now Sect. 12,601)[2]) of the 1994 *Violent Crime Control and Law Enforcement Act* authorizing the Department of Justice (DOJ) Civil Rights Division to investigate local and state police departments for 'patterns-of-practice' that violate the US Constitution. The legislation allowed DOJ attorneys to compel state and municipal governments to enter into court-supervised 'consent decree' agreements, in which local governments agreed to pay government contractors to monitor their department's operations, provide technical assistance in implementing consent decree[3] changes, and report to the federal court on the progress of the agreed-on reform. In this way, the DOJ acquired a direct role in overhauling police departments through court-supervised consent decree reforms.

Three years after the 1994 crime bill was signed into law, in 1997, the Civil Rights Division at DOJ entered into its first-ever consent decree with the City of Pittsburgh,[4] which agreed to reform its police department through specific changes to its organizational structures that would be paid for by the city and overseen by a federal court and the court-appointed private police monitors. The reform would last five years. Later, when DOJ entered into a second consent decree with the City of Pittsburgh to reform its still-troubled police department a second time, critics wondered why the first reform effort had not 'stuck' and why the second would be any different (Stolberg, 2017). Police reformers,

---

[2] https://uscode.house.gov/view.xhtml?req=(title:34%20section:12601%20edition:prelim).

[3] A consent decree is a settlement agreement approved by a judge with agreement by all parties to a case. It is a binding agreement that the court can enforce and is only appealable in a small set of circumstances. Government attorneys often use consent decrees to force defendants to change organizational conduct; if they agree, the consent decree is concluded to stop further litigation that could result in the court issuing a judgment (see Cornell LII 2022 for more).

[4] Consent Decree (Feb. 26, 1997), U.S. v. City of Pittsburgh (U.S. District Court for the Western District of Pennsylvania) https://clearinghouse.net/doc/5314/.

including the Pittsburgh police chief from 2017, who had since gone into business helping to monitor other cities' police departments, including New Orleans,' and report to the court on whether the overhauls were working, insisted that better technology could cure the ills that the original reform efforts had failed to address. Other reformers simply said the reforms worked for a time, but once the federal monitors went away, reformed agencies would slide back into trouble (Stolberg, 2017).

Over time, federal consent decree police reform would touch the lives of most Americans, many of whom worked, lived, or regularly traveled through areas policed by departments that the federal government had reformed using pattern-of-practice investigations and consent decrees (see DOJ 2017 for a list of police departments investigated and reformed by DOJ and description of DOJ's police reform work). Between 1994 and 2017, DOJ investigated 69 state and local police departments, signed 20 consent decree agreements, and concluded 20 additional memoranda of understandings not overseen by a federal judge (Walker, 2022). Though the targeted departments are just a fraction of approximately 15,000 local and state departments that police the United States, the outsized number of big-city police the DOJ reformers have focused on means that most Americans are policed at least some of the time by an agency that underwent or is currently undergoing federal reform.

These reforms do not just bring attention and pour tax money into police accountability efforts; they also introduce new techniques, technologies, and codes of police accountability practice that give meaning and shape to the calls for reform that both publics and government officials make in response to police violence, corruption, and abuse. As a social anthropologist interested in how law, institutions, science, technology, and political economy inform state violence and community efforts to reign it in, in the early years of the Movement for Black Lives I followed how civil rights discourse in the mid-2010's—especially that propagated by Obama administration officials and some BLM activists—presented federal consent decree police reform and the DOJ as an antidote to police killings and abuse. Reading the news, I noticed that the Obama Administration officials repeatedly returned to one solution—the promise of DOJ-led pattern-and-practice investigations followed by federal court-monitored consent decrees—to quell protestors, plead with them to leave the streets, and promise DOJ would address the violence and abuse that the protestors were spotlighting in their stead (e.g., Nicks, 2014).

Yet, federal consent decrees, the first of which Pittsburg signed with DOJ in 1997, did not, two decades later, seem to effectively reduce police violence, carceral governance, or corruption and abuse in the departments activists and government officials continued to call for changes in, as evidenced by federal reformers returning to the city and still finding pattern-of-practice abused (Stolberg, 2017). Moreover, few researchers or even journalists spoke to patrol officers, other low-level department employees, or community members about the various reform efforts that federal officials were bringing to America's cities and towns, preferring instead to interview DOJ officials, court-appointed police monitors, and police chiefs in charge of the reforms (with perhaps a perfunctory media quote from a police union leader contesting the cost and wisdom of consent decrees). Such figures create a police violence and corruption aesthetic that mediates problems and solutions through the voices of reform industry professionals and profiteers (*see* Kuldova et al., 2024, pp. 1–30, for a discussion of the aesthetics of anti-corruption governance).

Ostensibly, city leaders and DOJ officials stand opposed to one another, agreeing to federal court-monitored reforms to put a stop to continued and costly litigation. But there is often agreement and large degree of consensus, if not in every detail, among city and federal leaders that consent decree reforms are needed. The same goes for the direction of the reforms, especially because municipal police chiefs who dissent from the reform agenda are sometimes replaced by those who can more productively work to resolve government concerns and end their city's consent decree. Due to this broad agreement between the two most powerful parties to consent decrees, DOJ and police and municipal leaders, I wondered what police department employees—officers and others who were typically the subject of the reform effort and the primary agents of change through compliance processes and who remade policies that the reforms introduced—and the publics who were the intended beneficiaries of the federal reforms, thought about the changes consent decrees brought? I questioned why consent decrees did not 'stick' and the changes they brought seemed to disappear once the agreements concluded and federal judges and monitors ended their oversight. And if third-party monitors who oversaw consent decrees were failing, what might their failures tell us more generally about how organizations bring about and monitor compliance to make needed changes?

New Orleans: America's Longest Federal Police Reform

To address these questions, I spent twelve months from 2016 to 2017 embedded in a consent decree unit in the headquarters of the New Orleans Police Department (NOPD), a troubled agency in the United States with a long history of violence, abuse, and criminal malfeasance including officers dealing drugs, protecting dealers, and hiring a hitman to kill a citizen who filed a complaint against an officer; disposing of files tracking rape allegations without investigating (the latter after the department signed its consent decree); and sexually assaulting numerous children, at one point appointing an officer convicted of child sex crimes to head its juvenile sex crimes unit (Contrera, 2024). I worked at police headquarters as a consent decree auditor while also speaking to criminal defense attorneys, community activists, and an independent police monitor's office operating independently of the federal reform effort. From the outset, I informed police leaders that I was writing about police reform in the course of my doctoral research in social anthropology, though I did not inform them of my findings as these took shape over the course of my year in New Orleans. This reportage was separate from my doctoral dissertation research, though both are related to state violence, governance, and similar topics.

What I found in New Orleans is (1) that consent decree reforms focus almost exclusively on the actions of low-level officers. In New Orleans, police higher-ups were not even required to use the body-worn cameras police reformers introduced to such fanfare as a consent decree win. (2) That these officers were sometimes held accountable for wrongdoing while police leaders, supervisors, and policies that often led them to take the actions that they were punished for were overlooked. And (3) that police reformers on the for-profit monitoring team that the City of New Orleans employed to oversee its police department, help it define and institute the consent decree's agreed-on changes, and report on the progress of reforms to the federal court, and the department's internal consent decree unit that I had joined, were colluding to both manipulate reform metrics and at times blatantly cheat on how they measured progress and compliance with the consent decree. Effectively, they created a theater of police reform that was very different than what many police officers, some of the publics that they policed, and I too observed happening.

Elsewhere, I wrote about the multi-million-dollar police reform industry that is corrupt, costly for towns and cities, and largely ineffective at bringing about meaningful change (Nesvet, 2019). My account of this industry sheds light on the revolving door of local police leaders, DOJ officials, and the for-profit consent decree monitoring teams that they employ to reform police in New Orleans and elsewhere. It illuminates how (1) local police leaders and DOJ officials often become for-profit monitors themselves, either after or even in between stints in police departments and DOJ, and (2) how, in New Orleans, NOPD leaders colluded with court-appointed monitors to manipulate reform metrics and the consent decree compliance audits that used such metrics to measure the department's progress complying with the consent decree, all while sidelining the local police monitor's office who would outlast the federal reform and may be the best hope for making lasting change in New Orleans (Nesvet, 2019). Following my initial story, I also wrote about how one NOPD unit, the police department's troubled drug crime lab, and its misuse of a machine to identify illicit drugs to support city prosecutions, reveals that 'fast and cheap' justice in police investigations is a sign of the cheapness of life that mass incarceration inculcates—and not merely a technical problem or example of corruption or malfeasance that new and better technologies and expertise introduced by technocratic reformers can fix (Nesvet, 2021).

As I researched, wrote about, and spoke to print and television media about my findings, particularly after the return of new consent decree reforms under the Biden DOJ (the Trump DOJ halted new pattern-of-practice investigations and new consent decrees), I noticed that the number and scale of digital products the police reform industry was producing were growing in size, cost, and prominence. I also noticed that some of the key police employees and government contractors involved in implementing consent decree reforms were reappearing as makers, sellers, and consultants involved in developing or selling compliance systems and as scholars or pracademics researching their efficacy. This includes police reform experts moving between police departments and the police reform industry outside of New Orleans, as in the case of two former NOPD employees, one its data analytics director, the second a data analyst who worked for him, who went on to form a company, Datalytics, that sells data services used to combat crime and manage compliance to police agencies. Such pracademics blur the line between making knowledge, making profits, and advancing their careers implementing systems they also purport to objectively evaluate, such as when the federal judge in New Orleans overseeing the city's consent decree reforms, a police consent decree monitor paid to 'independently' assist and report on reforms, and the NOPD employee who then-headed the department's Compliance Bureau together wrote an article that was published in a peer-reviewed journal about the success of the NOPD consent decree reform, focusing on data-driven compliance management. They asked me to peer review this article, which was for a special issue of a criminal justice journal. I gave comments to one of the authors but did not submit my review to the editor out of ethical concerns. To add to the absurdity, the special issue of the journal, about consent decrees, was co-edited by a professor who was also paid to serve as an NOPD monitor, and apparently suggested to my boss at NOPD that I non-anonymously peer review their article. This is but one example of how those profiting from police consent decrees are also purporting to independently monitor and conduct research on them, and why this raises questions about the evidence base for police reform knowledge and practice (see: *Police Quarterly* 20:3, September 2017, and Morgan et al., 2017, pp. 275–294).

Unlike the Department of Defense (DOD), Food and Drug Administration (FDA), and other agencies that have also been criticized for the revolving doors that help private industry capture public acquisition and policymaking processes, local and federal criminal justice agencies, the academic criminal justice field, and court-appointed consent decree monitoring teams have few standards or transparency that can effectively wall off DOJ reformers and teams of court monitors from the cities and police agencies they are charged with advising or overseeing or the industry supplying compliance solutions to police departments (for a discussion of the revolving door of government 'watchdogs' and those they are meant to monitor, *see* Wedel, 2014).

Building on these insights and questions about the role of digital technology in police reform, this chapter interrogates one prominent police reform tool: an 'early warning' or 'early intervention' software that police leaders use to identify problem officers before it is too late. Turning away from the question of relationships and incentives and how police consent decree reforms unfold and are declared successful in concerning ways, which I have addressed elsewhere (Nesvet, 2019), in this chapter, I 'read' the key algorithm that a popular early intervention system uses. This means considering how police compliance systems and algorithms may produce norms and incentives that run counter to either reducing state violence and abuse or implementing democratic control and constitutional policing. One of the tools I examined for this chapter was put into use during my time in New Orleans. Similar tools are used by police agencies elsewhere, though they are certainly systems I do not examine here that may be in development or in use that do not have the features and problems that the software I examine has. This chapter was informed not only just by my work in New Orleans, but also by time spent visiting or speaking to police leaders and employees at other US agencies using early intervention compliance systems; examining manuals, memos, and other internal police documents; observing supervisors call up the software on their computer screens and viewing screenshots of what it looks like to do so in training slides; and talking with the early implementors of one large urban police department's early intervention system now in wide use.

Automating Police Risk

Early intervention systems draw on banks of police data to 'flag' potential problem officers. Police first implemented early warning systems in Miami and soon thereafter in other American cities in the 1970's (Shjarback, 2015). Just as police departments were developing risk management tools in the 1970's, private industry and financial service firms increasingly focused on risk prediction as key to business success (Ericson & Haggerty, 1997). That decade, the value of planning for fluctuations in interest rates, stock market returns, exchange rates, and the cost of commodities came into focus amidst the tumult of global economic and geopolitical crises of that decade (Dionne, 2013, p. 5). In the 1970's, companies were also experimenting with using mainframe computers to track employee time and performance and manage their payrolls, an effort that began with the development of IMB punched card equipment (which, by the 1970's, had made Babbage's programmable computer a reality). A decade later, the financial industry embraced automation to manage risk, an effort that began in postwar America when companies first started to self-insure against future risk and the first textbooks appeared that taught engineers and financiers how they could evaluate and manage financial and engineering risks (Dionne, 2013). These innovations in corporate management made automated risk prediction tools available to American police along with personnel whose experience managing financial and industry risk gave them the skills, concepts, and experience that they then used to figure police officer absenteeism, corruption, and abuse as organizational risks that departments could utilize automation to measure and manage.

The systems police departments purchased or developed to track employee performance and assess their risk for absenteeism, corruption, and abuse are called early warning or early intervention systems (EIS).[5] EIS generate a numerical picture of a police employee's performance, revealing both an officer's productivity and the presence of risk factors for corruption or abuse. Critics have argued that EIS systems do little to

---

[5] See for instance: https://counciloncj.foleon.com/policing/assessing-the-evidence/xv-early-intervention-systems-eis.

distinguish between amount of policing officers engage in and abuse, flagging proactive officers regardless of how many non-problem cases they are involved in due to the raw number of complaints they draw or use of force incidents they contribute to (Lersch et al., 2006). EIS rely on two types of data: employee data such as age, gender, or number of sick days taken, and policing data such as average number of stops an officer made per shift or number, how many instances of police violence an officer has committed (called 'use of force'), or number of citizen complaints the department received. In 1994, the same year Congress authorized DOJ to reform local and state police agencies using consent decrees, Len Davis, a onetime NOPD officer who led a ring of New Orleans police dealing illicit drugs under protection of their badges, hired a hitman to kill Kim Groves after she lodged a police brutality complaint against him with NOPD. Davis, now serving a life sentence for Groves' murder, demonstrates that even in a troubled agency that protected its own, citizen complaints represented either a real risk to a rogue officer or a source of annoyance that led Davis to order Groves' murder.

Soon after early warning systems first came about, software makers renamed them 'early intervention' software to win support from officers, chiefs, and police unions. In New Orleans, as the NOPD implemented early intervention software for the first time in 2017, department leaders pointed out that the system they were adopting could trigger an intervention, not a warning or punishment. These interventions were designed to identify emerging problems and prevent officers from committing acts of future wrongdoing. Though many patrol officers told me that they were skeptical of this claim, flyers dotted the walls of police headquarters and precinct stations (called 'bureaus' in New Orleans) saying much the same. As the Police Chief (Harrison) in New Orleans at the time when the early intervention system was being implemented told a reporter, the new early intervention system 'is not a disciplinary management tool, it is a human resource management tool. It is designed to alert supervisors when we see trends that need some type of supervisory intervention' (Steen, 2017).

The early warning system that the NOPD purchased and implemented at the urging of the private contractors monitoring the department was made and customized for NOPD by a company called Sierra-Cedar. Sierra-Cedar, initially an independent company called Sierra Systems that went on to become the Vancouver, Canada-based subsidiary of a larger technology and government services corporation, first developed its EIS in 2003. That year, they won a twelve-million-dollar (USD) contract to supply Los Angeles Police Department (LAPD) managers with an automated risk management and 'use of force' event tracking system. According to the LAPD contract with the then-900 employee company, Sierra Systems would develop software that would do two things: draw from 12 LAPD systems to merge and analyze employee performance and policing data and create a digital database of police use of force incidents that would replace the department's paper-based system for tracking police violence (Welsh, 2003). Sierra Systems and Sierra-Cedar would go on to update the system they developed for the LAPD to sell to other police departments such as the City of Oakland's still-troubled police department as well as prisons and courts in its Justice and Public Safety division.

In 2014, the City of New Orleans, as part of the changes it had agreed to make in the city's consent decree agreement with DOJ, signed a 34-month contract with Sierra-Cedar to adopt their EIS system for use by the city's police, with an option to extend the contract for three additional years. The city has continued to contract with Sierra Systems for the last decade through the new Vancouver, Canada-based corporate entity, Quartech Systems[6] that purchased Sierra-Cedar's Justice division in 2020; the city is likely to continue purchasing the system for years to come.[7]

In New Orleans, the city council-appointed independent police monitor's office was skeptical of some aspects of the federal reform effort, particularly some of the claims that the monitors and NOPD were making about the department's progress. While in New Orleans, I

---

[6] Sierra-Cedar was a subsidiary of Quartech: https://quartech.com/solutions/justice-public-safety/.

[7] NOPD contracting document with Quartech Corrections and its subsidiary, Sierra-Cedar Inc.: https://cityofno.granicus.com/MetaViewer.php?view_id=&event_id=23773&meta_id=626681.

spent time talking with this office to learn about how a local agency was approaching police monitoring and reform while also being sidelined by the federal police monitoring team.

Also skeptical about the federal reform was a local activist group, Voices of the Experienced [formerly 'of the incarcerated']-NOLA. Group leaders focused on disrupting police violence and abuse and helped formerly incarcerated persons restore their voting rights and access housing and employment. They also worked with family members of those who were incarcerated. I spent most of my year in New Orleans regularly talking to leaders and activists from this and other groups and attending some of the group's meetings. I worked with activists to understand how the federal police reform effort that group leaders once demanded the former US Attorney General bring to their city was understood by leaders and group members after years of the consent decree being in force. VOTE-NOLA leaders and members were also excluded from many aspects of the reform effort after initially meeting with DOJ officials during their investigation of NOPD.

The independent police monitor and the city activists told me that the monitoring tools the city had purchased were opaque. To their knowledge, no one outside of the NOPD, Sierra-Cedar, and the criminal justice academics, ex-police chiefs, lawyers, and others who made up the federal monitoring team seemed to either be involved in its development or know much about it. The city council-appointed independent police monitor's office,[8] different from the government contractor the city employed to monitor its police and report back to the federal court enforcing the consent decree, was ignored by DOJ reformers, even as this office could be key to lasting change after the federal monitors leave the city and the court ends its oversight. Meanwhile, the NOPD's consent decree unit and police leadership actively thwarted the work of the independent police monitor, including misrepresenting departmental data capacities to avoid releasing information. For example, the independent police monitor found out that the then-NOPD chief misrepresented to them that it would be impossible to obtain information that they

---

[8] New Orleans' Office of the Independent Police Monitory is an independent, civilian police oversight agency, created in 2008 with more than 70% of New Orleans voters approving its authorization. See: https://nolaipm.gov/about-oipm/.

sought from NOPD information systems. Finding out that an employee had informed the office this information was easy to access in internal NOPD systems, NOPD ordered police employees to not interact with the independent police monitor without first obtaining prior written permission from NOPD leaders (Nesvet, 2019). A few years later, the city council would also learn that NOPD leaders had misrepresented the department's surveillance program to them in a bid to escape public oversight.

New Orleans' EIS system is named *Insight*. I first learned about Insight while embedded in NOPD headquarters, where I was in part charged with auditing *Insight's* rollout. I went on to learn more about *Insight* and similar systems from officers and other police agencies implementing the Sierra-Cedar system that the company customizes for NOPD and other departments. Drawing on ideas and analytical practices from critical algorithm studies, critical security studies, and political, legal, and economic anthropology, I will now move toward a reading of the semiotics of police reform inscribed in *Insight* and other police agency EIS. This reading aims to both elucidate police reform practice and analyze why EIS and similar tools have failed to more effectively reduce police violence, corruption, and abuse, even as other public services are sacrificed to pay for police reform industry-led changes. New Orleans agencies have systematically seen their budgets reduced to pay for the city's police reform, which after more than a decade is the country's most expensive court-enforced consent decree police reform effort.

To read police EIS systems, I highlight and discuss key features of the Sierra-Cedar system. These features point to how algorithmic governance and technocratic expertise have largely come to replace principles and practices that liberal political thinkers point to as essential for democracy, including transparency, deliberation, and public control over public agencies and state violence.

Threshold Governance

Josh Scannell, writing about the New York Police Department (NYPD) surveillance network, the Domain Awareness System (DAS), calls asking what an algorithm does 'absurd' (Scannell, 2016). 'An algorithm is a series of instructions,' and therefore to apprehend its meaning, one must ask what it *does*, not what it is' (Scannell, 2016). For Scannell, an algorithm is a 'political object... an assemblage of forces that imprints itself on the social as something like "algorithmic governance"' (Scannell, 2016). The algorithm, that is, is a particular node in a decisional network. To understand the algorithm, its readers should describe the decision the algorithm expresses and the network that makes and enforces such decision.

Echoing Scannell, ethnographer and STS scholar Nick Seaver writes that algorithms are 'heterogeneous and diffuse sociotechnical systems,' not simple formulas (Seaver, 2017, p. 1). To analyze the workings of an algorithm, we should describe how the algorithm—like any rule—is enacted. In other words, who conceives the rule, how the algorithm expresses it, and what networks of actors and events the algorithm is embedded within are key to its meaning and operations. Like laws, algorithms do not exist in isolation, most scholars in critical algorithm studies say. Rather, they are expressive utterances that should be read in the context of the particular practices, institutions, and events they come about within (e.g., Besteman & Gusterson, 2019).

In police departments, the 'algorithmic culture' (Striphas, 2015) such rule-oriented assemblages cultivate does not enter police agencies from afar, replacing, say, different modes of thought with rule-based decisions. Such is the way that Striphas and other STS scholars sometimes discuss how algorithms supplant other cultural processes. Rather, rule-based thinking has long been key to how police represent their work. Like other bureaucratic organizations, police express power, maintain hierarchical order, and enforce public codes of conduct and behavior by making constant reference to algorithmic decisions, such as when a police officer tells a suspect that their behavior triggered the officer to stop and search or incarcerate them. In the United States, police officers must be able to 'articulate' the reasons why they have 'reasonable suspicion' to stop a person or 'probably cause' to arrest them. Whether or not the officer's reason is what actually motivated them to make a stop, conduct a search, or make an arrest, the law and courts compel them to have, utter, and write down such a reason. In this way, police agencies mobilize sets of algorithms to narrate how they achieve goals, conduct operations, and explain their conduct. When publics contest criminal and municipal codes or argue that they are not uniformly and impartially (that is, seemingly automatically) applied to all, or when a person stopped, searched, or arrested or their attorney challenges what led to the stop, search, or arrest, police and prosecutors respond by figuring law enforcement as algorithmic. In this way, policing, figured as the application of a rule to a situation, like Gillespie describes algorithms when they become political objects, 'becomes' culture and strategic action (Gillespie, 2016).

In New Orleans and other cities that purchased computational compliance software systems like *Insight* to try to reign in police, the algorithmic governance that the federal contractors monitoring police tout to federal judges and publics often prominently pertain to police 'use of force' incidents. Just like a police officer's age, gender, rate of absenteeism, years on the force, number of citizen complaints received, and other data, every time the officer behaves in a way that their department classifies as using force, they must report what they did. Use of force can include strongarming or tasering a suspect; unholstering and aiming weapons; or using lethal force (killing someone). These are then computed as part of an officer's personnel record. In *Insight*, when an officer exceeds the threshold for maximum acceptable use of force incidents, just like when they exceed a certain number of sick days or citizen complaints, EIS automatically flags them to their supervisors.

Insight flags these potentially problem officers by outputting an automatic email message to the officer's direct report supervisor and adding their name to a system dashboard that supervisors can access. In this way, the compliance system's approach to reducing police violence and stopping problem officers before they commit more serious acts of unwarranted violence is built around a single decision: when to alert a supervisor to an officer's behavior. Officers, supervisors, and the public can also file complaints or open investigations of officers, but this occurs separately from EIS and is a more traditional internal compliance tool.

Internal affairs departments manage such efforts, though they have mixed results at finding and stopping problem officers.

How many times is too many is the 'threshold' that police departments must select to alert their supervisors to potential problems after they purchase an EIS. As NOPD leaders and internal *Insight* staff members worked with Sierra-Cedar employees to customize and roll out the software and train supervisors to use it, agency leaders and the contractors on the consent decree monitoring team met to decide the appropriate thresholds for when the system would flag officers' behavior. This decision, and the subsequent work of encoding it in *Insight*, created the algorithms that now govern NOPD officer behavior, monitoring each officer and warning (notifying) their supervisors to intervene when they surpass a given threshold.

Sometimes, the algorithmic thresholds that agencies use to flag officers for intervention are based on empirical studies. Thresholds for alerting supervisors to employee absenteeism are based on academic criminal justice and human resources studies that demonstrate a statistical association between absenteeism and alcoholism for workers (e.g., Bacharach et al., 2010). Alerting supervisors to high rates of absenteeism is supposed to trigger an intervention that can disrupt substance use disorder and get police employees help before potential substance abuse leads to serious problems at work and illegal behavior.

Other thresholds—particularly those having to do with officer performance—require agencies implementing EIS to decide what is acceptable and not acceptable without extant studies to guide their decision making, and, as in the case of NOPD, no clear organizational objective that might have been supplied by the consent decree. How such decisions are made has profound impacts on how EIS systems are configured in practice and reveals much about the politics of their algorithms and the reform efforts that center them in agency overhauls.

In New Orleans, the department's internal consent decree unit— led by an Assistant Chief who went on to help lead Baltimore Police Department's consent decree reforms—and the DOJ attorneys and federal contractors monitoring the department worked together to devise acceptable use of force policies and thresholds for *Insight* to flag officers. Together, they changed the consent decree's call for NOPD officers to only use force as a last resort. Instead of implementing the use of force as last resort policy called for in the consent decree, the department and monitoring team worked together to create a vaguer metric that allowed police to justify using force whenever they claimed to 'run out of time,' a key exception. Since NOPD officers almost always had other calls to answer while confronting suspects, they could always be 'out of time' (Nesvet, 2019).

Police, DOJ attorneys, and federal monitors then devised the NOPD's threshold for use of force incidents that, when exceeded, would trigger *Insight* to email supervisors that an officer under their command met the threshold for early intervention. But the algorithm they made did not set a goal for the department or even individual units as a whole, and it did not aim to measure or reduce overall or unit-level use of force incidents. Rather, NOPD, DOJ, the federal monitors, and Sierra-Cedar created an algorithm that flagged officers who were found to significantly deviate from the *mean* number of use of force incidents within their units. This was seen as appropriate to avoid whole units of officers meeting intervention thresholds due to the types of work their units engaged in or avoid officers more violent than their peers going unnoticed if their unit engaged in policing activities that were less prone to uses of force than other units.

Reading this algorithm and attending to the work of algorithmic governance in police reform efforts can elucidate the ways in which the EIS algorithms configure reform, delimiting how efforts to overhaul police can take shape while foreclosing other paths to change.

First, the EIS system implemented in New Orleans, which is the same system that Los Angeles, Oakland, and other departments have adopted for their use before and after the NOPD customized the Sierra-Cedar system, does not hold unit supervisors, agency policies, or police and leadership accountable for police violence. Instead, the system, by design, positions supervisors as problem solvers and the officers they supervise as the source of all problems. If an officer is especially and frequently violent, or elicits frequent citizen complaints, EIS charges the supervisor with holding the officer accountable or otherwise intervening with him. EIS proponents claim the system is not about accountability, but rather intervention and retraining. Officers and low-level supervisors themselves often challenged this claim to me. But the system does not flag the unit or its supervisor to higher-ups for them to intervene with unit leadership. And this is by design: Sierra-Cedar sells the system to police leaders so they can hold officers accountable, not so they themselves can be called to account. And neither the company, which aims to sell the system to departments, nor the federal monitors, who themselves use letters of reference from police chiefs to win their next monitoring jobs, have any incentive to try and introduce accountability to the city and police brass who buy their products and recommend them to other cities for monitoring work (Nesvet, 2019).

According to many officers I spoke with, this meant that *Insight* and other EIS had little power to create change when the supervisors could easily dismiss system warnings. Moreover, supervisors, officers claimed, were themselves often responsible for much of the behavior the system alerted on, deploying officers in certain ways or giving orders that sometimes led to violence. By the same token, *Insight* and other EIS are little capable of holding department brass accountable for violence, because the thresholds for intervention that the system enforces only contains individual officer thresholds, not department-wide ones. For *Insight* and other EIS to help consent decree reformers reduce agency violence—a major goal, sometimes *the* major goal, of consent decree reforms, these systems would have to track the direction in uses of force for police departments overall and within their units. This would mean flagging units and supervisors, not just individual officers, when department violence ticks upward or does not tick downward, while perhaps controlling for the number of police encounters that an agency engages in. (Statistically controlling for the number of citizen encounters police have when evaluating how much force they use may help identify officers who engage in higher rates of violence. But by controlling for the number of encounters an officer participates in, police agencies may also miss the opportunity to show declines in police-civilian violence by limiting overall police-civilian encounters. This is a strategy to limit overall use of force incidents in a department.)

But *Insight* did no such things. Instead, hyper-focusing on individual officer behavior, *Insight* and other EIS, like other aspects of consent decree reforms, protect supervisors, leaders, and policies. By placing higher-ups outside the purview of EIS, agencies are prevented from making meaningful changes to police operations at the same time as reform efforts are discredited in the eyes of many police officers and their unions. The only aspect of *Insight* that NOPD or its monitoring team made supervisors accountable for was knowing how to use the system. Meanwhile, the NOPD consent decree implementation unit and *Insight* unit provided critical aspects of system training only to the supervisors who would be present when the federal monitors went to check their knowledge, something the consent decree unit learned about in advance under the guise of coordinating the monitors' visits, but actually used to manipulate inspections (Nesvet, 2019).

Second, *Insight* and other EIS systems that create thresholds for flagging officers normalize the very police violence that consent decree reformers promise to reduce. In New Orleans, so long as a unit's mean level of violence is high, *Insight* will neither flag individual officers in the unit nor alert anyone that the unit's leadership is overseeing high rates of violence. This may create the perverse incentive for unit leaders and officers who are prone to violence to encourage their fellow officers to increase their own uses of force, thus making other officers' violence acceptable to the system. Meanwhile, EIS does not give anyone—police and city leaders, federal monitors, or the public—any capacity to track or reduce overall violence within individual units or for police departments holistically.

Third, *Insight's* threshold for interventions related to uses of force makes assumptions that may not be based in evidence (as discussed above, evidentiary claims about police reform systems are also undermined by the lack of ethical controls over police reform scholarship.) The primary assumption many EIS systems make is that officers who participate in many use of force incidents are at greater risk for future illegal violence than their counterparts who are less frequently violent. There is no credible evidence that frequently violent officers engage in more illegal, or even more avoidable (in the moment given their deployment instructions, not if these varied) violence than other officers, especially for lethal incidents which are hard to statistically model due to their rarity.

Fourth, by the same token, EIS' that enact algorithms through threshold governance are built to create compliance with enduring and binary rules, not encourage stepwise change and progress. If police EIS algorithms tracked changes over time in mean department and unit uses of force, the algorithms could alert the organization, the federal court, and the media and public to how agencies are succeeding or not in reducing violence. By not tracking change over time or in comparison to other police agencies, the algorithms police EIS' use are better at tracking and holding accountable officers (or retraining and 'redirecting' them) than they are at creating systematic changes to police operations and practices.

Fifth, these algorithms are made by a small number of people empowered by departments, courts, and DOJ to govern police reform. The algorithms are largely invisible to publics or police officers themselves when under development. Cities operating under police consent decrees often boast that they are implementing one or another compliance tool, from introducing EIS' to equipping officers with wear body-worn cameras (Kang, 2023). But few details about how these systems are built and operated are ever revealed, and the algorithms that set thresholds for police violence are rarely made available for public scrutiny or visible to the public. By purchasing EIS from for-profit government contractors who develop algorithms as part of proprietary systems, these companies offer publics little information about the algorithms they use or a chance to dig deeper into them, even if there is such capacity to investigate the technical customization of an EIS. And police leaders are often happy to limit public scrutiny, simply reporting that the systems flag bad behavior.

Ironic Algorithms

In New Orleans, most patrol officers and even supervisors told me that they did not know how *Insight* is triggered—that is, what the exact threshold of missed workdays, citizen complaints, or uses of force is that would cause the system to notify supervisors to intervene. The system was in its early days then, not quite working reliably when I spoke to most officers and supervisors about it. Police leaders and the monitoring team were rushing to declare the system a success before it was even implemented, eager to show the court and public their success in implementing *Insight* despite not having done so.

But at other agencies, officers and supervisors I have spoken to seem to know what triggers EIS to flag officers, likely because the systems were functioning in these other agencies. In some cases, I spoke to officers outside New Orleans who strategized to avoid EIS flagging them. In other cases, officers I spoke to told me the intervention notifications meant very little to frontline supervisors who are well aware of what was going on among their officers. Few frontline supervisors I spoke to in New Orleans or elsewhere reported finding EIS useful, as they already knew exactly which employees show up or not to work, engage in excessive violence, or elicit the most complaints. In the view of many officers I spoke to, violence, complaints, sometimes even missed work have as much to do with supervisors' decisions and behaviors as anything else. And because EIS systems do not ask department brass, who genuinely have little knowledge of what happens within small units of officers, to hold the units' supervisors accountable for change, there may be little point to EIS. Except, of course, that EIS operates as a public communications tool that enriches its makers and the consultants and contracting firms helping agencies implement it. Meanwhile, the software normalizes violence in police-civilian encounters, police avoid making real changes to agency policies and practices, and courts and publics are shown evidence of organizational change when little may actually be changing.

At the same time, it is ironic that many patrol officers do not like EIS algorithms. Several officers in New Orleans told me that these systems are crude expressions of a much more complicated social reality that the officers experience on the streets. An officer in another city told me that the algorithms his agency uses frustrate him because no one asks him what he thinks should or should not trigger an agency review; the algorithm seems to decide this on its own. This is ironic because so many officers cite similar algorithmic logics when making arrests, issuing tickets, and enforcing carceral orders, even if they may approach situations with more nuance when using their discretion to *not* give a ticket or *not* make an arrest. EIS, like the criminal and municipal codes police enforce, seem to replace public deliberation about state violence, incarceration, enforcement decisions, and the like with thresholds of organizational behavior that are obtuse to the public and not open to scrutiny or debate and deliberation.

If algorithms EIS use were made visible to the public and city leaders and informed them about the operations of police, the direction of police reforms, and the decisions made by police agencies undergoing reforms—such as the debate about increasing police encounters while also exposing officers and those they encounter to greater risks of violence, or reducing police-civilian encounters but also limiting the tasks police may be asked to carry out—EIS might be an effective tool for reform, deliberation, and democratic oversight. But this is not how actually existing EIS' like *Insight*'s algorithms are made or what they do.

Police officers' dislike for the algorithms that *Insight* and other EIS software use to compute their personnel and policing data (even when officers call in sick, they continue to output more data) is not surprising. Many employees in many industries object to being managed by inflexible rules they have little input into, little room to agree or disagree over, which largely deflect organizational problems to low-level workers from problem policies and problem leaders. Such strategic attention to low-level workers' behavior 'responsibilizes' workers while letting higher-ups off the hook, a feature that is typical of neoliberal governance that Foucault-inspired scholarship often draws out (e.g., Pyysiäinen, 2017). Such dislike for the transformation of organizational problems into the workers' problem without giving police employees a real way to change much of what occurs in their agency means police officers share the experiences other workers have: they have little insight into how police departments govern officers' behavior; no power to scrutinize, involve themselves in, or actually be responsible for the policies and decisions higher-ups in police agencies and cities make; and no way to inform publics and courts that behind their frontline actions are decisions and policies that often influence what officers do.

Community activists, reform-minded police leaders, and the police reform industry figure police officers and their unions, and police reform, as opponents. But a closer look at police reform and accountability processes and EIS systems reveals possible new directions for communities and the police officers who are sometimes part of these communities to pursue, starting with (a) devising systems that elucidate decision making chains and leadership policy choices and not create policy myopia by spotlighting only the actions of frontline officers; (b) finding ways to reform algorithms to support transparency and informed deliberation as publics learn about what police do, not 'lock in' single decisions about what is desirable and acceptable for police to be doing made at an original moment of EIS design the same way that constitutions and other systems of rules may lock in policy and practice design choices that discourage publics from updating these; and (c) considering what systems—algorithmic or otherwise—might be devised to guide and regulate state violence and criminal law enforcement that the revolving door of profit-oriented police reform contractors and companies and city and federal leaders have not yet offered.

Funding and Ethics Statement   This chapter is based on reportage undertaken from 2015–2016 in New Orleans and 2016–2018 nationally. The chapter reflects on the algorithmic aspects of federal police reform in the United States and police accountability software systems, drawing from the author's and others' published accounts of police compliance algorithms and further investigation into one early intervention system in widespread use by police agencies. The author informed all interlocuters about his intent to write about consent decree police reform.

References

Bacharach, S. B., Bamberger, P., & Biron, M. (2010). Alcohol Consumption and Workplace Absenteeism: the Moderating Effect of Social Support. *The Journal of Applied Psychology, 95*(2), 334–348. https://doi.org/10.1037/a0018018

Besteman, C., & Gusterson, H. (2019). *Life by Algorithms: How Roboprocesses are Remaking our World.* University of Chicago Press. https://doi.org/10.7208/chicago/9780226627731.001.0001

Christie, N. (2017). *Crime Control as Industry: Towards Gulags*. Routledge. https://doi.org/10.4324/9781315512051

Colley, L. (2021). *The Gun, the Ship, and the Pen: Warfare, Constitutions, and the Making of the Modern World*. W.W. Norton and Co.

Contrera, J., Abelson, J., & Harden, J. (2024, March 14) A Police Officer Took a Teen for a Rape Kit. Then he Assaulted her, too. *The Washington Post*. https://www.washingtonpost.com/dc-md-va/interactive/2024/new-orleans-police-child-sexual-abuse-rodney-vicknair/

Department of Justice, Civil Rights Division. (2017). The Civil Rights Division's Pattern and Practice Police Reform Work: 1994-present. https://www.justice.gov/crt/file/922421/dl

Dionne, G. (2013). Risk Management: History, Definition and Critique. *Risk Management and Insurance Review, 16*(2), 147–166. https://doi.org/10.1111/rmir.12016

Ericson, R., & Haggerty, K. (1997). *Policing the Risk Society*. University of Toronto Press. https://www.jstor.org/stable/10.3138/9781442678590

Gillespie, T. (2016). Algorithm. In B. Peters (Ed.), *Digital Keywords: A Vocabulary of Information Society and Culture*. Princeton University Press.

Jefferson, T. (1802). From Thomas Jefferson to Joseph Priestley, 19 June 1802. *Founders Online,* National Archives, https://founders.archives.gov/documents/Jefferson/01-37-02-0515 [Original source: *The Papers of Thomas Jefferson*, vol. 37, 4 March–30 June 1802, ed. Barbara B. Oberg. Princeton University Press, 2010, pp. 625–627.]

Kang, I. (2023). How does Technology-Based Monitoring Affect Street-Level Bureaucrats' Behavior? An Analysis of Body-worn Cameras and Police Actions. *Journal of Policy Analysis and Management*. https://onlinelibrary.wiley.com/doi/full/10.1002/pam.22493#:~:text=body%2Dworn%20cameras.-,THE%20CASE%20OF%20THE%20NEW%20ORLEANS%20POLICE%20DEPARTMENT,a%20body%2Dworn%20camera%20program

King, R. (2012). *The Riot Within: My Journey from Rebellion to Redemption*. Harper Collins.

Kuldova,T. Ø., Østbø, J., & Raymen, T. (2024). *Luxury and Corruption: Challenging the Anti-Corruption Consensus*. Bristol University Press. https://doi.org/10.56687/9781529212426

Legal Information Institute (LII). (2022). *Consent Decree*. Cornell University. https://www.law.cornell.edu/wex/consent_decree

Lersch, K. M., Bazley, T., & Mieczkowski, T. (2006). Early Intervention Programs: An Effective Police Accountability Tool, or Punishment of the

Productive? *Policing: An International Journal 29*(1), 58–76. https://doi.org/
10.1108/13639510610648485

Morgan, S, Murphy, D., & Horwitz, B. (2017). Police Reform Through Data-driven Management. *Police Quarterly 20*(3), 239–249. Special Issue: Consent decrees, edited by G. Alpert. https://doi.org/10.1177/109861111
7709785

Nesvet, M. (2019, July 30). Notes on an Anthropologist's Year as a Consent Decree Police Insider. *The Appeal.* https://theappeal.org/my-year-as-a-new-orleans-consent-decree-insider/

Nesvet, M. (2020). Anatomy of a Crime Lab: Winning Convictions 'on the Cheap'. *The Crime Reporter*, City University of New York John Jay College. 15 December 2020. https://thecrimereport.org/2020/12/15/anatomy-of-a-crime-lab-winning-convictions-on-the-cheap/

Nicks, D. (2014, August 19). Attorney General Holder Appeals for Calm in Message to Ferguson. *Time Magazine.* https://time.com/3145690/eric-hol
der-ferguson-message/

Pyysiäinen, J. (2017). Neoliberal Governance and 'Responsibilization' of Agents: Reassessing the Mechanisms of Responsibility-shift in Neoliberal Discursive Environments. *Distinktion: Journal of Social Theory, 18*(2), 215–235. https://www.tandfonline.com/doi/full/10.1080/1600910X.2017.
1331858

Sabol, W. J., & Johnson, T. L. (2020). The 1994 Crime Bill: Legacy and Lessons - Impacts on Prison Populations. *Federal Sentencing Reporter, 32*(3), 153–156. https://doi.org/10.1525/fsr.2020.32.3.153

Scannell, J. (2016). What Can an Algorithm Do? *Dis Magazine.* http://dismag
azine.com/discussion/72975/josh-scannell-what-can-an-algorithm-do/

Scharback, J. (2015). Emerging Early Intervention Systems: An Agency-Specific Pre-Post Comparison of Formal Citizen Complaints of Use of Force. *Policing, 9*(4), 314–325. https://doi.org/10.1093/police/pav006

Seaver, N. (2017). Algorithms as Culture: Some Tactics for the Ethnography of Algorithmic Systems. *Big Data & Society, 4*(2). https://doi.org/10.1177/
2053951717738104

Steen, M. (2017, May 4). Do Intervention Systems Amount to Scrutiny of Police Departments? *Government Technology.* https://www.govtech.com/em/
safety/scrutinizing-cops-with-intervention-systems.html

Stolberg, S. G. (2017, April 9). 'It did not stick': The First Federal Effort to Curb Police Abuse. *The New York Times.* https://www.nytimes.com/2017/
04/09/us/first-consent-decree-police-abuse-pittsburgh.html

Striphas, T. (2015). Algorithmic Culture. *European Journal of Cultural Studies,* *18*(4–5), 395–412. https://doi.org/10.1177/1367549415577392

Walker, S. (2022). The Justice Department's Pattern-or-Practice Police Reform Program, 1994–2017: Goals, Achievements, and Issues. *Annual Review of Criminology, 5*(1), 21–42. https://doi.org/10.1146/annurev-criminol-030 920-102432

Wedel, J. (2014). *Unaccountable: How the Establishment Corrupted our Finances, Freedom and Politics and Created an Outsider Class.* Pegasus Books.

Welsh, W. (2003, August 25). Sierra Systems to Build LAPD risk Management System. *Washington Technology.* https://washingtontechnology.com/ 2003/08/sierra-systems-to-build-lapd-risk-management-system/353341/

11

The Platformization of Policing: A Cross-National Analysis

Simon Egbert[ID], Vasilis Galis[ID],
Helene Oppen Ingebrigtsen Gundhus[ID],
and Christin Thea Wathne[ID]

For several years now, police authorities have been increasingly using data and algorithms to improve their work, trying to make it more efficient. For example, attempts have been made to predict crime with forecasting software to preventively control anticipated risk locations and risk groups

S. Egbert (✉)
Bielefeld University, Bielefeld, Germany
e-mail: simon.egbert@uni-bielefeld.de

V. Galis
IT-University of Copenhagen, Copenhagen, Denmark
e-mail: vgal@itu.dk

H. O. I. Gundhus
University of Oslo, Oslo, Norway
e-mail: h.o.i.gundhus@jus.uio.no

C. T. Wathne
OsloMet—Oslo Metropolitan University, Oslo, Norway
e-mail: wach@oslomet.no

349

T. Ø. Kuldova et al. (eds.), *Policing and Intelligence in the Global Big Data Era,
Volume I*, Palgrave's Critical Policing Studies,
https://doi.org/10.1007/978-3-031-68326-8_11

or individuals more intensively (Brayne, 2021; Egbert & Leese, 2021). Furthermore, different data collecting and data analysis tools are used to enhance the police's investigative methods and consequently their evaluation capabilities, such as license plate documentation and recognition systems (Koper et al., 2022), gunshot detection systems (Max, 2023), digital DNA procedures (Kaufmann, 2023) as well as 'smart' surveillance cameras with behavioral pattern analysis (Usha Rani & Raviraj, 2023; see also Diphoorn, in this volume) and/or facial recognition functionalities (Smith & Miller, 2022; *see also* Narayan, in this volume; Terra, in this volume).

Against this backdrop, we focus in this chapter on one of the latest and probably the most momentous developments in the field of digitalized police: the spread of data integration and analysis platforms. We will focus on one of the most prominent software solutions in this area, the Gotham[1] software by US-company Palantir Technologies (Brayne, 2021; Iliadis & Acker, 2022; Munn, 2017). Since this platformization trend has taken place in different (European) countries, we will conduct our analysis in a comparative way, investigating the introduction and implementation of such platforms in Germany, Denmark, and Norway. Comparing here is not a means of reaching causal-linear explanations but a way for us to delve deeper into data integration and analysis practices adopted by the police in different countries (cf. Krause, 2016). The selection of these countries is based on the fact that the authors of this paper have already collected empirical data on these countries regarding the procurement (Germany, Denmark, Norway) and implementation (Germany, Denmark) of customized versions of Palantir's Gotham. Therefore, the analysis of the empirical material can provide us with important insights about the impact of alternative versions of the same platform on police work in the countries under investigation. Notably, the platform has been customized and differently evaluated by different actors involved in both the procurement and use of the platforms, which enables us to shed light on the epistemic and practical consequences of the platforms for the police in three different national and cultural (police) contexts.

---

[1] https://www.palantir.com/platforms/gotham/.

Our argumentation is structured as follows: First, we will describe the basic idea and functionality of data integration and analysis platforms in more detail, with special emphasis on the Gotham software of US-company Palantir Technologies. After that, we introduce the methodological framework of our analysis, the research style of 'comparative policing' as proposed by de Maillard (2022), adding methodological insights about the three case studies. Following this, we present our three cases, the implementation and usage of Palantir Gotham software by the police in Germany, Denmark, and Norway. In the subsequent section, we present the commonalities and differences, with special emphasis on the implementation and adoption processes of these platforms.

Palantir's Gotham as the Role Model of Data Integration and Analysis Platforms for Police Agencies

The growing amount of data is a challenge for every organization. However, it is a particularly difficult and important challenge for the police. This is because police organizations have always, and especially after the turn to intelligence methods (Ratcliffe, 2016), accumulated and worked with high volumes of information and sometimes deal with legacy and usually remarkably complex IT infrastructures. Furthermore, in many cases, it is particularly important for the police to establish correlations from data as quickly as possible to take pre-emptive action. Against this backdrop, it is not surprising that many police departments in the world make use of data integration and analysis platforms to interconnect their databases to facilitate a more effective, efficient, and interoperable information generation process (Bigo, 2020).

Palantir Technologies

The international role model and most prominent example of data integration and analysis platform stems from the US-company Palantir Technologies (Brayne, 2021; Iliadis & Acker, 2022; Munn, 2017).

Accordingly, several European police forces (among other institutions of the public sector) also rely on the platform technology from Palantir when it comes to data analysis and integration. Palantir Technologies, founded in 2004, is a software company which is generally considered one of the most secretive as well as publicly controversial (e.g., Sherman, 2020) companies of its kind in the world. This public controversy is largely due to the support of surveillance practices of governmental agencies (Brayne, 2021; Iliadis & Acker, 2022; Knight & Gekker, 2020) as well as because of its founding background closely related to the venture capitalist branch of the Central Intelligence Agency (CIA), In-Q-Tel, and the dubious investor and Trump supporter Peter Thiel (Greenberg & Mac, 2013). Palantir has been open about their agenda of providing the United States and its allies with the most effective software platforms for intelligence operatives on the front lines, casting nets of criticism of competitors working with US adversaries (Palantir, 2023, 2022, 2020). What is relevant here is that the idea of understanding Palantir as a shadowy and authoritarian creature misrepresents both the company and the role that security plays in the context of a liberal western state. And this is how we should treat Palantir: an authentic offspring of contemporary liberal capitalist democracies. Palantir's business model is like that of many other IT companies; initially, they sell their products rather cheaply or even through zero-cost contracts and earn money in the long term from training and license fees, aiming to establish a vendor lock-in, that is making it hard or excessively costly for the client to change the platform after using the initial platform for some time (Howden et al., 2021).

Palantir Gotham

The Palantir platform for security agencies in general and police departments in specific is called Gotham (Palantir, 2023). This type of data integration and analysis platform is characterized by its status as interface as well as infrastructure. Its goal is 'desiloing' databases, that is breaking up data silos by interconnecting numerous as well as different data banks; this is supposed to enable cross-database analyses at high speed from a central virtual location (Brayne, 2021; Egbert, 2019; Palantir, 2023). Palantir Gotham is basically designed as an internet search engine, enabling to search for specific keywords from a superordinate search mask that has access to all connected databases in the background (see Fig. 11.1). This type of platform is inscribed with the goal of promoting an enhanced technical infrastructure and database architecture to upgrade the quality and availability of the digitized information available to the police, by facilitating interoperability and visualizations. At the same time, this development implies and promotes a comprehensive process of platformization of police work (Poell et al., 2019), meaning the increasing usage of platform in police work and inevitably linked to this, the increased influence of the values and assumptions embedded in these platforms on the work of police officers and analysts (Egbert, 2019).

From an epistemological perspective, Palantir Gotham is driven by the idea that relevant information for police officers and analysts arises

Fig. 11.1 Palantir Homepage LAPD (Brayne, 2017, p. 995)

from associations between data (see Fig. 11.2). The interconnection of data(-bases) shall enable the linking of persons with other persons, with objects (like license plate numbers or houses), activities (like flights or telephone calls) or spaces (areas that high score in specific crime rates) to generate actionable information from these associations (Brayne, 2021). Based on an approach that can be called 'suspicion/risk by association', based on the guilt by association principle, those persons are classified as at least interesting, possibly even suspicious, who have been in contact with persons already documented by the police as suspects or criminals (Ferguson, 2017, p. 200).

After this short introduction of Palantir's Gotham platform for police departments, we will now turn to the presentation of our methodological approach, after which we will present our three case studies of the utilization of Palantir's Gotham application by the police in Germany, Denmark, and Norway.

GOTHAM: GRAPH

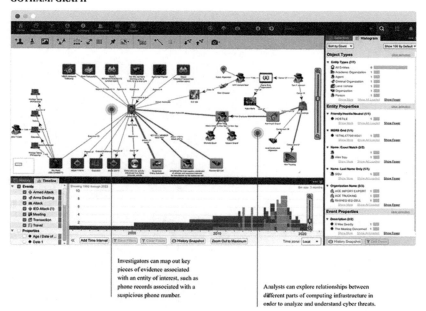

Investigators can map out key pieces of evidence associated with an entity of interest, such as phone records associated with a suspicious phone number.

Analysts can explore relationships between different parts of computing infrastructure in order to analyze and understand cyber threats.

Fig. 11.2 Palantir Gotham's graph application (Palantir, 2020, p. 134)

Methodology

Our cross-national analysis should be understood against the background of the comparative policing approach that has been increasingly discussed in recent years (Maillard, 2022; Roché & Fleming, 2022). The main goal of comparative policing is the explanation of similarities and differences of different national police systems and the associated uncovering of overarching patterns and trends in police work (Roché & Fleming, 2022, p. 256; *see also* Maillard, 2022, p. 3). In relation to our cases, this means that we are interested in how platformization takes place in Germany, Denmark, and Norway and what differences and similarities can be uncovered and what this tells us about the trend that we call, following Egbert (2019), the platformization of police work.

The selection of our cases did not follow a systematic search for suitable comparative cases but was the result of the authors' joint work on digital policing when they realized that Palantir software was being used by the police in all three countries and that empirical data was already available in this regard. This data is based on projects that the authors carried out independently of each other and that were not originally intended for a comparative analysis of Palantir platforms in police work. As a result, the material of the available case data varies in quantity and quality. Nonetheless, we believe that the similarities are significantly sufficient to provide a robust basis for a comparative analysis.

The data from the German case stem from the ongoing research of Simon Egbert on algorithmic policing in Germany. In addition to around 100 qualitative, semi-structured interviews, 55 field protocols, and of 400 + documents which were collected and analyzed in the course of the research on predictive policing in Germany and Switzerland, two demonstrations, one semi-structured interview and 100 + documents specifically on data integration and analysis platforms were analyzed.[2]

The data from the Danish case stem from the ongoing research of Vasilis Galis on predictive policing and the international research project Critical Understanding of Predictive Policing (CUPP), partly carried out

---

[2] More information on the data and methods can be found in Egbert and Leese (2021, pp. 6–10) as well as Egbert and Esposito (2024).

in collaboration with Björn Karlsson (Galis & Karlsson, forthcoming). In this work, Galis draws upon ethnographic interviews and documents such as programmatic reports published by Palantir on their website as well as transcripts of parliamentary debates, written presentations of the program in law drafts, police reports on POL-INTEL (the customized version of Gotham for the Danish police), reports on state security strategies, and PowerPoint presentations by the police at various conferences. Galis additionally draws on eight interviews (four with high-ranked officers within the Danish police organization, two with Palantir employees from the Copenhagen office, one with a former Ministry of Justice employee, and one with a former member of the Danish parliament). The empirical material also includes a comprehensive review of Danish newspaper articles on POL-INTEL.

The study of the implementation of Gotham in Norway is part of a broader project investigating digitalization and the use of technology by Norwegian police from 2021 to 2024 led by Helene Gundhus and Christin Wathne. The empirical data includes analysis of documents relating to police digitalization, interviews, and observations of police officers on patrol in two related projects, 'Algorithmic Governance and Cultures of Policing' (AGOPOL) and 'Critical Understanding of Predictive Policing' (CUPP). Since 2021, Gundhus, Wathne, and their project colleagues have interviewed 56 (38 in AGOPOL, 18 in CUPP) officers from four police districts and spent 174 hours observing police practice. Of the 56 interviewees, they have interviewed six police ICT employees (Oslo Police District, Police Directorate, Police IT center) and four lawyers working on the topic of data integration and prediction. Another inspiration was historiography—attention to the historic values and imaginaries informing the political-legal discourse on the digitalization of law enforcement. This approach also draws on news media and articles, political strategies, policy documents, reports, and public procurement processes around police data-driven technologies.

From Predictive to Platformized Policing: Data Integration and Analysis Platforms in Germany

From Predictive Policing to Datafication

The platformization of the police in Germany cannot be understood without referring to the hype surrounding the implementation of predictive policing from 2014 onwards (Egbert, 2018; Egbert & Leese, 2021). This hype has not only led to a rather rapid introduction of police prediction technologies but has also sparked a development toward a much more holistic algorithmization of police work (Egbert, 2019). While predictive policing in Germany, was always very narrowly focused— police data is utilized to predict residential burglaries so that patrols can increase patrols there—current algorithmic developments in the German police have a much broader aim, in fact they potentially cover all areas of police work. The hype around predictive policing and the much broader datafication of German policing are closely connected because police and political leaders were sensitized by the hype about the introduction of crime prediction software to the promises of modern data analytics and especially data analysis and integration platforms (Egbert, 2018).

One symptomatic as well as important element of this datafication trend is the 'future program' (Kaller, 2019) Police 2020 (now called P20) of the German Federal Ministry of the Interior launched in 2016, which is framed as a 'milestone in police work' (Bundeskriminalamt, 2018), as it aims to thoroughly restructure the police IT landscape, especially by connecting intra-office databases. The goal of this project is nothing less than a 'common digital platform to which all police officers in Germany have access' (Lezgus, 2019, p. 26). At the same time, following the chief of the Federal Criminal Police Office in Germany, Holger Münch, Police 2020 shall ultimately provide a 'development platform and a kind of app store' (Münch, 2019, p. 15), intending to enable the collaborative development of 'skills, tools, and instruments' (Münch, 2019, p. 14).

The datafication efforts of the police have a high potential for transforming the day-to-day practices of police officers, since the police forces in Germany have so far worked very little with modern data analytics, with the effect that essential personnel, technical, legal, and official prerequisites for this are not yet in place. In a predictive policing research project of the State Office of Criminal Investigation of German Federal State Hamburg, it was for example found that the existing data was only used by police officers to a very limited extent. Moreover, they observed that important prerequisites for predictive police work were lacking since the necessary awareness that data must be entered as correctly and promptly as possible to be able to conduct data analysis at all did not prevail (Hauber et al., 2019). In response to this, the application-oriented project 'Development of a Job Profile in Crime Analysis' was initiated in Hamburg (Mahnken & Rabitz-Suhr, 2019), pointing clearly toward the transformative potential of algorithmic analysis for police work in terms of changing job profiles and updated professional competences of police officers (*see also* Gundhus et al., 2022; Waardenburg et al., 2022). The relevance of this development is also demonstrated by the fact that the project was taken over in fall 2023 by the German Police University, which is responsible for the training and further education of police managers centrally for the whole of Germany (DHPol, 2023).

Datafication as Platformization

Upon closer inspection, the current trend toward datafication of police work in Germany turns out to be largely a process of platformization. That is, the trend of datafication leads to police authorities increasingly relying on data integration and analysis platforms. This can be observed already in several empirical examples: Since the summer of 2018, the Hessian police have been using the software 'hessenDATA' to generate time-critical information on 'terrorists and serious criminals' by means of cross-database research accessing heterogeneous sources and correlation-based context analyses and to implement this information directly in police operations (Hessisches Ministerium für Inneres & Sport, 2018, p. 59). The program is based on the software Gotham of the company Palantir Technologies (Hessischer Landtag, 2019). Similar approaches are conducted in North Rhine-Westphalia with the system DAR ('system for cross-database analysis and research' [Datenbankübergreifende Analyse und Recherche]) since 2021 (Landeskriminalamt Nordrhein-Westfalen, 2020) and in Bavaria with the system VeRA ('Cross-process search and analysis system' [Verfahrensübergreifende Recherche und Analyse]) since 2022 (Bayerisches Landeskriminalamt, 2022). Both platforms also rely on the Gotham software from Palantir Technologies. Remarkably, VeRA was intended to be integrated in the Police 2020/P20 program and, in doing so, should be made available to all police departments in Germany through a framework agreement, which would have made a respective new tender obsolete. This was perceived as a potential 'breach of the dam' (Brückner, 2022) in terms of the algorithmization of German policing. What are the reasons for the given federal states to implement data integration and analysis platforms based on Palantir's Gotham? We will illustrate this using the example of hessenDATA.

In Hesse, reference was made to a tense security situation about Islamist terrorism. In the committee of inquiry of the Hessian state parliament, which investigated the awarding of the contract to Palantir in relation to hessenDATA, it is stated: 'In the course of 2016, the security situation was significantly exacerbated by the dangers of Islamist terrorism. This also presented the Hessian police with increasing challenges. In particular, deficits in the area of data evaluation and analysis became apparent' (Hessischer Landtag, 2019, p. 50).[3] A witness from the Hessian State Police Headquarters, who was involved in the award process, additionally specified:

> At the time, we looked very closely at the Hessian security strategy and, in the context of the scenarios that we had to reassess there, we reviewed how the Hessian police force was set up and in which areas we still had a need for development. This resulted in us tackling the security strategy again in the years 2016 to 2020 and developing it further. (Hessischer Landtag, 2019, p. 50)

As a result, not only was the contract awarded to Palantir, but this was also announced in the form of a direct award of contract, due to urgency.

---

[3] All translations are by the authors.

The committee of inquiry should precisely investigate this award procedure, as there must actually be a proper public tendering procedure for such contracts (e.g., Hanack, 2019).

The representatives of the police and the Ministry of the Interior, who were responsible for awarding the contract for hessenDATA directly to Palantir, also comment on the concrete operational hopes they have placed in the platform. One representative from the hessenDATA development team says:

> (L)arge amounts of data are a reality, period. And the police have to face up to these amounts of data. And we are currently being shown this reality on a daily basis, because we have now had this procedure and are ourselves so impressed by the amount of data that is actually coming our way within a very short space of time and handling it at all, storing it sensibly, dealing with it in accordance with the law, these are major, major challenges for the security authorities over the next few years. (Interview hessenDATA)

In the report of the inquiry committee, a delegate from the Hessian police is cited concerning the specific advantages of hessenDATA:

> The first advantage is that we are incredibly fast with analyses. That helped massively with the attack in Eschwege [Hessian town], and we are deeply convinced: Without the optimization of the analysis capability, we would not have been able to prevent it. The second point. We have a better overview of our data. You must imagine it like this: The different cooking pots, the different data pots are normally queried individually and one after the other. With the platform, we are now able to make a query across the pots. The third thing is particularly important to me: collaboration. We have improved cooperation between evaluators, investigators and operatives has improved noticeably and significantly. That is one aspect. The other aspect is that we have also significantly improved cooperation in Hesse from north to south between one organization in a large state. (Hessischer Landtag, 2019, p. 18)

This idea of using data integration and analysis platforms to interconnect data silos and to hereby enable a cross-database analysis can also be heard from the other two federal states in which Gotham is used. The tender for DAR in NRW, for example, states:

> The authorization-dependent, comprehensive, simultaneous analysis and research functions for analysis and research in different databases of the NRW police is critical to the success of the police's fight against crime in NRW and is of outstanding importance. The intention is therefore to acquire a state-of-the-art system for cross-database analysis and research (DAR). (Landeskriminalamt NRW, 2019)

And the Bavarian tender for VeRA states almost verbatim:

> The simultaneous, authorization-dependent, and comprehensive analysis and research in different police databases is of enormous importance for averting danger and fighting crime, in particular for investigating and uncovering facts relevant to criminal and anti-crime law for common structures, patterns of action, groups of people as well as temporal, factual, organizational, personal and situational contexts. The intention is therefore to acquire a state-of-the-art cross-procedural research and analysis platform (VeRA). The core competence of this VeRA system is the direct access, merging and evaluation of data from different sources. (Bayerisches Landeskriminalamt, 2019)

Although the Federal Minister of the Interior and Community, Nancy Faeser, in summer 2023 announced that VeRA—and thus Palantir's Gotham—is no longer favored by the Federal Ministry of the Interior and that the development of its own software is being pursued, the desire for a data integration platform continues unabated (Zierer et al., 2023). According to a debate in the German Bundestag at the beginning of December 2023, the main reason given for the move away from Gotham is the software's background as an American software solution with links to the CIA and Peter Thiel, which is increasingly perceived as problematic. Reference is also made to a ruling by the Federal Constitutional Court in early 2023, in which the police regulations in Hamburg and

Hesse, which were declared partially unconstitutional with regard to the (intended) use of Palantir's Gotham (Deutscher Bundestag, 2023).[4]

In view of the current developments in Germany, at least two things are observable: First, the quasi-sole dominance of Palantir software in the platformization of the German police seems to be coming to an end. It seems that the arguments that civil society critics have long used against Palantir are now increasingly taking hold within the responsible police forces and ministries. The introduction process of VeRA in Bavaria already shows that the climate toward Palantir has become increasingly critical. In contrast to Hesse and North Rhine-Westphalia, the Bavarian police have commissioned an external research institute to check the source code of Gotham to ensure that the platform is clean and, for example, does not contain an invisible back door that could allow Palantir to access data unnoticed (Bayerisches Landeskriminalamt, 2023). Second, despite all the criticism of Palantir, it is clear that the desire for a powerful data integration and analysis platform is unbroken and that intra-European and/or self-developed solutions are being sought to make the corresponding functionalities available to the local police forces.

Data Integration and Analysis Platforms in Denmark: A Story of Scientification

The platformization of the Danish police is the result of a long period of structural transformations in the organization and operational philosophy of the police, technological developments, as well as critical events, such as the 2015 shootings in Copenhagen (see also Sausdal, 2021). These transformations are also discernible in the outspoken political ambition toward *scientification through intelligence* of police practices. Technologies and intelligence techniques have always been an integral part of police work and restructuring (Stevnsborg, 2013). For example, the 2007 major police reform in Denmark aimed at the

---

[4] More information about this ruling of the Federal Constitutional Court can be found in Bundesverfassungsgericht (2023).

modernization of the police by establishing initiatives to strengthen the analytical capacity of law enforcement and to create a more technically savvy police force (Diderichsen, 2017). Moreover, the 2007 reform was inscribed with specific visions, such as economic efficiency, safety and security, peace, and order (see the document drafted by the Vision Committee prior to the reform, Visionsudvalget, 2005). This reform resulted in additional police officers 'on the street', the reduction from 54 to 12 geographic districts (Diderichsen, 2017), centralized management (Holmberg, 2019), teams organized across professional divides to produce solid intelligence (Christensen, 2021), and the implementation of different technologies (e.g., global positioning system and electronic 'fleet monitoring') (Holmberg, 2013).

With the police reform of 2007, the police were reshaped by the New Public Management approaches to organizational governance and policy, as was the case with several public institutions in Denmark (Mikkelsen & Conrad, 2018; Stevnsborg, 2010). This also signified a critical shift from the previous bureaucratic and fragmented police structure in terms of divisions and specializations, into a flexible and complex organization that would conduct intelligence-based or problem-solving policing (Christensen, 2021). In turn, this opened for new groups of personnel beyond the classical distinction 'uniformed police and detectives' as well as for new (digital) technologies (Stevnsborg, 2013) and policing techniques. Concretely, the reform moved the emphasis on crime prevention and the so-called intelligence led policing (ILP) (Balvig et al., 2011), enabling the increasing involvement of the private sector in policing in Denmark (Kruize & Bislev, 2012).

When Intelligence-Led Policing Comes to Cop-town

ILP constitutes one of several law enforcement streams manifesting a strong change in the philosophy of policing: from a reactive to a proactive focus. One of its main proponents, Jerry Ratcliffe defines ILP as a system that.

emphasises analysis and intelligence as pivotal to an objective, decision-making framework that prioritises crime hot spots, repeat victims, prolific offenders, and criminal groups. It facilitates crime and harm reduction, disruption and prevention through strategic and tactical management, deployment, and enforcement. (Ratcliffe, 2016, p. 5)

ILP, *problem-oriented*, *smart*, *holistic policing*, all these strategies describe with marginal difference the same tendency in policing, that is, the shift from a case-by-case focus and criminological attention to cases that have already occurred to preventing/disrupting criminal activities, as well as the management of the risk of crimes (Fyfe et al., 2018). According to a senior intelligence analyst in the Danish police, ILP is a way for the police organization to manage and prioritize the right fields of crime and this is not an easy task: 'It is difficult to implement, and it is also difficult to choose the right tools, given that it is imperative that the strategic aims are also known. Prioritizing is a political issue' (Interview with Senior Intelligence Analyst, May 2022). The turn to ILP has been portrayed as a remedy to mitigate the police's criticized tendency to rely on intuition and experience, to react rather than act (Sausdal, 2022). Turning to intelligence is considered equivalent to adopting norms of (positivistic) science, rationality, and objectivity (Rønn, 2022). The former project owner of the current Danish digital police platform explained that whereas experience is very important, the police force needed to modernize and systematize their future analytical ability. Therefore, in 2012, the Danish police decided to go ahead with working intelligence led in the future, meaning new education for police officers, new ways of investigating, and new concepts of how to collect, analyze, and disseminate information in the police organization. This also led to the establishment of intelligence and analytic units in every police district in 2013 (interview with POL-INTEL project owner, September 2021).

Concretely, ILP enables 'cross-sectional information analyses', that is, the police are allowed to cross-check data effectively and systematically from its own sources (e.g., the general crime register) with other external sources (e.g., EUROPOL). Former director of the Danish National Police explained that there was a tremendous need within the police 'to being able to access information that you have in your system, but also in the longer run to be able to add new data sources and have even more information available to people working in investigation to whatever' (interview with Svend Larsen, March 2021). In other words, the transition to an ILP approach also opened for or even required a technological lift of the police, both by purchasing a digital tool as well as training officers processing data as part of their tasks.

In this context, ILP is not only considered a value-free and legitimate criminological method, but also gives substance to the belief that many police authorities across the world.

'have a lot of faith in "technoscientific miracle fix[es]" (see Egbert & Leese, 2021)—hoping that the next methodological or technological development will be that which finally puts policing at the forefront of things.' (Sausdal, 2022, p. 123)

A Super ... Search Engine

In the case of Denmark, the need for a new IT system, a technoscientific fix, related to, implicated with, and inspired by ILP was documented in several reports, but it was accelerated and consolidated after the shooting incidents in Copenhagen in February 2015. After the attack, the government issued the anti-terror plan 'A Strong Defence Against Terror: 12 New Initiatives Against Terror' [Et stærkt værn mod terror] that also strongly argued for the need of increasing the analytic capacity of the police (presentation of POL-INTEL, September 2021).

In connection to the plan, the government allocated 150 million DKK for the purchase of a new data fusion platform (Regeringen, 2015). The Copenhagen attack, the ensuing anti-terror plan, and ILP's proviso for advancing the analytical capability of the police 'pushed things a lot', according to POL-INTEL's former project owner (Interview, September 2021). In 2015, the Danish government proceeded with a public procurement process for a data integration and analysis platform for the police that would allow them to process vast amounts of data more effectively (Regeringen, 2015). In 2016, the Danish state signed a

160 million DKK contract with the American software company Palantir for the development of POL-INTEL (Rigspolitiet, 2016). According to Volquartzen (2018), POL-INTEL signifies in material terms the transition of the Danish police to an intelligence-led, smart policing and embodies a techno-optimistic idea that algorithms and automation can revolutionize police work.

Even in the Danish case, the data integration and analysis platform POL-INTEL is a customized version of Palantir's Gotham. POL-INTEL integrates several siloed IT systems already at the disposal of the police. The police's case processing system POLSAS, the criminal record register, license plate registration system, gun permits register, drivers' license database, passports, the EUROPOL database, and several others are interconnected in POL-INTEL. The platform consists of two siloed subsystems, *Finder* and *Analyse*, meaning that there are different levels of access. *Finder* is accessible to 10.000 users within the police and allows for rapid look ups on data available about a given individual, an event, a place, or an object. *Analyse*, accessible to 1200 users, constitutes a tool for operational analysis, visualizations, and investigations.

To start with, several media articles as well as the police themselves portrayed POL-INTEL as a 'super weapon' to combat terrorism and predict crime (Holst & Kildegaard, 2017; Kulager, 2021; Toft, 2018). Soon after, however, these techno-optimistic headlines were downplayed. Several informants from the police organization and Palantir describe POL-INTEL as an advanced 'google search engine for police officers'. Regardless of the maximalist or reductive headlines, POL-INTEL provides the Danish police with a platform that allows for different silos of data to communicate/be combined with each other and to produce analysis and visualizations. The platform does not perform predictive tasks if predictive policing refers to targeting individuals. Nevertheless, POL-INTEL does engage with identifying 'future high-risk areas on the basis of historic crime patterns' (Egbert & Mann, 2021, p. 26).

Does POL-INTEL Conduct Predictions?

The SmartSpot, for example, is a place-based component in POL-INTEL that performs map visualizations of integrated data (hot spots), and it is also used for planning patrols and composing threat analysis. According to an employee of the intelligence unit in one of the 12 police districts, SmartSpot allows analysts to identify concentrations of crime in specific areas and to recommend preventive patrols. These patrols are supported by ILP in a sense that officers in place receive a so-called threat analysis of the area that allows them to act and prepare accordingly (interview, September 2022). For a Palantir employee that we interviewed, the whole discussion on whether POL-INTEL performs predictive tasks is irrelevant and banal. He argues that in modern democratic societies, the state monopoly of violence is well-established and defined. According to his view, among the tasks of the police is prediction, that is, how one prevents crime:

> by having your uniformed officers who are walking around, walk down streets where crime is more likely to happen, or anything else. So, from our point of view, we obviously want our software to be used for any purpose that society has come together and decided this is a good use of this capability in society (interview with Palantir Manager, September 2021).

Following the quote, Palantir acts as the State's representative in society, being one with the police to execute its will (see also Kuldova, in this volume). In that sense, any other (non-technical, non-technocratic) discussion about the police is insignificant or/and political. What is important is that the digital technology obtained by the Danish police should not constrain police work, but on the contrary, it should enable the police organization to analyze data in a coherent, holistic, protected, and transparent way avoiding 'automation that tends to suggest a conclusion to a human' (interview with Palantir Manager, September 2021). The establishment of the institution of the police a priori presupposes the predictive element in police work. Indeed, there is not enough academic debate about whether and, if so, how predictive policing can be separated from earlier forms of crime analysis, intelligence, forecasting, and other computer-supported police tactics (Egbert & Leese, 2021).

Nevertheless, as the (Palantir) narrative goes, prediction or preventive police work stemming from intelligence (ILP) and/or supported by digital platforms (POL-INTEL) do not come into being in a presumptuous way, assuming authority and enacting things on their own; rather, they are depended on a scientific method, they are one with science, and they properly represent science. This is not a coincidence. Quite the opposite, the platformization of the Danish police follows the long international 'scientification of the police' trajectory, dating back to the 1980s.

A Platform Against the Copper's Nose

Police work refers to a 'form of action with attendant symbolic and rhetorical features, used to discover the truth and settle problems by constructing a view that satisfies certain criteria of rational acceptability' (Ericson & Shearing, 1986, p. 132, cited in Egbert & Leese, 2021). According to our informants from Palantir, POL-INTEL constitutes a kind of professional cultural change for the police, where the platform nudges the police as an organization toward being driven less by the so-called copper's nose and more by solid data (interview with Palantir Manager, September 2021). During an interview with a Palantir engineer, it was stated that part of Palantir's engineering is to simulate and represent reality in code. The previous source systems acquired by the Danish police poorly and fragmentally represented reality. Palantir's mission was to empower and make the Danish police force more efficient by creating a platform ontology that encoded police officers' reality as 'it lives in their heads' (interview with Palantir Senior Engineer, March 2022).

The case of POL-INTEL is not unique. Wang argues that the radical scientification of policing and the introduction of evidence-based law enforcement (including sophisticated digital platforms) has led to a 'rebranding of policing in a way that foregrounds statistical impersonality and symbolically removes the agency of individual officers' (Wang,

2018, p. 236). The veneer of scientific validity serves to obscure power relations, societal explanations and rationalizes police power through the development of an allegedly neutral police platform (see also Narayan, in this volume). In this way, police activity is constructed as neutral, unbiased, rational, and thus impervious to scrutiny.

In view of the recent history of the police in Denmark, it shows at least two things: First, the platformization of the Danish police is attached to a process of intelligentization/scientification. While several proponents of intelligence doctrines and data integration and analysis practices, even within the Danish police, all describe scientific rationality as a central norm of police work, POL-INTEL is far from value-free and value-neutral platform. How intelligence hierarchizes crimes, how software translates reality into a digital landscape, and how digital landscapes produce visualizations and forecasts about crime occurrence are deeply political processes (Završnik, 2021). This is also depicted in the discussions/interviews with users of the platform. Second, despite all the criticism of Palantir, the political choice of the leadership of the Danish police is in favor of developing and further integrating the POL-INTEL platform in police work. For Palantir, the collaboration with the Danish police constitutes 'a model for future engagement'. It is thus worth exploring what is the actual (quantitative and qualitative) effect of integrating POL-INTEL in police and intelligence work.

From Prüm to Everything—Data Integration and Analysis Platforms in Norway

Data analysis and interoperability are high on the agenda in the Norwegian police (DFØ, 2022, Gundhus et al., 2022; Klepper et al., 2020; Office of the Auditor General of Norway, 2023; Police Directorate, 2017; Wathne, 2020). Intelligence-led policing has been at the center of police work since 2000 and has been the police's main strategy since 2014. The aim is to utilize the data in police registers to become more objective, neutral, and knowledge-driven (Police Directorate, 2014, 2020). ICT is also key to streamlining police work by automating routine work and reducing manual labor. An important purpose of streamlining the police is to ensure citizens' legal protection and utilize police resources by fleet steering the patrols where they are needed. The Norwegian police have 19 different computer systems—some of them contain registers in accordance with the Police Register Regulations (Politiregisterforskriften, 2013), others are tools for producing data for police registers, or simply tools for performing work tasks (Eklund, 2023).

The international IT case management system from the early 1990s was perceived as outdated. The criminal intelligence register Indicia, implemented in 2007, was also lacking data integration, data visualization and analysis capacity (Politiregisterforskriften, 2013). However, Indicia provides process support for prevention and intelligence-based police work and serves as a tool for planning and managing investigations. It contains registers of concern for young people and digital tips, and a search engine with access to 14 other police systems/registers.

In 2015, a major internal police project called the Value-Added Programme (Merverdiprogrammet), which was supposed to be revolutionary and include a data analysis module, ended in failure (Sletteholm & Ekroll, 2015). It was supposed to be a large-scale case management solution for the Norwegian police. Between 2010 and 2015, the Norwegian Police Directorate spent NOK 240 million on preparations: on concept selection, preliminary projects, and quality assurance. The Minister of Justice claimed that although very large projects have a high risk of failure, the termination of the Value-Added Programme in 2015 meant that the risk of cost overruns and delays was limited (Office of the Auditor General of Norway, 2023). After the project was shelved, new services had to be added to computer systems that were described as vulnerable and outdated. The police needed a success story, and this was a key background factor for Palantir becoming such an all-encompassing project in the Norwegian police force.

Handling the Prüm Commitment

Unlike the all-encompassing POL-INTEL project in Denmark, the Norwegian police bought Palantir Gotham for NOK 81 million in

2016 when Norway entered the EU's Prüm agreement. The official story was that the police decided to buy Gotham because the Norwegian Police Directorate assumed that there would be many more international investigations when Norway joined the European Prüm cooperation. The Prüm agreement enables police forces in Europe to cooperate and exchange information with each other. The agreement was originally established in the German town of Prüm in 2005 by seven EU countries: Germany, Belgium, the Netherlands, Luxembourg, France, Spain, and Austria (European Commission, 2023). Norway and Iceland followed suit in 2009, but due to legislative work, court proceedings, investigations, and frequent changes of justice ministers, it took seven years before Norway's agreement was approved by the Norwegian parliament.

To meet the response time for hits in the database, the Norwegian police needed better case management software to check and forward DNA profiles, vehicle information, driving licenses, and fingerprints. The Norwegian Police Directorate wanted to use Gotham to link several police registers, which contain fingerprints, DNA profiles, and information about vehicles and driving licenses. Terrorism was excluded, and big data was not to be used. The government procurement system weighted the bids according to quality, expertise, and price. It was also decided how much weight should be given to each of the criteria. According to our informants, Palantir won on price and quality, but the key reason they won was that they priced all data integration work at zero.

Project Omnia

The project of integrating the Palantir software Gotham in the Norwegian police for this purpose was entitled Omnia meaning 'everything', and the system was supposed to be ready for operation in 2018. The Omnia project was run by the Norwegian Police Directorate (POD) and aimed to support the police in handling international police work. The project was organized under the National Criminal Investigation Service (Kripos). The ambition with Gotham was to be able to look for links between clues, find connections between criminal cases, and solve them faster by analyzing people, networks, and events. The goal was to break up data silos in the police, so-called de-siloing of databases. Omnia would provide an intelligence analysis based on information retrieval in all the police's associated registers and provide access to different police registers from one platform. It was particularly important to be able to match DNA profiles. Gotham was therefore to link data from 19 major police registers and the DNA database, for everything from vehicles to DNA. This was a much broader goal than what was needed to fulfill the Prüm agreement. A data analysis platform that allows agencies to integrate data stored in different databases from internal and external sources was something completely different from the original need.

After winning the contract, Palantir's engineers moved into Kripos, as they usually do (Iliadis & Acker, 2022). Project Omnia was scheduled to be ready for use in 2018. As earlier mentioned, terrorism was not included, and big data was not to be used; the aim was for the police to be able to look for connections between clues, find links between criminal cases, and solve them more quickly by gaining access to analyses of people, networks, and events and retrieving information from the DNA database.

Expanding the Platformization Logic

Our interviews show that different actors in the police had different views on how comprehensive the Omnia project should be. Some hoped that Prüm could eventually be expanded, but the basic need of implementing Prüm was not resolved. Time passed, and the DNA employees grew impatient. Several informants said that the police wasted resources and expensive consultancy hours on tinkering with legacy IT systems. Interviews with participants in the 2017 project and the investigation report summarize the year as follows: 'Omnia grew' (see also Østli, 2022). Registers were added, others removed, but the total number of police registers increased—from five to nine, then to fourteen—without the police's internal audit having found documentation on what information should be entered into Omnia and why. Palantir continued to integrate more and more data. They were to receive the same payment, no matter how many registers were connected to Omnia. This ambition motivated the police chiefs to collect everything, connect everything and see what they got.

Palantir's IT engineers were perceived as outsiders in the police organization and were not integrated into the established police environment. Police DNA specialists and police IT and data processing staff, who experienced the project as end users, experienced problems with data visualization and integration of police databases. Palantir's IT team continued to work on data integration and creating interoperability. However, there was too much resistance from various stakeholders. The totalizing tendencies of platform-based policing may explain why the project went on for so long before it was stopped.

In February 2020, the Norwegian Police Directorate announced that the project would be terminated without being finalized. The original implementation budget was NOK 49 million. When the contract was signed, around NOK 100 million had been spent without anything being achieved (Østli, 2022). The police 'super weapon' was a failure, and it still did not fulfill the Prüm obligations. An internal audit concluded that project management had too much faith in Palantir's ability to deliver integrations and interoperability. There were several clashes between the professionals involved and the platformization processes. Competition in the market between the old suppliers, as Genus, and Palantir also played an important role. Loyalty to professional competence among police employees collided with the managers' loyalty to the system, and a more decentralized distribution of professional power clashed with a more self-regulated expansion of the platform. There was friction between managers' loyalty to the system and the professionals' loyalty to the result. The project continued despite criticism from the professionals, and the tensions were reinforced by the managers' lack of collective responsibility and organizational loyalty. The managers and other leaders were too distanced to deal with disputes while the platform was being built, and the manager lost the power to lead the project.

There was also disagreement among employees and managers in the police and the Data Protection staff at Kripos about the legality of integrating the data. Critics of the project believed that Omnia ultimately violated Norwegian law. Both the Data Protection Act and the Police Register Act state that the police should only process information when there is a clear purpose, and that they should process as little information as possible to fulfill the task. However, stakeholders and managers claimed in interviews that it was internal tensions and power games that put a stop to the project, not the questionable legality of the data integration. In December 2019, the Omnia steering group still did not know whether the disclosure of personal data in the system was legal (Mortvedt, 2020).

The implementation of ICT systems must be understood as a social restructuring process involving new actors, logics, and management systems in interaction with established institutional logics. The analysis of conflicting institutional logics emerging from socio-technical and material objects shows how police employees' experiences of the symbolic, material, and cognitive aspects of the logics are important in domestication processes. The struggle for market dominance also fueled the conflict between established IT suppliers and the new suppliers. The reorganization of the police is thus a political issue, and not just a choice of tools, as claimed in the proposition to the Parliament on amendments to the Police Act (Prop. 61 LS (2014–2015)). A key point is that the introduction of a new surveillance structure and logic can affect underlying power structures in the organization and trigger power struggles.

Platformized Policing in Comparative Perspective

When comparing the three presented Palantir-Gotham-cases, we will focus on three questions: How important are the societal as well as inner-institutional contexts in which the platform was implemented? What are the key expectations tied to the implementation of the platform? How is the existing IT infrastructure of the police affected by the platformization process?

Implementation Contexts

First, the case studies illustrate the importance of understanding how the contextual aspects impact procurement, development, and implementation of new platforms like Palantir's Gotham. These processes are engrained with and products of specific political and historical contexts. They are inscribed with specific visions of policing, management, and social order at the same time as they bear technopolitical components, socio-technical and market logics.

In all three cases, there were specific reasons behind the initial efforts to introduce Palantir's Gotham (even if it may not have been clear at the beginning that it would be this software). While in the case of Norway, the starting point for adoption was the need to implement the Prüm Agreement, in Denmark and in Germany/Hesse it was terrorist attacks that prompted the response. In Denmark the attacks in Copenhagen in 2015 and the ensuing anti-terror plan accelerated the procurement of a digital platform that would strengthen the analytical capabilities of the police. In Hesse, the reason for the introduction of hessenDATA was, on the one hand, related to the terrorist attack by Anis Amri in Berlin in 2016, which, according to a subsequent review, was not prevented primarily because the security authorities had not connected their available data well enough. On the other hand, an increased risk of attack was perceived in Hesse due to two further attacks in Ansbach and Würzburg—it is noteworthy that both cities are in Bavaria—in the same year, which increased the perceived need to enhance the analytical capabilities and accelerate the data research processes.

What is also different is that in the cases of Norway and Denmark, the implementation of Palantir's Gotham platform was part of broader police reorganization and reform projects, namely a conscious scientification of policing in Norway and an adaptation of intelligence-led policing and scientification through intelligence in Denmark. In Germany, however, the adaption of data integration and analysis platforms was not part of a deliberate strategy, but rather a singular digitization measure. Although it can be understood from a research perspective as part of a broader datafication of police work, it was not framed in this way by the police. The

Norwegian police in turn have been rather reluctant to rely on technological solutions in the past. This has been a recurrent theme at Norwegian Police University College, for example (Gundhus, 2012).

What all cases have in common, though, is that they demonstrate another iteration of the well-known techno-solutionist thinking (Morozov, 2013) or what has been called 'techno fix' in science and technology studies—the belief that one single technological tool is powerful enough to solve challenging societal problems (e.g., Rosner, 2004). Particularly the police managers appear as techno-optimists. Even if the platforms do indeed have the real potential to generate operational advantages, the role of the political-discursive dimension in this matter should not be neglected: by adopting platforms, one can present oneself as innovative and progressive and as willing to do everything possible to put crime in its place. Accordingly, regarding hessenDATA, then-minister of the interior Peter Beuth stated that hessenDATA is a 'modern software' that has 'lifted police work into a new digital age' and due to this platform, they are a 'nationwide pioneer in the fight against modern crime' (as cited in Hessisches Ministerium des Innern, für Sicherheit und Heimatschutz, 2023).

Additionally, in Norway and Germany, another dynamic can be observed, namely that after an initial almost uncritical introduction of Palantir platforms, the focus gradually shifted to in-house developments. In Norway, this undoubtedly has to do with the failed Omnia project and the scaling up of the Police IT Centre from 2020, in Germany with the announcement by the Federal Ministry of the Interior to move away from commercial solutions, especially from the United States, for reasons of data sovereignty and transparency (Zierer et al., 2023). Denmark, however, stands out in this context, as the thrust there is still to bind itself even more strongly to Palantir contractually and to equip even more security authorities with their platforms.

As shown, the three cases have different conditions in terms of the framework conditions for implementing the platforms. The fact that Palantir managed to land contracts everywhere, at least at the beginning, speaks for the company's negotiating skills as well as for the flexibility of the platforms, which can fulfill different functions and tasks and can therefore also be framed differently in terms of discourse.

Expectations and Adaption Processes

There are also several commonalities in the three cases related to perceptions of expectations in connection with the acquisition of the platform. As already indicated, the primary goal of the police representatives was to enhance analytical capabilities by making the available data more easily searchable and interoperable. That is, the main goal was desilosation, the breaking up of isolated data sources (silos), to enhance analytical efficiencies and, hence, speed. All departments shared at least subliminally the idea that a large amount of data and its improved likability guarantee better information and rapid information collection. They therefore also, on a more general level, shared the belief in the totalizing tendencies that come with platformization: the more data, the better the police (Egbert, 2019). These totalizing tendencies were, however, embraced differently in the various cases in the development processes, leading to a smooth adaptation in Denmark, ambivalence in Germany and conflicts in Norway.

At the macro-level, it is of importance to what extent the national legal system allows for data integration, including what type of data can be collected and integrated from different sources. This is because basically the principle of data minimization also applies to the police, meaning that they should use as little data as possible (e.g., Van Der Sloot, 2013). Data integration and analysis platforms are fundamentally at odds with this principle. This had to be responded to in the three cases, which was done in different ways. In Norway, legal obstacles was one of several reasons for not implementing it. In Denmark, the relevant law was modified. And in Germany, the use of Palantir, after it had been used in Hesse since 2017 without intervention, was restricted in Hesse by the German Constitutional Court in early 2023 and completely prohibited in Hamburg (where, however, no software was used up to that point in time). The proceedings concerned the newly created legal paragraphs in the respective police laws of Hesse and Hamburg to enable the use of Palantir platforms. Because they do not define a sufficient threshold for interference and contain unclear wording, the provisions were classified as unconstitutional by the Federal Constitutional Court, as they violated the general right of personality in its manifestation of the right to informational self-determination (Bundesverfassungsgericht, 2023). HessenDATA did not have to be completely shut down as a result, but there was a requirement to introduce a new law by the end of September 2023. This law was passed in the summer, with opposition parties criticizing the fact that it was an inappropriate fast-track legislative process (DIE LINKE. Fraktion im Hessischen Landtag, 2023).

In Norway, police professionals were concerned about how data was stored after being deleted, and how it would meet the Data Protection Agency's standards. Moreover, no privacy assessment was conducted when procuring the potentially invasive tool, which has subsequently been criticized (NOU, 2022, p. 11). During development, questions were raised as to whether the integration of personal data in the system was within the limits of the law. It was argued that Palantir's data integration is powerful, and the mass collection of personal data violates the principle of purpose limitation. The privacy commission assessing privacy challenges in the field of criminal justice in general and Palantir in particular, argues that data separation is a good way to achieve purpose limitation, as well as improper linking and linking between different data sets (NOU, 2022, p. 11). All in all, privacy had not been sufficiently addressed before the Palantir project began, and when it ended it was still not known whether the solution would become legal or not regarding privacy.

In Denmark, the Danish Ministry of Justice (MoJ) submitted a draft law, the so-called Palantir-law[5] [Palantir-loven], on amending the Police Act with new data analysis provisions, in February 2017. The law enabled a legal basis for processing personal data in the POL-INTEL system, which uses the legal framework of the existing Data Protection Act as a reference. The new law provided a very general legal basis for combining existing police databases in the POL-INTEL system, irrespective of the purpose limitations of these databases, and for collection and processing of information, including personal data, from open sources (EDRi, 2017). The Palantir-law was drafted by the National Police, instead of the MoJ that usually develops legislative proposals. According to a former employee of the Ministry, the MoJ did not acquire the momentum

---

[5] https://hoeringsportalen.dk/Hearing/Details/60330.

to draft the legislation and required expertise to deal with this kind of sophisticated legislation about the processing of personal data. This expertise was found at the Data Protection Officer at the Danish police, who also worked closely with the procurement of POL-INTEL. In this way, the Danish police succeeded in pushing and rushing the implementation of POL-INTEL (Interview with former Ministry of Justice employee, April 2022).

This leads us to a discussion of why resistance to Palantir came up in Norway, but not in Germany and Denmark? In the Norwegian example, the resistance to Palantir began already early in the development phase. Why was there so much resistance in Norway and not in the other countries? In Norway, the criminal intelligence police register Indicia had already a strong support, and the competition between the old suppliers and Palantir made it more difficult for Palantir to succeed. The internal IT specialists were satisfied with current contracts with the software firms. Among the key players that Palantir was considered to threaten were the established IT suppliers to the police, who now had a new rival or competitor. IT personnel representing the old and new suppliers competed for the market by promoting solutions inspired by their own logic, bureaucratic, and agile respectively. The traditional values and norms of the bureaucratic logic left little room for agile processes and gave high priority to data security, while the logic of digital agile processes saw the quality of data as a question of quantity. Furthermore, the police working with knowledge led policing in Norway was critical to the process of rushing for data analysis and integration—before structuring and cleaning the data. The output was very inaccurate, and they needed accurate data for applying it to profiling in investigating cases. ICT staff at Kripos warned the police chiefs, urging the need for specificity in data and stressing that flawed data was clearly an obstacle to integration. They emphasized that the aim of the project was to gain accurate output and optimalization of data exchange. The Palantir consultants working at Kripos were considerably less well-informed than insiders about the complex history of the different police registers. Palantir had not considered that there will always be uncertainty about identification based on name, date of birth, and ethnicity.

And these small differences led to huge mistakes when data were integrated. They tried to solve this problem by using shared children as a proxy for relationships, but that was criticized by the data protection environment for being too unreliable. There was also growing mistrust in the Norwegian development group because Palantir told the managers that they were trying to solve quality problems whereas they actually they kept working on data integration and interoperability. The project therefore failed since Palantir was only working on the interoperability, analysis, and data visualization aspect of the Gotham application, when the real problem was the bad quality of the data.

In Germany, there was opposition to the use of Palantir platforms in police work from civil society and the media (e.g., Brühl, 2018) right from the start, but for a long time, there was no significant criticism within the police and among the relevant ministers at state and federal level. This ultimately changed with the above-mentioned ruling by the Federal Constitutional Court. Independently of this, party political reasons certainly also played a role when the Federal Minister of the Interior, Nancy Faeser, who was campaigning in the Hessian state elections at the same time, announced in the fall of 2023 that she did not want to pursue the federal VeRA option any further (Zierer et al., 2023). Within the police force itself, however, criticism of Palantir remains remarkably low. Not only in comparison to the introduction of prediction software at the time, which was always criticized within the police (see e.g., Egbert & Leese, 2021), it is striking how unanimously operational police officers in particular speak positively about the platform and would like to use it in their day-to-day work. This certainly also has to do with the fact that the IT equipment of German police authorities can at least be rated as capable of improvement and that there is repeated criticism from those involved that the data infrastructure is too heterogeneous and complex. It is therefore hardly surprising that a platform that links all these numerous and scattered databases in the background and makes them searchable across the board is attractive to operational forces. To concretize by referring to the example of hessenDATA: The platform brings together seven data sources, including POLAS (POLizeiAuskunftsSystem), a system for wanted lists, CRIME (Criminal Research Investigation Management Software), a preventive case processing system, ComVor (Computer-assisted case processing), the standard case processing system, data from telecommunications surveillance, including data from providers, forensic extracts, e.g., from confiscated mobile phones (call lists etc.), police telexes, internal e-mail system for formal communication for high-ranking cases, as well as, upon request and court order, social media sites, e.g., Facebook (both publicly viewable and non-publicly viewable data). Being able to analyze up to seven data sources at once and in a uniform environment is undoubtedly an asset for the police officers involved—provided, of course, that the data is good enough and is displayed correctly. It is therefore hardly surprising that although the Federal Minister of the Interior is moving away from Palantir, she still considers the idea of a data integration and analysis platform for the police to be relevant and wants to support the development of an own solution (Zierer et al., 2023).

In Denmark, three concrete reasons contributed to reduced opposition to the collaboration with Palantir. First, a delegation of members of the Danish police had encountered Palantir executives in at least two occasions: (1) during the annual meeting of Interpol in Monte Carlo in 2014, where Palantir pitched Gotham for the Danish delegation (Kulager, 2021) and (2) during a field trip to the United States also in 2014, where Danish police officials pronounced Palantir Gotham 'suitable for the needs of the police in Denmark' (Howden et al., 2021; Rigspolitiet, 2014). The shock caused by the 2015 shootings in Copenhagen accelerated the already advanced contacts between the Danish police and Palantir and what was perceived as too expensive during the initial negotiations, became a matter of rapid procurement process soon after. The effect of the shootings was enormous in the ensuing public debate and enabled the Danish government to procure for and implement POL-INTEL without significant opposition. This was also depicted in the parliamentary debate for the ratification of the so-called Palantir-law.

Second, during the parliamentary debate and public hearing for the amendment of the Police Act, submitted by the Ministry of Justice, 'no questions ever came' (interview with former Ministry of Justice employee, April 2022). At the same time, a former member of the Danish parliament involved in the ratification of the Palantir-law explained that very few politicians are sufficiently informed and competent to assess the content of the bills introduced in the parliament, especially those about complicated technical systems, such as POL-INTEL. They lack technical skills and are constrained by time pressure and huge workload related to law-making processes that has a great cost on political reflection as well as democratic transparency and insightfulness. In other words, there was no time and not enough competence to assess the POL-INTEL-law before its ratification (interview with former member of the Danish parliament, February 2022). In this context, not only was opposition impossible, but also even a basic scrutiny of what the Danish government had procured was unrealistic given the inability of elected politicians to audit what they were voting for, denoting a serious democratic deficit in the procurement, implementation, and ratification of complex technical systems by the public administration.

Third, the Danish police and public administration had already attempted to develop a digital handling system before POL-INTEL to replace the outdated POLSAS in the years 2007–2012. The development process turned out to be a fiasco, since the new IT system, POLSAG, never got further than pilot operation due to technical problems and it was completely scrapped in February 2012, even though over half a billion DKK had been spent on the project at that time. This created considerable pressure on the Danish government and pushed toward the direction of purchasing an off-the-self system. Considering this previous budgetary fiasco, the Danish police and the POL-INTEL project in general could not afford significant public opposition (interview with former Ministry of Justice employee, April 2022).

Conclusion

In this chapter, we analyzed the implementation and utilization of data integration and analysis platform from US software company Palantir Technologies in policing in Germany, Denmark, and Norway. Following a comparative lens, we showed that these platforms are implemented with the hope of enhancing the efficiency of policing, especially when it comes to data handling and data analysis. We argue that these kinds of platforms will very likely have a prominent role in policing practices in the future, since also police organizations—like all other organizations—find ways to manage the ever-increasing volume of data properly. However, these platforms pose challenges for the police, as we saw in the case of Omnia, the Palantir Gotham-project of the Norwegian Police. This project has not only become more and more expensive, but it was also ultimately canceled after three years without any concrete results. The main reason for this was internal criticism of the continuous testing without results, insufficient quality of the data visualization and uncertainty about the legality of the project. And in Germany, although Palantir currently appears to be increasingly criticized as a provider, the idea of a data integration and analysis platform is still considered very relevant, which is why the Federal Ministry of the Interior is now planning its own development. In Denmark, despite organizational challenges, the signs are clearly pointing to uncritical expansion and therefore even a broader cooperation with Palantir.

What is important to note is that the platforms presented in this chapter do not simply assist police institutions with analysis and visualization tools, but they also restructure, and reprogram the police organizations and work by (re-)introducing a new type of scientific rationality based on the desire for a powerful data integration. To this end, data integration and analysis platforms do not only incorporate and develop intelligence techniques such as risk analysis and visualizations but also make intelligence possible as well as the population subject to calculations, control, and prediction. In this sense, they are to be understood as 'mediators' (van Dijck, 2013, p. 29) and not just as (passive) intermediaries, analogous to the large internet platforms (Facebook, Google, Amazon, etc.), which are mainly discussed in platform studies and to which van Dijck refers to. From this perspective, data integration and analysis platforms serve as infrastructural devices for enabling conjunction, fostering interactions of third parties—although not only humans—thereby being raising the issue whether integrating these platforms with human work constitutes a deskilling process or a skill acquisition opportunity for police officers (Gundhus et al., 2022; Waardenburg et al., 2022). Against this backdrop, data analysis and integration platforms undoubtedly have the potential to reconfigure work practices and employment conditions, which ultimately challenge the long-standing professional culture in regulating law enforcement work environments.

Funding and Ethics Statement   The work of Simon Egbert was funded by Fritz Thyssen Stiftung (grant agreement number 10.16.2.005SO) and European Research Council (grant agreement number 833749). He was also supported by Weizenbaum Institute for the Networked Society in Berlin. The work of Helene Gundhus and Christin Wathne was funded by funded by the Research Council of Norway (grant: 313626, *Algorithmic Governance and Cultures of Policing: Comparative Perspectives from Norway, India, Brazil, Russia, and South Africa;* AGOPOL), and by Nordforsk (grant: 106,245, *Critical Understanding of Predictive Policing;*CUPP). The work of Vasilis Galis was funded by the aforementioned Nordforsk grats as well. Each of the research projects had complied with the relevant national ethics research guidelines, which means, among other things, that all data collected was documented with the explicit consent of the research subjects.

References

Balvig, F., Holmberg, L., & Højlund Nielsen, M. P. (2011). *Verdens bedste politi: politireformen i Danmark 2007–2011.* [World's best police: police reform in Denmark 2007–2011]. Jurist- og Økonomforbundets Forlag.

Bayerisches Landeskriminalamt. (2023). *Projekt VeRA: Ergebnis der Quellcodeüberprüfung.* https://www.polizei.bayern.de/aktuelles/pressemitteilungen/045266/index.html

Bayerisches Landeskriminalamt. (2019). *Database Software Package 2021/ S 011–023694.* https://ted.europa.eu/udl?uri=TED:NOTICE:23694-2021: TEXT:EN:HTML&src=0

Bayerisches Landeskriminalamt. (2022). *Noch erfolgreichere Polizeiarbeit— Zuschlag für neues Recherche- und Analysesystem der Bayerischen Polizei: Höchste Ansprüche an Datensicherheit und Datenschutz.* https://www.polizei.bayern.de/aktuelles/pressemitteilungen/025971/index.html

Bigo, D. (2020). Interoperability: A Political Technology for the Datafication of the Field of EU Internal Security? In D. Bigo, T. Diez, E. Fanoulis,

B. Rosamond, & Y. A. Stivachtis (Eds.), *The Routledge Handbook of Critical European Studies* (1st ed., pp. 400–417). Routledge. https://doi.org/10.4324/9780429491306

Brayne, S. (2017). Big Data Surveillance: The Case of Policing. *American Sociological Review, 82*(5), 977–1008. https://doi.org/10.1177/0003122417725865

Brayne, S. (2021). *Predict and Surveil: Data, Discretion, and the Future of Policing.* Oxford University Press. https://doi.org/10.1093/oso/9780190684099.001.0001

Brückner, A. (2022). Dammbruch! Palantir gewinnt den Rahmenvertrag für Data Mining in der deutschen Polizei. *Police-IT.* https://police-it.net/dammbruch-palantir-gewinnt-rahmenvertrag-data-mining-in-der-deutschen-polizei

Brühl, J. (2018, October 18). Palantir in Deutschland: Wo die Polizei alles sieht. *Süddeutsche Zeitung.* https://www.sueddeutsche.de/digital/palantir-in-deutschland-wo-die-polizei-alles-sieht-1.4173809

Bundeskriminalamt. (2018). *Das Programm 'Polizei 2020'—Ein Meilenstein in der Polizeiarbeit.* https://www.bka.de/SharedDocs/Kurzmeldungen/DE/Kurzmeldungen/180126_Polizei2020.html

Bundesverfassungsgericht. (2023). *Legislation in Hesse and Hamburg regarding automated data analysis for the prevention of criminal acts is unconstitutional.* 16 February 2023. https://www.bundesverfassungsgericht.de/SharedDocs/Pressemitteilungen/EN/2023/bvg23-018.html

Christensen, M.J. (2021). Battles to Define the Danish Police. In J. Appiahene-Gyamfi, M. Baylis, M. F. Briskey, M. J. Christensen, M. Dai, S. G. Davies, F. del Castillo, G. Fabini, L. E. Grant, R. Hendy & D. Kekić (Eds.), *Global Perspectives in Policing and Law Enforcement.* Rowman & Littlefield.

Deutscher Bundestag. (2023). *Antwort der Bundesregierung auf die Kleine Anfrage der Fraktion der CDU/CSU—Drucksache 20/8205—Entscheidung des Bundesministeriums des Innern und für Heimat bezüglich der Einführung der polizeilichen Analyse-Software Bundes-VeRA.* https://dserver.bundestag.de/btd/20/083/2008390.pdf

DFØ. (2022). *Evaluering av nærpolitireformen – en vurdering av resultater og effekter.* (DFØ-rapport 2022:6). https://dfo.no/rapporter/dfo-rapport-20226-evaluering-av-naerpolitireformen-en-vurdering-av-resultater-og-effekter

DHPol (Ed.). (2023). *DHPol und LKA Hamburg starten Fortbildung "Kriminalitätsanalyse".* https://www.dhpol.de/die_hochschule/aktuelles/news-2023/news_30_10-2023.php

Diderichsen, A., (2017). Renewal and Retraditionalisation: the Short and Not Very Glorious History of the Danish Bachelor's Degree in Policing. *Nordisk politiforskning, 4(2),* pp.149–169. https://doi.org/10.18261/issn. 1894-8693-2017-02-04

DIE LINKE. Fraktion im Hessischen Landtag. (2023). *Regelungen zu HessenData im Schnellverfahren verabschiedet.* https://www.linksfraktion-hes sen.de/presse/mitteilungen/detail-pressemitteilungen/regelungen-zu-hessen data-im-schnellverfahren-verabschiedet/

EDRi (2017). *New Legal Framework for Predictive Policing in Denmark.* https://edri.org/our-work/new-legal-framework-for-predictive-policing-in-denmark/

Egbert, S. (2018). About Discursive Storylines and Techno-Fixes: The Political Framing of the Implementation of Predictive Policing in Germany. *European Journal for Security Research, 3*(2), 95–114. https://doi.org/10.1007/s41125-017-0027-3

Egbert, S. (2019). Predictive Policing and the Platformization of Police Work. *Surveillance & Society, 17*(1/2), 83–88. https://doi.org/10.24908/ss.v17i1/2.12920

Egbert, S. and Mann, M., (2021). Discrimination in Predictive Policing: The (Dangerous) Myth of Impartiality and the Need for STS Analysis. In A. Završnik, & V. Badalič (Eds.), *Automating Crime Prevention, Surveillance, and Military Operations* (pp. 25–46). Springer, Cham. https://doi.org/10. 1007/978-3-030-73276-9_2

Egbert, S., & Leese, M. (2021). Criminal Futures: Predictive policing and everyday police work. *Routledge, Taylor & Francis Group.* https://doi.org/ 10.4324/9780429328732

Egbert, S., & Esposito, E. (2024). Algorithmic Crime Prevention. From Abstract Police to Precision Policing. *Policing and Society, 34*(6), 521–534. https://doi.org/10.1080/10439463.2024.2326516

Eklund, L. H. (2023). *Politiets registre.* Kripos.

Ericson, R. V., & Shearing, C. D. (1986). The Scientification of Police Work. In G. Böhme, & N. Stehr (Eds.), *The Knowledge Society: The Growing Impact of Scientific Knowledge on Social Relations* (pp. 129–159). Springer Netherlands. https://doi.org/10.1007/978-94-009-4724-5_9

European Commission. (2023). *Strengthening the automated data exchange under the Prüm framework.* European Commission.

Ferguson, A. G. (2017). *The Rise of Big Data Policing: Surveillance, Race, and the Future of Law Enforcement.* NYU Press. https://doi.org/10.2307/j.ctt1pw tb27

Fyfe, N., Gundhus, H. O. I., & Rønn, K. V. (2018). Introduction. In N. Fyfe, H. O. I. Gundhus, & K. V. Rønn (Eds.), Moral Issues in Intelligence-led Policing. In *Moral Issues in Intelligence-led Policing* (pp. 1–22). Routledge. https://doi.org/10.4324/9781315231259

Greenberg, A., & Mac, R. (2013). How A 'Deviant' Philosopher Built Palantir, A CIA-Funded Data-Mining Juggernaut. *Forbes.* https://www.forbes.com/sites/andygreenberg/2013/08/14/agent-of-intelligence-how-a-deviant-philosopher-built-palantir-a-cia-funded-data-mining-juggernaut/

Gundhus, H. I. (2012). Experience or Knowledge? Perspectives on New Knowledge Regimes and Control of Police Professionalism. *Policing, 7*(2), 178–194. https://doi.org/10.1093/police/pas039

Gundhus, H. O. I., Talberg, N., & Wathne, C. T. (2022). From Discretion to Standardization: Digitalization of the Police Organization. *International Journal of Police Science & Management, 24*(1), 27–41. https://doi.org/10.1177/14613557211036554

Hanack, P. (2019). Licht ins Dunkel. *Frankfurter Rundschau.* https://www.fr.de/rhein-main/licht-dunkel-11413308.html

Hauber, J., Jarchow, E., & Rabitz-Suhr, S. (2019). *Prädiktionspotenzial schwere Einbruchskriminalität − Ergebnisse einer wissenschaftlichen Befassung mit Predictive Policing.* Landeskriminalamt Hamburg.

Hessischer Landtag. (2019). *Zwischenbericht des Untersuchungsausschusses und Abweichende Berichte. Drucksache 19/6864.* https://starweb.hessen.de/cache/DRS/19/4/06864.pdf

Hessisches Ministerium des Innern, für Sicherheit und Heimatschutz. (2023). *Polizei-Analyseplattform zum Schutz vor Terroristen und Schwerstkriminellen.* https://innen.hessen.de/presse/polizei-analyseplattform-zum-schutz-vor-terroristen-und-schwerstkriminellen

Hessisches Ministerium für Inneres und Sport. (2018). *Jahresbilanz 2018* [Jahresbericht]. Hessisches Ministerium des Innern und für Sport. https://innen.hessen.de/sites/innen.hessen.de/files/2021-10/jahresbilanz_2018_160119_web.pdf

Holmberg, L. (2013). Scandinavian Police Reforms: Can You Have Your Cake and Eat It, Too? *Police Practice and Research, 15*(6), 447–460. https://doi.org/10.1080/15614263.2013.795745

Holmberg, L. (2019). Continuity and change in Scandinavian Police Reforms. *International Journal of Police Science & Management, 21*(4), 206–217. https://doi.org/10.1177/1461355719889461

Holst, H. K., & Kildegaard, K. (2017, February 10). Dansk politi advarer forbrydere: Vi er klar med et "supervåben". *Berlingske*. https://www.ber lingske.dk/politik/dansk-politi-advarer-forbrydere-vi-er-klar-med-et-superv aaben

Howden, D., Fotiadis, A., Stavinoha, L., & Holst, B. (2021, April 2). Seeing Stones: Pandemic Reveals Palantir's Troubling Reach in Europe. *The Guardian*. https://www.theguardian.com/world/2021/apr/02/seeing-sto nes-pandemic-reveals-palantirs-troubling-reach-in-europe

Iliadis, A., & Acker, A. (2022). The Seer and the Seen: Surveying Palantir's Surveillance Platform. *The Information Society, 38*(5), 334–363. https://doi.org/10.1080/01972243.2022.2100851

Kaller, S. (2019). Das Zukunftsprogramm der Polizei in Deutschland—Polizei 2020. *Polizei Verkehr + Technik, 64*(1), 6–9.

Kaufmann, M. (2023). DNA as in-formation. *Wires Forensic Science, 5*(1), e1470. https://doi.org/10.1002/wfs2.1470

Klepper, K. B., Greve, B. M., Ousdal, S., Paulsen, J. P., Rjaanes, M., Strand, M., & Thorsberg, L. (2020). *Teknologiutviklingens betydning for politiet, PST og Den høyere påtalemyndighet*. FFI (FFI-RAPPORT 21/02532).

Knight, E., & Gekker, A. (2020). Mapping Interfacial Regimes of Control: Palantir's ICM in America's Post-9/11 Security Technology Infrastructures. *Surveillance & Society, 18*(2), 231–243. https://doi.org/10.24908/ss.v18i2.13268

Koper, C. S., Lum, C., Wu, X., Johnson, W., & Stoltz, M. (2022). Do License Plate Readers Enhance the Initial and Residual Deterrent Effects of Police Patrol? A Quasi-randomized Test. *Journal of Experimental Criminology, 18*(4), 725–746. https://doi.org/10.1007/s11292-021-09473-y

Krause, M. (2016). Comparative Research: Beyond Linear Casual Explanation. In J. Deville, M. Guggenheim, & Z. Hrdličková (Eds.), *Practicing Comparison: Logics, Relations, Collaborations* (pp. 45–67). Mattering Press.

Kruize, P., & Bislev, M. (2012). Recent Trends in Policing and Managing Urban Security in Denmark. In A. Kohl (Ed.), *Recent Trends in Policing in Europe, Reports from Denmark, The Netherlands and the UK* (pp. 24–36). Andreas Kohl.

Kulager, F. (2021, May 4). For fire år siden fik politiet et "supervåben". Her er, hvordan det har transformeret ordensmagten. *Zetland*. https://www.zetland.dk/historie/sO9kBG7W-aOZj67pz-04ca0

Landeskriminalamt Nordrhein-Westfalen. (2020). *LKA-NRW: Polizei NRW setzt bei Verbrechensbekämpfung und Gefahrenabwehr zukünftig neue Analysetechniken ein.* Presseportal. https://www.presseportal.de/blaulicht/pm/58451/4490593

Landeskriminalamt NRW (Ed.). (2019). *Beschaffung eines Systems zur Datenbankübergreifende Analyse und Recherche (DAR) für die Polizei des Landes Nordrhein-Westfalen.* https://ausschreibungen-deutschland.de/550095_Beschaffung_eines_Systems_zur_Datenbankuebergreifende_Analyse_und_Recherche_DAR_fuer_die_2019_Duesseldorf

Lezgus, A. (2019). Ein gemeinsames Datenhaus entsteht. *Moderne Polizei, Polizist der Zukunft: Kompetent-Digital-Vernetzt, 1,* 26–27.

Lindsay, C. (2023, October 17). UK government slammed for Palantir 'free trial period' deal in Ukraine housing scheme. *The Register.* https://www.theregister.com/2023/10/17/uk_government_slammed_for_palantir/

Mahnken, J., & Rabitz-Suhr, S. (2019). Auswertung und Analyse 4.0.: Das Projekt 'Entwicklung Berufsbild Kriminalitätsanalytik'. Teil 1: Entstehen und Analyse der Ausgangssituation. *Der Kriminalist, 51*(12), 21–26.

de Maillard, J. (2022). *Comparative Policing.* Routledge. https://doi.org/10.4324/9781003108399

Max, B. (2023). SoundThinking's Black-Box Gunshot Detection Method: Untested and Unvetted Tech Flourishes in the Criminal Justice System. *Stanford Technology Law Review, 26,* 193–249.

Mikkelsen, L. N., & Conrad, M., (2018). The Role in Society and Changing Assignments of the Danish Police in the Three Phases of Modernity. In *NSfK's 60. Research Seminar* (pp. 184–195). https://www.nsfk.org/wp-content/uploads/sites/10/2018/11/NSfK-Research-Seminar-report-2018.pdf

Morozov, E. (2013). *To save Everything.* The Folly of Technological Solutionism. PublicAffairs.

Mortvedt, O. M. (2020). Bråstopp for prestisjeprosjekt. *Politiforum.* https://www.politiforum.no/kripos-nyhet-palantir/brastopp-for-prestisjeprosjekt/158144

Münch, H. (2019). Kriminalitätsbekämpfung weiterdenken. Phänomene—Herausforderungen—Handlungsoptionen im Zeitalter von Big Data, Algorithmen und autonomen Systemen. *Kriminalistik, 73*(1), 11–16.

Munn, L. (2017). Seeing with Software: Palantir and the Regulation of Life. *Studies in Control Societies.* https://studiesincontrolsocieties.org/seeing-with-software/

NOU 2022:11. *Ditt personvern - vårt felles ansvar.* Oslo: DSS.

Office of the Auditor General of Norway (2023). Riksrevisjonens undersøkelse av digitalisering i politiet Dokument 3:7 (2023–2024). digitalisering-i-pol itiet.pdf(riksrevisjonen.no)

Østli, H. (2022). *Palantir i politiet. Metode-rapport - Skup 2022. SKUP.* https:// www.skup.no/sites/default/files/2022-02/palantir-metoderapport.pdf

Palantir. (2020). *S-1 Prospectus.*

Palantir. (2023). *Gotham.* https://www.palantir.com/platforms/gotham/

Poell, T., Nieborg, D., & van Dijck, J. (2019). Platformisation. *Internet Policy Review, 8*(4). https://doi.org/10.14763/2019.4.1425

Police Directorate. (2014). *Etterretningsdoktrine for politiet.* Versjon 1.0. Oslo: Politidirektoratet.

Police Directorate. (2017). *Overordnet plan for gevinster i nærpolitireformen.* Oslo: Politidirektoratet.

Politiregisterforskriften. (2013). Forskrift om behandling av opplysninger i politiet og påtalemyndigheten. (FOR 2013–09–20–1097). *Lovdata.* https:// lovdata.no/dokument/SF/forskrift/2013-09-20-1097/KAPITTEL_11#KAP ITTEL_11

Prop 61 LS. (2014–2015). *Endringer i politiloven mv. (trygghet i hverdagen – nærpolitireformen).* DSS.

Ratcliffe, J. H. (2016). *Intelligence-led Policing.* Routledge. https://doi.org/10. 4324/9781315717579

Regeringen. (2015). *Et stærkt værn mod terror: 12 nye tiltag mod terror.* Regeringen. https://www.regeringen.dk/media/1312/et_staerkt_vaern_ mod_terror.pdf

Rigspolitiet. (2014). *Projekt: Platform til operativ analyse og efterforskning Refer-encebesøg i USA uge38,* 2014. Retrieved by Freedom of Information Act Request.

Rigspolitiet. (2016). Danmark-København: Programmering af software og konsulentvirksohed. Bekendtgørelse om indgåede kontrakter på området 'forsvar og sikkerhed'.

Roché, S., & Fleming, J. (2022). Cross-national Research. A New Frontier for Police Studies. *Policing and Society, 32*(3), 256–270. https://doi.org/10. 1080/10439463.2022.2037560

Rønn, K. V. (2022). The Multifaceted Norm of Objectivity in Intelligence Practices. *Intelligence and National Security, 37*(6), 820–834. https://doi.org/ 10.1080/02684527.2022.2076331

Rosner, L. (Ed.). (2004). *The Technological Fix: How People use Technology to Create and Solve Problems.* Routledge.

Sausdal, D. (2021). Terrorizing Police: Revisiting 'the Policing of Terrorism' from the Perspective of Danish Police Detectives. *European Journal of Criminology, 18*(5), 755–773. https://doi.org/10.1177/1477370819874449

Sausdal, D. (2022). A Cult(ure) of Intelligence-led Policing: On the International Campaigning and Convictions of Danish Policing. In M. J. Christensen, K. Lohne, M. Hörnqvist (Eds.) *Nordic Criminal Justice in a Global Context* (pp. 111–127). Routledge. https://doi.org/10.4324/978100 3195504-9

Sherman, N. (2020, October 1). Palantir: The Controversial Data Firm now worth £17bn. *BBC News.* https://www.bbc.com/news/business-54348456

Sletteholm, A. & Ekroll, H. C. (2015, July 7). Brukte 200.000 på internreklame for skrotet IT-prosjekt, *Aftenposten.*

Smith, M., & Miller, S. (2022). The Ethical Application of Biometric Facial Recognition Technology. *AI & SOCIETY, 37*(1), 167–175. https://doi.org/10.1007/s00146-021-01199-9

Stevnsborg, H. (2010). *Politi 1682–2007.* Samfundslitteratur.

Stevnsborg, H., (2013). The Police from Plush and Bread to the Investigation of Criminal Offenses–A Danish Historical Perspective. *Bergen Journal of Criminal Law & Criminal Justice, 1(2),* 120–130. https://doi.org/10.15845/bjclcj.v1i2.539

Toft, E. (2018, May 17). Nyt supervåben I politiet: Mand pågrebet for to voldtægter. *DR.* https://www.dr.dk/nyheder/indland/nyt-supervaaben-i-pol itiet-mand-paagrebet-voldtaegter

Usha Rani, J., & Raviraj, P. (2023). Real-Time Human Detection for Intelligent Video Surveillance: An Empirical Research and In-depth Review of its Applications. *SN Computer Science, 4*(3), 258. https://doi.org/10.1007/s42 979-022-01654-4

Van Der Sloot, B. (2013). From Data Minimization to Data Minimummization. In B. Custers, T. Calders, B. Schermer, & T. Zarsky (Eds.), *Discrimination and Privacy in the Information Society* (Vol. 3, pp. 273–287). Springer Berlin Heidelberg. https://doi.org/10.1007/978-3-642-30487-3_15

van Dijck, J. (2013). *The Culture of Connectivity: A Critical History of Social Media.* Oxford University Press. https://doi.org/10.1093/acprof:oso/978019 9970773.001.0001

Visionsudvalget. (2005). *Fremtidens politi.* Justitsministeriet.

Volquartzen, M. (2018). Forskydninger mellem det private og det offentlige. In Rønne, K.V. & Stevnsborg, H. (Eds.), *RetSMART: Om smart teknologi og regulering*, Jurist- og Økonomforbundets Forlag.

Waardenburg, L., Huysman, M., & Sergeeva, A. V. (2022). In the Land of the Blind, the One-Eyed Man Is King: Knowledge Brokerage in the Age of Learning Algorithms. *Organization Science, 33*(1), 59–82. https://doi.org/10.1287/orsc.2021.1544

Wang, J. (2018). *Carceral Capitalism.* MIT Press.

Wathne, C. T. (2020). New Public Management and the Police Profession at Play. *Criminal Justice Ethics, 39*(1), 1–22. https://doi.org/10.1080/0731129X.2020.1746106

Završnik, A. (2021). Algorithmic Justice: Algorithms and Big Data in Criminal Justice Settings. *European Journal of Criminology, 18*(5), 623–642. https://doi.org/10.1177/1477370819876762

Zierer, M., Kartheuser, B., Schöffel, R., & Harlan, E. (2023). Bund rückt von Software Palantir ab. *Tagesschau.de.* https://www.tagesschau.de/investigativ/br-recherche/palantir-software-analyse-polizei-100.html

Index

Printed by Printforce, the Netherlands